Dancing with the Devil

DANCING WITH THE DEVIL

The Political Economy of Privatization in China

YI-MIN LIN

Oxford University Press is a department of the University of Oxford. It furthers
the University's objective of excellence in research, scholarship, and education
by publishing worldwide. Oxford is a registered trade mark of Oxford University
Press in the UK and certain other countries.

Published in the United States of America by Oxford University Press
198 Madison Avenue, New York, NY 10016, United States of America.

© Oxford University Press 2017

All rights reserved. No part of this publication may be reproduced, stored in
a retrieval system, or transmitted, in any form or by any means, without the
prior permission in writing of Oxford University Press, or as expressly permitted
by law, by license, or under terms agreed with the appropriate reproduction
rights organization. Inquiries concerning reproduction outside the scope of the
above should be sent to the Rights Department, Oxford University Press, at the
address above.

You must not circulate this work in any other form
and you must impose this same condition on any acquirer.

CIP data is on file at the Library of Congress
ISBN 978–0–19–068282–8 (hbk.); 978–0–19–068283–5 (pbk.)

9 8 7 6 5 4 3 2 1
Paperback printed by Webcom Inc., Canada
Hardback printed by Bridgeport National Bindery, Inc., United States of America

Contents

List of Illustrations   vii

Introduction   1
    Privatization as a Process of Endogenous Institutional
        Change: Toward an Eclectic Perspective   5
    Driving Forces of Privatization   9
    Political Actors as Change Agents: The Main Storyline   21
    Note on Statistical Analyses, Data Sources, and
        Chinese Materials   27

1. The Changing Fate of Private Ownership since 1949   28
    Socialist Transformation and the Mao Era   29
    From *Getihu* to "Equal Protection" of Public and
        Private Property Rights   31
    Reversal or Moderation of Privatization?   36
    Broad Trends of Change   39
    Summary and Questions   59

2. Demographic Pressures   60
    Structure and Change of the Post-1949 Population   61
    Buildup of Employment Pressures   67
    Labor Market: Occupational and Spatial Movements   71
    Aging and Old-Age Support   76
    Summary   80

3. The Evolving Structure of Public Finance   82
    "Unified Revenue and Spending"   83
    Fiscal Contracts   86
    Revenue Partitioning   93
    Implications   102

4. Careerism and Moral Hazard in Early Marketization 106
   Large Is Beautiful: Political Performance Assessment
      under Economic Decentralization   107
   The TVE Spectacle   116
   The SOE Sideshow   128
   Summary   135

5. Rule Bending for the Necessary Evil 137
   Uneven Paces of Early Privatization   138
   The Wenzhou Story Retold   141
   Beyond Wenzhou   161
   Summary   167

6. FDI and Privatization 169
   Centrally Imposed Constraints and Local Rule Bending   170
   FDI Entry Mode and Resource Dependence   183
   Bipolar Concentration of Risk Taking   187
   Summary   193

7. The Tipping Point and Beyond 195
   The Triggers   196
   The Political Bandwagon   202
   From Industrial Development to Urbanization   211
   Asset Stripping and Insider Control   216
   The End Game: SASAC and the Remaining SOEs   221
   Summary   229

Conclusion 231
   Institutional Stability and Unintended Consequences
      of Rule Compliance   233
   Noncompliance and Political Risk Management   235
   Path Dependence in Endogenous Institutional Change   238

Bibliography 243
Index 263

Illustrations

Tables

1.1.	Categorization of nonfarm economic organizations	42
1.2.	Number (millions) of industrial and commercial organizations	44
1.3.	Shares (%) of public and nonpublic enterprises in industrial assets, 1993–2014	45
1.4.	Shares (%) of public enterprises in secondary and tertiary sector assets	46
1.5.	Shares (%) of contributions by public enterprises to GDP	48
1.6.	Estimates of contribution (%) by the nonpublic sector to GDP	49
1.7.	Changing significance of public entities and quasi-private entities in nonfarm employment	51
1.8.	Share (%) of publicly owned entities in secondary and tertiary sector employment	52
1.9.	Sectors with dominant SOE shares (%) in economic census years	53
1.10.	Number of industrial sectors with paid-in capital dominated by different owner groups, 2013	54
1.11.	Selected statistics on the relative significance (%) of entities with FDI in the economy	55
1.12.	Selected statistics on the geographic and sectoral distribution of FDI	56
1.13.	Organizational forms of FDI in the industrial sector, 1978–2008	58

2.1.	Selected statistics from population censuses	63
2.2.	Cultivated land and per capita shares	66
2.3.	Distribution of workforce in selected years	73
2.4.	Urban retirees on old (mainly work-unit-based) benefit schemes, 1978–1998	78
3.1.	Selected statistics of public finance, 1978–2010	88
3.2.	Taxes due and paid by township and village enterprises (RMB billions)	92
3.3.	Revenue partitioning between central and provincial governments in 1994	94
3.4.	Acreages (1,000 hectares) of different types of land use right transfer, 1993–2005	101
4.1.	Financial liabilities of public enterprises versus equity and government revenue	125
5.1.	Selected indicators on economic conditions in 1978	144
5.2.	Selected statistics on cities and counties in Wenzhou	159
5.3.	Selected statistics on privatization and initial economic conditions in prefectural cities of Zhejiang	162
6.1.	Selected statistics of foreign-invested industrial enterprises	177
6.2.	Selected statistics on wholly foreign-owned enterprises and joint ventures in the industrial sector	180
6.3.	Percentage of joint ventures with more than 50% of equity capital held by local partners	181
6.4.	Selected statistics (%) on fiscal conditions of counties	189
6.5.	Selected statistics on foreign-invested industrial enterprises in Guangdong, 1995	191
7.1.	Redundant and furloughed employees in urban public enterprises (millions)	197
7.2.	Selected financial indicators of industrial SOEs, 1980–1997	198
7.3.	Percentage of remaining industrial SOEs relative to previous year's, 1996–2002	203
7.4.	Decline of TVEs in Jiangsu province	210

7.5.	Industrial enterprises centrally located in urban areas	215
7.6.	Insider control of former industrial SOEs after privatization	219
7.7.	Selected statistics on industrial SOEs before and after ownership restructuring	223

Figures

2.1.	Natural rate (‰) of population growth, 1949–2009	62
2.2.	Estimates of net addition (millions) to workforce pool, 1949–2010	67
2.3.	Percentages of graduates able to enter next level of school, 1949–2010	69
2.4.	Number of persons in (intercounty) "floating population" (million persons), 1982–2010	76
3.1.	Major components (%) of tax revenue, 1978–2010	89
3.2.	Extrabudget revenue and SOE-related funds (100 million yuan), 1978–1992	90
3.3.	Enterprise income tax paid as percentage of gross profit of industrial SOEs, 1985–1997	92
3.4.	Land sale proceeds as percentage equivalent of local budget revenue, 1995–2010	99
4.1.	Taxes and profits versus sales, 1984–1990	121
4.2.	Sales growth rate (five-year moving average) of TVEs, 1980–1998	122
4.3.	TVE output, sales, and GDP, 1985–1998	122
4.4.	Taxes and profits as percentage of TVE sales, 1978–1998	123
4.5.	Debt, sales, and profit of TVEs, 1984–1998	123
4.6.	Sales growth rate (five-year moving average) of industrial SOEs, 1980–1997	130
4.7.	SOE taxes, profits, and sales	132
4.8.	Taxes and profit as percentage of industrial SOE sales, 1978–1998	132
5.1.	Share of public enterprises in nonfarm workforce, 1984–2004	155
5.2.	Size of Wenzhou's public sector, 1978–1997	158

6.1.	Percentage of newly registered JVs with foreign investors holding more than 50% of equity capital	181
6.2.	Number of foreign-private joint ventures in the industrial sector, 1992–2001	182
6.3.	Foreign investment in Guangdong: FDI (%) versus processing contracts (%) 1979–1996	182
7.1.	Ratio of unhealthy assets to equity (%) by province: Nonfinancial SOEs, 1997–1998	199
7.2.	Ratio (%) of nonperforming loans to bank lending, 1995–2012	200
7.3.	Total number (1,000s) of TVEs in Jiangsu, 1984–2004	209
7.4.	Urbanization and tertiary sector growth, 1978–2010	212
7.5.	Share (%) of secondary and tertiary sectors in city GDP	213
7.6.	Share (%) of public enterprises in total real estate investment, 1997–2012	214

Maps

5.1.	Map of Zhejiang province	142
5.2.	Map of Wenzhou	142

Introduction

THE AUTUMN OF 1949 saw the end of China's three-year-long civil war. With the military force of the ruling Kuomintang (KMT) in defeat, the rival Chinese Communist Party (CCP) was poised to take over the national government. On September 25, CCP chairman Mao Zedong (1893–1976) presided over a meeting of the Chinese People's Political Consultative Conference, which was convened to make preparations for the creation of a new political regime—later known as the People's Republic of China (PRC). Among the matters decided at the meeting was the design of the new national flag. It featured a big star flanked by four small stars, all in yellow and set against a red backdrop. According to the summary statement from the contributing designer (Zeng Liansong 1949), the big star symbolized the CCP as the country's leading political force, and the small stars symbolized the four classes that Mao had defined in *On People's Democratic Dictatorship* (June 30, 1949) as the social forces that the CCP must unite during *and* after the revolution: the proletariat, the peasantry, the urban petite bourgeoisie, and the national (indigenous) bourgeoisie.

The political symbolism of the new national flag reflected the thinking of the incoming rulers. Devastated by a century of conflicts and wars and deeply anchored in a premodern mode of production, the Chinese economy was underdeveloped. That reality was clearly incompatible with Karl Marx's depiction of the material conditions necessary for initiating a transition into communism. So CCP leaders were prepared to oversee a largely private economy for an extended period of time after the revolution, as Mao had envisioned in an earlier treatise entitled *On New Democracy* (1940). What transpired in the following decade, however, substantially shortened that time frame.

Emboldened by the speedy economic recovery and the effective consolidation of political power during 1950–1953, Mao pushed for an accelerated process of socialist transformation. By 1959, private ownership of economic resources was virtually eliminated. Gone with it were the two capitalist classes represented on the national flag, which nonetheless remained the country's most important political symbol. During the 1960s and 1970s, public ownership provided the foundation for a Soviet-style, centrally planned economy. Yet since the late 1970s, private ownership has made a comeback, first re-emerging as an element supplementary to the overwhelmingly dominant public sector, but gradually overtaking the latter as the leading force in the fast-growing economy. Today, the nonpublic sector produces some two-thirds to seven-tenths of China's GDP and employs about 90% of the workforce. And capitalists, big and small, are exerting a significant influence on politics and socioeconomic life, arguably increasingly more than the two working classes represented on the national flag.

Reflecting on the vicissitudes of private ownership in China since 1949, one may get a strong sense of déjà vu. Mao's "new democracy theory" defined, ex ante, the mixed economy of the 1950s. Thirty years later, its essential spirit was resurrected by the "theory of socialism with Chinese characteristics" that the new paramount leader Deng Xiaoping (1904–1997) articulated in the 1980s. Deng's central claim was that private ownership and capitalism could play a limited role in China's development during "early-stage socialism" but would eventually be eliminated in an indeterminate long run. This so-called theory, however, was more of an expedient pretext for pragmatic strategies to cope with new realities than a coherent blueprint for the post-Mao transformations. The expansion and institutionalization of private ownership, among other things, are largely the result of ex post adjustments and adaptations to a series of unintended changes resulting from earlier reforms, rather than being the outcome of CCP leaders' premeditated calculations. In fact, these changes and policy responses have even stretched beyond the limit set by Deng's own theory, forcing the post-Deng leaders to scramble for justifications.

Ideologically, public ownership would have been far more consistent with the CCP's continued claim to build a classless society as envisioned by Marx. From a practical point of view, it would also have provided the state with continuous and more direct channels to allocate resources and control socioeconomic activities. In fact, the ascent of private ownership since 1978 has by no means been a smooth process. Revived on a limited basis as a stopgap measure to address acute pressures for job creation and fiscal shortfalls, the private sector faced severe restrictions and discrimination in the early years of reform, when the state sought to marketize and internationalize the economy, mainly through a restructuring and expansion of public enterprises. That undertaking initially showed seemingly promising results but subsequently exhausted itself. Since the mid-1990s, the vast majority of public enterprises have been sold off or closed down, reducing the dominance of state ownership to a handful of strategically important sectors, such as banking, telecommunications, utilities, energy, air and rail transport, warehousing and storage, tobacco, and armaments. In the meantime, the government has not only relaxed or removed an increasing number of restrictions on the private sector, but also introduced new laws and policies to protect private property rights and facilitate their use and exchange. Since 2001, ironically, the CCP has increasingly welcomed and even encouraged private business people to become party members.

These developments, as well as their apparent tendency toward perpetuation, directly contradict the Party's proclaimed commitment to socialism. The expansion of private ownership and capitalism under weak legal and regulatory constraints on negative externalities and opportunism also compounds many coevolving problems, such as growing inequalities, pervasive political corruption, increasing economic insecurity, environmental decay, and sinking moral standards. Together, they contribute to the growth of popular discontent with the CCP and undermine its legitimacy and ability to govern.

This fundamental predicament sets the case of China in sharp contrast with ideologically and politically motivated privatization movements in the former Soviet bloc and beyond.[1] Why, then, have Chinese leaders had to come to terms with an institutional arrangement that they initially suppressed and still loathe deeply? The short answer, I argue, is that privatization of the post-Mao economy is largely due to the state's increasing inability to rely on the public sector to address two critical concerns for regime survival: employment and revenue. How and why this inability has grown and consequently redefined the choice sets of the CCP is the focus of this book.

Here, I use the term *privatization* broadly. It refers to a process where private ownership becomes increasingly significant in the economy via two convergent mechanisms: the growth of genetically private economic entities, including those funded with foreign capital, and the conversion of existing public enterprises into purely or predominantly privately owned entities. This

---

1. For a survey of the broad literature on this issue, see Megginson and Netter 2001. Djankov and Murrell (2002) offer an overview of studies on enterprise restructuring toward private ownership in transitional economies. Hamm, King, and Stuckler (2012) explain varying economic consequences of mass privatization in postcommunist countries. Obinger, Schmitt, and Traub (2016) provide an analysis of privatization in more mature capitalist systems.

immediately raises a question. If state actions in reaction to the growing failure of public enterprises to address employment and revenue imperatives hold a key to explaining privatization, what has been the role of entrepreneurs and citizens-at-large in overcoming the obstacles to private ownership in market-oriented economic reforms and opening?

In fact, there are numerous accounts of the persevering, oftentimes ingenious efforts by economic actors to defy the odds and pursue profits by pushing beyond the boundaries of direct state ownership and control during the past four decades. The common story about the resultant growth of private economic activities is one that celebrates the triumph of entrepreneurship and markets. There is indeed much truth to it. What this study seeks to offer is a close examination of the changing structural contexts in which the roles of these essential forces have played out under the reign of political actors. The intended outcome is a more revealing view of the causal mechanisms at work.

The structural contexts that I analyze mainly concern the demographic characteristics of the country and the fiscal infrastructure of the state system. Both bear deep imprints of postrevolution history and have had profound implications for political and economic decisions and actions in the reform era. In particular, cumulative pressures to provide jobs for China's baby boomers forced CCP leaders to take the first step toward privatization in the late 1970s, when they moved toward legalizing self-employment. Such pressures have since persisted and continued to accentuate the need for jobs beyond the accommodating capacity of the public sector.

The fiscal structure carried over from the Mao era, on the other hand, featured divisions and flows of revenue and spending under a multitude of stratified and fragmented government property rights over economic organizations. Efforts to restructure these complex relationships in the reform era altered the self-interest calculus of political actors at various levels of the state system. A major consequence was the growth and multiplication of opportunism in such forms as moral hazard in the supervision of public enterprises, rule bending in favor of private business and foreign capital, and direct use of public office for personal gain, all of which undermined the vitality and dominance of public ownership.

Entrepreneurs, including some of those initially serving as public enterprise managers; foreign investors; and their local agents were part of the story. Their economically and politically risk-taking behavior in pursuit of private profits contributed to creating and expanding markets and competition, developing alternative sources of employment and revenue, and exacerbating financial and governance problems in public enterprises. In the meantime, the emerging markets provided a platform on which to test out the institutional choices preferred by leading political actors for addressing employment and revenue imperatives on the basis of public ownership. As the inherent weakness of these choices was laid bare, and as the vitality of the alternative (albeit least preferred) choice—that is, privatization—was more evidently demonstrated, the degree of freedom enjoyed by the top decision-makers became increasingly limited. This, in essence, was how and why private ownership took hold as a necessary evil and eventually prevailed against the political will of the CCP leadership.

Privatization as a Process of Endogenous Institutional Change: Toward an Eclectic Perspective

Privatization is one of the most fundamental changes that have redefined the economic institutions of post-Mao China. It is a complex process for which existing theories of institutional change do not have directly applicable explanations. The main insights of these theories, however, can be synthesized to form a discerning perspective that helps understand the mechanisms at work. The fact that the ascent of private ownership has taken place under a communist regime is analytically puzzling and indeed politically ironic, as the CCP is ideologically mandated to strive for a society without private ownership. Looking at the entire span of the PRC's history, one may also see this contradictory development as an institutional reversal—what has been unfolding since 1978 is in essence a resurrection of the mixed economy in the early 1950s.[2] It contrasts with the institutional reversals elsewhere that have taken place by design, by force, or by negotiation, such as adoption of Western-style systems in postcommunist Eastern Europe, return to dictatorship in inchoate or unstable democracies, or deregulation in Western countries. The Chinese case instead involves a largely endogenously derived process that has evolved and prevailed against the political will of rulers who command an organizationally potent authoritarian state.

To be sure, this process is not simply a matter of resuming what had been truncated at an earlier point of time in history. What had happened during

---

2. Here the term "institutional reversal" means resurrection of an erstwhile institutional order. This usage differs from the way Acemoglu, Johnson, and Robinson (2002) use the term, by which they refer to the reversal of the relative levels of economic development among countries as a result of the adoption of different types of institutions.

the first three decades of the PRC had profound implications for how the process of privatization evolved in the post-Mao era. According to a prominent view in the literature on institutional change (e.g., Sewell 1996; Hausner, Nielson, and Jessop 1995), the orientation of institutional change is subject to the lasting influence of institutional legacies of the past, which are often too deep-rooted to be swept away, even by torrent events like war, revolution, or regime collapse. In contrast, a narrower view of path dependence emphasizes the role of contingencies in triggering and orienting the change in an existing institution. Extending the research on the "lock-in" phenomenon in technological change (e.g., Arthur 1989; David 1985), for example, some scholars seek to illuminate the mechanisms of institutional change by accounting for the positive feedback that may develop in an initially fluid process (e.g., Mahoney 2000; Pierson 2004). The basic argument is that incremental positive feedback (such as newly generated political and economic interests) may make it increasingly costly or difficult to reverse the process of change along certain institutional path.

These seemingly contrasting views of path dependence, while differing in focus, can be complementary. Positive feedback is an important channel through which the influence of institutional legacies may play out, whereas the sources of positive feedback are rarely limited to factors newly derived from the changes (oftentimes in response to a "shock" event) in a particular institution per se. A question that may help join the historical-contextual view and the contingency view is whether the forces that set in motion the process of change and/or build up the momentum therein also have certain temporal and/or structural characteristics that define their influence on the path of the institutional change under investigation. Another question is whether initially strong positive feedback for a newly emerging institutional order may herald the beginning of its ultimate demise. In this study I will show that China's changing demographics after the 1949 revolution and the prereform fiscal system were among the key triggers for the movement toward private ownership and have since shaped the path of the subsequent process of change. I will also show that the leading role of public enterprises in early marketization generated and disguised forces leading to their subsequent self-destruction.

To explain why Chinese communist leaders have had to accept what they initially suppressed or resisted in the restructuring of property rights institutions, it is important to examine the behavior of change agents, including both economic and political actors. Such behavior is seen as particularly catalytic and consequential during times of institutional instability (e.g.,

Katznelson 2003; Swidler 1986). A predominant view (also known as the "rationalist view") in economic analysis of institutional change regards exogenous shocks as the main cause of such instability.[3] The underlying rationale is that institutions are self-enforcing, equilibrium phenomena, where "each player's behavior is a best response . . . no one has an incentive to deviate from the behavior associated with the institution" (Greif 2006, 159). It follows that change comes when self-sustained institutional reproduction breaks down.

This view is questioned by the "historical institutionalists" in political science (Hall and Taylor 1996; Mahoney and Thelen 2010). They argue that institutions embody different patterns of power-distributional relations that are fraught with tension and conflict. Change is perennial and oftentimes endogenously derived, as noncompliance is an inherent feature of institutional life, especially when rules are ambiguous, weakly reinforced, and/or vigorously contested. Such deviant behavior, open or covert, stems from diverse motivating sources, and its cumulative and sometimes transformative effects may lead to different outcomes of institutional change in different contexts.[4]

Both views are useful in that they draw attention to different forces that shape the fate of institutions. An issue that is recognized by both views but remains underexplored is that compliant behavior with existing institutions may lead to unintended consequences that increase institutional instability from within (Greif and Laitin 2004; Mahoney and Thelen 2010). In my analysis I will investigate how this scenario materialized as a result of growing moral hazard among the stewards of public ownership that significantly undermined the financial and organizational health of public enterprises in the 1980s and early 1990s. I will also seek to explain institutional change by understanding what renders institutions relatively stable in light of a modified version of the rationalist view. That is, institutional stability hinges on making the vast majority of players, rather than *all of them*, consider it to be

---

3. A revisionist view allows for endogenous sources of institutional instability by redefining some exogenous factors as "quasi-parameters" that may reinforce existing institutions in the short run but gradually move in the opposite direction (Greif 2006; Greif and Laitin 2004).

4. See Mahoney and Thelen 2010 for an elaborate discussion of diverse outcomes, such as "layering," "drift," "displacement," and "conversion." It should be noted, though, that noncompliance with dominant institutional rules does not necessarily bear a linear correlation with institutional change, as deviations from such rules may create behavioral regularities that reinforce rather than undermine the reproduction of existing formal institutions. Illicit pursuits of redistributive gains in "rent-seeking societies" (Krueger 1974), for example, may well contribute to perpetuating the established institutional order instead of subverting it. A challenge for institutional analysis is to identify the conditions under which the effects of noncompliance on institutional stability change directions, as well as the mechanisms whereby these effects play out. I will reflect on this issue in the concluding chapter.

in their best interest to follow, most times if not always, dominant institutional rules, provided that the unintended consequences of rule compliance are contained. This will broaden the space for investigating what the historical institutionalists emphasize—that is, the role of change agents, who often are among the noncompliant actors and play an instrumental role in subverting the existing institutional order. In order for institutions to be relatively stable, not only do most actors need to be motivated to follow dominant rules, but the erosive and contagious effects of noncompliant behavior need to be deterred and contained. Otherwise the opportunities for institutional change will significantly increase, which is what happened during the process of privatization in China. To account for institutional change, therefore, it is important to consider the incentives and constraints faced by both rule followers and noncompliant players. In particular, what shapes the risks faced by change agents merits close analytic attention.

A relevant factor to consider in this connection is the ability of rule breakers to justify their behavior.[5] Assuming individuals are risk-averse, the stronger such ability, the weaker the coherence of the institutional order concerned and vice versa. This brings up questions about what may be called the homogenizing function of institutions, which legitimizes (e.g., through coercive, normative, and/or mimetic mechanisms) and thereby diffuses and routinizes rule-abiding behavior while deterring deviance through pressures or punitive sanctions on risk-takers.[6] Such a function is a central issue addressed by the "new institutionalism" in sociology and organization studies (Powell and DiMaggio 1991; Scott 2001, 2013). Yet this school of institutional analysis has been criticized for overemphasizing the tenacity of institution and falling short of providing a useful theory for explaining change (Hall and Taylor 1996; see also Greif 2006). Indeed its generalizations are mostly based on cases where institutions are strong enough to constrain noncompliance. There is only scant coverage of institutions that are weak and unable to contain rule breaking effectively. It also is largely silent about the conditions under which justification of noncompliance is rendered difficult.

---

5. Rule breaking is not the only way change agents subvert institutional stability, though. Problematic institutional designs may leave open space for change agents' opportunistic pursuit of self-interest that complies with formal rules (hence involving low risk) but generates unintended destabilizing effects on the existing institutional order. I will further discuss this in chapter 4 and the concluding chapter.

6. Considering the effect of such communally or societally induced behavior contrasts with but does not necessarily contradict the emphasis that rationalist perspectives place on the role of private order, reached and maintained through voluntary exchange or association among interacting individual actors, in the development of institutions (e.g., Greif 2006).

Despite these inadequacies, however, the main insight offered by the sociological view should not be dismissed. That is, the difficulty or costliness of justifying noncompliant behavior holds a key to understanding institutional stability, which is the flip side of the story about institutional change. As I will show in this book, a major contributing factor to the deepening of privatization in post-Mao China is the growth of a gray area in the institutional space for property rights. It undermines the enforcement of existing rules and greatly reduces the risk of rule breaking. Investigating how such a gray area grew and what affected the cost function of justification for noncompliance therefore will enrich the understanding of what drives the institutional change under investigation.

To sum up, it is possible and useful to synthesize some of the main thrusts in institutional analysis that are often presented as antitheses. In particular, the study of the mechanisms of endogenously derived institutional change may benefit from (*a*) a comprehensive view of path dependence that incorporates both the lasting influence of historical legacies and the possibility of sequentially opposing effects rendered by contingencies arising from the process of change; (*b*) a revisionist view of institutional stability that does not require universal rule following and considers subversive effects from both rule compliance and deviation to be key to understanding institutional change; and (*c*) an extended view of the homogenizing function of institutions that recognizes the costliness of justifying noncompliance as well as the variations in the pertinent cost in different contexts. This eclectic perspective will guide and inform my research on the driving forces behind the decline of public ownership in post-Mao China. I will discuss the theoretical implications of my findings for institutional analysis in the concluding chapter. Let me begin my search for explanations with a brief review of the existing empirical scholarship on China's privatization.

Driving Forces of Privatization

When CCP leaders initiated economic reforms in the late 1970s, they never thought that the limited steps that they took would eventually lead to the predominance of private ownership. As noted above, the unfolding of this transformation in the ensuing thirty years followed three convergent paths: the growth of genetically private economic entities, the conversion of public enterprises into private or predominantly private companies, and the expansion and deepening of foreign (private) ownership. The driving forces behind the changes along these paths have attracted considerable analytic attention.

Three prominent explanations stand out in the pertinent literature: the entrepreneurship thesis, the budget constraint thesis, and the foreign direct investment (FDI) thesis.

A central theme in the research on privatization in post-Mao China is that entrepreneurship has played an essential role in the growth of genetically private economic entities (e.g., Bruun 1993; Huang 2008; Kraus 1991; Krug 2004; Nee and Opper 2012; Odgaard 1992; Tsai 2002, 2007; Wank 1999; Young 1995). This not only involves economically innovative and risk-taking behavior, but encompasses various strategies, such as the evasion, neutralization, and engagement of local officials, to cope with the political constraints and channel influence and resources from the state. As private entrepreneurs pressed their way forward from the initially adverse institutional environment, they contributed to the creation and expansion of markets and competition, as well as the development of informal institutions to govern the new economic space. Over time, the CCP has had to reckon with these realities and, in order to influence them, to co-opt private entrepreneurs into a new alliance of political and economic interests (Chen and Dickson 2010; Dickson 2008; Tsai 2007).

The budget constraint thesis offers an explanation for the privatization of public enterprises (e.g., Brandt, Li, and Roberts; Cao, Qian, and Weingast 1999; Li 2003; Park and Shen 2003; Qian and Roland 1998; Whiting 2000). Its basic argument is that public enterprises, especially state-owned enterprises (SOEs), entered market reforms under soft budget constraint—easy credit and fiscal subsidies for inefficiencies and operating losses. The lack of strong financial discipline fostered imprudent decision-making and led to the accumulation of increasing amounts of debt among these latecomers to market-oriented economic activities. In the mid-1990s, banking reforms heightened the profit goals of state-owned banks and drove them to tighten lending practices. In the meantime, comprehensive tax and fiscal reforms drastically changed revenue streams in favor of the central government and thereby weakened the fiscal capacities of local governments that controlled the vast majority of public enterprises. The result of these concurrent developments was a hardening of the budget constraint faced by public enterprises. Coupled with growing competition, this change pushed many of these enterprises into serious financial crisis. In view of the mounting cost of continuing to finance them, the government had no choice but to resort to a massive sell-off around the turn of the century.

The FDI thesis draws attention to a link between the expansion of foreign investment in China and the resurgence of private ownership. While there is a large body of studies on the growing role of foreign investment, especially FDI, in the Chinese economy (e.g., Gallagher 2005; Howell 1993; Lardy 1994; Moore 2002; Pearson 1991; Shirk 1994; Zweig 2002), Huang (2002) was perhaps the first to make an explicit argument about the privatization function of foreign capital. The gist of the argument is that inefficiencies of SOEs and ideologically and politically motivated discrimination against domestic private enterprises left open extraordinary opportunities for FDI to expand up until the turn of the twenty-first century. The influx of capital from abroad represented a growth of the significance of private (albeit foreign) ownership in the Chinese economy. It also facilitated the growth of domestic private enterprises disadvantaged by legal-regulatory constraints and inadequate financial access, mainly through joint ventures that added property rights security and much-needed capital, though this was sometimes achieved at the expense of local partners' ceding the rights of control. Moreover, for some poorly performing SOEs, FDI provided an exit through the cannibalization of their remaining assets into equity shares in joint ventures dominated by foreign investors.

Each of these theses illuminates an important part of a big and complex puzzle. They also complement one another in that each accounts for a different avenue of privatization. More research, however, is needed to weave their insights into a fuller and more revealing account of the mechanisms at work.

Local Rule Bending and National Policy Constraints and Changes

The entrepreneurship thesis draws mainly on findings from studies of the entrepreneurial drive and savvy of private business people in face of the initially adverse political environment. As Tsai (2002, 264) succinctly puts it, these entrepreneurs devised diverse and ingenious ways to conduct and grow business "behind the state, with the state, and despite the state." A large part of their political strategies, however, involved efforts to neutralize and/or manipulate state authorities, as invisibility from the state tended to decline with the growth of a business and there was a limit to what could be achieved through open defiance or confrontation with an organizationally potent state apparatus. Indeed much of the pertinent analytic attention focuses on how private business people interacted with local officials and secured from them tolerant or even facilitating administrative and regulatory actions and policies beyond centrally imposed restrictions. The common story is that such rule-bending behavior stemmed from a convergence of shared interests between local officials and private entrepreneurs. In some instances, the rule bending by local officials even facilitated the creation of informal institutions that served as the prototypes for eventual conversion or evolution into formal institutions (e.g., Tsai 2007).

This is a useful perspective, focusing primarily on the role of mutual *benefits* between local political and economic actors. To enhance its explanatory power, however, an in-depth analysis of the *costs* of pursuing such benefits is necessary. In particular, it is important to further investigate how local officials justified their rule-bending behavior, which involved various degrees of risk (and hence cost) under the ideological and political constraints imposed by the CCP. Understanding how such risk was contained and managed in different local contexts will not only clarify what shaped the cost-benefit calculus of local officials and why genetically private enterprises were able to grow despite the initially adverse institutional environment. It will also help explain the varying paces of their growth across space and over time.

A widely shared view about regional variations in the development of the private sector is that local government policies are path dependent (e.g., Liu 1992; Tsai 2002; Whiting 2000). Locales that entered economic reforms with a strong preexisting base of public enterprises tended to have more restrictive policies on the private sector than those without such a base. This is by and large true, especially in rural areas. But it tells us more about why some local governments favored public enterprises over private enterprises than why some local governments actively promoted the private sector during the first two decades of reform. In fact, governments in locales with similarly weak legacies of public enterprises demonstrated a wide range of differences in terms of their tendency to promote the private sector. A narrow view of path dependence focusing on initial organizational endowment, therefore, is an inadequate explanation for the variations among poorly endowed locales, which encompass more space than organizationally well-endowed locales. As I will show in chapter 5, a broader view that incorporates local demographics, public finance, and entrepreneurial forces before and after the revolution offers a more revealing account of such heterogeneity in causal effects, as these factors directly conditioned how local officials perceived the benefits of rule bending and dealt with the political risks associated with policies favoring the private sector.

While interactions between private business people and local authorities are important for understanding the expansion of private business, it should be noted that sweeping policy changes at the national level, where regime survival is a much greater concern than at local levels, have also played an important part in redefining the institutional environment for genetically private entities. Examples include the landmark decisions to legalize self-employment in 1979–1980, to remove the size limit on private employment in 1988, to further legitimize the private sector as part of China's "socialist market economy" in 1992, to provide constitutional recognition for the status of private business in 1999, and to place public and private property rights under "equal protection" in 2007, as will be elaborated in chapter 1.

Not all these national policy changes can be adequately explained with an account of the entrepreneurial pursuits of private business people in local contexts. The decision to legalize self-employment, for example, was made at a time when the revival of entrepreneurial forces was still inchoate and could not possibly have been the predominant driving force. The trigger for that decision, as I will show in chapters 2 and 3, came both from growing pressures to create jobs and from fiscal shortfalls, which had resulted from population policies and development strategies of the Mao era. Understanding these historical factors and their national policy implications helps illuminate the beginnings of the changing fate of private business.

Where local influence did lead to national policy changes, questions remain as to how the micro-macro causality played out. As will be elaborated in the following chapters, a key factor in this connection is how both local and central leaders perceived and assessed the seriousness of the growing crises in job creation and public finance in light of the coping capacities of public enterprises at different times and various levels of the system. To account for the gradual relaxation of restrictions on genetically private enterprises, an analysis of the interactions between local officials and private entrepreneurs needs to be complemented by an understanding of concurrently emerging problems in the public sector. Furthermore, decision-making by central leaders about private business was also an incremental process in which earlier decisions made at the national level engendered responses from various actors—including local authorities and private entrepreneurs—according to their own self-interest calculus. A large number of such responses went beyond the initial limits but nevertheless managed to hold on, oftentimes in the name of experimental reforms to address key policy imperatives, thereby both creating pressures and signaling directions for further change. A careful examination of what went into the argument to justify local rule bending is therefore necessary.

The tempo of national policy change toward the private sector can also be better understood through a broader view that incorporates both historical structural factors and the consequences of interactions among local political and economic actors and between local and central authorities in the reform era. The drastic relaxation of restrictions on private business in the second half of the 1990s provides an example. For reasons to be discussed below, by the mid-1990s the financial performance of the public sector had seriously deteriorated. Coupled with a fiscal recentralization aimed to tackle problems spawned or exacerbated under the fiscal decentralization before 1994, this reality generated a strong motivation for local governments to jettison the vast majority of public enterprises under their purview. At the same time, as a result of entrepreneurship and local rule bending, the private sector had grown beyond centrally defined limits and proved to be a viable alternative for the state's employment and revenue imperatives. Moreover, public-sector employees who joined the nonfarm workforce during the massive industrial buildup in the 1950s and 1960s began to retire in large and increasing numbers, exacerbating the financial plight of the public sector and accentuating the need to shift the growing responsibility for social security provision away from the public sector. What followed was a massive and precipitous wave of privatization.

The Political Benefits of Soft Budget Constraints, and Then Some

While the entrepreneurship thesis emphasizes mutual benefits to local political and economic actors as an explanation for the growth of genetically private enterprises, the budget constraint thesis is mainly concerned with the issue of *cost* in the administration of public enterprises. In particular, it focuses on cost considerations as an explanation for the central government's changing policies for the privatization of public enterprises. Its basic argument is that privatization was a result of the increasingly unbearable cost of continuing to finance the vast majority of these enterprises. This is indeed true. And the emphasis that the thesis places on the linkages between fiscal and banking reforms and the massive privatization of SOEs and township and village enterprises (TVEs) in the late 1990s is especially useful for understanding the triggering mechanisms for the decline of the public sector. Yet there are gaps in the analysis of the underlying forces at work. A key issue that needs closer scrutiny is why the budget constraint in many public enterprises not only continued to be soft but was actually further softened during the transition from central planning to markets, which presumably would tend to harden (e.g., with profit orientation and competition) rather than soften the budget constraint. There also remain questions as to whether the soft budget constraint problem provides a sufficient explanation for the deterioration of the financial health of the public sector, and what shaped and reshaped the calculation by local authorities of the opportunity cost for maintaining public enterprises up to the tipping point of massive privatization and beyond.

In his original formulation of the soft budget constraint problem in socialist economies, Janos Kornai (1979, 1980) attributes its cause to the need to internalize the social costs of unemployment and/or organizational restructuring under an all-encompassing, "paternalistic" state. Broadening the use of the term to market economies, Shleifer and Vishny (1994) further point out that a soft budget constraint may result from the active pursuit of political benefits (e.g., votes in exchange for excessive employment or other unprofitable investments) that accrue to politicians in control of public enterprises. Shifting the focus from politics to information cost, Dewatripont and Maskin (1995) present a scenario of adverse selection in which the authority that softens the budget constraint does so not by choice, but by necessity. What causes this is that under a centralized structure of financing, information asymmetry renders it difficult for the fund provider to ascertain, ex ante, and devise effective deterrence against the fund user's undertaking inefficient activities, making the continuation of financing a rational way to recoup sunk costs ex post facto.

Accounts of the soft budget constraint problem in China's economic transition invoke both the political-benefit perspective and the information-cost perspective (e.g., Qian and Roland 1998; Bai and Wang 1998; Li 1998; Li and Liang 1998). Such analysis, however, largely stays at a theoretical level and has yet to be contextualized in regard to the concrete characteristics of China's changing political economy. The utility of these perspectives may be enhanced if one uses them as launch pads for investigations into more probing questions on the complex forces that weakened the financial discipline and health of public enterprises in market-oriented reforms. What, for example, constituted the political benefits from softening the budget constraint in the post-Mao era? And why did the soft budget constraint problem persist or even worsen under an increasingly decentralized structure for the supervision of public enterprises, which presumably would have alleviated information asymmetry and hence hardened the budget constraint?

Kornai's emphasis on employment retention as a major political benefit associated with soft budget constraint offers a useful point of departure. It derives from his prototypical case of Hungary, which had a relatively stable population size and a high degree of urbanization from the 1950s to the 1980s. In contrast, the main challenge faced by post-Mao Chinese leaders was not employment retention but the need to create jobs by leaps and bounds. China had experienced fast population growth in the Mao era while accumulating large numbers of underemployed workers in the rural sector due to a capital-intensive strategy of industrialization and restrictions on the occupational and geographical mobility of the workforce. In the face of mounting pressures for nonfarm job creation after agricultural decollectivization in the late 1970s and early 1980s, government authorities relied heavily on public enterprises to expand nonfarm employment, which oftentimes eclipsed the goal of profit making despite the fact that these enterprises were moving away from central planning to markets.

The pursuit of profits by public enterprises during the early years of reform faced further interference from their supervising authorities. As will be discussed in chapters 3–4, although the reform of public enterprises aimed to turn them from passive takers of bureaucratic orders into market-oriented profit makers, supervising officials focused on the growth of sales as the main avenue to generating fiscal revenue. What fostered such behavior was a longstanding structural bias in the fiscal system, where government budget revenue was derived mainly from indirect taxes and levies tied to sales volume rather than direct taxes on profits and income.

As employment and revenue were often among the key criteria used in the assessment of the performance of leading officials, who typically had transient tenures, and since there was a lack of clear cost accounting and intertemporal tracking of responsibility in such assessment, softening the budget constraint to enlarge the workforce and boost sales without close links to profitability became a convenient tool to maximize the short-term political benefits of control over public enterprises. The moral hazard that led many public enterprises down this path of overexpansion and eventual implosion cannot, therefore, be fully accounted for without a close examination of the political incentives faced by supervising officials, as well as the demographic and fiscal conditions that defined the parameters of their decision-making.[7]

The moral hazard story also sheds some light on the link between budget constraint and information cost. The fast expansion of public enterprises orchestrated by local authorities for quick political benefits posed a parallel

---

7. Following the usage in economic analysis (Arrow 1963), I employ the term "moral hazard" to describe the tendency to be less risk-averse when one is shielded from the consequences of risk-taking. In the context of this study it refers to the tendency of state officials to risk without accountability the financial and organizational health of public enterprises for the pursuit of political and economic (including private) benefits for themselves.

challenge to the enforcement of financial discipline. That is, when the number and scale of public enterprises outgrew the monitoring capacity of their supervising authorities, the budget constraint could be further softened due to the increased information asymmetry, which nevertheless resulted mainly from a significantly broadened span of control rather than centralization of control, as emphasized by the pertinent theory.

While a closer examination of the forces that softened the budget constraint will be useful, it may still fall short of yielding a sufficient explanation for the deteriorating financial health of public enterprises. A fuller account requires the consideration of a concurrent contributing factor, the self-seeking behavior of political actors. Examples of such behavior, as I have illustrated in an earlier study (Lin 2001) and will further discuss in chapter 4 and chapter 7, include the use of public enterprise accounts to manipulate revenue flows and finance personal expenditures, the diversion of resources to officials' private profit centers, and outright asset stripping. These problems were particularly serious in the 1990s, when the decline and death of the vast majority of public enterprises occurred.

The fiscal system, again, provides a window into what led to the growth of opportunism in the administration of public enterprises. In particular, there are revealing clues from the changing opportunities and constraints faced by political actors during the fiscal decentralization in the 1980s and early 1990s, which saw a drastic expansion of off-budget revenue and spending as well as increasing inconsistencies (hence "gray areas") in fiscal and financial regulation and supervision during the transition away from central planning (chapter 3).

Moreover, changes in the fiscal system also hold a key to understanding the shifting attitudes of local authorities toward public enterprises. Perhaps the most telling example, to be discussed in chapter 3 and further shown in chapter 7, was a reform in the mid-1990s to replace the fiscal contract system adopted in the preceding decade with a revenue-partitioning system. It significantly increased direct control by the central government of revenues from the industrial sector, which had been dominated by public enterprises. At the same time, local governments were forced to rely more on revenues from other sectors, especially the tertiary sector, which had long been given low priority under central planning and therefore posed relatively lower entry barriers to private enterprises during the early years of reform. In view of this fiscal restructuring, many local authorities began to refocus their economic policies from the industrial sector to other economic activities that could boost revenue. What followed was a rising and spreading wave of efforts throughout the country to promote urbanization and real estate development as the main stimulus for the expansion of local services (and hence government revenue and job creation). Weak initial presence, intense competition, and consideration of monitoring costs combined to limit the role of public enterprises in this undertaking, leaving open opportunities for private enterprises to proliferate. Given the growing importance of the private sector for local revenues of both the formal (budgetary) and the informal (off-budget) kinds, and in view of the deteriorating financial health of many public enterprises, the resolve of local authorities to hold on to these enterprises rapidly diminished. Consequently, the tempo of privatization greatly accelerated.

The Entry and Expansion of FDI

A comprehensive account of privatization in post-Mao China must also include a close look at the role of foreign capital, especially FDI, which has become an increasingly important force in the country's new economy. A major feature of the entry and expansion of FDI in China is that, while the central government has held the authority to set the rules, local governments, especially subprovincial governments, have been the main gatekeepers and regulators. In the first three decades of reform, especially before China's accession to the World Trade Organization (WTO) in 2001, there were significant entry barriers in terms of sector, region, and organizational form. Over time, however, many of these barriers were lowered or weakened, resulting in the expansion of the space for internationally related private economic activities. The driving forces for such change came not only from shifts in the central leadership's own strategic calculations and growing international pressures for greater degrees of opening, but oftentimes from the behavior of local gatekeepers and regulators that deviated from centrally defined rules and mandates.

What drove local authorities to go beyond centrally imposed limits, according to Zweig (2002), was regional competition. By bending the rules on foreign investment local authorities sought to increase the attractiveness of the institutional environments under their purview, thereby gaining first mover's advantage in the rivalry for external resources. There were variations, however, in the intensity of such efforts. To explain this, Huang (2002) looks to the preexisting conditions of reform. He argues that China's regional economic fragmentation hindered the geographical flow of financial resources and thus raised the demand for the use of external capital to finance local economic development. During the early years of reform, private enterprises were denied access to credit and faced regulatory discrimination, whereas SOEs were inefficient and administratively barred from organizational integration across jurisdictional boundaries. This created a niche for foreign investors to emerge as a leading source of capital supply, and consequently local dependence on FDI grew. The higher the demand for foreign capital, the more concessions local authorities had to make to foreign investors, hence deepening the degree of privatization.

These explanations are useful in that they help us understand the interplay of internationalization and privatization by illuminating an important link between the political and economic benefits of foreign capital and the behavior of local officials. Yet there is more to the story. The rule-bending behavior of local officials was not free of political risk. As will be shown in chapter 6, without the help and support of local officials many foreign investors would not have been able to bypass national regulatory approval requirements, enter sectors with centrally imposed restrictions or even bans, take organizational forms (e.g., wholly foreign-owned venture, joint venture with minority or declining public ownership, and joint venture with domestic private enterprises) discouraged or disallowed under existing policies, and locate themselves in the same regions and sectors already populated by central or provincial SOEs. Facilitating these pursuits inevitably violated or deviated from the norms of administrative conduct and, if not properly defended and justified, could have negative consequences to the local gatekeepers concerned.

To be sure, unlike the domestic private sector, foreign investment was generally encouraged by the central leadership from the very beginning of economic reforms. This left local authorities with greater degrees of freedom to manipulate around centrally set rules. In comparison with domestic private enterprises, foreign investors were also more mobile in site selection—especially in the early years of reform, thus having greater bargaining power versus local gatekeepers. The question is how far the latter would go beyond the existing policy limits to attract and accommodate foreign capital. In fact, not all of them were noncompliant with the rules. Different tendencies toward such behavior therefore provide a useful window on the mechanisms whereby privatization deepened through localized economic internationalization.

As a major consideration in the self-interest calculus of local officials, dependence on foreign capital is a factor relevant to explaining the variations. But it is insufficient because understanding how the political risk generated in the interactions with foreign investors was tackled requires an examination of the interactions between local and higher-level authorities, which are interdependent. The ability of a local government to buffer or alleviate the political risk of rule bending depends greatly on the strength of its bargaining power with higher-level authorities. As I will show in chapter 6, during the first three decades of reform such bargaining power tended to be particularly strong in two diagonally different types of locales: those that contributed significantly to the revenue bases of higher-level authorities and, interestingly, those that relied heavily upon fiscal subsidies to cover the perennial gaps in basic public spending. The leverage came from the fiscal dependence of higher-level authorities on the former and from their need to contain or reduce the fiscal burdens posed by the latter, especially when the shortfalls were further compounded by significant local unemployment pressures. A close analysis of fiscal flows—especially various remittance and transfer arrangements, therefore, will be useful for unveiling the dynamics of the bargaining relationships within the state system, as well as their implications for local FDI policies. Given the importance of vertical bargaining to political risk management over the full spectrum of ownership-related issues, the investigation along this line of inquiry will also yield more clues to understanding the attitude and behavior of local officials toward the domestic private sector.

Summary

In short, the entrepreneurship thesis can be strengthened with an explicit analysis of the risks (and costs) of unauthorized local government actions to facilitate or promote private enterprise. The role of entrepreneurship can also be more clearly understood from a broader view that incorporates the causes, dynamics, and effects of central policymaking regarding the private sector. The budget constraint thesis can benefit from closer attention to the moral hazard associated with the pursuit of political benefits through softening the budget constraint on public enterprises. It can also be complemented with an account of self-seeking behavior of party-state officials as a concurrent cause for the deteriorating financial health of public enterprises, as well as by an analysis of the changing opportunity costs of maintaining and relying on these enterprises. The FDI thesis can be reinforced with an account that considers not only the benefits but the costs of local deviations from centrally defined rules and examines how such costs were dealt with by extending the analytic focus from the dependence on foreign capital to the interdependence between different levels of political authority. Demographics and public finance, as pointed out above, provide useful coordinates for these further explorations of the decision-making and behavior of political actors, whose roles loom large but remain somewhat blurry in each of the three theses.

Political Actors as Change Agents: The Main Storyline

The political actors examined in this study are decision-makers throughout the hierarchy of public administration in China.[8] My analysis centers on officials in the executive branch of the state, known as the People's Government. In terms of both personnel and range of functions it is by far the largest among the four constitutionally defined branches of power in the Chinese state system,[9] and the actions undertaken by officials in the executive branch have had the most immediate impact on the decline of public ownership and the evolution of private ownership. Despite inconsistencies and contradictions between the institutional logic of the CCP and that of the government (Zheng 1997), in practice the CCP has been the guiding and integrating force of governmental decision-making throughout the reform era. In this study, therefore, I will not explicitly treat them as separate analytical units.

In terms of their roles in the economy, the political actors in public administration can be categorized into four groups: (*a*) political leaders at each level of government, (*b*) economic bureaucrats who have broad regulatory, extractive, or allocative authority over economic activities in each jurisdiction, (*c*) administrators of agencies overseeing public enterprises, and (*d*) noneconomic bureaucrats with other government functions (in education, cultural and religious affairs, social services, etc.). I assume these political actors to be self-interested decision-makers who take calculated risks, though none of the groups is internally homogenous. Differences in rank, administrative function, ideological predispositions (e.g., regarding communist orthodoxy versus pragmatism), role differentiation between the CCP and the state apparatus, factional divisions, personal rivalry, variations in time discount rate, and so forth may all result in considerable heterogeneity in the interest calculus used

---

8. Here I define a decision-maker as a cadre (*ganbu*) with some kind of rule-making, enforcement, allocative, extractive, or supervisory authority at or above the rank of deputy division chief (*fu ke ji*) in the nomenclature system of the party-state proper. Managers of public enterprises, decision-makers in government-funded establishments like hospitals, schools, and research institutions, and heads of communal organizations such as village residents' committees and urban neighborhood committees are not included.

9. The four branches of power of the Chinese state as defined by the constitution are People's Congress, People's Government, People's Court, and People's Procuratorate.

by the actors in each group and thereby affect the coherence of their decisions and actions. What is interesting, however, is that over time the effects of their decision-making driven by diverse motivating forces have converged in the direction of creating increasing space for the growth of private economic activities.

The story began with post-Mao CCP leaders. Despite internal differences, they shared a common concern about collective survival, which was rendered highly precarious by the disastrous consequences of Maoist radicalism. In face of the threat posed by serious job creation pressures and fiscal shortfalls at the end of the Cultural Revolution (1966–1976), they expanded the space for self-employment and initiated fiscal decentralization. They also made the historic decision in 1978 to shift the focus of policy from class struggle to economic development, which was followed by a corresponding retooling of the performance assessment system for local political leaders. These centrally initiated measures set off a chain of responses and interactions that contributed to the decline of the public sector in the 1980s and 1990s. They opened the door for new players—private entrepreneurs and foreign investors, whose efforts to seek further growth not only diluted public ownership in the economy but posed competition to public enterprises and demonstrated a viable alternative. The initial measures introduced by central decision-makers also changed the incentives and constraints faced by local political actors. While these actors were driven to focus their policies on the economy, three types of opportunism grew and consequently combined to expand the space for private ownership and paved the way for the massive privatization around the turn of the century.[10]

First, public enterprises were overexpanded as a way to facilitate the pursuit of careerist and revenue-related benefits for local officials. Second, similar agendas drove local officials to bend centrally set restrictions on private business and foreign capital. Third, illicit use of public office for self-enrichment by political actors of different ranks and administrative functions became a widespread phenomenon. What led to the overexpansion of public enterprises was a widely used strategy by local officials to promote, with the aid of financial leverage, the growth of industrial sales delinked from profitability. It boosted the expansion of output, revenue, and employment, all of which were important for the self-interest of local officials. The strategy was shaped by two important features of the fiscal system: heavy reliance on indirect taxes (realized in or through sales) and existence of gray areas for revenue

---

10. These types of behavior were opportunistic in that they advanced self-interest at the expense of compromising the formal agendas of the CCP.

manipulation through off-budget and (public) enterprise accounts. It was further reinforced by a high time discount rate among local political leaders who faced periodic rotation, transient tenure, and lack of clear administrative cost accounting. Moreover, it was also seemingly consistent with the centrally defined mandate of making public enterprises the leading force of marketization.

Yet the abilities to carry on the strategy varied among different locales. Where it fell short or faltered, alternative or parallel strategies, such as use of unauthorized measures to promote private business and foreign investment, assumed greater potential importance. These strategies involved political risks, however. Where the risks could be contained or managed, the space for private ownership tended to experience early expansion. At the same time local rule-bending for private capital was often intertwined with private exchanges for political actors' self-enrichment at the expense of public ownership. Similarly damaging effects also resulted from the pursuit of the initially dominant strategy (of promoting sales growth among public enterprises), which not only undermined the financial health of public enterprises but weakened their organizational governance due to increased monitoring cost and collusion between supervising officials and managers.

By the mid-1990s the (over)expansion of the public sector reached its limit. Financial liabilities became increasingly unbearable, which was compounded by a series of centrally adopted measures to address dysfunctional consequences of earlier (especially fiscal) reforms. The problem was also exacerbated by a triple crunch from demographic factors—the swelling of personnel redundancy in public enterprises, the persistence of vast job creation pressures, and the rising wave of urban retirement. To cope with the challenges, in 1997 the central leadership resorted to ownership restructuring among SOEs. But both the tempo and the scope of what followed went far beyond their initial plans. Within six years the entire collective sector collapsed, and SOEs laid off some half of their workforce and lost the leading positions in the majority of the economic sectors they had dominated. Among the forces that contributed to such precipitous decline were a political bandwagon effect from among "laggard locales" of earlier economic development, a shift in the focus of the self-interest calculus of local officials from industry to urban development, and asset stripping by insiders. The following decade saw continuing erosion of the public sector, though the state tried to "rationalize" the new economic order by consolidating and reinforcing the remaining SOEs in a handful of strategically important sectors while letting private and foreign capital dominate the bulk of the Chinese economy.

The central theme of this story is that political actors have been important change agents in China's ownership transformation. With a close bearing on jobs and revenue, demographic forces and the evolving fiscal system have had significant influence on the decision-making of these actors and shaped the consequences of their behavior. Both national and local officials have played important roles in the decline of public ownership. My account of this decline focuses on the first three decades of the post-Mao era (1977–2007), when private economic activities gradually became the mainstay of the economy and took hold in an increasingly free and institutionalized space. I must stress that recognizing this phenomenon should by no means be interpreted as negating the fact that public ownership still dominates a number of important economic sectors and accounts for a sizable part of the country's economic assets and output. Nor should it be seen as indicating the state's unwillingness and inability to hold onto and support the remaining public enterprises and to even reclaim some of the territories already dominated by private capital. What I seek to explain is why the state was unable to retain the overwhelming majority of public enterprises into the twenty-first century and what has constrained its ability to curb the growth of private enterprises in most economic sectors.

I begin my exploration with an overview of the changing fate of the private sector. Chapter 1 traces the evolution of private ownership since 1949, with a focus on several major twists and turns that profoundly changed the space of private business during and after the Mao era. This survey is further substantiated with a descriptive statistical mapping of a number of important features of the re-emerging private sector and foreign investment, including organizational forms, geographic variations, sectoral distributions, and changes over time. In so doing, the chapter brings up a number of key questions that will be addressed in the ensuing chapters.

Chapter 2 provides a macro analysis of the implications of China's evolving demographics for policymaking. The main story is that the pressure to create jobs was both a most important initial trigger and a persistent force for the shift in government policy—especially central government policy—toward the private sector. The lasting impact of Maoist policies on population and economic development, the aftermath of political radicalism during the Cultural Revolution, structural changes in the economy, and the cohort effects of the population were among the factors that constrained the choice set of CCP leaders and shaped the orientation and timing of their decisions on the private sector.

In chapter 3, I examine the evolution of the fiscal system, with a view to setting up a backdrop for the analysis of its implications for privatization in subsequent chapters. What the chapter illustrates is that the post-Mao fiscal structure was path dependent in that it continued to bear some essential features of the old system while seeking to address some of its main problems through decentralization and with the incorporation of a contractual element in fiscal relations. These features and changes had a profound impact on the economic strategies of local governments concerning public and private enterprises. Unintended consequences of earlier reforms led to a major fiscal restructuring in the mid-1990s. It redefined the self-interest calculus of local political actors, whose responses hastened the decline of public enterprises.

Chapter 4 explores the ramifications of the evolving demographic conditions and fiscal reforms for the careers of local political leaders. The focal issue is the moral hazard embodied in these leaders' opportunistic use of public enterprises for career advancement and revenue control and manipulation during the 1980s and early 1990s. Their dominant strategy was to promote sales growth without a close link to profitability among the public enterprises under their purview. This strategy helped grow output, revenue, and employment, thereby contributing to the political and economic interests of local officials. Yet it also undermined the financial and organizational health of public enterprises and pushed them down the road to destruction.

Chapter 5 investigates the strategies of local officials in places where the sales growth strategy faltered in the early years of reform. An alternative strategy was to tolerate and even facilitate the expansion of private business beyond centrally set limits, as illustrated by the much-studied case of Wenzhou in Zhejiang province. Echoing a prevailing view on the important role of entrepreneurship in early privatization, the chapter goes further to investigate how and why local entrepreneurial forces survived Maoism in the peculiar local setting, and how their interplay with extraordinary economic hardship developed into both a driving force for local policy change and a shield against the political risks that had to be contained. This re-examination of the case material also sheds light on why Wenzhou was an "aberration" and why many regions that lagged in public-enterprise-led growth did not actively promote private business before centrally initiated ownership restructuring.

Chapter 6 extends the analytic logic of this investigation to the privatization function of FDI. The focal issue is how and why foreign investors were able to overcome centrally imposed regulatory and policy constraints on their entry, expansion, and organization before the implementation of trade liberalization associated with China's WTO accession in 2001. Again, rule bending by local governments was the centerpiece of the story. As in the case of locales experiencing early privatization, local officials took calculated political risks by using economic hardship and the benefits of FDI for addressing revenue and employment imperatives as justifications. The extent of their deviations from centrally set boundaries nevertheless varied, depending greatly on the bargaining power of local political leaders vis-à-vis their supervising authorities. In particular, I will show that whether a locale was perceived as a major fiscal burden or an important resource contributor to higher-level authorities was a major differentiating factor.

The convergence of the erosive forces discussed in chapters 4–6 culminated in a massive sell-off and closure of public enterprises, as well as wide-ranging relaxation of restrictions on private economic activities, in the second half of the 1990s and beyond. Chapter 7 explores how the tipping point came about and what set the tempo and shaped the scope of the precipitous changes that followed and spread beyond the initial limits set by central leaders. It shows that the trigger came from a confluence of challenges rendered by the sales growth strategy, the 1994 fiscal restructuring, and persistent and evolving demographic forces. The pace and extent of subsequent ownership change were greatly influenced by a political bandwagon effect, a shift in the focus of local officials' self-interest calculus, and an intensification of insider manipulation in the public sector. The interplay among these forces represented a continuation of the same opportunistic rationality that had driven the behavior of political actors up to the tipping point and beyond, including CCP leaders who, in seeking expedient solutions to historically and structurally engendered problems and challenges, kept sidestepping ideological principles to look after their greatest interest of all—immediate regime survival.

The process of privatization, therefore, mirrors the decline of communism in China. Revealing the underlying mechanisms at work in this fundamental transformation not only enriches the understanding of China's economic transformation but may yield useful clues for addressing many issues of broader theoretical interest and empirical relevance. The concluding chapter discusses the implications of the findings of the book for institutional analysis. I will show how a mechanism-focused view can make integrative and fruitful use of the analytical tools furnished by the existing literature. In particular I focus on the role of unintended consequences of rule-compliant behavior, the sustaining factors for noncompliance and its consequences to institutional instability, and the causal channels of path dependence in an evolutionary process of institutional change. It is the forces associated with these mechanisms that have contributed to defining and redefining the choices of political and economic actors and fashioning the outcomes of their strategies and interactions.

Note on Statistical Analyses, Data Sources, and Chinese Materials

The original manuscript of this book contained elaborate presentations and discussions of statistical analyses (in chapters 4–7), detailed descriptions and documentations of data sources, and a full listing of the page numbers of published statistics used in tables and figures. To make more efficient use of the limited space available and to avoid distraction for general-interest readers, these materials, along with notes on interviews with informants and additional information items, are posted at a website created and maintained for this book: https://www.privatizationinchina.ust.hk/. The main text instead focuses on summarizing and interpreting the results of data analyses. The tables and figures in the book only indicate the titles and the years of the statistical sources used.

The bibliography lists materials in Chinese separately from those in English. Throughout the book authors of Chinese materials are cited by full name instead of surname only. Following the Chinese convention, surnames of these authors are placed before their given names. For brevity, Chinese statistical publications are referenced by abbreviated titles instead of authors.

1

The Changing Fate of Private Ownership since 1949

SIX DAYS AFTER the Chinese People's Political Consultative Conference decided on the design for the new national flag, Mao took the podium at the Gate of Heavenly Peace in Beijing and proclaimed to the world the founding of the People's Republic of China. In keeping with Mao's "New Democracy Theory," the new political regime retained private ownership. During 1950–1953 the CCP made good on what it had promised during the civil war—confiscating the land owned by landlords and redistributing it to poor peasants who had little or no land. That move solidified the rural base of popular support for the CCP and helped the economy to make a quick recovery. In urban areas, the government relied heavily on private industry and commerce for the supply of essential goods and services and for the military provisions used by the Chinese troops fighting the Korean War (1950–1953).

The ensuing six years, however, ushered in drastic changes in the ownership of economic resources. In rural areas, peasants were first coerced to give up family-based farming and join government-controlled cooperatives; then they saw a quick erosion and eventual loss of the essential rights to make decisions on, to derive income from, and to dispose of the land, draft animals, and farm tools that they had brought into the cooperatives. In 1959 the government reorganized the cooperatives as people's communes, where "collective" ownership replaced the nominal private ownership of cooperative members. In urban areas, the government made use of massive Soviet aid and newly added investment to expand the public sector, which had been formed with the assets accumulated in CCP-occupied areas before 1949 and those taken over from the KMT or left behind by foreign and Chinese capitalists who had fled the revolution. In the meantime, it forced private industrial and commercial concerns to give up private ownership through mergers with public enterprises or conversion into cooperatives controlled and ultimately owned by the government in the newly created "collective sector." By 1959 state-owned enterprises and collective enterprises occupied the entire landscape of urban industry and commerce.[1]

This process of "socialist transformation" and the subsequent total dominance of public ownership throughout the 1960s and 1970s are well documented in many existing studies (e.g., MacFarquhar and Fairbank 1987; Shue 1980; Solinger 1984); so are the processes of the resurgence of private ownership since 1978 (e.g., Dickson 2008; Garnaut et al. 2001; Garnaut and Song 2004; Garnaut et al. 2005; Tsai 2002, 2007; Young 1995). What I want to highlight here is the incompleteness of the elimination of private ownership before 1978, which has implications for understanding the transformations since the end of the Cultural Revolution (1966–1976). I will also highlight sweeping policy changes adopted by the central authority that represented major turning points or landmarks in the process of post-Mao privatization despite recurrent attempts at retaining public ownership to the extent possible. I will then provide a statistical mapping of that process, including an account of the increasingly important role of FDI in the spread and deepening of private ownership.

Socialist Transformation and the Mao Era

The acceleration of "socialist transformation" during the mid-1950s was not what CCP leaders had planned for.[2] The drastic change in strategy was probably due to a number of developments after the revolution (MacFarquhar and Fairbank 1987; Riskin 1987). Euphoria from the success in economic recovery and political power consolidation in the early 1950s boosted Mao's confidence in the ability of the new state to push through fundamental social transformation sooner and deeper than anticipated. Power struggles within the CCP and growing tension with the Soviet Union might have driven Mao to step up the effort to eliminate private ownership so as to showcase the "superiority"

---

1. Both SOEs and urban collective enterprises were government-owned entities. Their main difference lay in the fact that SOEs were controlled by generally higher-level authorities and given greater priority in resource allocation than collective enterprises (Lin 2001).

2. See the memoir of Bo Yibo (Bo 1991, vol. 1), who was in charge of public finance in the early 1950s, for an insider's account of top CCP leaders' decision-making on major issues during 1949–1966.

of his radicalized view of socialist development. Depriving citizens of independent means of living for the purpose of behavioral control (Schurmann 1968; Walder 1986), which Mao emphasized and many CCP leaders felt an accentuated need for after becoming rulers, was another possible contributing factor.

It should be noted, however, that the end of the 1950s did not see a complete elimination of private ownership in China. Owners of private companies that had merged with public enterprises during the socialist transformation continued to receive a fixed dividend (at 5% of their equity shares) annually until September 1966—four months into the Cultural Revolution (Fei Kailong and Zuo Ping 1991, 85–86). More importantly, despite the overwhelming dominance of the *danwei* (work unit) system institutionalized in urban China at the end of the 1950s (Lu and Perry 1997; Walder 1986), the government was unable to provide full employment to all work-age urban citizens. During the 1960s and 1970s, a small number of urban citizens were allowed to be self-employed as supplementary providers of urban services (Fei Kailong and Zuo Ping 1991). Among the activities that they undertook to earn a meager living were repair services (e.g., for bicycles, timepieces, radios, and various household appliances), personal services (e.g., hair cutting, tailoring, furniture making, etc.), sanitary work, and recycling. They were closely monitored by local offices of the State Administration for Industry and Commerce (SAIC). Their income was unstable and, for housing and other basic social service provisions, they had to rely on family members who held regular jobs in government-controlled work units. Their self-employment was irregular too, and many of them were absorbed into SOEs or urban collectives when additional vacancies opened up.[3]

In rural areas the people's communes were organized to produce agricultural output according to government plans. Grain was the most important product. But in most farming communities each family was allotted a small plot of public land, known as *ziliu di* (land set aside for self-use), to produce supplementary food items (vegetables, fruits, pigs, chickens, etc.) for consumption by household members. Despite collectivization of farmland, housing remained privately owned as part of the means of living, though it was illegal to sell private housing or use it for profit making. Unlike the urban sector, however, rural communities were not given formal allowances for

---

3. In 1952 there were 7.24 million self-employed individuals registered with the SAIC; in 1959 the number was reduced to 1.06 million (*CLWS a*, 5). The total number crept back to 2.31 million in 1964 but steadily declined in subsequent years, with only 0.15 million remaining in 1978 (*CLWS a*, 5).

self-employment. Four types of private economic activities nevertheless struggled to persist under the commune system (Fei Kailong and Zuo Ping 1991).

Some rural residents sold part of the produces from *ziliu di* to gray (with organizational buyers) or black (with individual buyers) markets in urban areas. Some—especially those in areas with scarce farmland—drifted away from their home communities to urban areas (where they had relatives and/or acquaintances through communal ties) to take up illicit odd jobs in construction and transportation, to peddle farm produces and/or handicraft products, or to provide various repair or personal services. Still some others made small sums of money by illegally obtaining and selling products (especially consumer goods) that were in short supply at state-controlled rural distribution outlets. Such activities were labeled *touji daoba* (speculative buying and selling) and faced periodic crackdowns by the government. In addition some rural nonfarm organizations, known as commune and brigade enterprises, broke the rules and farmed out part of their work to individual households with private wages, as will be discussed in chapter 5.

From *Getihu* to "Equal Protection" of Public and Private Property Rights

The resurgence of private ownership in the reform era started out as an outgrowth of the remnant private economic elements on the margins of central planning. Soon after the historic decision by the CCP leadership to reform China's economic system in December 1978, nonfarm self-employment activities expanded in both urban and rural areas.[4] In the ensuing three decades, such expansion converged with the growth of more formal and sizable private enterprises of different ownership forms. Many factors contributed to this process, which will be discussed later. What I want to emphasize here is that a series of centrally adopted policy changes played a critical part in redefining and broadening the institutional space for private business.[5]

In November 1979 the CCP Central Party Committee decided to remove the political label "capitalist" that had been attached to the activities of

---

4. The agricultural sector was reorganized during 1979–1983, when family farming was restored to replace collective farming and the commune system at large (Perkins 1988; Yang 1996; Zweig 1989).

5. This account complements the various studies that emphasize the role of entrepreneurs in privatization. It, however, should not be taken to imply that the central leadership has taken a passive attitude to the decline of public ownership. As I will show in the following chapters, these changes are often responses to unsuccessful attempts by authorities at all levels of the state system to continue to rely on public enterprises to address essential policy concerns.

self-employed individuals during the socialist transformation in the mid-1950s. Such a symbolic move to destigmatize those individuals and their families signaled a more tolerant attitude toward the role of self-employment in the Chinese economy. In the following year the SAIC formally legalized self-employment by creating a new category of business licensing: *geti gongshang hu* or simply *getihu*, which means self-employment entities in industry and commerce. It nevertheless limited the size of the workforce in such entities to no more than seven employees, with one to two "helpers" and three to five "apprentices" allowed for each entity. The legality of self-employment was further codified in the 1982 constitution,[6] which stated that "economic activities undertaken by self-employed working people within the boundaries stipulated by law are a supplementary segment of China's socialist economy based on public ownership. The state shall protect the legal rights and interests of self-employed economic elements." In August 1987 the State Council issued the Provisional Ordinance on the Administration of Self-Employed Individuals in Urban and Rural Industry and Commerce.[7] It served as the main legal framework for the regulation of *getihu* until April 2011, when the State Council formally replaced it with the Ordinance on Urban and Rural Industrial and Commercial Self-Employment.

Back in 1979 the government enacted the Law on Chinese-Foreign Equity Joint Ventures. It marked the beginning of the open-door policy that encouraged the return of foreign capital and the expansion of international trade. In the following decade the inflow of foreign (private) capital via joint ventures with public enterprises became an increasingly important force to dilute public ownership in the economy. It received a major boost when the government enacted the Law on Foreign-Funded Enterprises in 1986, which further allowed foreign investors to form wholly foreign owned ventures. In 1988 the Law on Chinese-Foreign Contractual Joint Ventures was enacted to provide greater flexibility for foreign investors and their local partners to negotiate and define the relationship of equity capital to decision rights, profits, and liabilities (Pearson 1991).

In 1988 the National People's Congress adopted a constitutional amendment, which stated that "the state allows the existence and development of private economic activities within the boundaries of law. The private sector is

---

6. The constitution of the PRC was first enacted in 1954. It subsequently underwent substantial amendments three times—in 1975, 1978, and 1982 respectively.

7. The State Council is the command center of the executive branch of the Chinese state. It is also called the Central People's Government.

a supplementary element to socialist public ownership. The state protects the legal rights and interests of private business." In accordance with this expansion of the legal space for the private sector beyond self-employment, the government lifted the size limit (of employing no more than seven people) on private economic entities by creating a new category in the licensing and registration of industrial and commercial organizations: *siying qiye*, or private enterprise. According to the Provisional Ordinance on Private Enterprises adopted in the same year, a private enterprise can take one of three organizational forms: sole proprietorship, partnership, and limited liability company.

The June Fourth Incident in 1989 was followed by a significant slowdown of economic reforms and a more hostile policy environment toward private ownership for nearly three years.[8] Yet the institutional changes that had been introduced with regard to the private sector and foreign capital in the preceding decade were not reversed.[9] Indeed, even during this period of policy retrenchment an event of long-term significance for privatization took place. In 1990 the central government decided to establish two stock exchanges in Shanghai and Shenzhen. Initially all the listed companies were government-owned, and only a very small number of companies in the public sector were allowed to gain access. Nevertheless, allowing private citizens to purchase the stocks of these companies created a new avenue for the dilution of public ownership. Moreover, with gradual relaxation of entry restrictions, the stock market has subsequently grown and become an important venue for private companies to raise capital and expand, and to take over companies with initial predominance of government ownership.[10]

In the fall of 1992 the CCP held its Fourteenth Party Congress. That meeting took place in the wake of paramount leader Deng Xiaoping's "southern tour" (Fewsmith 2008), when he visited several provinces in South China and along the way made repeated calls for a speeding up of the process of

---

8. Huang (2008) argues that the impact of this policy entrenchment lasted for more than a decade. Evidence presented in this book does not seem to be consistent with that view, though I do agree that privatization in China should not be seen as a linear process.

9. To weather the sudden change in political climate, however, some private business owners resorted to a practice known as "donning the red hat"—falsely registering their companies as public enterprises, oftentimes with the help or consent of local officials (Shi Xiammin 1993; Young 1995).

10. Currently private or predominantly private companies account for about two-thirds of the listed companies (totaling some three thousand) in mainland China and overseas. Lists of domestically listed companies with and without controlling stakes held by the state are available at the official site of the China Securities Index Co. (http://www.csindex.com.cn/sseportal/csiportal/xzzx/queryindexdownloadlist.do?type=1).

reform and opening that had been stalled following the June Fourth Incident. At the party congress, the CCP leadership redefined the reforming Chinese economy as a "socialist market economy," in which the status of the private sector was elevated from a "supplementary element," as defined before, to an "integral part" of the new economy. Following the party congress, the government also made greater efforts to encourage foreign investment, including relaxation of entry restrictions on a large number of economic sectors, as indicated by a series of measures to further promote foreign investment (Lardy 2002). In 1995 the State Council issued a set of comprehensive and elaborate guidelines on where foreign investment would be encouraged, restricted, and banned. It expanded the sectors for foreign entry and showed clearer directions of opening to investors and gatekeepers.

In 1997 the CCP held its Fifteenth Party Congress. At that meeting it was declared that public ownership could take diverse forms (other than public sole proprietorship), hence formally opening the door for immediate dilution and/or subsequent decline of public ownership through various shareholding arrangements with private ownership. At the same time the status of the private sector was further elevated to "an *important* [emphasis added] integral part" of China's "socialist market economy." This redefinition of the role of private ownership was incorporated in a constitutional amendment by the National People's Congress in 1999. A concurrent change is that in 1997 the central government adopted a policy called *zhuada fangxiao*, or "holding onto the large and letting go of the small," to restructure and eventually privatize large numbers of small and medium-sized SOEs. That move, also known as *gaizhi* (ownership restructuring), soon spread to the urban and rural collective sector. Within six years, the vast majority of the public enterprises that had existed in the mid-1990s were sold off or closed down, as will be shown in chapter 7.

From 1997 to 2007, the State Council made four rounds of revisions to the 1995 guidelines on sectoral entry by foreign investors. In each round of revisions, greater space was granted for the inflow of foreign capital. The most noticeable change concerns the relaxation or removal of restrictions on foreign entry into a variety of service sector activities (e.g., banking, whole sale, professional services), especially after and as a concession for China's WTO accession December 2001. Another important feature of these revisions is a gradual increase in the sectors in which entry by wholly foreign-owned enterprises is permitted, as will be shown later in this chapter and then in chapter 6.

With the expansion of the private sector, the CCP gave further recognition to the political importance of this new economic force. On July 1 2001,

CCP general secretary Jiang Zemin delivered a keynote speech at the celebration ceremony for the eightieth anniversary of the founding of the CCP. During that speech, he formally welcomed private business people to join the CCP, which ironically has the ultimate goal of building a society without private ownership. To give further assurance to private owners, the National People's Congress adopted another constitutional amendment in 2004, which emphatically stated for the first time in the history of the PRC that "citizens' lawful property rights are inviolable."

In February 2005 the State Council issued "Guidelines on Encouraging, Supporting, and Guiding the Development of Self-employed, Private, and Other Nonpublic Economic Entities." Its basic spirit was to relax restrictions on the entry by domestic private economic entities to sectors that had been monopolized by SOEs, such as power, telecommunications, railway, air transport, oil, public utilities, infrastructure, social services, financial services, and even defense industries. It granted "equal" entry rights to foreign and domestic private companies to "legally allowed" sectors, correcting a long-standing entry policy bias in favor of foreign companies (Huang 2002). Both foreign and domestic enterprises were also encouraged to take part in SOE ownership restructuring and economic development in the western (underdeveloped) region of the country, whereas the government promised more fiscal, financial, and social service support for these entities. These guidelines were reiterated and further elaborated in a follow-up document issued by the State Council in May 2010, entitled "Guidelines on Further Encouraging and Directing Healthy Development of Private Investment." It also encouraged domestic private entities to take active part in global expansion and competition.

In 2007 the National People's Congress enacted the Real Right Law (*wuquan fa*), which is also translated as the Property Law in Western media. The drafting of the law started in 1993 and underwent eight rounds of rewriting amid considerable controversy and objections raised by conservative scholars and officials. It covers both publicly and privately owned entities. The most noteworthy part of the law is that in Article 3 it explicitly states that "the state shall oversee a socialist market economy and shall protect the *equal* [emphasis added] legal status and development rights of all market subjects," which include entities owned by the state, collectives, and private citizens. This represented the culmination of a series of changes that combined to form and institutionalize a new legal-regulatory framework for private ownership following the landmark decision in 1997 to downsize the public sector.

Reversal or Moderation of Privatization?

To be sure, what has been stated in law should not be taken at its face value. Indeed, in the wake of the enactment of the Real Right Law there was a heated debate in Chinese mass media and academia about whether the massive privatization at the turn of the century was followed by a reversing trend.[11] The debate revolved around the notion of *guojin mintui*, or "the state advances, the private sector retreats."[12] It was concerned with two major arguments by the proponents of the notion:[13] (*a*) the government increased its policy bias toward the remaining public sector in terms of regulation and investment; and (*b*) there were concrete attempts by the government to reclaim territories already ceded to private capital.

Despite a gradual lifting of entry restrictions on sectors that until recently were exclusively reserved for state-owned companies, private and foreign companies have continued to face formidable de facto barriers, especially in such forms as ad hoc restrictions on the scope of business,[14] granting of government contracts, and preferential regulatory treatment of the SOEs that have survived privatization (Naughton and Tsai 2015). During the 2008 global financial crisis, the central authority initiated a 4-trillion-yuan stimulation program of infrastructural investment. The bulk of the investment is widely claimed to have been channeled into state-owned companies.[15] A result of this and other types of financial transfusion is an expansion of many remaining state-owned companies not only in their traditional domains of operation but also in some sectors (such as real estate development) where competition between SOEs and private and foreign enterprises has been limited.

---

11. A collection of contending views can be found at http://www.aisixiang.com/data/related-51767.html. Parallel to this debate is a growing Western literature on "state capitalism" in China (e.g., Hsueh 2011, 2016; Naughton and Tsai 2015). See Lardy 2014 for a critique.

12. According to an article published in a CCP-run magazine and reposted at the website of the SASAC (http://www.sasac.gov.cn/n1180/n1271/n20515/n2697206/15065063.html), this notion first appeared in 2001, when massive privatization was still underway. It gained much wider currency during and after the global financial crisis, especially in 2009–2010.

13. A related (albeit less contentious) issue is whether government planning has made a comeback in the postprivatization era and how it has affected the roles of SOEs and private business (Naughton 2013).

14. Lardy (2014) argues that private enterprises face more restrictions in some service sectors (e.g., financial services and telecommunications) than in industrial sectors.

15. According to Wu Jinglian, a prominent Chinese economist, such bias led to an overflow of investment in SOEs (especially those under the SASAC) such that many of them channeled the funds to the real estate sector (http://www.cfi.cn/p20140421000944.html).

Indeed, a noticeable phenomenon in recent years is the rise of very large state-owned or controlled enterprise groups or multibusiness conglomerates. Mostly consolidated and reorganized under the purview of the State Assets Supervision and Administration Commission (SASAC) since 2003, many of these companies have experienced significant expansion through capital injection from the state and with funds raised from public listing on domestic and international stock markets. In 1997 only two mainland Chinese companies appeared on the list of the Fortune Global 500. Both of them were state-owned companies. In 2007 the number increased to eighteen, all of which had a 50% or higher equity share held by the state. In 2016 the number jumped to ninety-eight, eighty (or 82%) of which were state-owned or controlled.[16]

A concurrent development is that there have been several widely publicized incidences where privately owned companies were gobbled up by state-owned companies or lost their control rights to the state. Examples include the acquisition of Rizhao Steel Holding Group (a profitable privately owned company) by Shandong Iron and Steel Group (an SOE with operating losses) in 2009, the transfer of private controlling stake in Mengniu Dairy (then China's largest private dairy company) to COFCO (a state-owned conglomerate) in 2009, and the closure of several hundred small, privately operated coal mines and the takeover of some larger ones by state-owned companies in Shanxi in 2009–2010.[17]

What these developments clearly show is that the state has by no means taken a passive attitude toward the decline of public ownership and, wherever possible, has indeed tried to retain, reinforce, or even expand it. While it is evident that the remaining SOEs have received massive regulatory and financial support from the state, incidences of the state's reclaiming lost territories seem to have been limited.[18] Some scholars have questioned the overall magnitude of the alleged reversal effect of recent state actions on China's ownership structure. Based on a comprehensive analysis of official statistical data, for example, Hu Angang of the Chinese Academy of Sciences finds no evidence of any substantial change in the shares accounted for by public enterprises in

---

16. Annual information about the Fortune Global 500 is available at http://fortune.com/rankings/.

17. A sample of Western media reports on these incidences can be found at http://www.bloomberg.com/apps/news?pid=newsarchive&sid=a_ZaNgSyZNv8, http://online.wsj.com/news/articles/SB124684730489898749, and http://www.ft.com/cms/s/0/c1bb90ce-71c0-11e0-9adf-00144feabdc0.html.

18. In fact, following the "Resolution on Deepening Economic Reforms" adopted at the Third Plenum of the CCP's Eighteenth Central Party Committee in November 2013, a new round of SOE reforms has been underway, with such measures as greater allowance for private companies to enter sectors

terms of a variety of economic indicators in the industrial sector.[19] This finding is echoed in a data analysis on assets, GDP, and employment, conducted by Pei Changhong (2014), director of the Institute of Economics of the Chinese Academy of Social Sciences. An equally relevant question is whether the state has been able to rebuild and increase its ability to rely on the public sector for addressing the revenue and employment imperatives, which this book argues was fundamentally related to the massive ownership restructuring around the turn of the century.

In a recent study Lardy (2014) argues that the Chinese government's highly publicized attempt during the Hu-Wen era (2002–2012) to create so-called national champions via the SASAC and various industrial policies has been unsuccessful. The return on assets among centrally owned/controlled SOEs has plummeted since 2007 (when *guojin mintui* was about to become a contentious issue), raising questions about the sustainability of their further expansion.[20] As I will show later in this chapter and in chapter 3, the shares of public sector contribution to employment and government revenue have significantly declined since the mid-1990s. Although the pace of change has moderated in the past decade, the overall trend of erosion seems to have continued. A full analysis of what influences the relative significance between the public sector and the private sector in the postprivatization era is beyond the scope of this book. The focus of my study is instead on how and why the role of public enterprises in the economy experienced substantial shrinkage during the three post-Mao decades ending in 2007, when the enactment of the Real Right Law represented a pivotal landmark in the development of institutional protection for private ownership. This periodization notwithstanding, I will further argue and show in chapter 7 that the same analytic logic for explaining what led to the erosion of public ownership before 1997 as well as the massive privatization around the turn of the century also applies to the analysis of the behavior of political actors in the postprivatization era.

---

dominated by SOEs, public-private partnerships in social and infrastructural development projects, exit of SOEs from nonessential sectors, and dilution of state ownership in state-controlled companies (http://finance.sina.com.cn/china/hgjj/20131220/065917696154.shtml; http://finance.people.com.cn/n/2015/0914/c1004-27577910.html).

19. It is interesting that Hu's argument was presented in an article posted on the CCP's official website (http://theory.people.com.cn/n/2012/0716/c217905-18527967.html).

20. A report produced by the Unirule Institute of Economics (UIE 2011), a private think tank, claims that, net of implicit subsidies, the profit of SOEs was negative during 2001–2009. It nonetheless opines that the concurrent reinforcement of the monopoly positions of SOEs in select economic sectors represents a structural form of *guojin mintui*.

Broad Trends of Change

Ascertaining the magnitude and change of public ownership in the post-Mao Chinese economy is a challenging task. There are three major sources of measurement errors. First, the official classification of public versus private economic activities has been evolving and contains ambiguities concerning mixed-ownership organizations. Second, there are reporting errors regarding the true nature of ownership for a sizable number of economic organizations. Third, there is a lack of systematic information on the major indicators that are useful for a comprehensive and accurate assessment of the private sector's significance in the economy. Despite these problems, it is still possible to use existing data to piece together a clear enough picture of the general trend in China's ownership transformation.

Evolution of Ownership-Based Classifications

Before the start of economic reforms there were only two ownership-based categories of economic organizations outside farming (which was run by people's communes): state-owned enterprises and collective enterprises. In the 1980s the categorization was expanded to include *getihu*, private enterprises, joint (rural) household enterprises, Chinese-foreign joint ventures, wholly foreign-owned enterprises, joint ownership enterprises between public enterprises (state-state, state-collective, and collective-collective), and employee shareholding cooperatives. In government statistics, however, these heterogeneous organizational forms were oftentimes lumped together under an "other" category, especially before 1998.

Into the 1990s the categorization of economic organizations became even more complicated. The main sources of complication lie in the formation of new, mixed-ownership organizations under the shareholding system codified by the Company Law in 1994[21] and in the creation (under the concurrently adopted Ordinance on the Administration of Company Registration) of a new type of owners called "legal persons," or institutional owners, which may be entirely publicly owned, entirely privately owned, or co-owned by public and private owners with various distributions of shareholding and control rights. Starting from 1998, however, the National Bureau of Statistics (NBS) has used the label "state-controlled companies" to refer to limited liability

---

21. The Company Law governs two types of shareholding companies: limited liability company and joint stock company. From 1994 to 2005, with the exception of solely state-owned limited liability companies, these companies were required to have at least two or five shareholders respectively, which

companies and joint-stock companies where the state holds the controlling shares (above the 50% threshold or by agreement). In official (especially NBS) statistics, these companies are defined as SOEs and often grouped together with traditional state-owned sole proprietorships not (yet) (re)organized according to the Company Law. Solely state-owned limited liability companies organized according to the Company Law are sometimes listed as a sub-category under "limited liability companies" and therefore are identifiable. Limited liability companies and joint-stock companies founded or controlled by natural persons only or by legal persons with natural persons as the only founders or controlling stakeholders are categorized, along with private sole proprietorships (other than *getihu*) and partnerships, as "private enterprises" (*siying qiye*).[22] These measures help reduce some of the ambiguities concerning the classification of shareholding entities. But there remain difficulties in ascertaining the controlling stakeholders in Chinese-foreign joint ventures and those in shareholding companies that are not explicitly categorized as state-owned or state-controlled companies or as "private enterprises."

In the survey of aggregate data below I examine ownership change by defining the public sector as consisting of entities that are explicitly classified by the government as state-owned enterprises, state-controlled companies, solely state-owned limited liability companies, urban and rural collective enterprises, and joint ownership entities between public enterprises.[23] I use the term "quasi-private enterprises" to denote shareholding companies not classified by the government as SOEs, collective enterprises, or private enterprises. These entities, which I will call "label-less" shareholding companies, have various combinations of individual and institutional owners and controlling stakeholders that do not meet the above-mentioned "natural person test" for inclusion as private enterprises. I also include in this category all Chinese-foreign joint ventures, as it is difficult to ascertain from available data the extent of ownership and control rights held by the public sector partners in these entities. I treat

---

may include both public and private owners. In 2006 the law was amended to allow the formation of nonstate single-owner limited liability companies.

22. See http://www.stats.gov.cn/statsinfo/auto2073/201310/t20131031_450535.html and http://zcj.hnaic.gov.cn/html/article/4/40000998.html.

23. It should be noted that reporting errors about de facto private entities in the economy may cause exaggeration of the size of the public sector. From the late 1970s to the late 1990s, in order to contain political risk and leverage business opportunities, many private entities disguised themselves as public enterprises (Shi 1993; Young 1995; Dickson 2008). There were (and still are) also companies registered as "public enterprises" but in fact used by government officials and agencies as front organizations for their private profit-seeking activities (Duckett 1999; Lin and Zhang 1999; Lin 2001).

all other economic organizations as being private or predominantly private, including *gufen hezuo qiye*, or employee shareholding cooperatives, which are categorized by the government as a form of "collective" enterprise. A special kind of shareholding entity, these cooperatives pool truly private funds from members and thus fundamentally differ from traditional collective enterprises, which have nominally "collective" but individually indivisible (among members of the collective) assets and operate under an external "public" authority as the holder and controller of such assets. Table 1.1 summarizes the organizations in each of the three categories defined above.

A problem with this method of classification is that the size of the public sector may be underestimated by the inclusion as "quasi-private enterprises" of some "label-less" shareholding companies where the controlling stakes are held by institutional owners that are actually state-owned or controlled.[24] This distortion is likely to be more pronounced for the years since 2003, when the tide of massive privatization subsided and an increasing number of the remaining SOEs began to reorganize and expand their businesses by adding subsidiary companies, forming alliances, investing in existing companies, and even acquiring private companies (Fan and Hope 2013). It is important to recognize the resultant ambiguities in ownership and control. Yet it is also important not to treat these state-invested companies as similar to SOEs,[25] which are directly controlled by state authorities and faced with greater constraints on the pursuit of private interests and agendas. In fact the statistical distortion associated with "label-less" shareholding companies with state investment may be limited by a number of factors, thus not undermining the general validity of the "quasi-private" categorization.

---

24. A concern may also be raised about the predominance of public ownership in some Chinese-foreign joint ventures. Before 1993 the main organizational form of FDI was joint venture with public enterprises, where control power often tilted toward Chinese partners (Pearson 1991; Huang 2002). When public enterprise partners indeed had greater say in decision-making, however, foreign partners were unlikely to resemble generally powerless small shareholders in large (especially listed) companies. Instead they could seek to protect and address their interests through negotiation and/or with the threat of exit. So the term "quasi-private" still applies even when foreign partners were not predominant decision-makers in joint ventures with public enterprises. Moreover, the situation has changed since the mid-1990s. Firm-level data from the industrial sector, to be presented in the next section, reveal a subsequent decline of the importance of the joint venture form relative to wholly foreign-owned enterprises, along with a decline of the equity shares of public sector partners in joint ventures and a rise of the relative significance of (domestic) private-foreign ventures. As a result, underestimation of the significance of predominant public ownership in this group of quasi-private enterprises becomes a lesser issue.

25. For an opinion that extends the notion of SOEs to "label-less" shareholding companies with state ownership, see http://www.aei.org/publication/chinas-soe-sector-is-bigger-than-some-would-have-us-think/.

Table 1.1 Categorization of nonfarm economic organizations

Type	Category in official statistics
(1) Public enterprises	
	State-owned enterprises (sole proprietorships not organized according to the Company Law)
	State-controlled companies (limited liability companies and joint stock companies with controlling stakes held by the state)
	Solely state-owned limited liability companies
	Urban collective enterprises
	Rural collective enterprises (township and village enterprises, or TVEs)
	Joint ownership enterprises between SOE(s) and(/or) collective enterprise(s)
(2) Quasi-private entities	
	Limited liability companies not classified as SOEs or private enterprises
	Joint stock companies not classified as SOEs or private enterprises
	Chinese-foreign joint ventures
(3) Private or predominantly private entities	
	Private sole proprietorships
	Private limited liability companies
	Private joint stock companies
	Private partnerships
	Joint (rural) household enterprises
	Employee shareholding cooperatives
	Wholly foreign-owned ventures
	Foreign-invested joint stock companies
	Joint ownership enterprises between private entities
	Getihu

First, there are clear regulations by the SASAC, SAIC, and NBS that classify state-invested companies into three types of shareholding: solely state-owned (*guoyou duzi*) (type 1), state-controlled (*guoyou konggu*) (type 2), and those with state-held shares (*guoyou cangu*) (type 3).[26] Registering or

---

26. For a sample of these rules, see http://www.gov.cn/zwgk/2005-05/23/content_152.htm; http://www.china.com.cn/policy/txt/2008-10/29/content_16680911.htm; http://www.sdsgzw.gov.cn/channels/ch00167/200803/F9319286-1823-4AB1-BD24-77F879A8495F.htm; http://www.stats.gov.cn/statsinfo/auto2072/201311/t20131104_454901.html.

reporting a type 1 or type 2 company as a type 3 company is a violation of the rules. This imposes a constraint on the extent of misidentification. Second, where the rules are violated or not followed closely for reasons other than administrative oversight, the companies concerned are likely to be less closely monitored by state assets supervision authorities and thus more prone to the manipulation by insiders and outsiders for private agendas (hence likely being "quasi-private"). Third, when a company with both private and state-owned shares is controlled by private owner(s), it tends to follow the logic of private ownership more than state agendas despite the lack of the registration label "private enterprise." In fact it is not uncommon for SOEs to make investment in "label-less" shareholding companies that does not amount to a controlling stake.[27] While in general such investment may not cause the kind of statistical distortion mentioned above, potential problems may arise in a much less common scenario, where different SOEs constitute the largest shareholders of a "label-less" shareholding company that does not have a clearly established controlling stakeholder. But even in that case one needs to take precaution before coming to the conclusion of de facto state control, as it may be foiled by insiders (e.g., the management team) holding much smaller amounts of shares.[28]

Measurement Issues and General Patterns

Table 1.2 provides a glimpse of the changing landscape of nonfarm economic organizations in the post-Mao era. It shows that the number of public enterprises increased substantially before the mid-1990s but experienced contraction in the next two decades, when private and quasi-private entities demonstrated significant growth, especially during the last decade shown. To go beyond this broad view for a closer assessment of the magnitude of private economic activities, it would be useful to examine data on three major indicators: assets, output value, and workforce. Unfortunately, the Chinese government has never published full and detailed information that can be used to

---

27. China Life (an SOE), for example, was one of the founders and until mid-2015 one of the largest shareholders of the Minsheng Bank, a predominantly private joint stock company without an official registration status as private enterprise.

28. A case in point is China Vanke, one of the largest real estate companies in the country. An SOE spin-off and a "label-less" joint stock company without a clearly established controlling stakeholder, it has been controlled by its founder Wang Shi and his associates despite the presence of larger shareholders that are SOEs. For an interesting discussion of the recent disputes and struggles over control rights at Vanke, see http://finance.ifeng.com/a/20160625/14525547_0.shtml.

Table 1.2 Number (millions) of industrial and commercial organizations

Year	SOEs	Collective enterprises	Shareholding companies	Foreign-invested enterprises	Private enterprises	*getihu*
1984	0.8	2.85		0.002 (63%)		9.33
1994	2.17	5.46	0.09	0.21 (78%)	0.43	21.87
2004	0.92	1.39	1.22	0.32 (46%)	4.02	23.51
2014	0.35	0.45	1.33	0.46 (17%)	15.46	49.84

Notes: (a) SOEs include traditional (pre-1994) SOEs, state-controlled companies and solely state-owned limited liability companies; (b) figures in parentheses are shares of joint ventures in foreign-invested enterprises.
Sources: SICA 1994, 2004, 2014; SFYCICA.

cross-tabulate these indicators with different ownership types and compare the results over time.[29]

In the case of assets, no systematic data exist on the farming sector (Pei Changhong 2014), where farmland has remained publicly owned and been contracted out to rural households since the dismantling of the people's commune system in the late 1970s and early 1980s, while other farm assets have been mainly privately owned. Limited information is available on the assets of nonfarm economic organizations. Before the accounting system reform in 1993 (Wu and Patel 2015), no balance sheet data were reported by domestic industrial and commercial enterprises, as the old accounting system was designed to record and track fund use and flow for a centrally planned system based on public ownership. Nor were land and intangibles (copyrights, trademarks, brand names, etc.) valued and included as asset items. Except for the industrial sector and nonfinancial SOEs, most of the asset data collected since 1993 are not released. It was not until 2004, when the first economic census was conducted (and then followed by the second and third ones in 2008 and 2013 respectively), that asset data were collected on all economic organizations in the secondary and tertiary sectors, thus providing a baseline for assessing the relative significance of public enterprises. However, the government has withheld much of the ownership-related information that can be used for cross-tabulation, with the data on the financial sector being most closely guarded. Despite these limitations,

---

29. The quality of published data is another issue, which cannot be addressed in this book. See Holz 2014 and Rawski 2001 for assessments of the quality of China's GDP data.

from the data available it is still possible to discern some general patterns and trends.

Table 1.3 shows that the shares of public enterprises in industrial assets have declined. Although the scope of the time series varies for different periods, it is still clear that the decline was more drastic around the turn of the century and that collective enterprises have lost much of their significance.

Table 1.3 Shares (%) of public and nonpublic enterprises in industrial assets, 1993–2014

Year	SOEs	Collective enterprises	"Label-less" shareholding co.	Sino-foreign joint ventures	Private entities
(1) Coverage: industrial enterprises with independent accounting status at or above the township level					
1993	71.9 (65.9)	19.7 (16.9)			
1994	61.5 (56.7)	19.1 (16.3)			
1995	59.9 (59.1)	18.1 (14.8)	5.5	13	3.5
1996	58.6 (58.1)	17.4 (14.2)			
1997	57.1 (55.9)	16 (13.2)			
(2) Coverage: all industrial SOEs and non-SOEs with annual sales of no less than 5 million yuan					
1998	68.8 (67.8)	10.4 (16)			
1999	68.8 (68.5)	9 (12.9)			
2000	66.6 (66.2)	7.6 (6.7)			
2001	64.9 (64.5)	5.9 (5.2)			
2002	60.9 (60)	5 (4.4)			
2003	56 (55.5)	4.1 (3.8)			
2004	50.9 (52.6)	3.7	10.3	14	21.1
2005	48.1 (49.2)	2.2	9.5	13.5	26.7
2006	46.4 (47.5)	1.9	10	12.4	29.3
(3) Coverage: all industrial enterprises with annual sales of no less than 5 million yuan					
2007	44.8 (45.8)	1.6	9.8	12.8	31
2008	43.8 (42.4)	1.2	11.1	12	31.9
2009	43.7 (41.2)	1	10.5	11.8	33
2010	41.8 (39.1)	0.9	11.5	11.4	34.4

(continued)

Table 1.3 Continued

Year	SOEs	Collective enterprises	"Label-less" shareholding co.	Sino-foreign joint ventures	Private entities
(4) Coverage: all industrial enterprises with annual sales of no less than 20 million yuan					
2011	41.7 (38.7)	0.8	13	11	33.5
2012	40.6 (37.5)	0.7	14.7	10.2	33.8
2013	40.3 (36.4)	0.7	15	9.9	34.1
2014	38.8 (34.8)	0.6	17.3	9.5	33.8
(5) Coverage: all industrial enterprises in economic census years					
2004	40.5	3	8.2	11.1	37.2
2008	39.5	1.1	10.1	10.8	38.5
2013	35.1				

Note: Figures in parentheses are shares in equity capital.
Sources: CSY (various years), *CECY 2004, 2008, 2013, FYC 2015; SSIC 1995*, vol. 1; *CIESY 2006*.

Table 1.4 Shares (%) of public enterprises in secondary and tertiary sector assets

Year	SOE share among nonfinancial entities	Share of collective enterprises
2004	34.9	5.4
2008	33.9	2.1
2013	33.8	

Note: The shares of SOEs in all secondary and tertiary sector assets as reported in the statistical summaries of the three economic censuses do not include those of state-controlled joint-stock companies and therefore cannot used as indicators for all state sector entities. The alternative measure reported in this table is derived by dividing the total assets of nonfinancial SOEs with the total assets of nonfinancial economic organizations reported in the three economic censuses reported in the *Finance Yearbook of China*.
Sources: http://www.stats.gov.cn/tjsj/tjgb/jjpcgb/; *CECY 2004, 2008, 2013; FYC 2010, 2015*.

The shares of "quasi-private" industrial entities stabilized after 2004, whereas the expansion of private enterprises continued until 2010. The more encompassing information reported in Table 1.4 confirms the overall shrinkage of SOEs after the turn of the century. It also suggests that the decline of SOEs may have eased in the postprivatization years, though. But there is no sign of a trend reversal—even during 2008–2013, which was the focal period of the *guojin mintui* debate. The widening gap between industrial SOEs' shares in assets and equity capital (reported in parentheses in table 1.3) after 2007 further indicates that the assets of SOEs consisted of increasingly more liabilities than those of private and quasi-private organizational types. An implication of this is that the easing in SOEs' declining asset shares during the past decade may have been at least in part aided by heavier use of financial leverage under continued preferential treatment by the state-dominated banking system.

Ascertaining the share of public enterprises in economic output is equally difficult. In 1993 the Chinese government replaced the Soviet-style "material product system" (MPS) with the Western-style "system of national accounts" (SNA) for accounting and output reporting. Since then it has compiled and reported gross domestic product (GDP) as the main indicator of economic output and reconstructed the data series for the years before 1993. But, again, the government has withheld information on many economic sectors, organizational types, and time periods. As a result, it is not possible to derive directly from published data an economy-wide view of the changing contributions from public and nonpublic entities. Nevertheless, one can still piece together a partial picture from two limited time series—one on the industrial sector and the other on nonfarm economic activities in rural areas.

Table 1.5 shows that the GDP contributions by publicly owned industrial enterprises and by rural collective enterprises both declined from their peak levels in the mid-1990s. Collective industrial enterprises and collective enterprises in the rural nonfarm sector experienced steady declines in both absolute terms and relative to the all-inclusive groups. In contrast, the decline of industrial SOEs reached a bottom in 1997, when massive privatization began. Interestingly, their GDP share edged up in the ensuing decade, though this was not enough to reverse the decline of the public sector's share in both industrial GDP and total GDP (see the next paragraph). It is unclear whether the trend continued after 2007 and whether it took place among nonindustrial SOEs as well. It also remains to be carefully investigated whether the limited bounceback during and after massive privatization was due to improvement in governance, monopoly positions held by remaining SOEs in upstream industries that rode on the economic expansion in the postprivatization era (Wang 2015), or both.

For GDP shares of public and nonpublic entities in the economy as a whole, no published information can be used for making a direct calculation. Estimates are legion, though. Table 1.6 provides a brief summary. It

Table 1.5 Shares (%) of contributions by public enterprises to GDP

Year	GDP % of industrial enterprises			GDP % of rural nonfarm entities	
	All	SOEs	Collective enterprises	All	Collective enterprises
1978					5.8
1980					6.4
1985				8.5	6.2
1990				13.4	8.9
1991				13.6	9.3
1992	38.2	19.3	7.1	16.7	11.2
1993	40.2	20.6	10.8	22.7	14.5
1994	40.4	16.4	8.6	22.7	14.5
1995	41	13.7	6.4	24	15.4
1996	41.4	12.3	7.3	24.8	14.4
1997	41.7	11.6	6.7	26.3	12.7
1998	40.3	13.1	3.9	26.3	11.8
1999	40	13.5	3.5	27.7	11.1
2000	40.4	13.9	3.1	27.4	9.5
2001	39.7	13.4	2.4	26.8	8.3
2002	39.4	13.2	2.1	26.9	4
2003	40.5	13.9	1.9	27	2.8
2004	40.8	14.5	1.8	26.2	1.8
2005	42.2	14.8	1.4	27.6	1.4
2006	43.1	15.4	1.2	27.3	1.3
2007	43	15.5	1.2	27.1	1
2008				28	0.8
2009				27.4	0.7
2010				28	0.7

Notes: (*a*) Contributions from industrial enterprises in the public sector are defined as shares of industrial value-added in GDP; (*b*) the scopes of coverage for publicly owned industrial enterprises during different periods are the same as those indicated in table 1.3; (*c*) breakdown figures on industrial value-added are unavailable for the years before 1992 and after 2007.
Sources: CSY (various years); *CIESY 2006, 2007, 2008; CTEY* (various years); *CTEAPPY* (various years).

seems clear that the overall share of publicly owned entities has declined. The two most recent estimates—by Pei Changhong (2014) and jointly by the World Bank and the Development Research Center of the State Council (2014, 104)—put the share of the nonpublic sector and that of the

Table 1.6 Estimates of contribution (%) by the nonpublic sector to GDP

Year	Estimate	Source
1998	50.4	OECD 2005
	51	Garnaut et al. 2005; Gregory et al. / IFC 2000
2000	55	Huang Mengfu 2005
2003	59.2	OECD 2005
	70	Fan Gang 2003
2004	61	Li Chengrui 2006
	63 (nonfarm)	Yang Xinming and Yang Jixue 2012
2005	65	Huang Mengfu 2005
2008	70 (nonfarm)	Yang Xinming and Yang Jixue 2012
	69.7 (nonfarm)	Pei Changhong 2014
2010	70	World Bank and Development Research Center of the State Council 2013
2012	67.6 (nonfarm)	Pei Changhong 2014
2014	70	World Bank 2014

Note: Li Chengrui was director (1981–1984) of the State Statistical Bureau; Fan Gang is director of the National Economic Research Institute (http://www.china.com.cn/chinese/OP-c/277946.htm); Huang Mengfu was chairman of the All China Federation of Industry and Commerce (http://theory.people.com.cn/GB/49154/49155/3981648.html); Pei Changhong is director of the Institute of Economics, Chinese Academy of Social Sciences.

nonstate sector at 71% (in 2012) and 70% (in 2010–2014) respectively.[30] If one uses the latter as the benchmark and deducts 2% from the non-SOE portion as the share of collective enterprises,[31] then a more conservative estimate for the share of the nonpublic sector in total GDP would be 68% for 2014.

There are more detailed and systematic (albeit not without gaps) data series about the workforce and its distribution among organizations of different ownership forms. Given such data availability and considering the importance of employment in socioeconomic life and to political decision-makers,

---

30. Pei's estimate is for the secondary and tertiary sectors. If one treats the contribution from the primary (farming) sector (which amounted to 10.1% of GDP in 2012—see table 2.2 of *CSY 2013*) as being all from nonpublic entities, then the share of the nonpublic sector would come to about 70%.

31. This 2% share is estimated by assuming that urban and rural collective enterprises had similar industry structures and capital-labor ratios in 2010, when rural collective enterprises contributed 0.7 of the country's GDP (table 1.5) and had a workforce equivalent to about 60% of that of urban collective enterprises (*CTEAPPY 2011; CSY 2011*).

I will focus more on this indicator for assessing the relative magnitude of the nonpublic sector in the remainder of the book. The summary statistics in tables 1.7 and 1.8 reveal several important facts. First, public enterprises made substantial contributions to nonfarm job creation from 1980 through 1995, yet the result was not strong enough to maintain their initially dominant position in nonfarm employment.

Second, the significance of public sector employment declined sharply in both absolute and relative terms during the ensuing decade, when massive privatization was in full force. Collective enterprises experienced much greater shrinkage than state-owned entities, as suggested by the rising percentages of the latter in the remaining public sector workforce. Although the pace of decline slowed down in the postprivatization years, the trend continued. By 2014 the share of public sector employment in the entire workforce had dropped below 10%.[32]

Third, the overall significance of quasi-private enterprises in nonfarm employment rose steadily from the mid-1990s onward. But this was solely because of the growth of shareholding enterprises, as the share of Sino-foreign joint ventures actually shrank. In the meantime the share of the residual category—private or predominantly privately owned entities—also substantially grew, most probably passing the 70% level in 2014.

Fourth, there were variations between urban and rural areas and among different provinces. Table 1.6 shows that during the first decade of reforms, public sector employment dominated urban areas but experienced serious erosion in rural areas. Within the rural sector, there were also considerable variations among different provinces. In the next decade, the growth of employment outside the public sector continued in rural areas, which was paralleled by a similar but more speedy trend of change in urban areas. These changes not only extended into the decade following the start of massive privatization in 1997 but were accompanied by greater variability within urban and rural sectors, as indicated by the increase in the coefficient of variation.

To sum up, the foregoing survey illustrates a steady growth of private ownership in the post-Mao era. It also highlights a concurrent process of change, where public enterprises initially experienced expansion in absolute terms but subsequently declined, with collective enterprises under local authorities leading the way, both up and down, and at uneven paces across regions.

---

32. According to *China Statistical Yearbook 2015* (table 4.2), the combined workforce in farming and nonfarming sectors totaled 772.5 million in 2014, which put the share of public sector employment at 9.4%.

Table 1.7 Changing significance of public entities and quasi-private entities in nonfarm employment

Year	Nonfarm employment in public entities (millions)	Share (%) of public sector employment in nonfarm workforce	Share (%) of state-owned entities in public sector employment	Share (%) of shareholding enterprises in nonfarm workforce	Share (%) of Sino-foreign joint ventures in nonfarm workforce
1980	133.5	99.4	60.1		
1985	164.6	83.2	54.6		
1990	184.9	70.3	56		
1991	190.6	71.7	55.9		2.4
1992	196.9	70.6	55.3		5.1
1993	200.8	67.1	55.4	0.5	6.7
1994	204.0	67.0	55	1.0	
1995	204.7	64.2	55	1.0	
1996	202.1	60.5	55.6	1.1	
1997	192.6	56.9	57.4	1.4	
1998	158.5	46.4	57.1	2.6	
1999	146.5	41.7	58.5	2.9	
2000	134.3	37.3	60.3	3.2	
2001	123.0	33.1	62.1	3.6	3.6
2002	120.9	31.4	59.3	4.2	
2003	91.1	22.9	75.5	4.7	
2004	86.1	20.9	78	5.0	3.5
2005	79.8	18.7	81.3	5.7	
2006	77.2	17.4	83.3	6.0	
2007	76.4	16.6	84.1	6.2	
2008	75.7	15.9	85.2	6.4	3.3
2009	74.2	15.2	86.5	6.9	
2010	75.0	14.8	86.8	7.2	
2011	76.7	14.7	87.4	8.5	
2012	78.0	14.6	87.6	9.4	
2013	73.2	13.3	86.9	14.2	2.8
2014	72.4	12.9	87.2	14.4	

Notes: (a) State-owned entities include both economic organizations and noneconomic organizations (including party and government agencies); (b) shareholding enterprises refer to limited liability companies and joint-stock companies that are not categorized as state-controlled companies or private enterprises.
Sources: CSY (various years); YICAC 1992, 1993, 1994; CTEY (various years); CTEAPPY (various years); CECY 2004, 2008, 2013; CSNCBU.

Table 1.8 Share (%) of publicly owned entities in secondary and tertiary sector employment

	1985		1988		1998		2008	
	Rural	Urban	Rural	Urban	Rural	Urban	Rural	Urban
Nationwide	60	96	51	96	38	51	3	24
Anhui	43	91	38	91	38	66	7	39
Beijing	88	99	83	98	80	80	16	24
Chongqing	93		89		64	74	2	29
Fujian	65	95	52	90	34	56	5	24
Gansu	62	95	42	93	36	71	9	55
Guangdong	63	94	52	89	61	60	7	21
Guangxi	37	93	28	90	21	70	4	44
Guizhou	28	93	21	92	29	72	6	53
Hainan	46	94	33	92	21	69	12	42
Hebei	42	98	37	97	28	73	7	48
Heilongjiang	72	95	65	94	35	87	4	50
Henan	39	95	30	95	36	76	4	48
Hubei	58	97	52	96	47	67	8	40
Hunan			52		30	65	11	39
Jiangsu	84	97	76	97	55	76	2	19
Jiangxi	48	97	45	95	30	68	2	42
Jilin	53	94	41	93	20	71	3	43
Liaoning	73	94	64	93	30	74	6	36
Neimenggu	38	96	31	95	14	75	2	42
Ningxia	37	98	36	97	19	76	3	43
Qinghai	66	95	43	93	29	65	10	44
Shaanxi	53	97	41	96	24	69	6	54
Shandong	70	98	60	97	44	52	3	35
Shanghai		96	87	94	85	56	8	22
Shanxi	59	98	54	95	52	76	8	56
Sichuan	55	96	43	95	30	82	3	38
Tianjin	88	98	84	97	62	73	6	31
Xinjiang	67		42		27	82	9	50
Xizang			57			86	19	43
Yunnan	58	96	51	95	28	76	5	37
Zhejiang	81	97	74	95	43	61	2	16
CV (%)	29.7	1.99	36.3	2.6	48.1	12.8	67.1	28.4

Notes: (a) 1985 is the earliest year for which provincial data on rural nonfarm enterprises are available: (b) CV stands for coefficient of variation, which is the ratio of the standard deviation to the mean.
Sources: CSY 1986, 1989, 1999, 2009; SCTE; CTEAPPY 2009.

Table 1.9 Sectors with dominant SOE shares (%) in economic census years

Sector	2004		2008		2013	
	Assets	Sales	Assets	Sales	Assets	Sales
Industrial						
Coal	89	69	75	53	63	(35)
Oil and natural gas	90	95	96	97	86	85
Metallurgy	91	90	54	(40)	(44)	(32)
Tobacco	100	100	99	99	98	99
Power generation and distribution	73	79	77	74	70	65
Gas production and supply	77	83	53	(49)	(41)	(45)
Water production and supply	81	83	68	55	(46)	(47)
Nonindustrial						
Air transport	84	100	82	96	76	98
Rail transport	~100	~100	~100	~100	~100	~100
Water transport	(46)	61	50	53	(43)	(43)
Warehousing and storage	>50	>50	>50	>50	76	94
Postal, telecom and IT services	54	75	>50	56	57	52
Banking	>50	>50	>50	>50	>50	>50

Notes: (*a*) Value-added data are unavailable, and sales data are used as proxies of (gross) output; (*b*) figures with "~" or ">" indicate approximate magnitude or range due to the lack of precise data; (*c*) figures in parentheses indicate drop of percentage below 50%.
Sources: CSY 2005, 2009, 2014; CECY 2004, 2008, 2013; FYC 2006, 2015.

Relatively more SOEs survived the wave of massive privatization around the turn of the century, though their presence in the economy was also substantially reduced. When the SASAC was established in 2003 to consolidate control over the survivors, the state had retreated to a handful of strategically important sectors, as shown in table 1.9. Even there, the leading positions held by the remaining SOEs in some sectors after the tidal wave of privatization, such as coal, metallurgy, gas, water, and water transport, significantly eroded during the following decade. By 2013 the vast majority of industrial sectors,

Table 1.10 Number of industrial sectors with paid-in capital dominated by different owner groups, 2013

Dominant owner group (with 50+% share)	Two-digit sectors ($n = 45$)	Three-digit sectors ($n = 200$)	Four-digit sectors ($n = 578$)
Grouping I			
State	4	7	18
Collective	0	0	0
Legal person/institutional	2	20	64
Private	3	9	65
Foreign	1	13	53
Without dominant group	35	151	378
Grouping II			
Public (state and collective combined)	4	10	21
Legal person/institutional	2	20	64
Private and foreign combined	23	115	392
Without dominant group	16	55	101

Note: The data cover all industrial enterprises with annual sales of no less than 20 million yuan.
Source: CECY 2013.

especially those identified by four-digit classification, were dominated by private and foreign-invested companies, as suggested by the statistics on paid-in capital in table 1.10.[33]

The Growth and Organizational Patterns of FDI

Foreign investment is an important contributing force to privatization because the entry and expansion of foreign (private) capital not only dilute

---

33. Paid-in capital is investment in the shares of a company. It is the basic element of equity, which also includes items like additional paid-in capital (e.g., IPO proceeds), accumulated earnings and profits, etc.

Table 1.11 Selected statistics on the relative significance (%) of entities with FDI in the economy

Year	Industrial assets	Industrial sales	Nonfarm workforce	Industrial and commercial taxes
1994	11.7	13		8.5
1998	19.6	24.3		14.4
2004	24.6	30.8	11	20.8
2008	26	29.3	11.5	20.9
2014	20.7	22.8	(9.8)	20.9

Note: Figure in parenthesis is from the 2013 economic census.
Sources: CSY 1995, 1999, 2005, 2009, 2015; CECY 2004, 2008, 2013; SFDIC 2015.

the significance of public ownership but, as I will discuss later, embody and stimulate institutional change. The re-entry of foreign direct investment began in 1979, when the government allowed joint ventures to be formed between public enterprises and foreign companies. From 1979 to 2014 China received a total of US$1.59 trillion of foreign direct investment (*CSY 2015*, table 11.13).[34] Table 1.11, based on limitedly available data, captures some facts about the important roles of foreign capital in the economy. It shows that FDI enlarged its presence, while public enterprises were in decline from the mid-1990s through the turn of the century. Its relative significance in the industrial sector and nonfarm employment may have peaked during the post-privatization years, when domestic private entities experienced faster growth. But its contribution to government revenue seems to have remained stable following massive privatization.

Spatially, FDI has concentrated in the coastal region, as shown in table 1.12. But it is important to note that over time FDI has spread both within the coastal region and among noncoastal provinces. In 1985 61% of the cities (inclusive of subordinate counties) in coastal provinces were recipients of FDI, whereas the percentage was only 26% for those in noncoastal

---

34. Some of the FDI reported in official statistics may have been "recycled" or "round-trip" capital—funds moved (often through illicit channels) by Chinese individuals or companies to offshore locations (e.g., Hong Kong, the British Virgin Islands, and the Cayman Islands) and then reinjected into the economy as "foreign" investment to take advantage of the tax breaks and other special regulatory treatment offered by the Chinese government. The magnitude of such investment is unknown. Since much of it is likely to be private or de facto private capital, it exerts a diluting effect on public ownership similar to that of "genuine" FDI.

Table 1.12 Selected statistics on the geographic and sectoral distribution of FDI

Year	FDI utilized ($ billions)	Share (%) of coastal provinces in FDI utilized	% of cities with FDI in coastal provinces	% of cities with FDI in noncoastal provinces	% industrial sectors with FDI	% of manufacturing in registered foreign capital of FDI firms	
						All	Current year
1985	2.0	90.1	61	26	20	43.8	44.4
1995	37.5	84.5	97	65	90.4	53.1	73.0
2004	60.6	86.6	97	85	96.2	63.1	65.2
2008	92.4	85.2	97	89	98.1	55.4	42.8
2014	119.6	82.1	100	90	(96)	44.5	24.6

Notes: (a) 1985 and 1995 were industrial census years, 2004, 2008, and 2013 were economic census years; 2014 was the year for which pertinent data are available from latest sources; (b) the percentages of industrial sectors with FDI for 1985 and 2014 are estimated using information on three-digit and four-digit industry classifications from the statistical summaries of the 1985 industrial census and the 2013 economic census respectively; the percentages for 1995, 2004, and 2008 are calculated directly from census data with four-digit industry classification.

Sources: CSY (various years); SSIC 1985; SSIC 1995; CECY 2004, 2008, 2014; CCSY 1985, 1995, 2005, 2015; SICA; SFYCICA; data of the 1995 industrial census and the 2004 and 2008 economic censuses.

provinces. A decade later, these shares rose to 97% and 65% respectively, and the rise continued among noncoastal provinces during the next two decades. Interestingly, a substantial part of the spatial spread had already taken place before the massive privatization and China's WTO accession after the turn of the century.

A similar pattern can be found in the sectoral characteristics of FDI, which only had a limited presence in the economy in the mid-1980s. By the mid-1990s, however, foreign capital had already propagated some 90% of the industrial sectors based on the four-digit classification. Table 1.12 further shows that from the mid-1980s through the turn of the century the distribution of FDI was increasingly skewed toward industrial activities, especially manufacturing. As will be shown later in the book, such a pattern was consistent with the fact that government economic policies (especially at local levels) focused on industrial development during that period of time. The trend gradually shifted during and after massive privatization, when the service sector rapidly overtook industries as the leading destination of FDI. China's WTO accession in 2001 was a major catalyst, as it was followed by a lowering and removal of many barriers to foreign entry in service activities. Equally noteworthy, though, is the growing importance of urban development to the self-interest calculus of the gatekeepers and regulators of FDI—that is, local political actors—following the restructuring of fiscal relations in the mid-1990s,[35] as will be detailed in chapter 3.

The geographic and sectoral expansion of FDI during the first decade of reform was largely achieved through forming joint ventures with public enterprises. That organizational pattern was subsequently redefined by three developments in the next two decades, which substantially reduced the significance of public ownership in the expanding foreign sector. First, wholly foreign-owned enterprise became the predominant organizational form of FDI. Second, private-foreign partnerships overtook public-foreign partnerships as the predominant group of organizations among joint ventures. Third, within the remaining public-foreign joint ventures the share of public ownership has been in decline. As can be seen in table 1.13, the shares of joint ventures in the total number of FDI entities declined over time relative to wholly foreign-owned enterprises, which are more "private" than joint ventures with public enterprises. Table 1.13 further shows concurrent declines in terms of investment and workforce shares. It also shows that among the FDI entities

---

35. The overwhelming majority of FDI entities are licensed by sub-provincial governments. I will discuss this in chapter 6.

Table 1.13 Organizational forms of FDI in the industrial sector, 1978–2008

Year	Share (%) of wholly foreign-owned enterprises (WFOE) in			Share (%) of private-foreign joint ventures (JV) in total JV industrial workforce	Share (%) of public ownership in equity capital of industrial public-foreign JV
	New foreign-funded projects	Newly added FDI	Industrial FDI work-force		
1979–82	3.5	7.2			
1983	3.2	2.3			
1984	1.4	3.8 (247)			
1985	1.5	0.8 (110)	11.3		
1986	1.2	0.7 (192)			
1987	2.1	12.7 (343)			
1988	6.9	9.1 (311)			
1989	16.1	29.5 (212)			
1990	25.6	37 (131)			
1991	21.5	30.6 (104)			
1992	17.8	27 (110)	43.1	5.8	
1993	22.7	27.3 (104)	48.2		
1994	27.4	26.6 (140)	43.9	20.2	
1995	31.8	36.8 (98)	40.8	22.4	55.6
1996	36.9	36.6 (76)			
1997	45.7	35.8 (66)			
1998	48.9	36.2 (65)	39.5	64.3 (44.8)	
1999	48.5	38.6 (57)	40.1	68.5 (48)	52.5
2000	54.6	47.3 (89)	41.7	74.5 (52.1)	51.4
2001	59.8	50.9 (52)	42.8	77.5 (56.6)	50.1
2002	64.9	60.2 (38)	42.8	82.2 (61.1)	49.8
2003	65.9	62.4 (40)	44	87.1 (65.6)	49.2
2004	70.3	66.3 (33)	49.1	91.3 (70.3)	52.2
2005	73	71 (33)	50.1	93.7 (72.7)	47.3
2006	72.7	73.4 (36)	51.2	95.1 (74.1)	43.7
2007	78	76.6 (33)	52.7	95.3 (73.8)	36.1
2008	81.4	78.3 (23)	64		

Notes: (a) Figures in parentheses of the third column are coefficient of variation for weighted average among provincial units (including centrally administered municipalities); (b) figures in parentheses of the fifth column are derived by classifying all joint ventures between institutional owners and foreign investors as public-foreign joint ventures.

Sources: CSY-2008 (various tables); *CFES; CEESY* (various years); data of NBS annual industrial surveys (1992–2008).

organized as joint ventures there was steady growth in both the importance of joint ventures with domestic private owners and the significance of foreign shares in joint ventures with public enterprises.

Summary and Questions

The foregoing overview illustrates a process of government policy change toward private ownership that started in the late 1970s, as well as a concurrent decline of the public sector that progressed at uneven paces across space and accelerated from the mid-1990s through the turn of the century. Without downplaying the role of entrepreneurial forces, I want to stress that accounting for the driving forces of this fundamental transformation requires close attention to the decisions and actions of political actors at both the national and local levels. The central government has been an important part of the story in that it has made a series of landmark decisions that have had sweeping and long-lasting impact on the revival and growth of private ownership. These include, among other things, legalizing self-employment and private enterprise, granting and expanding entry for FDI, initiating ownership restructuring among SOEs, and instituting legal, regulatory, and political measures that improve the ecological environment of private economic activities. Local governments, as I will show, are important players too, as most of the changes have taken place—oftentimes beyond centrally set limits—under their direct purview. To account for the mechanisms of this endogenously induced institutional change, a number of questions need to be addressed.

First, what drove the national leadership's decision to open up the space for private economic activities and gradually expand it? Second, what explains the tolerant and even facilitating measures that some local authorities took to make allowance for private business and foreign capital beyond what was authorized by the central leadership during the years before massive privatization began in the late 1990s? Third, why did so many public enterprises disappear from the mid-1990s through the turn of the century? Fourth, what explains the spatial and temporal variations in the pace of domestic private business growth across different jurisdictions? Fifth, what explains the sectoral and spatial spread and deepening of FDI beyond the initial entry barriers and regulatory restrictions? Sixth, what has been behind the changing organizational patterns (and the varying diluting effects on public ownership) of FDI? Last but not least, what has shaped the boundaries between public and private ownership following the tipping point of the precipitous collapse of public enterprises in the late 1990s? I will take up these questions in the ensuing chapters.

2

Demographic Pressures

ONE OF THE legacies that China carried into the communist era is the country's population, which for centuries had been the world's largest (Maddison 2007). In 1949 it totaled 542 million (Xu Dixin 1988, 493). In the ensuing three decades the population experienced substantial growth, surpassing 1 billion in 1981. To understand the role of the demographic forces associated with this growth in the causal mechanisms of privatization, it is important to consider several factors that influenced the structure and change of the population under Mao, which had long-lasting impact on the agendas and constraints of policymaking—especially at the national level—in the post-Mao era.

First, the 1950s and 1960s progressed in an essentially nonrestrictive policy environment for the growth of the population. Second, the economic development strategies of the state emphasized capital goods industries and made the underdeveloped rural economy the main repository for absorbing and supporting the vast majority of the growing population, resulting in pent-up demand for alternative avenues and spaces of job creation under increasing resource constraints. Third, the initially large base and young age structure of the population, coupled with the impact of the Maoist population and development policies, shaped the timing for the onset and persistence of the tidal wave of employment pressures in the late 1970s and thereafter, and for the pressing need to address the swelling size of retiring cohorts during the 1990s and beyond. Fourth, the politics during the Cultural Revolution (1966–1976) led to peculiar developments, such as restructuring of primary and secondary education and rustication of urban youths, that exacerbated the situation of job creation at the end of the Mao era, thereby triggering the initial decision by the central leadership to legalize self-employment in 1980. During the three decades following the end of the Mao era, the demographic pressures converging from these different directions forced the state to look beyond the public sector for solutions to job creation, thereby expanding the institutional space for private economic activities.

Structure and Change of the Post-1949 Population

The year 1949 was a major landmark in China's population history.[1] Before the revolution, the country had high birth rate and high death rate. A high birth rate persisted into the 1950s and the 1960s. Yet the death rate, especially infant mortality, decreased sharply after the revolution and continued to decline afterward, largely owing to the end of wars and the improvement of nutrition, sanitation, and healthcare. This paved the way for the next phase of demographic transition that began in the early 1970s and featured declining fertility and rising life expectancy.

There was no systematic family planning program before the early 1970s. During 1949–1952 the newly established government actually encouraged childbearing by women, in part to compensate for the huge loss of lives during the civil war (Xu Dixin 1988). In view of the underdeveloped economy and fast-rising fertility, however, the government retreated from the initial stance and began to experiment with measures to introduce family planning during 1953–1957. But that undertaking was sidetracked by the radicalization of politics during and after the Anti-Rightist Campaign (1957–1958), which was aimed at punishing and silencing people who were skeptical or critical of Mao's policies, especially his attempt to accelerate the pace of socialist transformation. Among the collateral victims of the campaign was Ma Yinchu, president (1951–1960) of Peking University. An economist by training, he was a major advocate for the adoption of fertility control measures. Although he was not labeled a "rightist," open discussion of his view on population policy was suppressed.

In the following decade, no effective family planning program was implemented. The massive deaths during the Great Famine of 1959–1961 briefly eclipsed the concern about fast population growth. But discussions about the need to control population size resumed at the highest level of policymaking during 1962–1965. Such discussions were disrupted by the onset of the Cultural Revolution (1966–1976). In 1971, when the most violent storms of the revolution had subsided, the reorganized central government decided to

---

1. For overviews of China's population history through early years of reforms, see Banister 1987; Lee and Wang 1999; Lu Yu 2004; and Xu Dixin 1988.

put family planning on the active agenda and initiated a nationwide campaign to raise the marriage age among young people, prolong the interval between births, and even limit the number of births per married couple. The campaign was carried out through government-controlled work units—the only form of formal organization—in urban and rural areas. It had a major constraining effect on the birth rate and heralded the eventual adoption of the one-child policy during 1979–1980.

Figure 2.1 shows the natural rate of population growth in the five decades following the communist revolution. The pattern mirrors the changes in the policy environment: the rising trend (briefly reversed during the famine years) prior to the early 1970s took place in the absence of systematic policy constraints, whereas the steady decline thereafter reflects the increasing impact of family planning programs. Table 2.1 summarizes further information from census data. An important fact it shows is that the vast majority of the population resided in rural areas throughout the Mao era and the early years of reform. It was not until the early 1990s that the pace of urbanization began to accelerate. This spatial pattern of population distribution was largely the result of the economic development strategy of the government.

When the CCP came to power in 1949, China was a predominantly agrarian economy, where the rural sector was home to some 92% of the workforce

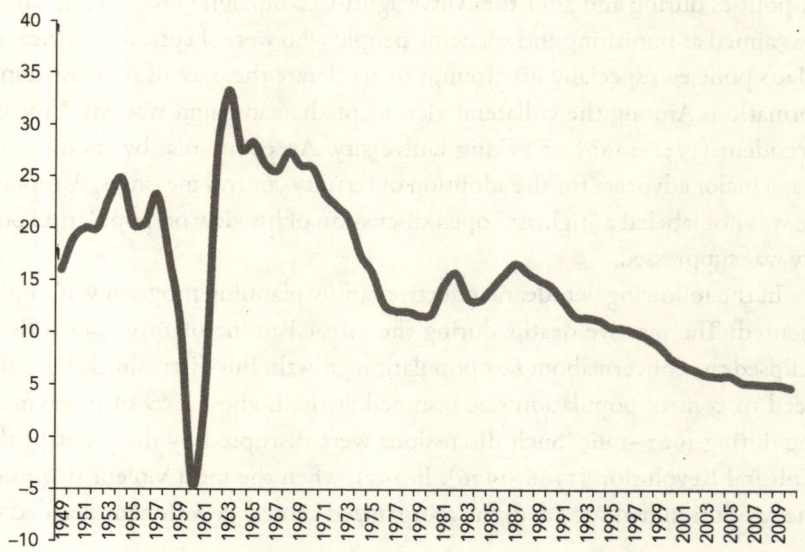

FIGURE 2.1 Natural rate (‰) of population growth, 1949–2009
Sources: CSY 2001, 2010.

Table 2.1 Selected statistics from population censuses

Year	Population (millions)	Urban %	% of age groups			Median age	People turning 15/65 (millions)	Dependency ratio	Rate of change (‰)		
			0–14	15–64	65 or above				Birth rate	Death rate	Natural rate of growth
1953	594.35	13.3	36.3	59.3	4.4	22.7	10.1/2.8	68.6	37	14	23
1964	694.58	18.4	40.7	55.8	3.6	20.2	13.5/2.6	79.4	39.1	11.5	27.6
1982	1008.18	21.1	33.6	61.5	4.9	22.9	22.8/4.8	62.6	22.3	6.6	15.7
1990	1133.68	26.4	27.7	66.7	5.6	25.3	21.6/6.2	49.9	21.1	6.7	14.4
2000	1265.83	36.2	22.9	71.2	7.0	30.8	20.0/7.8	42.7	14	6.5	7.6
2010	1339.73	49.7	16.6	74.5	8.9	34	18.0/9.1	34.2	11.9	7.1	4.8

Note: Data do not include the populations of Hong Kong, Macau, and Taiwan.
Sources: CSY 2010; CSA 2011; PSPRC; 1982PCC; T1990PC; MF2000PCC; T2010PC.

(*CLWS a*, 5). Prompted by encounters with Western powers in the mid-nineteenth century, the development of the modern sector had nevertheless been slow and heavily concentrated in consumer goods industries and limited urban services. As noted in chapter 1, the state eliminated private ownership by the end of the 1950s and became the sole allocator of resources. In view of China's economic underdevelopment, CCP leaders regarded acceleration of industrialization as a top priority. Yet they faced severe resource constraints. In 1950, despite US-led refusal to give political recognition to the new communist regime, Western countries still accounted for 60% of China's foreign trade (Zuo Chuntai and Song Xinzhong 1988, 87). But such economic ties were abruptly cut off in December of that year, when a Western embargo was imposed on China after Chinese troops entered the Korean War (1950–1953) in October. While Soviet aid during the early to mid-1950s played a vital role in broadening China's industrial base, it quickly diminished as the relationship between the two countries deteriorated toward the end of the decade. With limited domestic supply, CCP leaders decided to concentrate the allocation of scarce resources in the sectors that they considered to be of greatest strategic importance for the country's long-term development, namely, producer goods industries.[2]

To facilitate the official strategy of development, the state created a pecking order of resource allocation biased toward urban industries, and stratified economic organizations accordingly. Under the central planning system, there were three basic types of economic organization: state-owned enterprises controlled by national, provincial, and city/county authorities; urban collective enterprises exclusively controlled by sub-provincial authorities; and people's communes under the purview of county governments. State-owned enterprises and urban collective enterprises were the main carriers of nonfarm economic activities. Their size and complexity varied greatly, depending on the sector and the technology used, among other things. The level of direct supervising authority over an enterprise signified the importance the government attached to it. With the same level of direct government control, capital goods producers tended to enjoy higher priority in resource allocation than their peers producing consumer goods or providing services. People's communes were at the bottom of the system by both criteria,[3] though over time many of them also undertook some limited nonfarm economic activities,

---

2. During 1953–1980 some 89.3% of the investment for capital formation in the industrial sector was allocated to producer goods industries (*CSY 1981*, 300).

3. Although peasants made up some 75%–80% of the workforce, the agricultural sector only received 7.4% of bank loans and 6.9% of fiscal expenditure during 1952–1978 (*FSFYC; CSDMFYNC*).

which accounted for less than 10% of the rural workforce in 1978 (*CTEY 1987*, 245).

These realities of stratified resource allocation were sustained through several contemporaneous institutional arrangements (Riskin 1987). To squeeze out more resources for capital-intensive industrial development and to limit the demand for consumer goods and services, wages were maintained at very low and stagnant levels. The supply of essential daily necessities was rationed through a rationing coupon system. For urban employees and their families the provision of basic social services, such as housing, healthcare, and old-age support, was internalized or administered at the level of each and every formal organization, known as the work unit (*danwei*), whereas rural citizens had only minimal healthcare benefits under a cooperative medicine system. Closely coupled with such an employment practice was a household registration (*hukou*) system (Cheng and Selden 1994). Crafted after the revolution and institutionalized in the late 1950s, it classified citizens into urban and rural categories with spatially fixed residential status. Such status was combined with strict restrictions on intercategory change, extralocale employment, and even interlocale travel such that the allocation of human resources and their means of living could be centrally planned and extraplan provision and distribution of consumer goods and services (including transportation services) for working people and their families could be minimized.

An important implication of the state's economic development strategy is that the absorption of the rural work-age population into the urban workforce could not grow at very fast rate because of the capital-intensive nature of producer goods industries. Indeed from 1958 to 1978 the share of the rural sector in the total workforce only edged down from 80% to 77%, whereas the share of the industrial sector in GDP doubled from 21% to 42% (*LSYC 1987*, 5; *CSY 2010*, 36). Although there was considerable underutilization of the vast rural workforce—especially in the oversaturated farming sector (Perkins 1988)—the initial significance of underaged cohorts in the population somehow moderated the job creation pressure for the economy as a whole and thereby allowed a certain degree of freedom for CCP leaders to launch and implement their industrialization strategy.

When the CCP came to power, the population had a very young age structure. As shown in table 2.1, the median age in 1953 was 22.7 and dropped to 20.2 in 1964. It remained at that level for close to two decades. This long span of a young age structure was largely due to the initial significance of the cohorts below work age in the population and the high birth rate in the booming years that followed. With most baby boomers of the 1950s and

Table 2.2 Cultivated land and per capita shares

Year	Total cultivated area (billions of *mu*)	Share per person (*mu*)	Share per rural resident (*mu*)	Share per person in farm workforce (*mu*)
1952	1.619	2.82	3.22	9.35
1957	1.678	2.6	3.07	8.69
1978	1.491	1.55	1.89	5.27
1980	1.49	1.51	1.87	5.12
1985	1.453	1.37	1.8	4.67
1990	1.435	1.26	1.71	3.69
1995	1.425	1.18	1.66	4.01

Note: 1 *mu* = 0.067 hectare.
Sources: SYCLR 1996; CSY 1996, 2000.

1960s yet to reach work age, the share of the workforce in the total population remained under 60% throughout the 1950s, 1960s, and 1970s. It was not until after 1980, when the dependency ratio eased to 67% (which translates into a 59.9% share accounted for by the workforce in the total population), that the 60% mark was crossed and the demand for employment of new entrants into work-age cohorts began to escalate and intensify. Table 2.1 shows that the number of people turning fifteen was 13.5 million in 1964; it rose to 22.8 million in 1982, and the annual number subsequently persisted around that level for more than two decades.

Despite the moderating effect of age structure on the immediate pressure for employment growth in the Mao era, feeding the large and fast-growing number of underaged people was a formidable challenge. The fact that most of these people and their families resided in rural areas added to the pressure on China's limited arable land. Table 2.2 shows that per capita land cultivated steadily declined with the growth of the population after the revolution. Yet in the meantime agricultural productivity deteriorated during the Mao era,[4] largely because of the lack of modern farm inputs, poor organization, and incentive problems. From 1957 to 1977, grain output per capita never exceeded the level attained in 1956 (*ASFYNC*, 79), when the high tide of collectivization ascended. As a result, intrafamily reallocation of food and other essential daily supplies became the common means for the vast majority of the growing population to eke out a poor living in support of the country's accelerating industrialization.

---

4. See Wen 1993 for a summary of the total factor productivity (TFP) estimates by different economists.

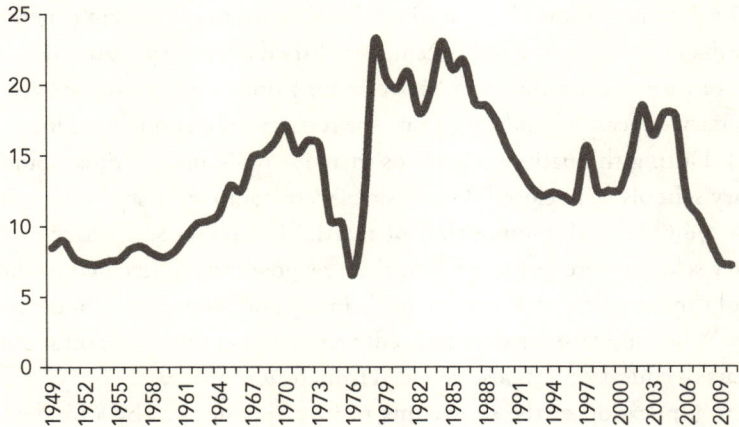

FIGURE 2.2 Estimates of net addition (millions) to workforce pool, 1949–2010
Note: Annual net addition to workforce pool is derived as the difference between people entering (at age 15) and exiting (at age 65) (estimated with census data on various age groups, adjusted for corresponding mortality rates) the workforce, plus the difference between entrants and graduates of high schools, vocational schools, and tertiary institutions.
Sources: CSDMSYNC; PSPRC; *1982PCC*; *T1990PC*; *MF2000PCC*; *T2010PC*.

Buildup of Employment Pressures

Over time the moderating effect of the initially young population structure faded with the growing up of baby boomers. With the increase of the rate at which people turning fifteen outnumbered those turning sixty-five, the net enlarging effect on the work-age population grew. Figure 2.2 plots estimates of the annual net addition to the workforce pool.

It shows a decade-long upward increase from the early 1960s to the early 1970s. The trend reversed briefly during the mid-1970s, reflecting the impact of the drastic decline in the natural rate of population growth due to massive deaths (including infant mortalities) during the famine years of the late 1950s and early 1960s.[5] That was followed by a decade with even higher levels of annual addition of new entrants. It was during that decade (i.e., the 1980s) that self-employment and private ownership were legalized by the central government, as described in chapter 1. Other than the cumulative demographic pressures, that timing was also influenced by politics.

---

5. Some 30 million excess deaths are estimated to have occurred during the famine (Kung and Chen 2011).

During the Cultural Revolution, China's educational system experienced some major changes. The old system, established after 1949, featured a curriculum of formal education with six years for primary education, six years for secondary education, and four years for tertiary education (He Dongchang 1996). During the nationwide chaos in 1967–1968, many primary and secondary schools were closed. Universities were completely shut down during 1966–1969. After the imposition of martial law in 1968, primary and secondary schools were reopened. But the new government decided to shorten school time to five and four years for primary and secondary schools respectively. When universities were limitedly reopened in 1970,[6] the total number of years of education was also reduced from four to three.

An implication of the shortening of formal education by a total of four years is that it could weaken the buffer of schooling against the employment pressure from new entrants into the workforce pool. This weakening effect was nevertheless moderated and postponed by a concurrent development during the Cultural Revolution. That is, while tertiary education languished, primary and secondary education was expanded, especially in rural areas, where significant numbers of school-age youngsters had been unable to continue their education beyond or even through primary school. That undertaking was intended to address the "elitist" bias in the education policy of the old government led by Mao's political rivals. The responsibility of financing the school expansion programs, however, fell largely on local governments, especially those in the rural grassroots. It became increasingly unbearable toward the end of the Mao era (He Dongchang 1996).

Soon after the regime transition after Mao's death, many local governments began to cut back on education and to limit secondary school enrolment. This, coupled with the continuation of the shortened school years, added to the difficulty of coping with the surge of new entrants into the work-age population during the late 1970s and early 1980s, when the central leadership began to relax the restrictions on private economic activities. It was not until the mid-1980s that the total length of primary and secondary education was restored to twelve years and that the expansion of secondary school resumed. An illustration of the fluctuations of school enrolment during different periods of the PRC's history is offered in figure 2.3. Among the

---

6. During 1970 and 1976 universities recruited students not on the basis of entrance exam scores but according to the recommendations from work units for select employees. In addition to the shortening and politicization of curriculum, there was also significant cut in the number of students enrolled, as well as majors and departments. See He Dongchang 1996.

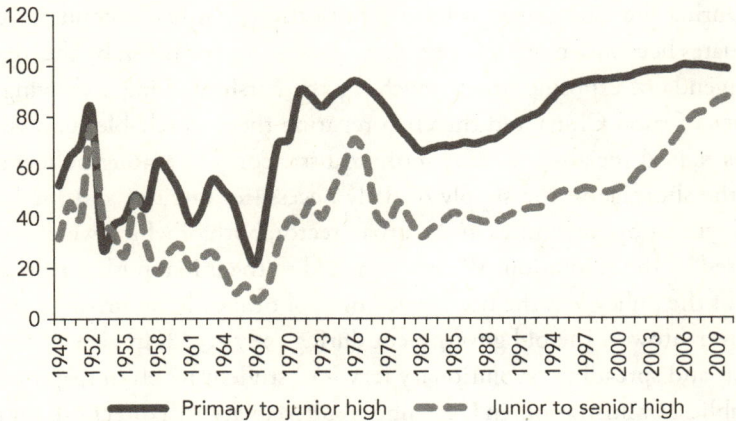

FIGURE 2.3 Percentages of graduates able to enter next level of school, 1949–2010
Sources: CSDMFYNC; CSDMSYNC; ESYC *1987, 1988, 1989, 1990, 2010*.

movements it shows is a decline of the percentage of primary school and junior high school graduates able to move to the next level of education in the late 1970s and early 1980s,[7] forcing many youngsters to become early participants in the workforce.

Another important phenomenon during the Cultural Revolution was the rustication of urban youths (mostly secondary school graduates), also known as the *shangshan xiaxiang* ("going up to the mountains and down to the villages") movement (Bernstein 1977). The origin of the movement can be traced to the mid-1950s, when some idealistic youths voluntarily gave up their urban resident status to live and work in poor rural communities and undeveloped frontier regions. Their intention was to help reduce the wide gaps between urban and rural economies. While their act was praised by the party-state and emulated by hundreds of thousands of secondary school graduates under the encouragement of, and ad hoc arrangement by, local authorities, there was no systematic migration program to transfer urban youths to the countryside.[8] By the end of 1966 a total of 1.3 million urban youths had settled in rural areas (*CLWS a*, 110).

---

7. The percentage of senior high school graduates able to attend college went up from the early 1980s onward. But the holding capacity of tertiary institutions remained limited, with fewer than 3 million students enrolled each year before 1995 (*CSY 2010*, table 20.8).

8. In a 1956 draft document on agricultural development, the Secretariat of the Politburo of the CCP indicated rustication as a possible option for the placement of urban school graduates (Lu Yu 2004, 543). But no nationwide policy followed.

During the Cultural Revolution, rustication of urban secondary school graduates became a government policy.[9] It was in part driven by the ideological agenda of exposing urban youths to the harsh working and living conditions of rural China and thereby preparing them as reliable successors to Mao's radical socialist cause. A more realistic concern among policymakers was the shortage in the supply of daily necessities in cities and the lack of employment opportunities in the urban sector, both of which were seriously affected by the revolution. What also added to the initial push for the adoption of the policy was the need to restore political order in urban areas after the overthrow of the old government during 1967–1968. In view of the persistent and spreading revolutionary fervor of student rebels in major centers of public administration, in December 1968 Mao issued a direct call for them to disperse into the vast rural grassroots, so as to facilitate the enforcement of the martial law imposed in the fall of that year. Under the policy implemented thereafter, urban secondary school graduates were required to go to the countryside to work as laborers in people's communes or state farms. The "sent-down" youth had to stay in the countryside for a minimum of two years before becoming eligible for limited opportunities of being recruited as urban work unit employees, army soldiers, or university students. Only one sibling—typically the youngest one—among the children of each urban family could be exempted from this policy (Liu Xiaomeng 1998).

From 1967 to 1977 a total of 15.8 million urban youths were sent to the countryside (*CLWS a*, 110). Over time some sent-down youth returned to cities, but the returnees were outnumbered by new "sent-downs." In 1977 there remained a stock of about 8.7 million sent-down youth. In October 1978 the central government convened a meeting to reassess the rustication policy. After extended debate it was decided that the policy should be gradually phased out (Liu Xiaomeng 1998). In 1979 large numbers of sent-down youth began to seek ways to leave the countryside (e.g., by faking illness, obtaining urban employment through personal connections, or taking the college entrance exam). Some simply flocked back to cities without permission. Attempts by local authorities to hold back or moderate the surging wave of self-initiated returnees triggered various forms of protest in twenty-one provinces, such as strikes, petitions, suicides, blocking of traffic, and even riots.

---

9. For a detailed account of the entire rustication movement, see a two-volume study by Ding Yizhuang 1998 and Liu Xiaomeng 1998. Bernstein 1977 provides an analysis of the politics that drove the early phases of the movement.

Accommodating the employment demand of the returning youths posed a formidable challenge to the government. The urban economy was still in an early stage of recovery from the chaos of the Mao era and did not have strong enough capacity to absorb all the returnees. Making matters worse was the fact that during the Cultural Revolution some 13 million native rural residents were recruited to take up newly created or vacated (by retirees) urban jobs that otherwise could have been assigned to the urban secondary school graduates who were rusticated (Liu Xiaomeng 1998, 801). Moreover, the growing constraint on the availability of further education for junior high school graduates due to the withering of the radicalist school expansion program, the continuation of the shortened (four-year) secondary school curriculum, and the discontinuation of the rustication policy for new secondary school graduates all added to the job creation pressures on urban authorities and compounded the issue of placement for rusticated youths.

To cope with the confluence of employment problems posed by the peculiar developments during the Cultural Revolution and the broader cohort effect of overall demographic change, the central government held a national labor policy meeting in August 1980. It was at that meeting that legalizing self-employment was adopted as a stopgap measure.[10] In accordance with the resolution of the meeting, the State Administration for Industry and Commerce (SAIC) created a new licensing category, *geti gongshang hu* (self-employment entity in industry and commerce), often known in abbreviated form as *getihu*. That, as discussed in chapter 1, was the first formal step toward legalizing private ownership in the post-Mao era.

Labor Market: Occupational and Spatial Movements

Throughout the 1980s the large number of annual new entrants into the work-age population continued to exert significant job creation pressures on the state. Such pressures were further accentuated by the rise of the labor market and the concurrently changing occupational and spatial characteristics of the work-age population, especially the movement of the existing labor force out of farming. Under the prereform system the state controlled the deployment

---

10. Professor Li Yining of Peking University was one of the economists convened by the central government to undertake preparatory work for the new national policy on self-employment. For an account, based on his personal experience, of the direct causal effect of the job creation pressures on policy change, see http://news.ifeng.com/history/zhiqing/comments/200912/1209_6852_1467798.shtml.

and organization of the entire workforce. The vast majority of working people were confined to agricultural activities, where productivity was low. Free movement of labor was strictly banned, especially between rural and urban areas, where the income gap widened because of the policy bias in resource allocation under central planning. Service activities in both urban and rural areas languished because of low income and concentration of investment in industrial activities, especially capital goods industries.

Table 2.3 shows that in 1978 more than three-quarters of the workforce were in rural areas, and 91% of rural working people were deployed in farming activities. Although receiving the bulk of government investment, the secondary sector only provided 17.3% of the jobs in the economy. The tertiary sector was the smallest employment provider, accounting for only 13.3% of the workforce. Overall, the labor distribution pattern in 1978 did not vary substantially from that in 1952, though a major difference is that the former was shaped mainly by state actions, whereas the latter reflected the state of the predominantly agrarian economy that the PRC inherited from history.

Decollectivization of agriculture during 1979–1983 created a push-and-pull effect on the allocation of the rural workforce, resulting in the rise and expansion of the labor market.[11] The return to family farming and the dismantling of the commune system allowed peasants to make increasingly freer cropping choices and to keep much of the gains from work. They also broke the state's monopoly on rural human resources. What followed was a major change in the incentive structure for peasants and a significant improvement in agricultural productivity (McMillan et al. 1989), thereby making available a sizable and growing number of surplus laborers for the pursuit of other activities. A study by the Ministry of Agriculture estimated that in 1985 surplus labor accounted for some 30%–50% of the agricultural workforce in most regions of the country, with the size of the surplus totaling 100 million (Lu Yu 2004, 552). On the other hand, the rising income from commercial farming boosted the demand for goods and services produced outside the economic space governed by government plans. From the periphery of the centrally planned economy, therefore, grew opportunities to deploy the surplus labor vacated from agriculture.

To capture and benefit from such opportunities, rural authorities promoted the development of publicly owned nonfarm enterprises, known as

---

11. For discussions of agricultural decollectivization and rural reforms, see Kelliher 1992; Yang 1996; and Zweig 1989.

Table 2.3 Distribution of workforce in selected years

Year	Total workforce (millions)	Sectoral share (%)			Rural/urban (%)	Rural breakdown (%)		Urban breakdown (%)	
		Primary	Secondary	Tertiary		Farm/nonfarm	Public/private sector share in nonfarm workforce	Local/migrant workers	Public/private
1952	207.3	83.5	7.4	9.1	88/12		1/99		65/35
1978	401.5	70.5	17.3	13.3	76/24	91/9	100/0	100/0	<99/>1
1988	543.3	59.3	22.4	18.3	74/26	81/19	60/40	87/13	95/5
1998	706.4	49.8	23.5	26.7	69/31	74/26	38/62	69/31	51/49
2008	755.6	39.6	27.2	33.2	57/43	67/33	3/97	55/45	24/76

Note: The primary sector includes agriculture, animal husbandry, fishery, forestry, and sidelines; the secondary sector includes industry (mining, manufacturing, and utilities excluding telecommunications) and construction; and the tertiary sector includes all service activities.

Sources: CSY 1999, 2009, 2010; CSA 2012; SCTE; CTEAPPY 2009; Liang and Ma 2002; National Population and Family Planning Commission (http://chinapop.gov.cn/xwzx/rkxw/200904/t20090401_168197.html; http://chinapop.gov.cn/xwzx/rkxw/201003/t20100330_195823.html).

commune and brigade enterprises (CBEs) before 1983 and township and village enterprise (TVEs) thereafter. These enterprises indeed played an important role in absorbing large numbers of working people transferred out of agriculture (Byrd and Lin 1990; Oi 1999). But they faced resource constraints (especially inadequate funding), lacked technology, and had limited and varying experiences in organization and management.[12] As a result, the jobs they created were insufficient to accommodate the large and fast-growing pool of rural laborers seeking nonfarm employment (Ma Jiesan 1991).[13] Private organizations had to be allowed to play a supplementary role and to expand beyond the initial size limit (of employing no more than seven persons) (Fei Kailong and Zuo Ping 1991).[14]

A major restriction faced by rural nonfarm enterprises during agricultural decollectivization is that their employees, like other rural residents, were not allowed to reside in what the government defined as "urban areas," even if their workplace was physically located there (in which case they had to commute between home and work). It was therefore difficult for rural residents to take up nonfarm employment far away from their home villages or to operate businesses (especially those related to urban services) in more densely populated areas. Fei Xiaotong (1983), a well-known sociologist who served as a vice chairman of the Standing Committee of the National People's Congress, once characterized (and indeed praised) such spatially confined nonfarm employment as "working off the farm but living in the countryside" (*litu bu lixiang*). Yet this restriction hindered the spatial movement of labor and other resources to nonfarm enterprises.

---

12. Local authorities in cities faced similar challenges throughout the 1980s. A major method they used to create jobs for the returning youths from the countryside and for new secondary school graduates (who were no longer required to be rusticated after 1978) was to establish "labor service companies" (*laodong fuwu gongsi*) in underdeveloped areas of urban services. Most of these companies were funded and run by urban work units for the work-age children of their employees. Started in 1980, labor service companies increased their workforce to 7.3 million in 1987 (He Guang 1990, 481), which was equivalent to some 28% of the urban residents with formally registered unemployment status during that period (*LSYC 2011*, 46).

13. According to statistics compiled by the Township Enterprise Bureau under the Ministry of Agriculture (*SCTE*, 71–74, 104–108), TVEs (then called CBEs) accounted for the bulk of the annual net gain in rural nonfarm jobs in 1979. But the contribution steadily declined. The percentage was 40% in 1986, 34% in 1993, and 19% in 1995. As of 1996 TVEs not only ceased to contribute to net job gain but began to cut jobs. A similar pattern existed among urban public enterprises, which accounted for 96%, 76%, and 11% of the net urban job gain in 1979, 1988, and 1990 respectively, and became net job losers starting from 1995 (*CSY 2010*, 118).

14. Before 1988 private nonfarm activities were either household-based or organized in the form of "joint household" operations with pooled familial resources.

In view of the mounting pressures for nonfarm employment that could not be adequately addressed within the rural sector, in 1984 the central government relaxed the restriction by allowing rural residents to both work and reside in urban areas on two conditions. First, they could only enter urban townships but not county seats or cities. Second, they were not eligible to receive any food subsidies—that is, a supply of grain at government-subsidized prices—that permanent urban residents were entitled to. Despite these limiting conditions, the lifting of the ban on rural-urban migration marked the beginning of a spreading process in which an increasing number of rural residents left their home villages to seek employment in urban places. The initial destinations were small towns. But it did not take long for the more daring and enterprising to break the rule of no entry into county seats and cities. By 1988 many cities, especially those in the coastal region, were faced with the influx of large numbers of rural migrants in search of economic opportunities.[15] Concerned about the overload of transportation and urban infrastructure, the difficulties of enforcing family planning among migrants, and the social problems (such as crimes) associated with uncontrolled migration, the central government issued a series of directives during 1989–1992 to tighten regulatory enforcement and push the so-called floating population (*liudong renkou*) back to the townships and rural communities in their home provinces.

The effects of these administrative measures were limited and faded quickly. They failed to deal with the fundamental driving forces behind economic migration, namely, the oversupply of labor in the countryside that could not be fully absorbed by nonfarm enterprises in the rural sector, and the wide income gap between rural and urban economies. Wherever the migrants were spatially oriented or channeled, they posed a growing challenge to the existing job creation capabilities of the local economies of their destinations, thereby casting a heavy shadow over government policymaking. At the same time, they also provided abundant supply of cheap labor for use by domestic and international private capital for profit making, thereby contributing to the expansion of the revenue bases of the local governments concerned. It is not surprising that in 1988 the central government removed the cap on the workforce size of privately owned economic entities. Despite the three-year retrenchment in economic reforms following the Tiananmen Incident in 1989, the private sector survived and continued to grow thereafter. With the

---

15. A widely cited estimate about the number of the migrants flocking to cities at that time is 30 million (Wei Jinsheng, Sheng Lang, and Tao Ying 2002).

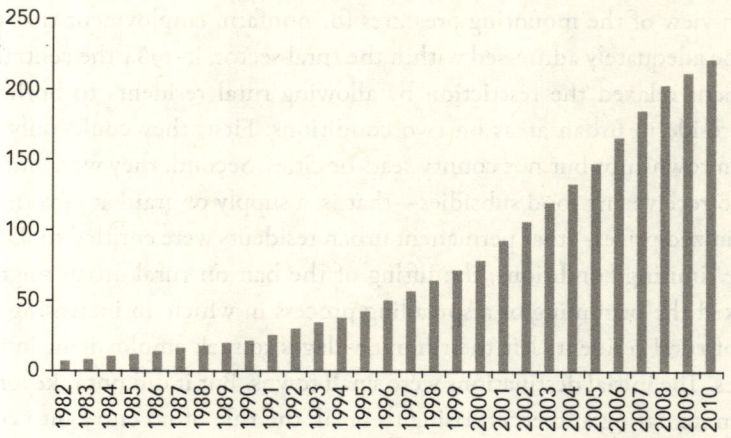

FIGURE 2.4 Number of persons in (intercounty) "floating population" (million persons), 1982–2010

Note: Interpolation is used to fill in some of the data gaps.

Sources: Liang and Ma (2002); statistical summary of the 2005 1% sample survey of the population; statistical summary of the 2010 census. (http://www.stats.gov.cn/tjsj/tjgb/rkpcgb/qgrkpcgb/201104/t20110428_30327.html)

deepening of reform and opening following Deng Xiaoping's southern tour in 1992, economic migration resumed its momentum and refocused on urban areas in more developed regions of the country. Figure 2.4 illustrates a steady upward trend throughout the decade and beyond. Along with it was a gradual process of further relaxation of restrictions on private economic activities, as discussed in chapter 1.

Aging and Old-Age Support

Still another factor that exacerbated the demographic pressures faced by the state was the urban retirement system. When the central planning economy was established in the 1950s, the government created separate systems of social benefits for working people in urban and rural areas. Urban employees were entitled to receive essentially free healthcare, subsidized housing, and a pension after retirement. Basic healthcare for rural residents was provided through a cooperative medicine system subsidized by people's communes. Housing was privately owned in the countryside. But there was no pension for those with rural resident status after they entered old age.

The official retirement age for the urban workforce was set at fifty for ordinary female employees, fifty-five for female administrative personnel (known as *ganbu* or cadres), and sixty for male employees.[16] After retirement an urban employee could receive a lifelong pension equivalent to 60%–100% of his or her basic wage or salary, depending on rank, seniority, and type of work organization. Housing and healthcare benefits would continue to be provided after retirement and to be extended to the dependent members of the retiree's immediate family. All the costs of these social benefits were borne by the work units of urban employees.

When the system was established in the 1950s, the work-age population was very young, as noted above. The urban sector absorbed only a small fraction of the total workforce. More importantly, the resource allocation bias under the central planning system throughout the Mao era provided the necessary funding for various urban work units to sustain the social benefits to their employees and employees' families.[17] Over time, however, these conditions changed. Although proportionally the majority of China's workforce continued to be deployed in the rural sector, the urban sector experienced significant growth under central planning. Into the 1980s, employees who had joined the urban workforce in the 1950s began to enter retirement, and their number steadily rose throughout the decade and beyond.[18] Table 2.4 shows that from 1978 to 1998 the total number of urban retirees increased by more than eleven times—from 3.1 million to 35.9 million. Unlike subsequent cohorts, these retirees were full-benefit recipients on the old social welfare scheme. Financing the related expenses became a growing challenge to the government, as can be seen from the rising costs in absolute and relative terms shown in the table.

Adding to the challenge was the fact that the old system was based on provisions by urban work units in the public sector, where the workforce-retiree ratio declined from 30.3 to 1 in 1978 to 4 to 1 in 1998. Starting from the mid-1980s, most of these organizations experienced a transition from central planning to markets (Naughton 1995). They faced more uncertainties

---

16. When this rule was formulated in the mid-1950s, the life expectancy of the population was under sixty (Banister 1987).

17. Aside from the inequalities associated with the urban-rural divide, there were also variations in the amount and quality of the social benefits among urban employees. More resourceful organizations, such as centrally controlled SOEs, tended to have better benefits than those at the bottom of the hierarchy of urban work organization, such as collective enterprises under the purview of county governments.

18. The positions vacated by retirees might have opened up some opportunities for new entrants into the workforce, thus moderating the pressures on job creation. This is especially true in the 1980s, when the workforce of the urban public sector was still expanding. But the effect is likely to have faded subsequently, when the urban public sector experienced employment contraction, as noted above.

Table 2.4 Urban retirees on old (mainly work-unit based) benefit schemes, 1978–1998

Year	Retired staff and workers (*zhigong*)			Expenditure on retirees		
	Total (millions)	Share (%) of public sector	Ratio of workforce to retirees	Amount (100 million yuan)	Expenses equivalent to % of fiscal spending	% of costs borne by work units (state-owned)
1978	3.1	100	30.3			
1979	6.0	100	16.7			
1980	8.2	100	12.8	86.8	7.1	92.4
1981	9.5	100	11.5	101.3	8.9	93.8
1982	11.3	100	10.1	117.5	9.6	94.8
1983	12.9	100	8.9	137.3	9.7	95.7
1984	14.8	99.7	8.0	161.5	9.5	96.5
1985	16.4	99.7	7.5	210.2	10.5	96.8
1986	18.1	99.7	7.1	257.1	11.6	97.7
1987	19.7	99.7	6.7	315.6	13.9	97.7
1988	21.2	99.6	6.4	426.3	17.0	97.0
1989	22.0	99.5	6.2	505.4	17.8	97.1
1990	23.0	99.5	6.1	622.6	20.1	97.7
1991	24.3	99.5	6.0	735	21.6	98.0
1992	26.0	99.3	5.6	896.7	23.8	98.1
1993	27.8	98.5	5.4	1147.2	24.3	98.1
1994	29.3	97.9	5.1	1218.9	20.6	98.0
1995	30.9	97.7	4.8	1522.4	21.8	98.2
1996	32.2	97.5	4.6	1797.7	22.1	98.5
1997	33.5	97.3	4.4	2043.8	21.5	98.4
1998	35.9	94.4	4.0	2330.9	20.4	98.3

Note: "Staff and workers" includes employees in state-owned enterprises, urban collective enterprises, share-holding companies, and foreign-invested companies.
Sources: LSYC 1996, 1998, 1999, 2000; SCTE; CTEAPPY 2009.

in government funding and sharp declines in profits due to both intensifying competition and moral hazard in the behavior of supervising officials (chapter 4). For many of them, supporting rising numbers of retirees became an increasingly unbearable undertaking.

To limit the social benefit responsibilities for urban employees, the government replaced the lifetime employment system with a contract employment system in 1986. But that change did not have any retroactive effect on existing public sector employees, who totaled 105 million in 1985 (*CSY 2011*, 45) and were slated to retire in the following decade and beyond. Nonetheless, in the meantime the government also began to experiment with pilot programs that aimed to transfer the provision of social benefits from urban work units in select locales to the corresponding local governments. What resulted from such experiments, however, was a shift of the administrative work of retirement account management to the local labor authority but not the financial responsibilities internalized to the public enterprises concerned. With the number of urban retirees and the cost of financing them continuing to rise, the government decided in 1991 to move to a system where the cost of financing pensions, bundled with that of financing healthcare, would be based on a combination of contributions from individuals, enterprises, and the government and the administrative work (concerning revenue collection and benefit dispensation) would be run by a unified authority.[19] Details of the new system were not finalized until 1997–1998,[20] when massive privatization of public enterprises began. It was first implemented in select sectors and locales and then gradually extended in the following decade to work organizations in the entire urban sector, including those outside the public sector.[21]

A proclaimed goal of the new social security system is to cope with the challenge of old-age support in face of China's accelerated transition from a young population to an increasingly aging population. It is also said to be conducive to reducing inequalities in society. But a more practical purpose it has served is the creation of a new pool of funds that can be utilized to finance, with future beneficiaries' contributions, the long-standing obligations of the

---

19. The new system has been run mainly by local governments at the city/county level. In 2000 the National Social Security Fund was established with a one-time allocation of seed capital (20 billion yuan) from the Ministry of Finance. It has since grown with IPO proceeds from SOEs listed on stock exchanges, lottery income, and investment returns. The main function of the fund is to provide backup support when the revenues of local social security funds are inadequate for covering spending.

20. Under the new system employees are required to contribute up to 8% of their wages to a pension fund, 2% to a healthcare fund, and 1% to an unemployment fund. Employers are required to make matching contributions equivalent to 20%, 6%, and 2% of the total wage bill to these funds respectively. Such contributions by employers are counted as operating costs. The implicit tax exemption constitutes the "contribution" from the government (Zhu Rongji 2011, 2:379). Upon retirement, employees having contributed to the pension fund for fifteen or more years will be eligible to receive a pension (equivalent to some 20% of the local average wage), plus an amount calculated as a fraction of the sum of the cumulative individual contributions. After enrollment, they are also eligible for discounts and/or partial reimbursements for certain healthcare services and can get an allowance for limited duration in the event of being unemployed.

21. In 2007 the government announced a plan to extend the system to the entire rural sector by 2020.

government to retirees on the old scheme.[22] Indeed, since their inauguration virtually all the local social security funds have tapped to the fullest, and continued to rely on, the contributions in the individual accounts of employees on the new scheme. These people mostly work outside the public sector and are either years away from retirement or not yet eligible for full benefits.[23] What is important for the state is that their contributions have helped cover the dispensation of benefits to existing retirees, who are overwhelmingly former public sector employees covered by the old benefit scheme (Jia Yingzi 2008). By the time the new system was introduced in 1997, it had become clear that the state could no longer count on poorly performing urban public enterprises to continue their traditional role in social benefit financing. New sources of financing had to be found, expanded, and sustained. The new social security system, coupled with privatization, would enable the state to spread the responsibility beyond the public sector and create a buffer against an immediate crisis in socioeconomic governance in the face of changing demographics.

Summary

At the end of the Mao era China entered a new phase of demographic transition, with an abundant and increasing supply of labor and a declining ratio of nonworking to working people. It coincided with the start of economic reforms. The timing of the coincidence was in part quickened by the family planning policy started in the early 1970s. The resultant potential of a "demographic dividend" not only represented enormous opportunities for economic growth but posed formidable challenges of job creation to the new CCP leaders. Like rulers in other political regimes, they could hardly afford to ignore these challenges, which were of essential importance to the livelihood of citizens and therefore to the CCP's attempt to shore up legitimacy after the turmoil and devastation of the Cultural Revolution. To accommodate the employment need of massive numbers of job seekers and to make

---

22. See, for example, the progress report on the new social security system presented by Zhang Zuoji, minister of labor and social security, to the Standing Committee of the National People's Congress in October 2001 (http://www.npc.gov.cn/wxzl/gongbao/2001-12/12/content_5281324.htm).

23. Under the new scheme a retiring employee who has not attained the fifteen-year threshold of cumulative contributions will not be eligible for a pension. Instead he or she will receive a lump-sum payment equivalent to the cumulative contributions to the individual account. This rule effectively limits the near-term pressures from new retirees for benefit dispensation, thereby creating an interim window for addressing the shortfalls in the funding for retirees on the old scheme.

productive use of the large and fast-growing workforce, a new economic space had to be created and expanded outside the existing institutional framework, especially the property right arrangements based on public ownership.

The trigger, extent, pace, and form of the policy responses in the years to follow were nevertheless conditioned by the spatial, occupational, and cohort characteristics of the population. These characteristics in turn had been shaped by the long-lasting impact of past institutions under the Maoist population policies and industrialization strategy, and by contingencies that immediately preceded the post-Mao reforms, such as the short-lived radicalization of schooling and rustication of urban youths. With greater concern than local governments about regime survival and as the main initiator of most of the relevant policies to cope with the challenges from demographics, the central government played an important part in this causal story of endogenously induced institutional change.

In face of the hardening constraints from changing demographics, it made a series of moves to reset the rules on private ownership, including the decisions to legalize self-employment in 1980, to lift the size limit on private enterprises in 1988, to give formal recognition to the private sector as an "integral part" of China's new economy in 1992, and to undertake ownership restructuring among public enterprises starting from 1997 while concurrently relaxing remaining restrictions on the private sector. Within the state system, it redefined the criteria of performance assessment for local officials and pushed them to pay closer attention to the issue of job creation and employment. As will be discussed in chapters 3–6, these moves set in motion and further fed into a process of interactions where the responses from local political and economic actors often went beyond the initial limits set by the central authority but many of the earlier deviations were amnestied and even incorporated as elements in subsequent central policy changes because they provided practical solutions to the existential concerns of CCP leaders.

Demographic constraints, however, are only part of the driving forces in the process of privatization. An important question that arises from the foregoing account is why the state became increasingly unable to tackle the challenges of demographic change within the institutional boundaries of public ownership. Addressing this question entails an understanding of the evolving public finance system and a close examination of the job creation capabilities of public enterprises. These are the focal issues of the next two chapters.

3

The Evolving Structure of Public Finance

WHEN THE MAO era passed, China faced serious challenges in public finance. The government had run a budget deficit for three consecutive years toward the end of the Cultural Revolution (1966–1976). After a brief interval of balanced budgets during 1977–1978—achieved largely through cutting back on some essential expenditures (Jia Kang and Zhao Quanhou 2008, 51) and booking unrealized revenues (Zuo Chuntai and Song Xinzhong 1988, 426–427), a budget deficit of unprecedented magnitude appeared in 1979. It totaled 17.1 billion yuan, which was equivalent to 15.2% of the current-year budget revenue (*CSY 1994*, 69), and ushered in a three-decade-long trend of fiscal shortfalls. To cope with the growing budgetary imbalances, the Ministry of Finance began to experiment with measures to restructure the rigid and highly centralized fiscal system in 1977, when political regime transition was still underway. What followed was a process of fiscal decentralization that fully unfolded in 1980 and had profound implications for intragovernmental relations as well as economic institutional change.

A pivotal component in this process was a fiscal contract system that ran through 1993. It reduced centralized control over local public finance by redefining the boundaries of the rights and responsibilities of local governments. In concurrence with it were three coevolving phenomena in the fiscal system: the decline and elimination of the role of (public) enterprise profit remittance in revenue generation, the expansion of revenue sources under various "regional property rights" regimes, and the growth of off-budget funds. These developments, coupled with a new focus of political performance assessment on economic development, changed the incentives and constraints faced by local political actors. Their responses nevertheless varied, as will be discussed in the following chapters. Such variations led to different local policy environments for domestic private business and foreign capital in the first decade and half of economic reforms. They also generated and compounded a host of problems, pressures, and challenges that drove the central leadership to undertake a major restructuring of the fiscal system in 1994 and, before long, to adopt sweeping measures of ownership restructuring.

"Unified Revenue and Spending"

The basic structure of the prereform public finance system was set up in the mid to late 1950s (Zuo Chuntai and Song Xinzhong 1988). Its main function was to facilitate centrally planned allocation of resources. To secure the necessary funding for the acceleration of industrialization in face of a weak domestic economic base and a lack of external sources of financing (especially after the withdrawal of Soviet aid in 1960), the central government imposed tight control over the extraction and utilization of fiscal revenue.

The anchor principle of centralized fiscal control in the Mao era was "unified revenue and spending" (*tongshou tongzhi*). What it meant is that lower-level governments were required to remit all their budgetary revenues to higher-level governments, which would then assess, authorize, and provide for the spending by lower-level governments. Public enterprises were also required to turn over all profits to their supervising authorities, which in turn would be responsible for financing the expenditures and covering the losses (if any) of their subordinate enterprises. In addition, all expenditures of nonadministrative and noneconomic units would be covered by a unified government budget.

In reality this principle was only strictly practiced in certain years of the Mao era—that is, 1950, 1961–1963, and 1968 (Jia Kang and Zhao Quanhou 2008). In the other years fiscal relations between different levels of government were governed by variant versions of the principle, which commonly made spending conditional on revenue and allowed for varying degrees of latitude in the use of fiscal resources by lower-level governments. With the exception of some brief periods of significant delegation of fiscal authority (e.g., during 1957–1958 and 1971–1973), however, the flexibility granted to lower-level governments was quite limited and the link between revenue growth and spending increase remained weak and unstable (Zuo Chuntai and Song Xinzhong 1988). The fiscal contract system adopted in the 1980s and early 1990s was aimed at relaxing these constraints through formalized contracts, instead of being a new institutional setup. Before getting to that issue, though, let me first highlight some other features of public finance in the Mao era.

Under the prereform system the bulk of government revenue came from two major sources: profits remitted by SOEs and a tax (known as *gongshang shui*, or industrial and commercial tax) on industrial and commercial transactions (with the exception of wholesale).[1] Together, they accounted for 86% of the total budget revenue in 1978, whereas the remaining 14% was derived from several minor taxes (*CSY 1983*, 67).[2] SOEs were the main contributors to the treasury. In 1978 the profits remitted and the taxes paid by SOEs made up 51% and 36% of total budget revenue respectively (*FSFYC*, 25).

While the revenues from SOEs were subject to centralized fiscal control, the majority of SOEs were not directly administered by the central government. As noted by David Granick (1990), nonfarm economic organizations in China's centrally planned economy were organized under a "regional property rights" regime, where public enterprises were stratified according to a pecking order of relative importance for resource allocation. The most important ones (e.g., large, capital goods producers) were "owned" by the central government or provincial governments, whereas the less important ones (e.g., small, consumer goods producers), including urban collective enterprises, were "owned" by authorities at the city, county, and subcounty levels. At the bottom of the pecking order were commune and brigade enterprises (*shedui qiye*) under people's communes in rural areas.[3]

When the degree of centralized fiscal control was moderated from the extreme of "unified revenue and spending," the level of enterprise "ownership" was used as a major benchmark for the division of fiscal flows between higher- and lower-level governments. The projected amounts of profits and taxes to be generated by public enterprises "owned" by different levels of government and the projected expenditures and costs to be incurred by these enterprises, for example, were among the key considerations in the setting of the annual

---

1. The industrial and commercial tax was introduced in 1973 by combining several taxes created in the 1950s. For details see Zuo Chuntai and Song Xinzhong 1988, 401.

2. These taxes were collective enterprise income tax, livestock sales tax, rural market transaction tax, agriculture tax, and import duty.

3. From 1954 to 1983 China had three levels of government: central, provincial, and city/county. Townships were added as a fourth level in 1984. Although without constitutionally designated status, prefectural cities under provincial governments have been treated as a separate level of fiscal authority and have (since 1982) been charged with the task of administering clusters of ordinary cities (including county-rank cities) and counties. Since 2002 reforms have been carried out in an increasing number of provinces to place cities and counties under the direct purview of provincial governments. A note on the ranks of cities and the evolution of various special status cities is posted at the book site.

targets of fiscal revenue and spending allowance for the government of the locale where these enterprises were situated. Regardless of the administrative ranks of their "owners," though, all public enterprises physically located in a particular city or county remitted their profits and paid their taxes to the local public finance authority. The latter in turn handed over the collected revenue, in full or after deduction of preauthorized amount for retainment, to higher-level authorities according to the prevailing fiscal rules of the time.

In addition to budget revenue there was a second category of fiscal resources generated and used by the government. It was called "extrabudget" revenue or fund (Deng Yingtao et al. 1990). It consisted of fiscal surcharges by local governments, administrative fees collected by government agencies, proceeds received by nonadministrative units (*shiye danwei*) (e.g., research institutes, cultural establishments, and schools), and funds retained by SOEs and their supervising authorities. The last category was by far the largest component of extrabudget revenue. In 1978 it made up 73% of extrabudget revenue (*FYC* 2011, 472). It included the depreciation charges and residual (postremittance) profits (if any) of SOEs, plus the proceeds from SOEs formed outside regular government budgets. The use of extrabudget revenue was directed toward supplementing centrally planned activities and was subject to pertinent regulations of the fiscal authority, though there was generally more latitude on the part of the government agencies that controlled them. In 1978 the total extrabudget revenue was equivalent to about 31% of budget revenue (*FYC 2011*, 472).

Through budget and extrabudget revenues the public finance authority on average extracted some one-third of the country's GDP for fiscal reallocation throughout the Mao era (Jia Kang and Zhao Quanhou 2008). The system nevertheless had two major problems: weak incentives for revenue expansion and high transaction costs. Because of the weak link between revenue and spending and the lack of flexibility in local appropriation of fiscal resources, government authorities responsible for activities related to revenue generation were not strongly motivated to expand their revenue bases. The same was true for public enterprises, where much of the accounting surplus was extracted by the government, which also subsidized all the financial losses. On the other hand, centralized micromanagement of public finance at all levels of the government system led to lengthy processes of decision-making and gridlocks of information flow. Frequent (oftentimes annual) negotiations over fiscal flows between higher- and lower-level authorities also seriously constrained the administrative capacities of the parties involved.

Fiscal Contracts

To tackle the problems in the old system the government implemented a series of changes throughout the 1980s and early 1990s. These changes were structured around an arrangement known as the fiscal contract system (*caizheng chengbao tizhi*). A fiscal contract was an agreement between a lower-level government and a higher-level government with regard to the fiscal rights and responsibilities of the two parties for a certain period of time (mostly two or more years). Its formulation typically involved three steps: (1) to assess, based on recent fiscal data and near-term projections, the spending needs and the revenue-generating capacity of the lower-level government; (2) to set the targets for revenue and spending during the contract period; and (3) to determine the share or amount of remittance to the higher-level authority or, in the event of projected local revenue being insufficient for covering projected spending, the amount of subsidies from the latter.

The first fiscal contract was adopted in the province of Jiangsu in 1977. Based on the information about past fiscal flows, a fixed percentage (42% vs. 58%) was set for dividing the revenue extracted by the province with the central government. The contract covered a period of four years. It set a precedent for subsequent experimentation of similar measures in other provincial entities and at sub-provincial levels. In 1980 the State Council introduced sweeping changes that made fiscal contract the basic mechanism governing central-provincial fiscal relations. The new practice was characterized in Chinese economic literature as "dining in separate kitchens" (*fenzao chifan*), which drew a metaphorical contrast with the old doctrine of "unified revenue and spending."

The actual form of fiscal contract varied by province and experienced adjustments over time during 1980–1993 (Jia Kang and Zhao Quanhou 2008).[4] A most widely used arrangement was known as "dividing revenue and expenditure and assigning full contractual responsibility to each level of administration" (*huafen shouzhi fenji baogan*). It defined the scope of central and provincial responsibilities for covering different spending needs in

---

4. There were three major rounds of fiscal contracts: 1980–1984, 1985–1987, and 1988–1993. The first round largely centered on the division of fiscal rights and responsibilities benchmarked to the revenues from basic extraction channels in the existing system—i.e., SOE profit remittance and industrial and commercial tax. The second round incorporated changes in the composition of revenues under the restructured tax system (see the discussion below) for ascertaining and determining central and local shares in fiscal flows. The third round featured greater emphasis on benchmarking these shares to the growth rate rather than the size of the revenues generated by local governments, so as to keep the central government from being blocked out of the above-target portions of revenue growth.

the pertinent province, and divided revenues into local and central categories benchmarked to the fiscal structure in a baseline year (oftentimes the year preceding the contract). When local revenue was projected to be greater than local spending, the extra amount would be shared with the central government according to a fixed percentage. When local revenue was projected to fall short of local spending, the central government would subsidize the deficit. Once the baseline figures on projected revenue and spending were set, they would hold for certain years. Any increase above the baseline figure on local revenue or in excess of certain growth rate would either be retained by the province concerned or shared with the central government according to a preset percentage, whereas any shortfall below the baseline revenue would have to be absorbed by the pertinent province through spending cuts. Similar and variant arrangements of this contractual form were also widely adopted between provincial and lower-level governments (Jia Kang and Zhao Quanhou 2008).

Parallel to the implementation of fiscal contracts was a restructuring of the tax system. In 1980 the Ministry of Finance began pilot programs in some six hundred SOEs to replace SOE profit remittance with an enterprise income tax. That experiment, known as the "tax for profit" (*li gai shui*) reform, was intended to provide SOEs with greater incentives by allowing them to retain part of their profits after paying income tax. Introduced to all SOEs during 1983, it was coupled with a reform (also known as "phase 2 of the tax-for-profit reform") in 1984 that decomposed and expanded the all-encompassing industrial and commercial tax into several taxes targeting different economic organizations and activities.[5] In the meantime, several concurrent or sequential steps were taken to expand tax categories (Jia Kang and Zhao Quanhou 2008), and to gradually free SOEs and other public enterprises from central planning and turn them into market players (Naughton 1995). As a result of these changes, taxes became the predominant source of budget revenue, as can be seen from the statistics in table 3.1.

A major feature of the restructured tax system is that the total revenue generated through income taxes (all but one of which—the collective enterprise income tax—were created in the 1980s) fell far short of the magnitude that SOE profit remittance had commanded. In contrast, the bulk of tax revenues

---

5. These taxes include value-added tax (on twelve categories of industrial products), product tax (on industrial products and select agricultural products), business tax (on service activities and construction), salt tax, (large and medium) SOE profit adjustment tax, resource tax, motor vehicle and vessel license tax, and SOE bonus tax.

Table 3.1 Selected statistics of public finance, 1978–2010

Year	Fiscal revenue as % of GDP	Budget deficit (billions of yuan)	Central share in revenue and spending		% in total budget revenue			
					Enterprise profit remittance	Taxes	Other	(SOE share)
1978	31.1	0	16	47	51	46	3	(87)
1980	25.5	6.9	25	54	38	49	3	(85)
1985	22.2	5.8	38	40	2	88	10	(72)
1990	15.7	14.7	34	33	<1	96	4	(45)
1995	10.3	58.2	52	29	0	97	3	(43)
2000	13.5	249.1	52	35	0	94	6	(41*)
2005	17.1	228.0	52	26	0	91	9	(37)
2010	22.5	677.3	51	18	0	88	12	(32)

Note: The "other" category consists mainly of various fees and surcharges. The figure with "*" is for 2001. SOE shares after 2000 do not include contributions from financial SOEs.
Sources: CSY 2012; FYC 1992, 1999, 2006, 2011.

after 1984 came from indirect taxes that were collected from or through the sale of products and services. Figure 3.1 illustrates the importance of these taxes both before and after the restructuring in 1984. Particularly noteworthy is the period from 1985 to the late 1990s, when the share of these taxes rose significantly and remained at very high levels and when public enterprises first experienced considerable expansion but then (after 1995) began to decline.

Also important to note is the fact that "regional property rights" continued to matter in the fiscal relations between different levels of government, as the boundaries between central and provincial fiscal rights and responsibilities (and those involving lower administrative levels as well) were still defined in connection with the "affiliation relationships" (*lishu guanxi*) of the economic organizations located in a province. That is, the central government retained all the fiscal revenues from centrally owned enterprises in the province, whereas the size of the fiscal revenues from local enterprises relative to local spending projections was a key determinant of the extent to which the province would be required to upload extra revenues to the center or receive subsidies from it. But there were two differences with the prereform system.

First, the profits of SOEs "owned" by different levels of government no longer made up the mainstay of budget revenue after 1984. Instead, it was the taxes paid or generated by these enterprises, along with those by other types

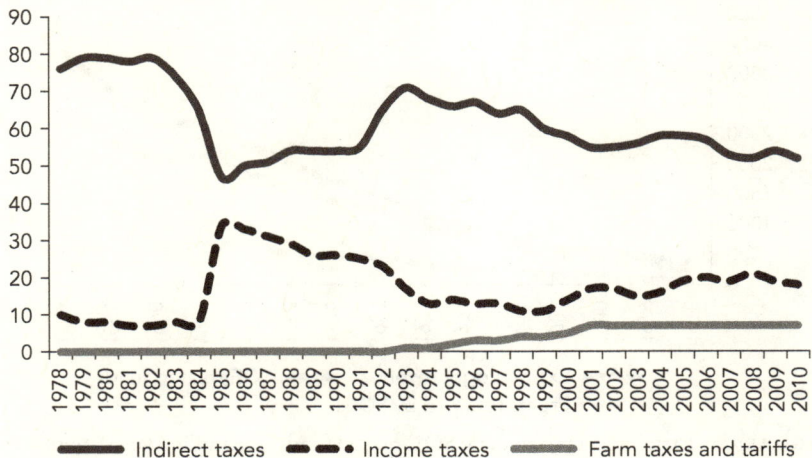

FIGURE 3.1 Major components (%) of tax revenue, 1978–2010
Sources: FYC 1992, 1999, 2011.

of economic organizations (including collective enterprises, foreign-invested entities, and private entities), that served as the benchmarks for setting the baseline figures on revenue and spending in fiscal contracts.

Second, the so-called affiliation relationships of revenue providers (enterprises) were no longer synonymous with "ownership" by different levels of government. Instead, they encompassed both public enterprises and some other types of economic organizations (i.e., shareholding companies, Chinese-foreign joint ventures) over which different levels of government held fiscal rights and responsibilities. Indeed the vast majority of those in the latter group were licensed by the governments of the cities or counties where they operated, and the fiscal extractions from them (including those without clearly defined "affiliation relationship" labels) combined to form "local" revenue.

Still another development under the fiscal contract system was the expansion of extrabudget funds, which lay outside the fiscal contracts between different levels of government. In 1978 they were equivalent to 31% of budget revenue; in 1992 the figure went up to 111% (*FYC 2011*, 472). The growth rate of extrabudget revenue was far higher than that of budget revenue. During 1979–1992 the average annual growth rate of extrabudget revenue was 19.1%, whereas budget revenue grew at an average rate of 8.6% (*FYC 2011*, 472). This expansion was in part the result of a multiplication of various fees charged by government agencies, over which centralized control became increasingly

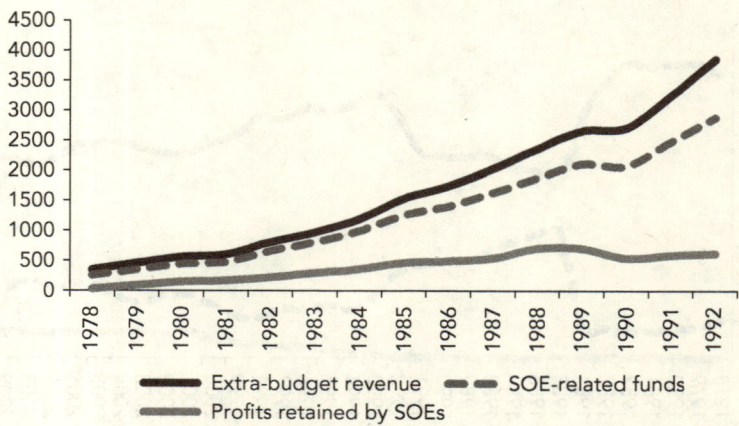

FIGURE 3.2 Extrabudget revenue and SOE-related funds (100 million yuan), 1978–1992
Sources: FYC 1992, 2011.

ineffective.[6] But the main driver came from SOE-related funds, which continued to be the mainstay (70%–80%) of extrabudget revenue, as shown in figure 3.2. These funds grew with the progression of SOE reforms.

Starting from 1978, SOEs were allowed to retain part of their profits to finance production, fringe benefits, and bonus schemes. During 1983–1984 the "tax for profit" reform further broadened the scope of profit retention after income tax payment. Yet not all the authorized retention was kept and used by SOEs. As indicated by the curve closest to the horizontal axis in figure 3.2, from 1978 to 1992 only about 20%–30% of the SOE-related funds in extrabudget revenue were booked to the accounts of SOEs, whereas some 70%–80% were held by various supervising agencies (*FYC 1993*, 684–685, 688, 691). The latter included depreciation charges, profits withheld from SOEs, proceeds from SOEs formed outside the state budget, and unspecified revenue categories. With the exception of depreciation charges, a major source of the growth of these funds was the diversion of fiscal resources from budgetary to extrabudgetary categories (Jia Kang and Zhao Quanhou 2008). A commonly used method for such diversion was to grant tax breaks to enterprises "owned" by local governments.

Under the fiscal contract system, revenue targets were mostly set as lump-sum figures. Although the target figures were derived by estimating the

---

6. See Lin 2001 for a discussion of the central government's largely unsuccessful efforts during the 1990s to curb the outgrowth of "three arbitrary charges" (*sanluan*) by government agencies—fees, fines, and ad hoc levies known as *tanpai*.

revenues from regular fiscal sources, such as profit remittance (before 1985), taxes, and fees, there was considerable maneuvering room for local governments. Given that above-target revenues were subject to sharing with higher-level authorities, local governments had the incentive to negotiate down the baseline target and not to overfulfill the contract greatly. During 1988–1993 (when pertinent data are available), for example, the average level of fiscal contract fulfillment by provincial governments was 111%.[7] Since all taxes were collected by the local tax authority and then divided with higher-level government, local governments could give tax reductions and exemptions to the enterprises they "owned" to any extent that would not affect the fulfillment of the fiscal contract. The tax breaks were then subject to "recall" for discretionary use by the local government concerned (Ma et al. 1994). From 1985 to 1993, for example, large and medium-sized SOEs were subject to an enterprise income tax at the rate of 55%, whereas small SOEs (and urban and rural collective enterprises) were faced with a progressive income tax rate ranging from 10% (for income under 1,000 yuan) to 55% (for income above 200,000 yuan). In reality, these tax rates were rarely applied.[8] In fact, figure 3.3 shows that the effective tax rate for industrial SOE profits trended down from over 55% in 1985 to less than 13% in 1993.[9] The uncollected tax revenue ended up in the pool of off-budget funds controlled by the supervising bodies of SOEs.[10]

SOEs were not alone. Township and village enterprises (TVEs) "owned" by rural authorities (see chapter 4) were also given substantial tax breaks as a way to divert funds away from the budgetary process. Table 3.2, based on published statistics, reveals a significant gap between "taxes due" (according to the prevailing tax rates) and "taxes paid" by TVEs during 1987–1992 (the

---

7. This figure is estimated by taking the ratio of "actually collected revenue" to "projected revenue" of different provincial entities, reported in the internally circulated material *Fiscal Statistics of Prefectures, Cities and Counties* for 1988–1993 (Ministry of Finance).

8. In 1994 enterprise income tax rate was reset at a unified level of 33% for all economic organizations. It was further lowered to 25% in 2008.

9. These rates are estimated by dividing the total enterprise income tax paid with the total amount of gross profits earned by industrial SOEs. The income tax here includes the SOE income adjustment tax, which was levied as a (firm-specific) percentage of the net profits (after income tax) of large and medium SOEs.

10. Under the new accounting system adopted in 1993, SOE-related funds previously defined as extra-budget revenue were reclassified as part of enterprise equity and therefore ceased to be categorized as extrabudget revenue. The removal of these funds from fiscal statistics, however, did not necessarily stop supervising authorities of SOEs from continuing their influence over the use of these funds. Moreover, remaining elements in the extrabudget revenue category continued to grow throughout the 1990s and into the new millennium (Jia Kang and Zhao Quanhou 2008).

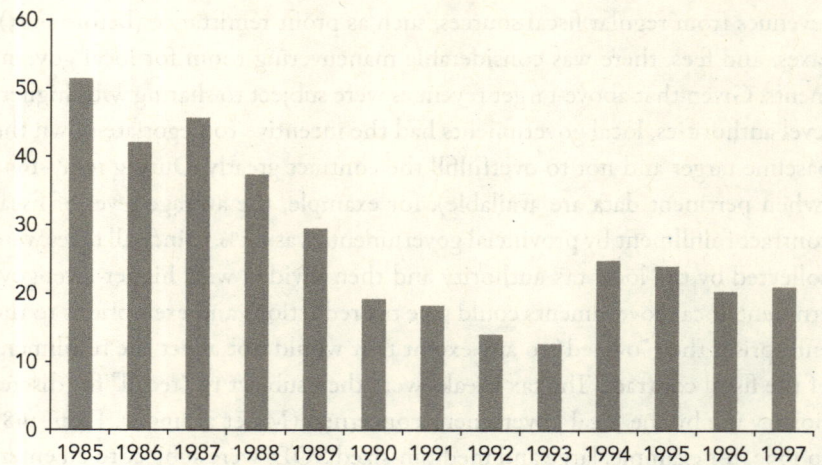

FIGURE 3.3 Enterprise income tax paid as percentage of gross profit of industrial SOEs, 1985–1997
Source: FYC 1998.

Table 3.2 Taxes due and paid by township and village enterprises (RMB billions)

Year	All taxes		Income tax		Indirect taxes	
	Due	Paid	Due	Paid	Due	Paid
1987	16.9	13.1				
1988	23.7	17.7	6	3.8	17.7	13.8
1989	26	19.6	6.1	3.8	19.9	15.7
1990	27	20.3	5.7	3.6	21.3	16.7
1991	33.4	24.2	6.8	4	26.6	17.3
1992	41.7	33.6	9.6	5.4	32.1	27.9

Sources: CTEY 1988, 1989, 1990, 1991, 1992, 1993.

period for which sufficiently detailed information is available). The tax breaks not only concerned income tax on enterprise profits but encompassed indirect (transaction) taxes that constituted the mainstay of budgetary revenue. Part of the unpaid taxes was parked in the accounts of TVEs for use by their supervising authorities; part became "self-raised funds" under township governments, which were not included in the statistics on extrabudgetary revenue until 1996 (Jia Kang and Zhao Quanhou 2008).

The outgrowth of extrabudget funds throughout the 1980s and early 1990s took place at the expense of budget revenue. As shown in table 3.1, the share of budget revenue in GDP steadily declined from 25.5% in 1980 to 15.7% in 1990 and further to 10.3% in 1995.

A concurrent problem under the fiscal contract system was the erosion of the central government's fiscal power. After an initial rise in the early years of reform, the share of the central government in budget revenue began to trend down after reaching an interim high of 40.5% in 1984. In 1993 it dropped to 22%. On the other hand, during most of the years under the fiscal contract system the responsibilities of the central government in total fiscal spending remained above the revenue it could dispose of, adding to the pressure to increase budget deficit (which indeed trended up, as shown in table 3.1). In 1993, for example, the central government was responsible for covering 28.3% of total spending but had only a 22% share in total revenue (*FYC 2011*, 459–463).

Governance costs also posed a problem. Although the fiscal contracts between the central government and provincial governments were set for multiple years, renegotiations for ex post adjustments after the start of a contract were commonplace, making contract enforcement and monitoring a formidable administrative task. Still another problem is that under the fiscal contracts local governments tended to promote sectors with high tax rates and/or large profit margins (e.g., tobacco and alcoholic products) and sought to protect their parochial revenue bases by creating trade barriers (e.g., through bans on the sale of locally produced raw materials and inputs to other, especially competing regions), resulting in overcapacity and segmentation of markets (Tao et al. 2009).

Revenue Partitioning

In face of the growing problems associated with the fiscal contract system, the central government began to experiment with measures in the late 1980s for a restructuring of the fiscal relations with provincial governments. In December 1993 it issued a directive to replace the provincial fiscal contracts with a new arrangement for central-provincial fiscal relations. It was called *fenshui zhi*, or system of tax separation. Effective from January 1, 1994, all fiscal revenues were partitioned along the lines of tax categories. Specifically, revenues were divided into three categories: taxes belonging exclusively to the central government, taxes belonging exclusively to provincial governments,

Table 3.3 Revenue partitioning between central and provincial governments in 1994

Revenue type	Tax categories
Central revenue	Import duty; excise tax; central SOE income tax and remitted profits; income tax on banks and nonbank financial institutions; combined revenues (business tax; income tax; remitted profits; urban maintenance and construction tax) from railway system and headquarters of national banks and insurance companies; (responsibility for covering tax rebates for exporters)
Local revenue	Business tax; local enterprise income tax and remitted profits; personal income tax; urban land use tax; adjustment tax on fixed asset investment; tax on motor vehicles and ship licenses; stamp duty; slaughter tax; agriculture tax; deed tax; animal husbandry tax; special agricultural product tax; urban (nonresidential) property tax; tax on nonfarm use of farmland; estate tax; land value appreciation tax; proceeds from state-owned land use right transfers
Shared revenue	Value-added tax (75:25); resource tax (offshore marine resources for central government and most other resources for local governments); security transaction stamp duty
Major post-1994 changes (through 2005)	Local enterprise income tax and personal income tax were redefined as shared taxes with a 50% central share in 2002 and 60% in 2003; export tax rebates were turned into a shared responsibility in 2004 (75% central and 25% local; adjusted to 92.5% central and 7.5% local in 2005); agricultural tax was abolished in 2005

Source: Contents of the table are based on descriptions in Jia Kang and Zhao Quanhou 2008.

and taxes shared by central and provincial governments according to fixed percentages. Table 3.3 summarizes the basic elements of this arrangement.

It should be noted that the 1994 restructuring was not a complete departure from the fiscal contract system. Under the new system, the central government nominally had a 100% share in the excise tax (converted from the product tax) and a 75% share in the value-added tax. Both taxes were created in 1984 as spin-off tax categories from the industrial and commercial tax (see note 5). To compensate for the "revenue loss" of local governments, the central government would annually repatriate to them a lump sum equal to the revenue they had collected through these taxes in 1993, plus a 0.3% equivalent of this lump sum for every 1% of the growth portion of these taxes. In 2002 the local enterprise income tax and the personal income tax were reclassified as shared revenue. Again, the sharing formula between the central government and local governments (initially 50:50 and then 60:40) would apply only to the growth portion of these taxes relative to the base year (2001) amounts retained locally, which the central government would repatriate to the pertinent local governments. Moreover, fiscal relations at sub-provincial levels were not covered by the new arrangement of revenue partitioning. By and large they continued to be governed by various fiscal contracts formed before 1994, albeit with adjustments reflecting the changes in central-provincial fiscal relations (Jia Kang and Zhao Quanhou 2008).

Despite these linkages and continuities, the 1994 restructuring did usher in many important changes with far-reaching implications. First, an immediate outcome of the new system was an increase of the central government's share in budget revenue, largely owing to its commanding the lion's share in the most important and stable tax—the value-added tax. As shown in table 3.1, the central share in budget revenue jumped to 52% in 1995 and remained at that level throughout the following decade and half. In the meantime, however, the share of the central government in direct budget spending trended down. Embodied in these movements is a growing ability of the central government to redistribute fiscal resources through various fiscal transfer programs, especially those to economically less developed provinces. Most of these transfers, though, had to be filtered by provincial governments, thus adding a new dimension in the bargaining relations between provincial and sub-provincial governments.

Second, to facilitate the implementation of the new tax system, the collection of taxes was divided into two separate authorities: the State Administration of Taxation (*guoshui ju*) and the Local Administration of Taxation (*dishui ju*). The former was directly controlled by the central government and would collect both central revenues and shared revenues and then download the local portions of the shared revenues back to pertinent provincial governments according to preset formulas.[11] The latter was placed under the control of pertinent provincial governments and would be responsible for

---

11. The State Administration of Taxation (SAT) has four levels of office: national, provincial, (prefectural) city, and county (including county-rank city).

collecting local taxes only.¹² This change significantly reduced the room for maneuvering by local governments to move budgetary revenues into extrabudgetary categories or nonbudgetary channels.

Third, although indirect taxes continued to be the most important source of budgetary revenue after the 1994 restructuring (as shown in figure 3.1), the fiscal property rights over them changed. Before 1994, the bulk of the indirect taxes came from three taxes: product tax, value-added tax, and business tax.¹³ Under the fiscal contract system they were mixed together with other taxes and fees in the larger pool of revenue that local governments collected and then shared with the central government. Accordingly, the property rights over them were not clearly defined. In 1994 the product tax was converted into the excise tax and the scope of the value-added tax was expanded.¹⁴ At the same time the central government locked in 100% and 75% of the growth portions of the excise tax and the value-added tax respectively. The business tax became the largest tax solely "owned" by local governments,¹⁵ accounting for 25%–30% of government budget revenue during the decade after the restructuring. Unlike the excise tax and the value-added tax, which are mainly derived from industrial activities, the business tax is in the main levied on service activities.¹⁶ Given the central government's dominant shares in the

---

12. The Local Administration of Taxation (LAT) is divided into three levels: provincial, (prefectural) city, and county (including county-rank city). The provincial-level tax authority is placed under the joint supervision of the pertinent provincial government and the central government, with the former being the locus of control and the latter mainly providing policy guidance. Lower levels of the local tax authority are controlled by the provincial-level LAT in terms of personnel, budget, and administration, though such control is to be done in consultation and coordination with the pertinent lower-level governments. The three levels of the local tax authority are responsible for collecting the revenues from the tax bases designated for provincial, city, and county governments, and the revenues they collect enter the treasuries of the corresponding levels of government (http://www.chinatax.gov.cn/n8136506/n8136608/n8138877/n8138997/n8353323/n8353921/8361035.html).

13. In 1993 they made up 69% of all indirect taxes (also known as industrial and commercial taxes) (*CTY 1994*, 15).

14. Before 1994 foreign-invested companies paid the unified industrial and commercial tax (*gongshang tongyi shui*) instead of the value-added tax. Also, dozens of products that had been subject to the product tax were redefined as products subject to the value-added tax. In 1986 a total of 260 types of products were subject to the product tax. By April 1991, the value-added tax was levied on 170 of them instead. In 1994 only 25 types of products were subject to the excise tax that replaced the product tax.

15. In 2016 the government announced plans, based on pilot programs in select sectors and locales, to replace the business tax with the value-added tax, hence eliminating the most important tax belonging to local governments.

16. During the decade after 1994, for example, over 90% of excise tax and over 70% of value-added tax came from the industrial sector, whereas over 80% of business tax came from the tertiary sector, and the bulk of the remainder came from construction (*CTY 2007*, 488, 497).

excise tax and the value-added tax, and with the decline of the relative significance of tax refunds in fiscal transfers, the 1994 restructuring phased in a process where the centrality of industrial activities in the revenue base of local governments experienced gradual erosion, which, as will be discussed below, had important implications for both public and private enterprises.[17]

Fourth, one of the changes in the 1994 restructuring that initially did not capture much attention but had far-reaching implications for local public finance and local government policies toward public and nonpublic enterprises is that the proceeds from the transfer of land use rights were categorized as local revenue. Under the prereform system, land was publicly owned and allocated administratively according to the needs of central planning.[18] Limited compensation was provided for converting rural collective land into state-owned land, so as to alleviate the negative consequences for rural collectives. But in the regular accounting of economic organizations, the value of land was not assessed or booked as part of their assets, nor was there any explicit charge for land use other than the agriculture tax in rural areas.

Explicit charges for land use emerged in the late 1970s and early 1980s.[19] That was followed by a gradual relaxation of the restrictions on the transfer of land use rights. In 1986 the government enacted the Land Administration Law and created a new agency, the State Land Administration,[20] to enforce the law. Among the changes the law introduced was allowing rural collectives to use, subjective to administrative approval, land as equity capital to form joint ownership enterprises with urban public enterprises. As a result of such self-arranged, lateral transfer of land use rights to a common resource pool,

---

17. In 1993 the value-added tax and the product (excise) tax combined to make up 50% of the tax revenue of local governments (*FYC 1994*, 353); in 1997 this share dropped to 21% (*FYC 1998*, 357).

18. After the socialist transformation in the 1950s, rural land was turned into a collective asset, whereas urban land, plus all uninhabited and unfarmed land outside the space of people's communes, became state owned. This reality was formally ratified in the 1982 constitution (Zou Yuchuan 1998).

19. After agricultural decollectivization (1979–1983), rural households were required to pay a land contract fee (also known as *cun tiliu* or *chengbao fei*) to the village for the use rights of farmland. Beginning in 1979 foreign-invested entities were required to pay a fee (rent) for the land they used if their local partners did not include in their equity shares the value of the land they had occupied. In 1987 a tax on nonfarm use of farmland was introduced, which was followed by a tax on urban land use by domestic industrial and commercial entities in 1988. In 1990 the deed tax was resumed after being suspended during the Cultural Revolution. A land value appreciation tax was added in 1993. All these levies belonged to local governments. In addition, after the start of reforms unauthorized renting (which represented a form of illicit charge) of urban land between existing occupants and space-deficient organizations also became increasingly prevalent despite repeated bans by the government (Zou Yuchuan 1998, 137–140).

20. The State Land Administration was merged into the newly formed Ministry of Land and Resources in 1998.

government acquisition ceased to be the only avenue for the transfer of rights, and administrative allocation began to be supplemented with other forms of such transfer.

Following a constitutional amendment on the transferability of land use right in 1988 the Land Administration Law was revised to allow the renting and sale of the use rights of both state-owned and collective land.[21] This further change marked the beginning of the rise of urban markets in land use rights.[22] In view of the fiscal implications of sales of land use rights, in 1989 the central government demanded a 40% share in the revenue generated. But the actual amount it received was miniscule, largely because of resistance from the "owners" (local governments) and the difficulty of ascertaining the net gains after deduction of requisition-related costs (which local governments could inflate) (Zou Yuchuan 1998). The sharing percentage was scaled down to 5% in 1992 and dropped altogether in the 1994 restructuring.

It is interesting to note that, unlike the taxes designated as local revenue in 1994, the proceeds from transfers of land use rights were not classified as budget revenue because of the ad hoc nature of their occurrence and therefore did not face close fiscal monitoring by the central government. Some of the proceeds entered the extrabudgetary accounts of local governments, but a large portion was not even booked as such.[23] The central government did require that the proceeds from the sale of rights be included in "special government-managed funds." But it was not until after 1999 that a small fraction of them began to show up in the local fiscal statistics on these funds. In 2000, for example, only 17% of the land sale proceeds recorded by the Ministry of Land and Resources was reported as "special government-managed funds" in the local fiscal statistics compiled by the Ministry of Finance (*SYCLR 2001*, 247; *FSPCC 2001*, 387). In 2005 the percentage edged up to 21% (*SYCLR 2006*, 177;

---

21. The law did not spell out the details of how to implement this allowance and left the matter to the State Council. In reality the subsequently adopted policies on transfers of land use rights restricted direct sale of the use rights of rural collective land (divided among residential uses, farming, and non-farming activities) for urban development. The only legal avenue for such conversion is to have the state (represented by city and county governments) rezone the boundaries between urban and rural areas, acquire the use rights of the affected rural land with compensation for existing owners/users, and resell the use rights to users for limited duration (e.g., seventy years for most residential development projects). See the discussion below.

22. In 1987 pilot programs were carried out in Shenzhen and a few other cities to sell the use rights of state-owned land with limited durations, which paved the way for the amendment in 1988.

23. In 1994, for example, the proceeds from transfers of land use rights recorded by the State Land Administration were equivalent to 176% of the funds in the "other" category in local extrabudget revenue, to which such proceeds, along with other miscellaneous funds, were supposed to be booked (*FSPCC 1994*. 76; *SYCLR 1995*, 98).

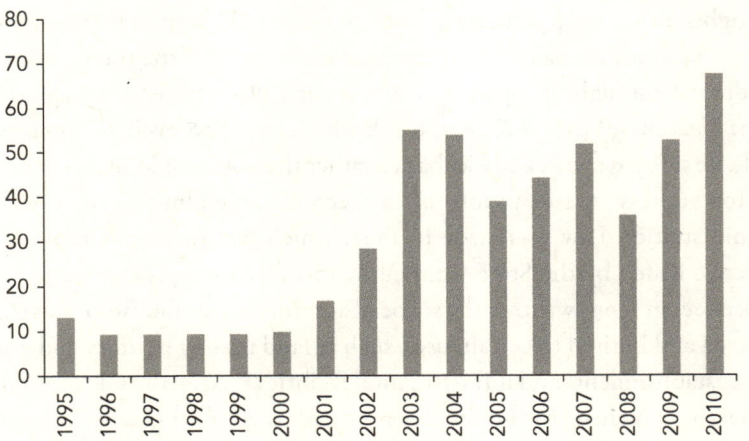

FIGURE 3.4 Land sale proceeds as percentage equivalent of local budget revenue, 1995–2010
Sources: FYC 1996, 1998, 2011; SYCLR 1995, 1996, 1997, 1999, 2006, 2011.

FSPCC 2006, 431). It was not until 2006 that the central government tightened monitoring and placed land sale proceeds under direct budgetary control.[24] What prompted that decision was a substantial growth of such proceeds after the turn of the century,[25] as can be seen from figure 3.4. There are several twists behind the pattern illustrated by the graph.

Following the 1988 amendment of the Land Administration Law, markets in land use rights began to emerge. By the end of 1992 a total of 56 billion yuan of land sale proceeds had been generated (Zou Yuchuan 1998, 164). But the pace of growth was not exceedingly fast, and administrative allocation (free of charge) remained the dominant mode of rights transfers, even after the 1994 restructuring. In 1994 the acreage of transfers of land use rights through administrative allocation was 1.85 times of that through sale. In 1999 the figure declined, but the ratio still stood at 1.2. According to the former head of the State Land Administration (Zou Yuchuan 1998), the main reason for this measured growth of the land sale market during the first decade of the law is that local governments could administratively allocate land use rights to companies that they "owned" and then rent out or sell through these companies the

---

24. The percentage rose to 25% in 2006, 57% in 2007, and 93% in 2008 respectively (SYCLR 2007, 298; 2008, 311; 2009, 272; FSPCC 2007, 977; FSPCC 2008, 266; FSPCC 2009, 321).

25. The absolute amount of land sale proceeds reported was 39 billion yuan in 1995; it rose to 130 billion yuan in 2001 and further to 808 billion yuan in 2006 (SLRYC 1996, 164; 1999, 136; SLRYC 1996; SLRYC 2007, 178).

use rights on secondary markets, for gains they could keep to themselves completely. Even for the sale of land use rights, over 90% of the transactions were conducted through an opaque arrangement called "transfer by agreement" (*xieyi zhuanrang*) (*SYCLR 2001*, 6–7), which could be easily manipulated to facilitate side payments and kickbacks, rather than open bidding or auction.

To address these problems, a second amendment to the Land Administration Law was made in 1998, which was further reinforced by a directive issued by the State Council in 2001.[26] Among the changes (which took effect in 1999) was that the scope of administrative allocation was sharply reduced and limited to certain uses, such as land uses by military and government establishments and infrastructural facilities.[27] Also, the sale of rural land (collectively owned) for urban uses now had to go through a two-step process: (1) conversion of rural land into state-owned (urban) land under city or county governments,[28] and (2) resale of the converted land on the primary market for urban land use rights.[29] These two changes made it difficult to use administrative allocation to channel urban land use rights to the secondary market or to transfer land use rights directly from rural to urban users. As a result, the market in the use of primary land assumed elevated importance for addressing the revenue concerns of local governments, and rural land requisition by local governments became the central avenue for the expansion of urban space and the main source of supply for primary land markets. The sharp rise of land sale proceeds after 1999 (figure 3.4) reflects the impact of these changes.

---

26. Among the demands reiterated and emphasized in the directive is that local governments should move from administrative allocation to market sale and from one-on-one negotiation to open competition (e.g., through bidding or auction) in the transfer of land use rights.

27. The amendment also broke the lock of local (i.e., city and county) governments on land revenue by stipulating that a fee be levied on the revenue from the sale of use rights for land newly added to the space demarcated for (economic) "construction" (*jianshe yongdi*), including rural land obtained through requisition. The fee would then be divided between the central government and the overseeing (provincial) government according to a ratio of 30 to 70. In 2009 this fee was equivalent to 6.5% of the total amount of reported proceeds from the sale of land use rights (http://www.mof.gov.cn/zhengwuxinxi/caizhengshuju/201004/t20100413_286852.html).

28. The law did not give township governments the authority to acquire land for urban development. They have therefore been facilitators rather than independent players in the urbanization drive. But they do have great influence and bargaining power in the process because much of the rural land acquired for urban development has been physically situated in the space under their purview.

29. Primary land markets in China refer to the markets where local governments sell the use rights of the (urban) land they "own" de jure or have obtained through requisition. Secondary markets involve exchanges of land use rights between buyers and existing users, including those that have purchased the rights from primary or secondary markets or have compensated the government for the land that has been allocated to them administratively (free of charge).

Table 3.4 Acreages (1,000 hectares) of different types of land use right transfer, 1993–2005

Year	Primary market sale	Administrative allocation	Secondary market sale	Secondary market renting	Mortgage collateral
1993	38	90	9	1	1
1994	49	91	7	1	8
1995	43	88	7	7	34
1996	34	70	6	24	244
1997	40	62	20	24	343
1998	43	58	27	23	392
1999	45	54	34	23	442
2000	49	81	50	27	1094
2001	90	74	139	10	2140
2002	124	88	67	17	2888
2003	194	65	70	9	1102
2004	182	62	67	8	3423
2005	166	65	51	6	4820

Sources: SYCLR 1995, 1996, 1997, 1999, 2006.

There are also some noteworthy developments in parallel to the changing patterns of land sale proceeds. Table 3.4 shows that secondary markets of land use rights experienced significant increases in the late 1990s and around the turn of the century. That was a period when massive privatization of state-owned enterprises and township and village enterprises took place in urban and rural areas. Furthermore, the table shows that there was significant growth in the total area of land mortgaged by existing users as collateral for obtaining bank loans. Many of the organizations involved in such dealings were actually "fundraising platforms" (*rongzi pingtai*) set up by local governments to obtain lending for urban development beyond the limit of their budgetary funds and/or for servicing existing debts.[30] Since until recently local governments in China were not allowed to issue public debt,[31] such land-leveraged

---

30. For a discussion of the roles played by these fundraising platforms in local public finance, see Walter and Howie 2012.

31. The central government began public borrowing through issuance of treasury bonds in 1981, but local governments were barred from doing so. During the Asian financial crisis in 1997–1998, the central government issued extra treasury bonds and relent the funds raised to local governments as an ad hoc measure to help sustain local economic growth. This practice was subsequently retained as a

borrowing became an important instrument to expand the fiscal resources of local governments. In addition, the growth of land sale revenue was accompanied by an upward trend in the importance of the taxes related to land use and urban development. These taxes were designated as local revenue in the 1994 restructuring. They include the land value appreciation tax, urban construction and maintenance tax, urban land use tax, urban (nonresidential) property tax, deed tax, and tax on nonfarm use of farmland. Together they accounted for 7% of the budget revenue of local governments in 1993. This share doubled to 14% in 1994 and further rose to 16% in 2005 (*FSPCC 1994*, 76; *FSPCC 1995*, 57; *FSPCC 2006*, 67).

Implications

It is important to note that the changes in fiscal relations highlighted above were not simply concerned with the division of revenue and spending between different levels of government. They also embodied redefined political responsibilities and were integrated with the changing practices of political performance assessment in the reform era. These practices experienced major shifts—from emphasizing political behavior to focusing on economic issues and from relying on broadly defined guidelines to using concrete metrics.[32] With the unfolding of fiscal decentralization and subsequent restructuring, how to raise revenue and manage fiscal flows became an important consideration in the self-interest calculus of local officials.

Under the fiscal contract system during the 1980s and early 1990s, fulfilling the revenue targets with higher-level authorities was key to the careers of local leaders and officials in charge of economic affairs. A common avenue through which to address this concern was to expand the local revenue base by promoting the growth of locally "affiliated" economic organizations, which were predominantly public enterprises during that period of time. More importantly, given that the bulk of locally extracted revenue came from indirect taxes on the volume of transactions, especially those in the industrial sector, boosting the sales of industrial enterprises became the dominant economic strategy of many local governments. Since such an undertaking necessitated

---

regular instrument to alleviate local fiscal imbalances. In 2009 the Ministry of Finance began to issue local public debts on behalf of select provincial governments. In 2012 Zhejiang, Guangdong, Shanghai, and Shenzhen were authorized to pilot direct issuance of local public debts. In 2014 the measure was extended to Jiangsu, Shandong, Beijing, Jiangxi, Ningxia, and the special-status city of Qingdao.

32. See chapter 4 for a discussion of the shifts of focus in political performance assessment.

an expansion of the industrial workforce and increased output value, it facilitated nonfarm job creation and output growth, which were also important factors included in political performance evaluation. Nonetheless, as will be shown in the next chapter, the pursuit of this strategy was not necessarily consistent with the agenda of improving profitability. Where competition was strong and local public enterprises' competitiveness was weak, political considerations and expediency often led sales growth to override the importance of profitability, resulting in extensive borrowing beyond the debt-servicing abilities of local public enterprises. As a result, the fundamental financial health of many public enterprises was compromised. *Understanding the basic setup and evolution of the fiscal system, especially the predominant importance of indirect taxes, therefore, helps explain the orientation and consequences of political actors' behavior.*

An interesting twist here is that, while there was a clear tendency on the part of local authorities to boost revenue growth, it did not lead to the maximization of formal revenue, as evidenced by the widespread phenomenon of fulfilling the fiscal contract to the "just right" extent (of moderately surpassing revenue targets). The setup of the fiscal contract system left open channels through which a sizable part of local revenue was stashed away in extrabudgetary revenue and other resource pools at the discretion of local officials. Sales growth of local enterprises, especially those in the local public sector that were more convenient tools than private enterprises (which tended to be more profit-conscious) for the manipulation of fiscal flows, therefore, served not only to help secure and advance the careers of local officials but to accommodate their self-defined agendas, including making private gains. The use of (public) enterprise accounts for revenue shuffling also entailed collusion between the enterprises concerned and their supervising officials and authorities. The outgrowth of such collusive ties was a precursor to the more explicitly private undertaking of asset stripping amid the deepening crisis of public enterprises in the mid to late 1990s.[33]

The 1994 restructuring represented a drastic overhaul of the fiscal contract system. But it did not fundamentally change the drive of local governments for revenue. In fact, efforts to promote sales growth of public enterprises continued through the mid-1990s. But the restructuring did prod local officials to adjust their fiscal strategies so as to reposition themselves favorably in political

---

33. Collusive ties among officials also grew with the expansion of off-budget funds, which further weakened their interest in the long-term financial health of public enterprises, as I have shown in a previous study (Lin 2001).

performance evaluation and in the generation and control of discretionary resources. In face of the hardened constraint on revenue diversion through tax exemptions and reductions under the system of revenue partitioning based on a separation of tax categories, local governments concentrated their attention on their redemarcated revenue bases and on new sources of revenue. Although the industrial sector remained an important revenue source, especially in the immediate aftermath of the restructuring, its relative significance gradually declined because the central government controlled the lion's share of the growth portion of the taxes from industrial activities. In the meantime, the sales expansion of public enterprises (especially those in the industrial sector) ran into increasing difficulties due to intensification of competition, tightening of credit under banking reforms that gained momentum in the mid-1990s, and cumulative liabilities. In contrast, the relative contributions from urban services and construction to local revenue assumed elevated importance in local public finance.

Coevolving with these shifting trends was a refocusing of local economic policies from industrial development to urbanization, with a growing emphasis on land-related transactions and land-leveraged resources. Along the way, the opportunity cost of keeping afloat poorly performing (and predominantly industrial) and overexpanded public enterprises became increasingly evident and unbearable. Also factored into the new self-interest calculus of local officials was the potential of redeploying the land use rights of existing public enterprises, especially those occupying central locations in urban or urbanizing areas, for more lucrative uses (i.e., generation of discretionary revenues and private gains). These considerations, coupled with the public sector's lack of an initial stronghold in service activities because Maoist economic policy favored industrial development at the expense of the tertiary sector, converged into the forces that led to the tipping point of massive ownership restructuring in the mid to late 1990s and quickened the demise of the vast majority of public enterprises thereafter.

I will lay out the empirical details underlying these general observations in the following chapters. It should be stressed here, though, that the unfolding of the aforesaid implications of the changing fiscal system was by no means uniform across space and over time. Some local governments, for example, pursued the strategy of public-enterprise-led industrial development until the onset of massive privatization. Some others began to deviate from it as early as in the mid-1980s. Governments of different locales and at different levels (i.e., provincial, city, county, and township) targeted and emphasized different revenue sources and streams (e.g., taxes vs. nontax revenues, revenues directly extracted from local sources vs. fiscal transfers from higher levels). Even after the clear authorizing signals from the central government in the late 1990s, the precipitousness and depth of privatization also varied among different regions. The next four chapters are devoted to detailing these differences. In particular, I will examine how the extent and pace of privatization were related to the varying responses of local governments to the common challenges from growing demographic pressures and to the evolution of the state's fiscal system. The goal is to reveal how the causal mechanisms of privatization played out in different historical and local contexts.

4

Careerism and Moral Hazard in Early Marketization

FROM THE LATE 1970s to the mid-1990s the Chinese economy experienced a fundamental transformation from central planning to markets (Naughton 1995, 2007). Public enterprises were the leading force of this process. Initially championed by township and village enterprises (TVEs) in rural areas and subsequently joined by urban state-owned enterprises (SOEs), marketization provided the main engine for fast economic growth through the mid-1990s. In the five to six years that followed, however, the momentum of public enterprises quickly dissipated, and their financial performance and sustainability seriously deteriorated. The debacle of public enterprises was accompanied by a rising tide of privatization, which drastically redefined the ownership structure of the economy. Why public enterprises were unable to carry on is what I seek to explore in this chapter.

The starting point of the exploration is the driving force behind the behavior of local officials. They controlled the overwhelming majority of China's public enterprises, and it was the enterprises under their purview that failed to survive beyond the early years of the twenty-first century. My basic argument is that both the initial expansion of local public enterprises and their subsequent implosion were closely related to the calculation and pursuit of self-interest by local officials. As political actors, they responded to the changing incentives and constraints in the evolving structural conditions of their decision-making. In face of the new focus on economic development in political performance assessment, many local officials actively promoted sales growth of local public enterprises, which had an immediate glossing effect on key performance indicators. This strategy helped secure and advance the careers of local leaders. It also contributed to the expansion of the discretionary resource pools that they and lower-ranked local officials controlled, therefore broadening the base for addressing the diverse concerns of different interest groups.

A major consequence of the sales growth strategy is that the expansion of public enterprises was gradually delinked from their profitability and organizational health. What drove it was the heavy reliance of the fiscal system on indirect taxes, and what sustained it was the supply of financial resources leveraged directly or indirectly from the banking system, which had weak profit agenda before 1994. Over time, however, the cumulative debts of local public enterprises grew way beyond their loan-servicing abilities, making them unable to withstand the credit tightening during banking reforms in the mid-1990s. The moral hazard inherent in this process was closely associated with the transient tenures of local leadership and the lack of clear cost accounting of administrative decisions. The sales growth strategy was also coupled with various revenue-hiding and diversion tactics that entailed collusion between local officials and public enterprise managers. Moreover, the fast expansion of local public enterprises increased monitoring costs, which further spurred the growth of agency problems, such as managerial corruption, and thereby added to the growing woes of public enterprises. In the end many of these enterprises fell victims to their own "success."

While widely pursued by local officials in the early years of reform because of the relatively low political risk involved and the property rights they held over local public enterprises, the sales growth strategy was nevertheless continued with varying degrees of tenacity among different locales. The tendency and ability to stay with it hinged on the varying strengths of local public enterprises and on the historical and geographic conditions of different locales. The use of alternative or complementary economic development strategies that involved greater political risks, such as measures to facilitate private business and promote foreign investment beyond the initial regulatory limits imposed by the central leadership, represented a parallel line of the story. They will be considered in the next two chapters.

Large Is Beautiful: Political Performance Assessment under Economic Decentralization

In December 1978 the CCP held the Third Plenum of the Eleventh Central Party Committee. Although no concrete reform measures were laid out in the meeting, it was decided that the focus of government policy should shift from class struggle to economic development. That decision is widely deemed to be the starting point of economic reforms in the post-Mao era. It also had important implications for the personnel policy and practice of the CCP, which had long focused on noneconomic considerations.[1]

During the three decades that followed, the CCP's Organization Department (CCPOD), which is the command center of personnel controls in the party-state, issued a series of directives and guidelines that redefined and tweaked the political performance assessment system of the party-state in line with the dominant policy agendas of the CCP leadership.[2] Four important changes are especially noteworthy.[3]

First, concrete criteria of performance were adopted, and quantified indicators were used to facilitate the assessment of party and government leaders at various levels of public administration. In particular, economic performance occupied the central place in the new metrics of assessment.[4] It was not until 2006 that more diverse criteria were adopted by the CCPOD to guide political performance assessment in a "scientific" manner. Second, political performance assessment was not only consequential to the career movements of leading officials but coupled with material incentives in such forms as performance-based bonus and salary.[5] Third, while central strategic control remained and ad hoc intervention from higher levels of authority was not infrequent, performance assessment and personnel decisions on local (sub-provincial) officials were delegated to provincial, prefectural, and county authorities over their immediately subordinate levels. Accordingly, centrally introduced guidelines and indicators were adapted to address local policy priorities that varied over time and across jurisdictions and administrative levels.[6] Fourth, subordinate officials' evaluative feedback on local leaders

---

1. For an analysis of personnel policies under Mao, see Lee 1991.

2. During 1977–1983 a series of personnel reshuffling took place throughout the party-state apparatus to replace officials purged for ties with Maoist factions and to fill the positions held by retiring officials. For accounts of the changes after the start of reforms, see Burns 1989; Edin 2003; Manion 1993; and Whiting 2004. Related discussions are also offered in Huang 1996; Cheung, Chung, and Lin 1998; and Landry 2008. Tao et al. 2009 provide a useful description of more recent developments.

3. A further note on the four changes highlighted here is posted at the book site.

4. The Chinese government did not compile GDP statistics until 1993. Industrial and agricultural output instead was the main output measure used in political performance evaluation before the mid-1990s.

5. For examples at the grassroots level, see Oi 1999 and Whiting 2000, 2004.

6. For examples, see Edin 2003; Landry 2008; and Whiting 2004.

was incorporated as part of the performance assessment process. This practice, known as *minzhu pingyi* (democratic appraisal), was initiated in 1983 and institutionalized in 1988 with the use of standardized feedback forms and procedures.

The relationship between economic growth and local officials' behavior under the new and evolving performance assessment system and the concurrent decentralization of economic (especially fiscal) authority has been analyzed from different angles. Oi (1992, 1999) discerns a positive link and explains it from a local developmental state perspective. Montinola, Qian, and Weingast (1995) (see also Maskin, Qian, and Xu 2000) argue that the combination of fiscal decentralization and political rewards for economic performance amounts to a form of federalism that induces promarket and progrowth policies of local governments. Zhou Li-An (2007) uses a tournament model to examine interlocale political performance competition as a key causal mechanism and expounds on its implications for local economic growth (see also Li and Zhou 2005).

Evidence in support of the positive link view mainly comes from data analyses on provincial leaders' promotion (e.g., Bo 2002; Chen, Li, and Zhou 2005; Li and Zhou 2005). Some other empirical studies of local leaders (e.g., Guo 2007; Landry 2008), however, reveal less definitive effects of economic output growth on elite mobility. Still other studies find no significant effects at all. An analysis of a revised set of the data used by Li and Zhou (2005), for example, yields results with sharply reduced significance in the effect of GDP growth on provincial leaders' promotion (Tao et al. 2010). Another study incorporating more variables (Shih, Adolph, and Liu 2012) finds no close link between economic output growth and political ranking among local leaders selected into the CCP central leadership. Instead, factional ties and factors like education and revenue are found to have mattered more in the allocation of political rewards.

Despite these different findings, none of the data analyses explicitly addresses the question whether economic growth was a necessary condition for upward political mobility. Indeed the focal concern they share instead is whether the political reward for local economic performance corresponds incrementally to variations measured on an interval scale. While a useful question, it may not lead to findings that will shed clear light on promotion decisions using much less differentiated (e.g., binary or ordinal) metrics. Such a situation is not uncommon, especially given the multifactor considerations involved in political performance evaluation and the temporal and spatial variations in local policy environment and priority under centrally defined guidelines that emphasize the importance of economic performance (Feng Junqi 2010; Wang Hansheng and Wang Yige 2009).

During 1995–2009 I interviewed a total of 137 officials at different levels of sub-provincial government.[7] Although there was no consensus as to whether those who excelled in local economic performance were more likely to be promoted, 135 of the interviewees agreed that poor management of the local economy in comparison with regional peers and with predecessors was a major negative factor in the assessment of political performance. In addition, 129 of them considered it imperative not to let local economic performance fall below the average level of regional peers and the attainment of predecessors. As one of them opined (informant, 29/1996), "You have to do well enough economically to move on, however important other factors may be [for promotion decisions]." More systematic evidence consistent with this opinion comes from a panel data analysis of the career movements of the party secretaries and mayors in 296 prefectural cities during 1990–2004 (Chen and Lin 2016). The results show that, other things being equal, local leaders failing to achieve economic performance at par with that of regional peers and predecessors had significantly lower probability of being promoted than those with better performance, though the difference among those with average and above-average performance was insignificant.

These findings suggest that, although local officials might not all strive to be stellar performers in economic growth, they had to be mindful of the implications of the "pass-fail" test, implied by the results reported above, for their careers. The means that they used to address this concern and related self-interest agendas during the 1980s and 1990s is the focus of the analysis in this chapter. What I seek to explore is how local officials responded to the new political incentives they faced under evolving structural conditions (especially fiscal decentralization) and what consequences their responses had for the decline of public ownership. Instead of separating their strategies into those seeking political (career) benefits and those seeking economic (e.g., revenue related) benefits (Li and Zhou 2005), I see them as closely related and oftentimes mutually reinforcing pursuits.[8]

---

7. A profile of the interviewees, including rank, age, gender, education, work history, etc., is posted at the book site.

8. Contrary to the more widely shared view mentioned earlier, Cai and Treisman (2006) argue that the new political incentive system and fiscal decentralization did not have a causal effect on China's economic growth. Rather, factional rivalry among central leaders holds the key to explaining it. Since the focal issue of my study is privatization rather than economic growth, I will not address that debate here.

The point of departure for my exploration is Susan Whiting's (2000) pioneering study of the evolution of rural property rights institutions from the start of economic reform to the mid-1990s. Based on comparative case studies, Whiting argues that the new political performance assessment system and fiscal revenue sharing with higher-level government in the 1980s and early 1990s drove rural officials to promote the growth of industrial output. Yet the extent to which rural officials pursued this strategy through local public enterprises (i.e., TVEs) depended on the strength of collectively owned rural industry before the reform. Locales with a strong organizational legacy tended to seek further expansion of TVEs. They also adopted tactics to hide fiscal revenue in public enterprise accounts that local officials could manipulate. Locales with a moderately strong organizational legacy shared the tendency to develop public enterprises, whereas at the same time they also granted limited tolerance to private businesses but made them absorb the transaction costs of revenue extraction. Locales with weak organizational legacy tended to take a more accommodating approach to private business. To tackle the transaction costs of revenue extraction they devised simplified metrics of tax estimation. The overall policy bias toward promoting output growth of TVEs led to dysfunctional consequences, however. The expansion of TVEs was facilitated with soft credit, which spawned inefficiency and overproduction and exacerbated the difficulties of centralized control over state bank lending. Revenue hiding contributed to the deteriorating fiscal capacity of the central government. These problems compelled the central government to restructure public finance and banking in the mid-1990s. Coupled with growing competition, the restructuring hardened the budget constraints of local governments and forced them onto the path of privatization.

This is an insightful analysis that has broad implications. It identifies political performance assessment and fiscal relations as key variables to explain local officials' behavior; it also relates the interplay of these variables to the initial conditions of the local political economy to account for spatial variations and illustrates important links in a complex process of endogenously induced institutional change. All these are useful analytic elements that can also be extended to the study of local political actors beyond the context of townships and villages. At the same time Whiting's work also points to several issues that need to be further explored for understanding and clarifying the causal mechanisms of privatization in the post-Mao era.

First, striving for industrial output growth, which Whiting emphasizes, represents a strategy different from promoting industrial sales growth, which is the focus of this chapter. Noting this seemingly minute difference is not a matter of splitting hairs. The former was practically difficult to sustain because of cash flow constraints in a marketizing environment (see next section). More importantly, it could have fallen short of serving the best interests of local officials. The main reason for this is that output by itself was not a revenue-generating tool. Although increasing industrial output would directly correspond to a key performance evaluation indicator (i.e., gross industrial and agricultural output before the mid-1990s and GDP thereafter) under the new political incentive system, any unsold output would not help address the revenue imperative under the reforming fiscal structure,[9] where some 70% of the budget revenue came from indirect taxes realized in or through sales during 1980–1993.[10] In contrast, promoting industrial sales would generate more immediate relief to the cash flow problem (although not without limit). And it could boost output growth *as a corollary* and at the same time address the revenue imperative, including the agenda of expanding discretionary resource pools (e.g., parking of exempted taxes in enterprise accounts). Still another benefit of sales growth is that could help generate and sustain nonfarm employment, which was another important policy imperative for local governments, as long as the volume of output sold could keep growing.

Second, Whiting's analysis notices that the "dysfunctional" consequences from the use of local public enterprises to boost political performance represented a moral hazard problem, yet why the problem was pervasive among local officials needs to be explained.[11] Part of the answer, I argue, lies in the broad interests that the strategy of promoting sales growth served to address. Other factors include transient tenures and lack of clear cost accounting in public administration, both of which further spawned opportunism.

While local leaders might be personal rivals and had different factional ties (Edin 2003; Shih 2008), promoting sales growth tended to be the dominant

---

9. As shown in the next section, there appears to be little evidence that TVEs had massive overproduction of output, which is often associated with output-maximizing behavior. Even SOEs were moving away from emphasizing meeting output targets to turning out marketable products during the second half of the 1980s, when the central planning system was in decline (Naughton 1995). What eventually brought down TVEs was not cumulative glut of industrial output—which is what Whiting's analysis alludes to, but sales expansion without a close link to profitability. Focusing on industrial output growth therefore may obscure this important causal linkage.

10. Whiting does pay attention to the role of the post-1980 fiscal system. But her discussion focuses on the impetus from the self-financing mandate for township governments rather than the composite structure of revenue sources.

11. Whiting brings up the issue of moral hazard in her book (2000) and a subsequent paper (2004) but offers no further analysis.

strategy not only because of its superiority in terms of narrow economic calculus but because of its low vulnerability to local politics. It had higher payoffs, for example, than subversive strategies that spoilers might pursue. The reason is that the common career benefits it furnished often assumed the key features of public goods—nonexcludability and nonrivalry (Samuelson 1954)—for those in the top echelon, especially given that achieving growth through local public enterprises was widely deemed as the most legitimate means to advance the new economy (hence also raising the political cost of opposition).[12] Moreover, local leaders were not the only beneficiaries of the expansion of discretionary revenue pools. Subordinate officials in charge of economic affairs had access too. Many of them were directly involved in the management and administration of local public enterprises and thus held a key to the implementation of the sales growth strategy. Under the new political performance assessment system, their evaluative feedback on local leaders was also a factor that local leaders could not afford to ignore. Promoting sales growth of local public enterprises provided an avenue for co-opting these political actors, thereby reinforcing the dominant strategy of local leaders.

Furthermore, the political performance assessment system itself was afflicted with inherent problems in the personnel practice of the party-state. An important feature of the CCP's nomenclatural system in the reform era is the transient tenure of local leaders.[13] Factors leading to transient tenures were many, including concerns about nepotism and factionalism, strategic positioning (e.g., in the name of *huoqu jiceng gongzuo jingyan*, or "gaining grassroots level work experience") of officials slated for subsequent promotion, alignment of loyalty with higher-level authorities and policies, rotation for diversification of work experience and environment, reduction of redundancy, responses to contingencies (e.g., personnel reshuffling in antigraft campaigns), repartitioning (merger or division) of administrative boundaries (of townships and urban districts), among others (Edin 2003; Feng Junqi 2010;

---

12. As to the discretionary pools of revenue resulting from the expansion of sales by local public enterprises, Whiting notices the use for private purposes but seems to de-emphasize this by pointing to the fact that part of it was used to finance regular public administration functions. What is interesting, though, is that the blurred boundary between public and private uses also created a cushion against the political risk involved and helped neutralize spoilers (Lin 2001).

13. Guo (2007), for example, reports that during 1994–2002 only 42% of the county chief executives completed their five-year terms and only one-fifth of them remained in the same county to serve as the local CCP secretary. Landry (2008) finds that the average tenure of prefectural mayors decreased from 3.2 years in 1990 to 2.5 years in 2001. A further examination of the data spanning 1990–2004 reveals that 60% and 70% of the CCP secretaries and mayors of prefectural cities had a tenure of no more than three years respectively (percentages are calculated from data set).

Wang Hansheng and Wang Yige 2009). A major consequence of transient tenures of local leaders is the prevalence of a high time discount rate in their decision-making. With short time horizons in their political expectations, incumbent local leaders tended to seek maximization of short-term political and personal benefits, even at the cost of creating or exacerbating longer-term problems, such as deterioration of the financial health of local public enterprises.

Adding to the growth of moral hazard among local officials was the lack of clear cost accounting for administrative decisions under the political performance assessment system. The system was geared toward assessing the tangible "achievements" by local officials on a yearly basis, rather than administrative efficiency in terms of cost-benefit comparison. There was a built-in mechanism called *yipiao foujue* (disqualification for promotion on account of one major dereliction), which was introduced in the early 1980s as a way to strengthen the implementation of family planning and subsequently extended to include other issues, such as major accidents, social unrest, food contamination, and so on. But it was event-specific and not well suited for ascertaining responsibilities for the cumulative negative effects of decisions by past local leaders, which was made even more difficult by transient tenures. In fact it was not uncommon for incumbent local leaders to gloss over growing problems (e.g., through borrowing new loans to service loans already incurred by local public enterprises to expand sales despite diminishing returns), to blame any exposed problems on their predecessors, and even to claim credit for finding "solutions" to problems that were part of their own doing.[14]

Third, the consequences of moral hazard for privatization need to be further explored. Whiting offers two useful pointers: growing financial liabilities of local public enterprises due to overexpansion, and post-1993 hardening of financial and fiscal budget constraint as a result of the central government's efforts to address problems such as lax banking controls and central revenue shortfalls, which had been exacerbated by local officials' opportunistic behavior in the early years of reform. The shocks from the 1994 banking and fiscal restructuring were indeed important for understanding the debacle of public enterprises after the mid-1990s, as I will discuss later. Yet there was more to the story. The decline of public enterprises was an uneven process. The sales growth strategy ran out of force in numerous locales even before 1994, which

---

14. For some interesting examples of the tactics used by local officials to finesse political credit and shed responsibilities, see the in-depth case study of a county government by Feng Junqi (2010).

therefore cannot be explained by the shock effect. Whiting traces the variations in the development of local public enterprises to the significance of commune and brigade enterprises in the local economy before the reform. The focus of such an account of path dependence, however, is on the initial policy preferences of local officials and their subsequent strategies of revenue extraction rather than the differences in the ability to carry forward the course of TVE-led growth. Nonetheless, it can be broadened to help illuminate the latter.

The adverse effect of moral hazard on local public enterprises could be enhanced by three major factors: poor ability of local officials to provide strategic guidance to local public enterprises, managerial corruption, and collusion between local officials and public enterprise managers for purely private purposes. As the stakeholder in local public enterprises, where and how the local government made its investment mattered greatly to the near-term sustainability of these enterprises. For the sales growth strategy to work, cash flow was critical. A minimum condition for this was to make products that could sell, which was by no means a matter of autopiloting in an increasingly competitive environment. Also important was the ability of the local government to monitor the behavior of enterprise managers and prevent them from engaging in self-seeking at the expense of their enterprises. This task would become more challenging when local public enterprises experienced fast expansion in number, size, and functional complexity. The sales growth strategy, therefore, generated forces that threatened the governance of local public enterprises. A further challenge came from the widespread practice of hiding taxes in the accounts of local public enterprises, which entailed collusion with managers. Although initially intended mainly as a way to stash away funds for addressing at least some public spending needs, such collusive relationship could degenerate into purely private pursuits harmful to the enterprises concerned.

Where and when local public enterprises suffered from poor strategic investment and/or serious deficiency in supervision, the sales growth strategy would run into difficulties unless there was unlimited supply of credit. A vicious cycle could kick in when supervising officials ceased to see local public enterprises as the goose able to lay golden eggs (i.e., facilitating the sales growth strategy) and thus slipped into full private collusion mode with managers to make a quick killing. For many local public enterprises, the 1994 restructuring of banking and public finance was probably what tolled their death knell. But for others the driving forces for movement to the final stretch might have come into play earlier, largely because of poor organization and management by supervising officials. In this connection, understanding the role of the organizational legacy from the prereform era in internal governance helps us discern the mechanisms at work (other than an extended proclivity in administrative behavior or policy preference), as locales with more experienced administrators and stronger organizational infrastructure would more likely have the ability to sustain the sales-expansion strategy for longer time on the road to self-destruction.

Last but not least, what explains the variations in local governments' initial tendency to pursue the sales growth strategy or in their ability to sustain it does not offer an adequate explanation for the variations in local governments' tendency to support private business. Whiting argues that the strength of commune and brigade enterprises (CBEs) in the prereform era holds a common explanation for the varying degrees of tolerance toward private ownership in different locales. Plausible as it may seem, this argument needs to be qualified. Supporting private business was not the fallback option by default for locales with weak organizational legacies from the Mao era. The main reason is that supporting private business beyond centrally set limits involved a political risk. The ability to manage this political risk did not bear any directional correlation with the strength of organizational legacy. Other factors, especially those that helped justify the need for supporting private business, should be considered. I will leave this issue to the next chapter, though. The focus here instead is how the sales growth strategy played out.

The TVE Spectacle

Township and village enterprises (TVEs), known as *xiangcun qiye* in Chinese,[15] were publicly owned companies that primarily undertook nonfarm economic activities in rural areas. They were the main driving force of China's transformation toward a market-oriented economy during the 1980s and early 1990s.[16] The predecessors of TVEs were commune and brigade enterprises (CBEs) formed during the people's commune era (1958–1983). In 1978 they were the only type of officially allowed off-farm economic organization in rural areas and accounted for 9% of the rural workforce and 17%

---

15. TVEs should not be confused with enterprises under township authorities, known as *xiangzhen qiye* in Chinese. The latter consist of both public and private nonfarm economic organizations in rural areas.

16. The rapid development of TVEs and rural nonfarm economic organizations in general not only diversified the rural economy but made the central planning unsustainable by creating and expanding markets, intensifying competition, and generating a demonstration effect on urban economic

of rural GDP (*SCTE*, 5, 7). In 2008 the percentages of the nonfarm sector (inclusive of both public and private entities) in these categories increased to 33% and 72% respectively (*CTEAPPY 2009*, 99; *CSY 2010*, 38, 117).

Throughout the 1980s and the early 1990s, TVEs led the expansion of the rural nonfarm sector, largely as a result of township and village authorities' active efforts to promote rural industrialization after agricultural decollectivization (Walder 1995; Oi 1999). There were three possible strategies for local authorities in this undertaking: focusing on output growth, maximizing profit, and expanding sales. Output growth was a major indicator in the performance assessment of local leaders. Profits of TVEs provided the basis for enterprise income tax, and the surplus after tax added to the pool of resources controlled by local officials. Expansion of sales helped generate indirect taxes, which constituted the main source of local revenue, as discussed in chapter 3. Nonfarm employment could also increase as a result of the growth of output and sales, which often required more labor input. Improvement in profitability did not necessarily lead to this, though, depending on whether it was achieved with a concurrent expansion of the nonfarm workforce. It would nevertheless have been ideal for TVEs to grow output, sales, and profits all together.

In reality, however, local officials faced constraints that tended to drive them to anchor their strategies in the growth of sales. A major challenge to focusing on the expansion of output by TVEs was cash flow, which would be seriously affected by large inventories of unsold products.[17] Recounting the experience of running TVEs in the late 1980s and early 1990s, for example, a township official I interviewed in Wuxi county in 1995 had the following observation (informant, 27/1995):

> Yes, output mattered greatly to our [local] leaders. But it's not feasible to grow output independent of sales. We were not part of the [centrally] planned economy, and there was no matching supply of capital for our output. . . . We had to work hard to sell our products, as much and as quickly as possible, even below cost in difficult times, so as to make sure that the cash flow would keep going.

---

organizations (especially SOEs) that were still bound by the central planning system in the 1980s. For discussions of the many-sided roles of TVEs in China's economic transformation, see Bramall 2007; Byrd and Lin 1990; Ho 1994; Jin and Qian 1998; Ma Rong et al. 1994; Naughton 1994, 1995; Oi 1992, 1999; and Whiting 2000.

17. See Ma Rong et al. 1994 for a sample of case studies that illustrate this problem.

Another factor that could accentuate the attention of local officials to sales was a built-in ratchet effect from the careerist pursuits of local leaders. The new political performance assessment system fostered an unintended incentive for local leaders to exaggerate the growth of economic output during their transient tenures (Cai 2000).[18] For an incumbent to outperform his or her immediate predecessor and peers elsewhere, there was pressure to deal with the gap between fabrication and reality. Even if the incumbent chose to refrain from further exaggeration, the bar had already been raised by his or her predecessor for subsequent assessments. Adding more exaggeration on top of it would inevitably increase the level of political risk. Maintaining sufficient maneuvering space between these constraints required real output to grow above the existing level,[19] which could hardly be realized without strong sales given the cash flow problem just mentioned. In fact there is no evidence that TVEs accumulated large amounts of inventories as a result of output growing at faster pace than sales. During 1993–1998 (when pertinent data are available), the average annual inventory turnover rate for TVEs was 7.3 (*CTEY*, various years), which was roughly at the same level as the concurrent average rate for companies listed on the Standard and Poor 500 Index.

On the other hand, promoting profit growth faced two major challenges. Despite local governments' efforts to help TVEs through regulatory laxity and resource support, the level of profitability was largely shaped by competition, which lay beyond the control of local officials and intensified with the deepening of reforms. A survey of TVEs ($n = 300$) jointly conducted by the Chinese Academy of Social Sciences and the World Bank in 1991–1992 found that 96% of them considered themselves to be operating in competitive (31%) or highly competitive (65%) markets.[20] The uncertainties in such environments made it difficult for local officials to anchor their economic strategy in

---

18. In 1993, for example, TVEs reported a total output of 2.065 trillion yuan, a total sales volume of 1.742 trillion yuan, and a total inventory value of 262 billion yuan (*CTEY 1994*, 367). The difference between output and sales was 362 billion yuan. Even if all the inventory consisted of current-year unsold output (with unused supplies and past unsold output being assumed as zero), one would still find a gap of 61 billion yuan unaccounted for, which most likely came from exaggerated output.

19. Debunking the statistical fabrication by the predecessor was another way to cope with this issue. But it was not without serious drawbacks. As one former township head in Shunde of Guangdong province (informant, 5/1996) pointed out: "You don't want to create new enemies unnecessarily; you may not be fully aware of how well connected your predecessor is in the county and even beyond; you don't know whether what you do will offend those (assessors) who have given a pass to his performance; and you don't want to trigger a close scrutiny of your own record—past and future; in short it (reporting exaggeration by predecessor) is a very risky move, even if he (the predecessor) is already in trouble."

20. Full documentation of the survey is posted at the book site.

profit growth. Moreover, profit maximization could be achieved through cost saving and even organizational downsizing, and thus it could be inconsistent with other important goals for local officials, such as output growth, revenue, and job creation. As a top economic official in a rural township of Suzhou put it (informant, 14/1995):

> Profits are important, but not absolutely important if we [the local government] consider the full range of issues we need to address. Actually our collective enterprises had a good number of years of high profitability back in the 1980s, when many SOEs were still bound by the old system and foreign companies were not in yet. Those days are long past. Not only is it more and more difficult to get high returns, but insisting on it may stand in our way forward. We need volume growth to boost the overall scale of our local economy, to broaden the bases for taxes and fees, and to expand employment opportunities. How can a local leader expect to be promoted without these?

What he meant by "volume growth," as he clarified at my request, was sales growth. This is not surprising. An examination of the economic statistics of the township reveals that during 1984–1995 the average annual sales growth rate of local TVEs was 25.9%, whereas industrial output, budgetary revenue, and nonfarm employment on average grew by 23.5%, 24.1%, and 13.8% per year respectively. Of the six party secretaries who led the township during this period, four were promoted, one retired, and one was laterally transferred to lead another township in the county (in the aftermath of the economic slowdown following the June Fourth Incident in 1989). Of the five township heads, three were promoted, one died in a car accident, and one left the government to take over the helm of a private business company owned by his extended family. Like those in many other locales in the region, TVEs in the township ran into deep financial difficulties in the following years and had to be privatized around the turn of the century. But none of those who had overseen the earlier boom were held accountable for that; nor were their successors. When I revisited the township in 2003 only three of the thirty-six township-owned enterprises that had existed in 1995 remained. Also, these survivors were all reorganized as shareholding enterprises with diluted stakes held by the township government.

The pivotal importance of TVE sales growth was also recognized by the overwhelming majority of the rural officials I interviewed in thirteen townships in Hebei, Liaoning, Shandong, Jiangsu, Zhejiang, Guangdong, and

Sichuan during 1995–1999.[21] Of the forty-eight interviewees, forty-four strongly agreed that it was clearly the focal strategy for promoting local TVEs during their booming years. One of them (informant, 9/1996), the head of the public finance department in a rural township in Heze of Shandong province, characterized sales growth as the "key link" that helped address multiple agendas of the local government. In particular, if and when sustained, it would help generate revenue that benefited different groups of local officials, as he explained:

> Making profit or not, our [collective] enterprises generate fiscal revenue as long as they can sell their products. They provide the basic stream of [fiscal] revenue we count on. This is not only because revenue is an important issue in the performance evaluation package for our township leaders, but because it also provides for the needs of everyone else—including those not even on the regular payroll—in the government, salaries, bonuses, fringe benefits, office supplies, transportation, entertainment of guests, not to mention things like roads, schools, and so on. . . . Why not count on private companies for these? Well, they may be helpful to a certain extent, but they are unwilling to stay the course for long without making money, especially during difficult times. Collective enterprises need to follow orders from the government, and we of course also need to keep them afloat and growing with all the necessary support for as long as we can.

Statistical evidence sheds further light. The 1991–1992 CASS–World Bank survey of three hundred TVEs mentioned above found that during 1984–1990 the sales volume of the sample enterprises on average grew by 17.4% per year, which had a Pearson correlation of .99 with output growth. The average ratio of sales to output in that period was 92.7%, with a standard deviation of 3.5. What these findings indicate is that output grew in close association with sales, but it did not outpace the latter significantly, which could have been the case if output expansion had been the dominant strategy. Sales growth therefore seems to have provided the bedrock for output growth (but not the other way around), which mattered to local governments too. Despite the strong sales growth, however, profits failed to keep pace with it. Figure 4.1 shows that the ratio of profit to sales trended down, whereas the ratio of taxes to sales held steady. The negative correlation of sales and profits suggests that

---

21. The basic biographic profile of these officials is posted at the book site.

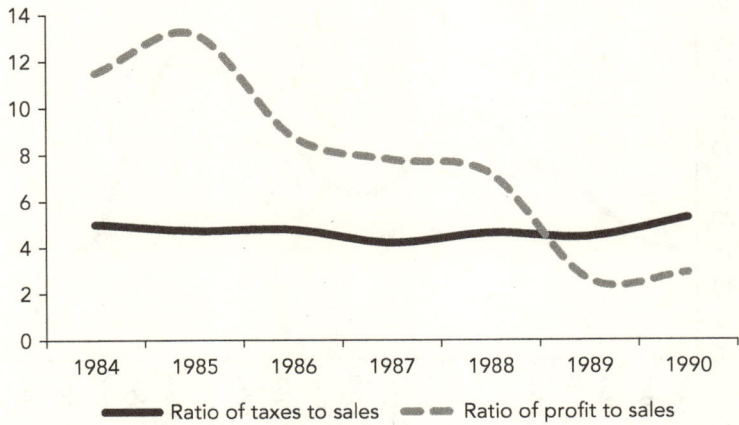

FIGURE 4.1 Taxes and profits versus sales, 1984–1990
Source: 1991–1992 CASS–World Bank TVE survey data ($n = 300$).

the growth of sales was unlikely to be the result of a profit maximization strategy.[22] Instead, the various (tax) revenues derived from the expansion of sales appear to have been the main driving force.

The larger picture at the national level was quite similar. Figure 4.2 shows the pattern of TVEs' sales growth rate up to the time of massive privatization. It demonstrated a strong upward trend in the mid to late 1980s. That was followed by a brief and moderate slowdown during the economic retrenchment in the aftermath of the June Fourth incident in 1989. But the upward trend resumed in 1992, with an even stronger tempo. It peaked in 1995 and then began a precipitous decline. On average the annual growth rate of TVE sales was 31% during 1984–1995. Figure 4.3 further shows a relatively stable trend in the correlation of sales to (gross) output and GDP during 1985–1998. On average the ratio of sales to output was 87% and the ratio of GDP to sales was and 29% (standard deviation = 1.8). There is no evidence of output significantly outgrowing sales. As mentioned in the preceding section, gross output was the leading economic indicator in political performance assessment until 1993, whereas GDP became the focal measure thereafter. The growth of sales therefore provided an essential platform for addressing the primary career concern of local officials in the first two decades of reform.

The relationship of sales to profit and taxes tells a different part of the story. Figure 4.4 shows that over time the tax revenues generated through

---

22. This, of course, does not imply that profits were unimportant to local governments. But, rather, declining profitability alone would not have undermined their dominant strategy.

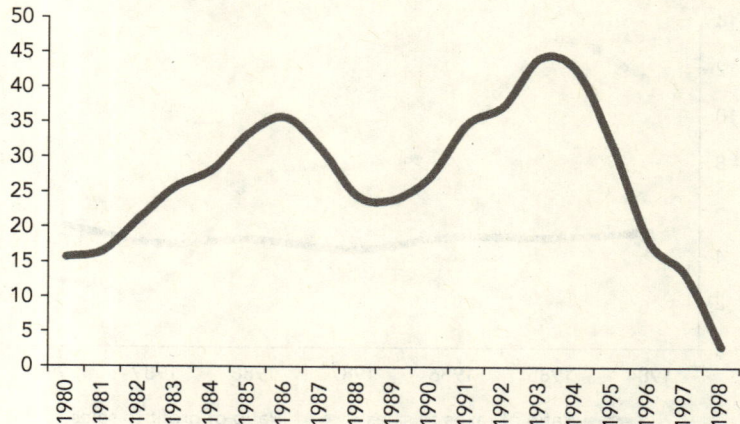

FIGURE 4.2 Sales growth rate (five-year moving average) of TVEs, 1980–1998
Source: CTEY, various years.

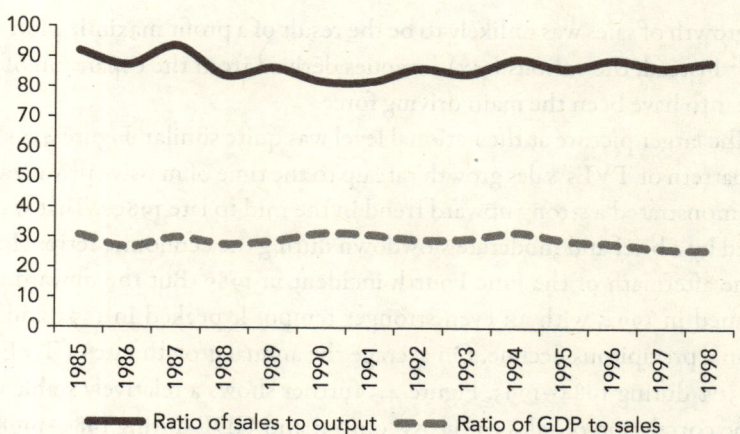

FIGURE 4.3 TVE output, sales, and GDP, 1985–1998
Source: CTEY, various years.

each unit of sales held steady but the profits generated through each unit of sales declined (through 1993) and then stagnated.[23] As discussed before, the bulk of the taxes generated by TVEs consisted of indirect taxes tied to sales (table 3.3). During 1987–1998 (when pertinent data are available) their share

---

23. Profit figures are adjusted to reflect the effect of tax exemptions booked as profits. An explanatory note on this is posted at the book site. It should be noted that this adjustment does not even account for the fact that as of 1993 a significant portion of what was booked as profit had to be used for interest payments on the loans that TVEs incurred to finance and sustain their expansion (see the discussion below).

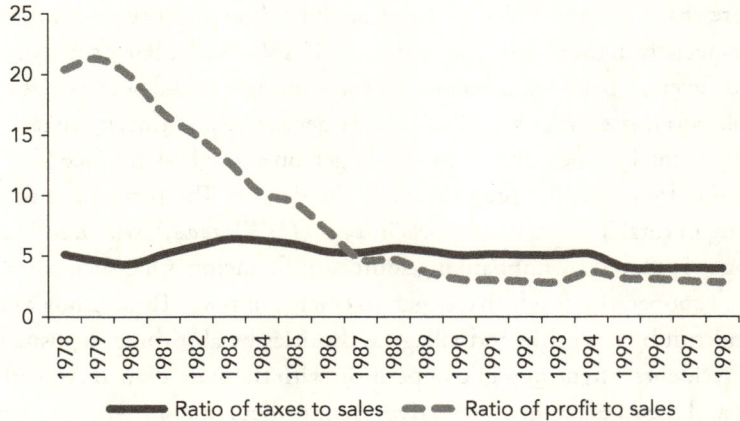

FIGURE 4.4 Taxes and profits as percentage of TVE sales, 1978–1998
Source: CTEY, various years.

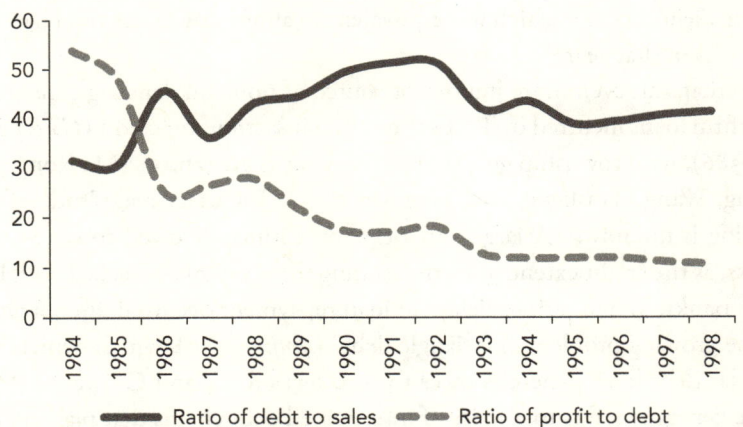

FIGURE 4.5 Debt, sales, and profit of TVEs, 1984–1998
Source: CTEY, various years.

in the total tax liability of TVEs ranged between 74% and 83% (*CTEY*, various years). Given such importance to the interests of incumbent local officials, it is not surprising that TVE sales kept expanding despite declining profitability.

What sustained TVEs' spectacular growth of sales despite declining and poor profitability throughout the 1980s and early 1990s was the supply of credit leveraged with the help of local authorities. Figure 4.5 shows that external borrowing kept pace with sales during the booming years of TVEs, which received the strongest boost in the late 1980s and early 1990s. It is interesting to note that the importance of direct bank lending declined in TVE liabilities, especially in the 1990s. The 1991–1992 CASS–World Bank survey reveals that on average bank loans accounted for some 81% of the borrowings of the sample enterprises, which tended to be larger in size and thus more resourceful than smaller ones. But even the larger ones might have faced increasing difficulties with the progression of the decade. The percentage of bank lending in total TVE debt was 38% in 1993 (*CTEY 1994*,), which indicates a strong role played by nonbanking sources of financing. One such source lay in rural cooperative funds that began to emerge in 1984. These funds were set up and run by township and village authorities by absorbing deposits from rural residents, oftentimes in competition with the state-owned Agricultural Bank and the rural credit cooperatives it controlled. In 1996, when the central government decided to crack down on rural cooperative funds, there were some twenty-one thousand township-run funds and some twenty-four thousand village-run funds. The amount of funds totaled about 150 billion yuan (Wen Tiejun 2000), which was equivalent to about 12% of the total liabilities of TVEs in that year.[24]

Perhaps an even more important source of nonbank lending consisted of interfirm loans incurred by TVEs through transactions on credit (*CTEY 1994*, 385–386), with township governments serving as guarantors (Ma Rong, John Wong, Wang Hansheng, and Yang Mu 1994). The exact magnitude of such lending is unknown. A large part of it was ultimately owed to state-owned banks, as the credit extended by the lending firms was often backed with loans from banks. When serious delays in loan repayment occurred, it contributed to the growing problem of "triangle debt" (*sanjiao zhai*), which depicts a triangular debt loop (where A owes to B, B owes to C, and C owes to A) but more generally refers to a series of intertwined debt chains that plagued public enterprises and state-owned banks alike in the early to mid-1990s (Lardy 1998). Indeed, the ability of TVEs to fuel sales growth depended greatly on cash flows facilitated by delays and rollovers in the repayment of principal.

In the 1991–1992 CASS–World Bank survey of TVEs mentioned above, 84% of the enterprises indicated that, when faced with difficulties in servicing their loans, they were able to obtain relief from local governments by deferring repayment, covering old loans with new borrowing, and/or using pretax profit for repayment. In 1995 the total principal repayment by TVEs was 9.7 billion yuan, which was equivalent to only 0.77% of the outstanding debts

---

24. This, of course, does not mean the full amount was channeled to TVEs. For an account of the rise and demise of rural cooperative funds during 1984–1999, see Wen 2000.

(of 1.25 trillion yuan) (*CTEY 1996*, 336, 341).[25] On the other hand, interest payment totaled 62.6 billion yuan, which was equivalent to 42% of the profits earned by TVEs in that year (*CTEY 1996*, 336, 341).[26] Apparently out of line with common practices of banking and financing, this peculiar structure of interest-principal amortization nevertheless reveals a major twist in the TVE growth story. With the accumulation of outstanding debts and the decline and stagnation of net profits relative to sales, the ability of TVEs to service their growing debts deteriorated. This is illustrated by the second curve (i.e., ratio of profit to debt) in figure 4.5. When the extensions for principal repayment could no longer be obtained or sustained, the sales growth strategy would inevitably run into difficulties.

Table 4.1 shows the debt level of TVEs relative to their total equity capital and to the revenues of township governments during 1993–1998 (when pertinent data are available). Although the debt-equity ratio of TVEs was generally lower than that of SOEs (to be discussed below) and registered some

Table 4.1 Financial liabilities of public enterprises versus equity and government revenue

Year	Debt-equity ratio			Debt-revenue ratio	
	TVEs	All SOEs	Local SOEs	TVEs	Local SOEs
1993	1.92	2.54	3.45	8.28	8.52
1994	1.78	2.41	3.47	12.19	14.96
1995	1.69	1.53	na	12.25	na
1996	1.63	1.91	na	11.66	na
1997	1.58	1.71	2.27	11.48	12.04
1998	1.52	1.67	2.12	10.30	11.3

Note: Debt-revenue ratio is defined as total TVE liability divided by total revenue of township governments (including budget revenue, extrabudget revenue, and "self-raised funds") for TVEs, and as total local SOE liability divided by budget revenue of provincial, prefectural, and county governments for local SOEs.
Sources: CSOAY (various years); *CTEY* (various years); *FSPCC* (various years).

---

25. Detailed breakdown figures are unavailable for earlier years. The percentages for 1996, 1997, and 1998 were 0.9% (of 1.45 trillion yuan), 0.88% (of 1.55 trillion yuan), and 0.88% (of 1.59 trillion yuan) respectively (*CTEY 1997*, 356, 367; *CTEY 1998*, 392, 297; *CTEY 1999*, 421, 427).

26. During 1986–1992 public enterprises were allowed to use part of their gross profit (before income tax) for repayment of loan principal. That practice, known as *shuiqian huandai* (repayment of loans before tax), was discontinued as of 1993.

decline from 1993 to 1998, it still exceeded their equity value by more than 50% in 1998. That implies that there would have remained a 34% gap had they been forced to liquidate all the assets of their own to pay off their debts. In fact the "improvement" shown by the downward movement of the debt-equity ratio in 1993–1998 reflects the changes resulting from early privatization of TVEs in an increasing number of locales during that period, which saw the disappearance of some 37% of all TVEs and, along with it, the financial liabilities on their books.[27] As I will show later, TVEs with more serious financial problems were more likely to be among the early dropouts (hence diluting the debt statistics).

The growing liabilities of TVEs also added to the fiscal strains faced by township governments, as can be seen from the debt-revenue ratio in the table. The problem was even more formidable than that faced by the "owners" of local SOEs, as the denominator for TVEs includes not only budget revenue but extrabudget revenue and "self-raised" funds (discussed in chapter 3). Moreover, the overleveraged growth of TVEs eventually turned them into casualties of their own earlier success in job creation. In 1978 they employed a total of 28 million workers; in 1995 TVE employment peaked at 61 million (*SCTE*, 103–105). Their inability to further contribute to nonfarm employment afterward was soon complicated by the need to accommodate large numbers of workers who were rapidly rendered redundant by the drastic shrinkage of sales growth. In face of the surge of combined financial and un(der)employment pressures, privatization became the only viable way out for local authorities, as will be discussed in chapter 7.

The deterioration of financial health and longer-term sustainability was not the only problem associated with the sales growth strategy that made TVEs increasingly vulnerable to major external shocks. The internal organization and governance of TVEs were also negatively impacted as a result of local officials' using them as instruments for careerist pursuits and revenue manipulation. A common practice adopted by township authorities during the booming years of TVEs was to hide taxes in enterprise accounts (Ma Rong et al. 1994), which had been particularly widespread before the 1994 fiscal restructuring.[28] What they did was to refrain from "overfulfilling" the fiscal

---

27. In 1993 the total number of TVEs was 1.69 million; in 1998 it dropped to 1.07 million (*SCTE*, 55–56).

28. As noted in chapter 3, the 1994 fiscal restructuring did not change the various arrangements of revenue sharing between township and county governments. But it did make the exemption of certain taxes (e.g., value-added tax) more difficult. I will discuss the constraining effect of this change on the incentives for local governments to continue the sales growth strategy in chapter 7.

contracts with higher-level authorities by not collecting the full amounts of taxes, especially indirect taxes, owed by TVEs so as to stash away revenues that otherwise would have to be shared with higher-level authorities, and even to inflate profitability (which could also be a plus in political performance assessment). As shown in table 3.3, there was a sizable gap between "taxes due" and "taxes paid" by TVEs. Although the taxes exempted had the effect of helping some TVEs to stay in competition, they were funds subject to recall by the (local) government rather than belonging to the enterprises concerned. Indeed the uses of such funds were oftentimes not for the longer-term development of the enterprises concerned, but for various discretionary purposes defined by local officials, ranging from private and collective consumption to the financing of activities (e.g., "image projects"—see Guo 2009 for a discussion) irrelevant to the pertinent account holders that provided the hiding service. Because of the shuffling of closely related accounting items in revenue manipulation, local officials sometimes even "conveniently" expanded these uses beyond the slush funds parked in TVE accounts, thus undermining the financial independence and health of the enterprises affected.[29]

On the other hand, the involvement of TVE managers in the manipulation of fiscal flows through enterprise accounts fostered a collusive relationship with local officials. Their collusion could degenerate into a common base for naked pursuit of private gains at the expense of TVEs.[30] Even without further slippage down this path, the elevation of informal dependence of local officials on TVE managers in revenue maneuvering could compromise their

---

29. A common observation that I made during my fieldwork trips to the thirteen townships (mentioned above) during 1995–1999 is that the bills for entertaining township officials' visiting guests were always paid by their subordinate TVEs. This, of course, was only part of the "bursary" service provided by TVEs. A TVE manager I interviewed in Shunde (informant, 12/1996) acknowledged having receiving tax breaks for the township government but claimed that "we purchased the Toyota car that chauffeurs the (township) party secretary; we share [with other enterprises] the expenses for some of their duty trips, as well as the gifts they carry along, to the county [government], the provincial capital, and other cities; we contribute to the fees and other expenses incurred by township leaders' children attending boarding schools in the county; last year we were asked to pay for the cement and sand used in the construction [at the suggestion of the county party secretary] of the monument commemorating revolutionary martyrs in the war of resistance against Japan; we shared the cost for replacing the water pipes for the canteen of the township government; we were one of the sponsors for the lantern fair after the Lunar New Year.... There are just too many items to list out in full. What I can say is that in return we have actually contributed more than what we have received."

30. In a previous study (Lin 2001) I have discussed how such collusion undermined the organizational health of public enterprises. For a sample of corruption cases involving collusion between township officials and TVE managers, see Wang Guangying 1996 and Jin Qiang 2005.

formal fiduciary role (as representatives of rural communities) in monitoring the behavior of the latter. This problem was exacerbated by a concurrent rise of monitoring cost amid fast expansion of TVEs driven by the sales growth strategy. From 1985 to 1995 the total assets of TVEs increased from 118 billion yuan to 1.99 trillion yuan, whereas the workforce grew from 42 million to 61 million (*CTEY 1988*, 273; *CTEY 1996*, 100). The resultant increase of organizational scale and complexity added to the information asymmetry faced by supervising authorities (Li and Rozelle 2004), leaving open more opportunities for opportunism to grow.[31] As I will discuss in chapter 7, managerial corruption and asset stripping were among the factors contributing to the decline of public enterprises, which was further hastened by insiders' strategic manipulation of enterprise asset valuation before and during massive privatization.

The SOE Sideshow

SOEs were latecomers to the process of marketization. In terms of resource allocation they were the main beneficiaries of the central planning system (Naughton 1995; Riskin 1987). Resistance from vested interests in the party-state bureaucracy, coupled with greater organizational complexity and concerns about potentially adverse impact on economic stability, held off the full start of reforms in the state sector until the mid-1980s (Naughton 1995; Perkins 1988). In the following decade, however, SOEs gradually moved away from central planning and became active participants in the new, market-oriented domain of economic activities.

Under the political performance assessment system and the fiscal contract arrangements in the 1980s and early 1990s, the behavior of the supervising officials of SOEs grew increasingly similar to that of township officials overseeing TVEs. Expanding output through sales growth became the dominant strategy, and financial leverage facilitated its implementation. Before the massive wave of privatization in the late 1990s,[32] the overwhelming majority of

---

31. According to a township official (informant, 21/1995) in Wuxi county—the heartland of the TVE boom—during 1993–1994 more than a dozen local TVEs had to be liquidated because of heavy losses and debts. Their remaining assets were taken over by private business people. "They expanded too fast such we could not keep a close eye on them. The managers took advantage of this and entered deals that benefited their friends and family members at the expense of their enterprises. Some of them have now been disciplined, and we are still investigating these cases."

32. Of the 70,342 industrial SOEs covered by the 1985 industrial census, 3,825 were "affiliated" with the central government, 31,254 with provincial and prefectural governments, and 35,263 with county governments (*SSIC 1985*, 6). The total number of industrial SOEs increased to 118,000 in the 1995

SOEs were "owned" by local governments.[33] Yet they had a major difference with TVEs, which were also situated under (even lower) local government authorities. That is, TVEs had weak bonds with the central planning system and thus quickly became market-oriented players after the start of reforms. In contrast, SOEs carried more baggage from the old system, where fulfilling output targets set by the government had been their main task. This preoccupation with output was also reinforced by the fact that output was recast as an important indicator under the new political performance assessment system.

A 1991–1992 CASS–World Bank survey of 967 SOEs in 40 cities of 10 provinces found that the top three objectives specified in the managerial contracts with government supervising authorities were output (35.4%), total taxes and profits (34.7%), and taxes and profits handed over to the government (27%).[34] Although the first objective might still be reflective of the lasting impact of the old mentality, the latter two both pertained to revenue concerns. More importantly, the operating environment that these enterprises had been used to was no longer there. Of these enterprises, 95% indicated that they faced competition; 66% of those facing competition said it was very intense and formidable. The growth of output, therefore, could not be sustained without selling products for the same reasons that drove TVEs to focus on sales growth. This is reflected in the remarks made by a top economic official (who had previously been the director of a large SOE) I interviewed in Foshan of Guangdong (informant, 19/1995):

> Things were quite routinized in the planned economy. There was no competition. The government arranged all the supply of input and capital; the [state-owned] enterprises followed the output plan to make our products and sold them to users specified by the government. The reforms have changed all that. Input supplies are no longer arranged by the government; enterprises have to find buyers for their

---

industrial census. Of these, 7,275 were classified as central SOEs, 43,039 as provincial and prefectural-level SOEs, and 67,686 as county-level SOEs (*SSIC 1995*, 8).

33. Even central SOEs had a "local" character of sorts due to the lack of a highly coherent line of command. Before the establishment of the SASAC in 2003 as the unified authority in charge of all nonfinancial SOEs directly controlled by the central government, central SOEs were affiliated with various industry-specific ministries and bureaus.

34. The information reported here is derived from the survey data set. Documentation of the survey is posted at the book site. The survey also covered 366 urban collective enterprises. Considering the limitation of space and given that these enterprises behaved like small SOEs (Lin 2001), I do not include them in the analysis here.

products. If they are to expand their output, they have to push it out to the market. Otherwise they will be dragged down. There is only so much capital they can spare for products sitting in the warehouse, not to mention it's difficult and costly to borrow money from banks now. For the [local] government, output growth among SOEs is a top concern, because they are the leading force of the [local] economy and have an uplifting effect on everything—our image, revenue, and even employment. But we do not focus on output per se. What we strive to do is to grow output based on sales. This is very different from producing output for the sake of doing it before the reforms.

The pattern of output and sales growth among the 967 SOEs mentioned above is consistent with this observation. There is no evidence of output expansion outpacing sales growth. In fact their growth rates were almost identical (at 10.5% and 10.9% respectively) during 1985–1990, when SOEs were brought under reform (and when pertinent data are available). Figure 4.6 shows the overall trend of sales growth for all industrial SOEs, which has a Pearson correlation of .99 with output growth rate.[35] It was similar to that of TVEs shown in the preceding section—rising sharply in the early to mid-1980s, hovering at high levels for about a decade, and then dropping

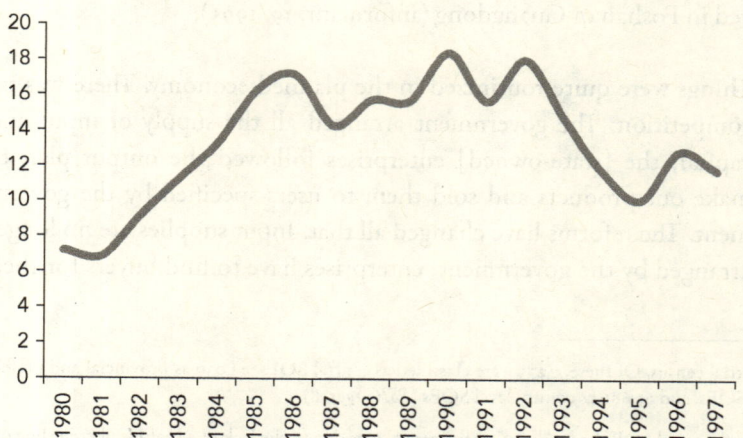

FIGURE 4.6 Sales growth rate (five-year moving average) of industrial SOEs, 1980–1997
Sources: *CIESY* (various years); *FYC* (various years).

---

35. The gap between output and sales among SOEs was actually narrower than that among TVEs. In 1985, for example, the ratio of sales to output for industrial SOEs was 94.3%; in 1995 it rose to 97.1% (*SSIC 1985; SSIC 1995*).

precipitously in the mid-1990s. While the absolute level of growth rate was less spectacular than that of TVEs, it is important to note that SOEs had a much larger initial base of sales value than TVEs and every percentage point of growth carried much greater weight.[36] Also noticeable is the fact that during the high-growth period of 1985–1995 industrial SOEs maintained an average sales growth rate of 15.4%, which was higher than the GDP growth rate of the economy as a whole (*FYC 1999*, 484).

Like TVEs, though, SOEs experienced a gradual delinking of profitability from the taxes generated through expanding sales. Figures 4.7 and 4.8 illustrate this phenomenon based on the data for the 967 SOEs covered by the CASS–World Bank survey and for all industrial SOEs. The lack of detailed data on tax exemption renders it infeasible to make adjustment for the distortions caused by the practice of booking exempted taxes as profits. But even with the inflated profits the pattern is still clear. That is, while taxes held steady relative to sales (which were expanding, as shown in figure 4.6), profits declined over time. SOEs, especially industrial SOES, tended to be more concentrated in sectors (e.g., tobacco) where indirect tax rates were higher than those where TVEs were concentrated (Lin and Liu 2000). This is probably why the problem looks more pronounced in figure 4.5 than in figure 4.4, though the underlying story remains similar. In fact despite their significant role in fiscal revenue generation, the profitability of SOEs seriously deteriorated into the 1990s. In 1985 9.6% of the industrial SOEs under state budget incurred a loss; the percentage rose to 29.8% in 1992 and further to 43.9% in 1997 (*FYC 1998*, 482). In 1996 the financial losses incurred by SOEs totaled 112.7 billion yuan, exceeding the net profits of SOEs (*FYC 1998*, 482).[37] The rationale for this seemingly irrational behavior resembled that for TVEs, as explained by the director of a state-owned machine tool maker in Nanjing that had been in the red during 1992–1995 but continued to operate and even expand (informant, 3/1995):[38]

> As a key enterprise (*zhongdian qiye*) of the city we probably overexpanded in the 1980s, with an increase of capacity by almost threefold.

---

36. In 1980 the total sales value of all TVEs was 5.96 billion yuan (*SCTE*, 253), which was equivalent to only 2.4% of the sales value of industrial SOEs alone (*CSA 1987*, 48).

37. Since the losses had already been factored in before the reporting of net profits in aggregate, what this means is that the total losses of SOEs were equivalent to more than 50% of the after-tax profits of SOEs. See Holz and Lin 2001 for a discussion of the pertinent accounting practice.

38. The strategy would look less irrational if one made a close examination of its revenue implications. According to the summary statistics of the 1995 industrial census (*SSIC 1995*, 23), for example, industrial

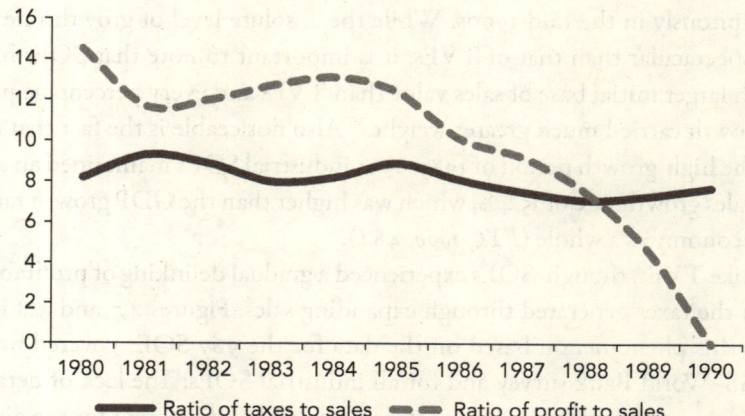

FIGURE 4.7 SOE taxes, profits, and sales (n = 967)
Source: Survey data.

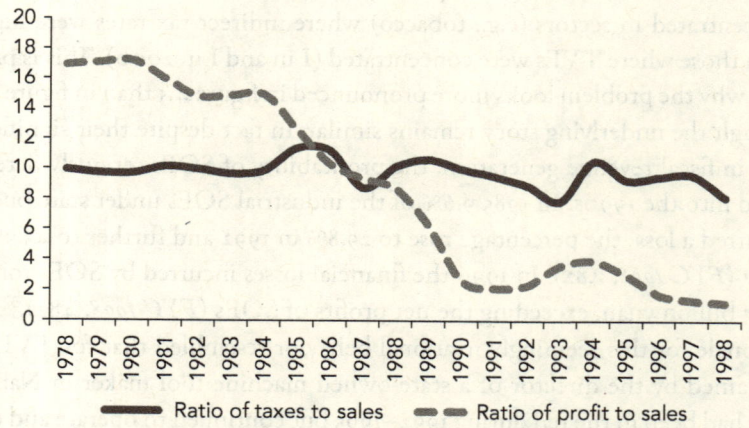

FIGURE 4.8 Taxes and profit as percentage of industrial SOE sales, 1978–1998
Source: FYC 1997, 1999.

But the government does not want us to reduce or stop production because it would affect the overall economic performance of the sector, which has certain binding targets to achieve for the city. Although we can barely sell our products at cost now, the [sales] volume itself generates fiscal revenue. We also have seventeen hundred-plus workers and staff, plus some 160 retirees. We cannot transfer them to other places or lay them off. We have no choice but to keep going. Hopefully we will be able to overcome the short-term difficulties with more reforms.

A major difference between TVEs and SOEs is that SOEs had easier access to bank lending. This was a legacy from the central planning era, when the entire state banking system was primarily geared toward serving SOEs.[39] In 1985, SOEs accounted for 77% of all the non-fixed-assets lending extended by state-owned banks.[40] The percentage trended down but remained above 67% through 1995, whereas the percentage of TVEs never exceeded 10%.[41] In comparison with TVEs, which (as shown in the preceding section) managed to minimize the principal repayment for their debts as a way to leverage funds for short-term growth, the principal repayment by SOEs was considerably larger. In 1995, for example, the repayment amount of industrial SOEs for their long-term loans was equivalent to 15% of the outstanding balance (*FYC 1999*, 485). This, however, was not the result of robust financial health, but rather the greater availability of bank loans and soft financial discipline imposed by their lenders. The repayment of the principal of 126 billion yuan in 1995 was largely covered with newly borrowed loans (totaling 200 billion yuan) (*FYC 1999*, 485). According to the 1991–1992 CASS–World Bank survey of industrial SOEs mentioned above, some 73% of the respondents indicated that when they had difficulty servicing their loans on time, they were able to either get an extension to the existing repayment schedule or obtain a new loan to address the immediate shortfalls.

The consequences of the financially leveraged expansion of SOE sales were similar to those of TVEs. Table 4.1 shows that in the early 1990s SOEs had accumulated massive financial liabilities. Their overall debt-equity ratio was higher than that of TVEs. Local SOEs had even higher ratio than central SOEs, which weighed heavily on their "owners," as can be seen from the high debt-revenue ratios. The seeming "improvement" during 1993–1998 was

---

SOEs generated a total of 256.3 billion yuan in taxes. Profit tax accounted for only 11.3% of this total, where the lion's share of the total consisted of various indirect taxes generated in or through sales. The total net profit of industrial SOEs, after deduction of a total operating loss of 36.5 billion yuan, was only 36.1 billion yuan (*FYC 1999*, 486). The short-term utility of maintaining sales growth despite poor profitability was obvious from a fiscal point of view.

39. Before 1983 most (approximately 80%) of the working capital of SOEs consisted of fiscal grants from the Ministry of Finance, whereas a small fraction (about 20%) took the form of basically interest-free loans from state banks. In 1983 the government decided to turn all working capital grants of SOEs into bank loans and to charge interests on such loans. See Shang Ming 1989 for an account of the prereform system and the subsequent changes.

40. Over time SOEs also became more dependent on borrowings to address their cash flow needs. In 1985 funds owned by industrial SOEs themselves was equivalent to 35% of the quota working capital they took out from state banks; in 1992 this percentage dropped to 22% (*FYC 1993*, 686).

41. Urban collective enterprises, agriculture, foreign-invested companies, and domestic private enterprises made up the remaining percentages.

in part due to the dropout of large numbers of failing SOEs from debt statistics. During 1995–1998, for example, the total number of industrial SOEs declined from 118,000 to 64,700 (*CIESY 2001*, 16). Also, during 1994–1995 SOEs underwent a major overhaul of their accounting practices. One of the major changes was the inclusion of assessed land value in enterprise equity, which had not been counted as such before. That led to an upward adjustment to enterprise equity value and thereby had an offsetting effect on the debt-equity ratio.

Furthermore, before the debacle of public enterprises in the mid to late 1990s, the sales-driven expansion of SOEs also helped grow their workforce, hence alleviating the mounting demographic pressures (discussed in chapter 2) that the country faced during the two decades after the Cultural Revolution. In 1981 the total employment of industrial and commercial SOEs was 49 million; in 1994 it rose to 116 million (*SFYCICA*, 3; *SICA 1995*, 21). This job creation effect quickly dissipated and reversed as SOEs' sales expansion faltered in the mid-1990s. Finding alternative placement for the large numbers of workers in overexpanded SOEs soon became a hard constraint that CCP leaders could not afford to evade.

The fast expansion of SOEs under the sales growth strategy also exacerbated governance problems. Like TVEs, local SOEs were often used by their supervising officials as instruments of revenue manipulation. In 1995, for example, the total taxes due for industrial SOEs were 256.3 billion yuan, but the taxes actually paid were 195.8 billion yuan, or 76.4% of the amount due (*FYC 1999*, 483; *SSIC 1995*, 23). The exempted taxes were often parked in enterprise accounts, which were at the discretionary disposal of their supervising authorities.[42] This practice blurred the boundaries between formal and informal resource pools and between public and private uses, which had a negative spillover effect on the financial health and independence of SOEs, as partly reflected in the growing complaints about local officials' encroachments into enterprise funds in the early to mid-1990s (SJSFGS 1995; see also Lin 2001). The softening of arm's-length relationships with enterprise managers also weakened the resolve and ability of supervising officials to monitor the behavior of enterprise managers,[43] which as in the case of TVEs became

---

42. During 1995–1999 I interviewed thirty-six SOE managers in seven different cities (details about the interviews are posted at the book site). Twenty-eight of them indicated that their enterprises had received tax exemptions with the help of their supervising authorities. They also acknowledged having provided various "bursary services" to government officials in connection with this special treatment.

43. When asked about the impact of fiscal manipulation through enterprise accounts, the chief accountant of a large SOE in Guangzhou (informant, 16/1996) opined: "Under the old system our

even more difficult because of an increase in information asymmetry associated with fast-growing organizational scale and complexity. From 1985 to 1995 the total assets of industrial SOEs increased by thirteen times—from 402.6 billion to 4.8 trillion yuan (*SSIC 1985*, 3:565; *SSIC 1995*, 25). It was during this period of time that the saying *qiong miao fu fangzhang* ("impoverished temple under self-enriched master"), which depicts asset stripping by public enterprise managers, gained currency. In a 2004 CASS-HKUST survey (n = 510) of private enterprises,[44] 45 respondents indicated that their companies were former SOEs; 36 of them agreed that overexpansion and poor monitoring over managers were among the major factors contributing to the decline and eventual privatization of SOEs. I will further discuss this issue in chapter 7.

Summary

Promoting sales expansion through local public enterprises was the dominant strategy of economic development among local governments before the mid-1990s. This strategy was lodged in the "regional property rights" structure carried over from the prereform era. It was ideologically consistent with the new thinking of the post-Mao leadership on market socialism and thus involved low political risk. It helped address the career concerns and resource control agendas of local leaders under the new political performance assessment system and fiscal structure. At the same time, it also accommodated the interests of many lower-rank local officials in charge of economic affairs. The pursuit of this strategy, however, undermined the fundamental financial and organizational health of public enterprises. Transient tenures, weak accountability of administrative behavior, and lax financial discipline combined to compound the coevolving moral hazard problem, which eroded the staying power of the strategy and ultimately rendered it self-defeating.

It is important to note, though, that the extent to which local governments pressed on with the strategy was not uniform over time and across regions. A separate study based on analysis using data from the industrial sector (Li and Lin 2016) finds considerable variation both among different sub-provincial locales and relative to the starting years of comparison for the same locales before massive privatization began. In some places, strong sales

---

management used to have a rather strict superior-subordinate relationship with the government. But now it is more like a relationship between senior and junior partners [*laoda he laoer*] who need each other for a variety of informal issues, and we are tacitly allowed some wiggle room to handle them."

44. Details about the survey are posted at the book site.

growth among local public enterprises lasted all the way to 1997, whereas in some other places growth rate peaked as early as in the mid-1980s. Yet the slowdowns were not accompanied by a reduction of financial leverage and improvements in profitability, suggesting the strategy might still have been in play for some time, but with poorer results. Nor was early slowdown alone a reliable predictor of early privatization. Indeed the public sector remained dominant in some laggard locales despite slowing growth and deteriorating financial health of local public enterprises. In the next two chapters, I will explore the conditions under which local officials ventured to develop parallel or even alternative strategies to address their self-interest. In particular, I will examine how they tackled the political risks of tolerating and facilitating private business and foreign capital beyond the limits set by the central authority, and how variations in this endeavor help us understand the diverse patterns of privatization prior to the tipping point in 1997.

5

Rule Bending for the Necessary Evil

THE CREATION OF China's new economy in the post-Mao era was a process driven by forces converging from different directions. The increasing difficulties of expanding public enterprises, as discussed in the preceding chapter, were accompanied by an accelerating growth of genetically private enterprises. This growth increased competition, filled in the gaps left open by faltering public enterprises, and demonstrated the vitality of private ownership as an alternative to the preferred institutional choice of CCP leaders. Key to this growth were the efforts of private entrepreneurs to defy and overcome the institutional constraints in an initially hostile political environment. In so doing, they reshaped the conditions of their own existence. The players who directly faced such challenge (and opportunity) were officials of the party-state who held allocative, regulatory, and extractive power over the local economic space. How they responded out of self-interest calculations had an important bearing on the cost of private business and thus affected the pace of privatization before the drastic policy change at the national level in the mid to late 1990s.

The self-interest calculus of local officials was subject to the influence of the postreform system of political performance assessment and fiscal relations, which made reliance on public enterprises for economic growth their dominant strategy. As a policy choice, therefore, early privatization would most likely occur where that initially dominant strategy had faltered.[1] This

---

1. There was a concurrent mechanism at work, though. Party-state officials could collude with private business people and among themselves to create and expand the space for the private economy, as I have discussed in a previous study (Lin 2001). Such collusion was nevertheless pervasive and spreading

condition, however, does not in itself establish a sufficient causal link. The reason, I argue, is that overseeing early privatization inevitably required local officials to bend the rules set by the central leadership on the private sector. Understanding how they tackled the inherent political risk of rule bending and why they did so differently in different local contexts is crucial for explaining the varying attitudes of local governments toward the private sector despite early exhaustion of sales-focused expansion of local public enterprises.

Uneven Paces of Early Privatization

Before the precipitous decline of public ownership in the late 1990s, gradual erosion had already taken place despite the initially predominant tendency of local governments to promote the growth of public enterprises. The erosion began right after the start of economic reforms. As shown in table 1.7 in chapter 1, from 1980 to 1995 the share of the public sector in the total nonfarm workforce declined from 99.4% to 64.2%. The decline occurred earlier and trended down to lower levels in rural areas than in urban areas. From 1985 to 1998 the share of the public sector in the rural nonfarm workforce went down from 60% to 38%, whereas that in the urban workforce dropped from 96% to 51% (table 1.8). There was also increasing variation over time, and the variability in the rural sector was greater than that in the urban sector among different provinces, as indicated by the coefficients of variation.

There are three major explanations for what led to early privatization in some locales of the country. The first one emphasizes the role of entrepreneurship. The central argument is that private entrepreneurs defied the restrictions imposed by the state and created new economic realities that the central leadership subsequently had to reckon with (e.g., Huang 2008; Nee and Opper 2012; Tsai 2002). A factor that facilitated this is that some local authorities bent the rules where the growth of private business could help boost local economic growth, though sometimes private entrepreneurs pressed ahead even without the acquiescence of local officials (Tsai 2002).

---

throughout the political system, and there is no clear evidence of significant variations across jurisdictions and administrative levels. For understanding the spatial variations in early privatization, therefore, one can hardly derive much additional explanatory power by looking at collusive dealings of political actors. Moreover, private exchange relations in the political process were often bundled with public policy issues and disguised as "normal" types of interaction. For this to be sustained, justifications had to be fabricated to contain the political risk involved, which is the focal issue here.

The second explanation focuses on the lasting impact of history on the composition and behavior of the local political elite. In Wenzhou of Zhejiang province, for example, Liu (1992) finds a close relationship between a thriving private sector in the early years of reform and a permissive policy environment for private business. She attributes this to the potent influence of native officials in the local party-state apparatus and traces the origin of such influence to the fact that the region was "self-liberated" by native-led guerrillas during the communist revolution rather than taken over by the regular armed forces of the CCP. With deep social and family ties in local communities, guerrillas-turned-officials shared a political culture that tolerated petty private economic elements during the Mao era. The supportive policy toward private business in the reform era was an outgrowth of that long-standing tradition, which was further reinforced by various personal benefits from collusive ties with private business people. Zhang (2011) echoes this view in a broader study on the evolution of the private sector in Zhejiang but adds that factional power struggles between native cadres and outside appointees solidified the alliance of the former with the local grassroots, thereby opening up more space for the growth of private business.

The third explanation is that early privatization was a second-best choice for some local governments. As noted in chapter 4, Whiting (2000) argues that locales with a weak presence of nonfarm public enterprises in the Mao era were in a disadvantageous position to compete with those with strong organizational legacies. In face of growing difficulties in relying on the expansion of local public enterprises for addressing their career and revenue concerns, officials in locales with poor organizational endowment in the public sector tended to hold a more tolerant or even supportive attitude toward private business. The initial weakness of public enterprises thus helps explain the strength of the private sector during the early years of reform, and vice versa.

All these explanations are useful but need to be further developed. The entrepreneurship argument points to a fundamentally important driving force of private economic activities. But it leaves open the question of why the degree of privatization varied across space. This question cannot be adequately explained by looking at the resilient behavior of entrepreneurs only, as the entrepreneurial spirit could be dampened or enhanced by the local institutional environment.[2] Political actors, who played an important part

---

2. Ningbo and Hangzhou, for example, are two regions in Zhejiang province with long-standing entrepreneurial traditions. But their local economies were mainly driven by public enterprises until the mid-1990s. See the discussion below.

in shaping the constraints and incentives faced by private business people, need to be brought into the picture. And, as I have argued in the introductory chapter, because of the political costs (risks) associated with different policies, the benefit embedded in mutual dependence between these two groups of actors is insufficient to explain the varying attitudes and behavior of local officials toward private business. Furthermore, entrepreneurship involves not only the propensity to innovate and take risk for profit making, but the ability to do so. Among the factors affecting such ability is the precommunist local business culture—that is, the stock of cumulative knowledge, understanding, experiences, strategies, and behavioral norms shared among locals in regard to the internal and external organization of private business. Both the level of development before the communist revolution and the depth of the socialist transformation afterward could have a major impact on the strength of the entrepreneurial forces in the local economy after the start of reforms.

This brings up the role of local history. The causal linkage emphasized by the argument about the composition of the local elite is that the tolerance or protection by native cadres kept prerevolution local business traditions alive, which in turn provided a launch pad for more intense synergetic interactions that propelled the growth of the local private sector after the start of reform. The gist of the story is that there was a symbiosis between local political actors and socioeconomic forces. To reveal the mechanisms of this possibility, three questions need to be further considered. First, why were petty private economic elements tolerated or even protected by local cadres to a greater extent in some locales than others before the reform, when different locales faced similarly strong structural constraints on petty corruption? Liu (1992) attributes this to a shared local political culture dating back to the prerevolution era but offers no further explanation. Second, were native cadres in local governments a homogenous group? This seems to be a key assumption of the thesis. If it does not hold, however, what explains the observed uneven distribution of remnant private elements? Third, regardless of the validity of this assumption, how did the sympathizers of private business defuse or fend off the ideologically legitimate and politically menacing challenges from their opponents (as individual or factional rivals) in the local political establishment? This question is important in that without a certain degree of acquiescence from the latter, the observed policy outcome could not have been sustained. Again there is a major gap in the analysis.

Local history is also a major concern of the organizational legacy argument. But its focus is on the implications of uneven postrevolution economic buildup for subsequent policy orientations in the reform era. Unlike the local elite composition thesis, it explicitly argues that the preferences of local officials were closely linked to their self-interest calculus with regard to career movement and resource control, which varied under different structural conditions. Such variation is then used to explain why in locales where pre-revolution business traditions were similarly strong (i.e., Shanghai, Wuxi, and Wenzhou) there were different policy outcomes in regard to private ownership. As pointed out in the preceding chapter, this account helps illuminate the varying abilities of local authorities to sustain the sales expansion strategy through local public enterprises after the reform. But it is not sufficient to explain the varying paces of early privatization among locales experiencing early slowdowns of expansion among local public enterprises. Again, how local officials justified their toleration or support for private business beyond centrally set limits needs to be considered.

Indeed I argue that political risk management holds a key to understanding the focal issues in all three arguments and to enhancing their explanatory power. I illustrate this by taking a close look at the case of Wenzhou, which has been analyzed to support or derive these arguments. The missing link I seek to add back to the story is the fabrication and sustainability of justifications for deviant administrative behavior of local political actors, which is an undertaking conditioned by local history and geography. The peculiar circumstances under which local entrepreneurial forces survived socialism—partly due to the damaging effects of highly divisive politics on local state capacity rather than "benevolence" of indigenous officials—and developed into a strong driving force of early privatization make Wenzhou an "aberration" among locales facing difficulties in sustaining the initially dominant strategy of promoting sales growth in the public sector. This peculiarity nevertheless provides a useful benchmark for understanding the different gradations of early privatization before the mid-1990s.

The Wenzhou Story Retold

Wenzhou is a prefectural city in the southern region of Zhejiang province. It governs four districts (Lucheng, Longwan, Ouhaiand, and Dongtou), two county-rank cities (Ruian and Yueqing), and five counties (Yongjia, Pingyang, Cangnan, Wencheng, and Taishun). Wenzhou's geography is 75% mountains and hills, whereas plains only account for 17.5% of the surface area (*WZSY 1985*, 13). Maps 5.1 and 5.2 show the location of the prefecture and the subprefectural administrative units mentioned above.

MAP 5.1 Map of Zhejiang province

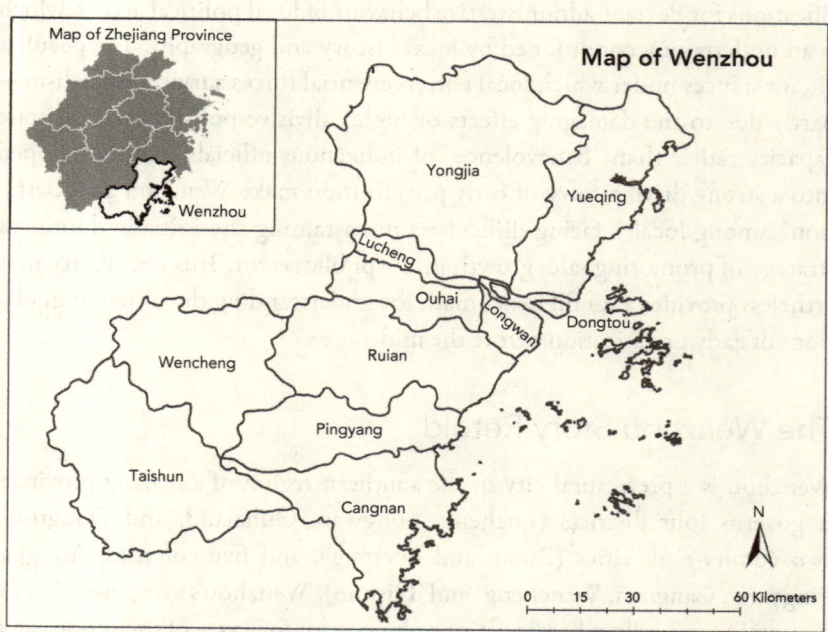

MAP 5.2 Map of Wenzhou

Wenzhou has always been the most populous prefecture in Zhejiang. When economic reforms started in 1978, it had a population of 5.61 million, which was twice the size of the local population (at 2.76 million) in 1949 (*WZSY 1999*, 20). But Wenzhou was also one of the poorest prefectures of the province. In 1978 90% of the local population resided in rural areas (*WZSY 1999*, 20). As shown in table 5.1, GDP per capita was only 238 yuan, significantly below both the provincial average and the national average. Of the three counties in Zhejiang classified by the central government as national poverty-stricken counties in the 1980s and 1990s, two were located in Wenzhou (i.e., Wencheng and Taishun). Table 5.1 further shows weak endowments of the prefecture in terms of literacy level and arable land availability.[3]

In the three decades that followed, however, Wenzhou became one of the most dynamic economic regions in the country and a spearhead of privatization, as widely noted in the literature. To explain this dramatic reversal, it is important to take a close look at the initial economic conditions of the prefecture. Despite the concentration of population in the rural sector, there was a sizable presence of nonfarm activities in the rural economy. Table 5.1 shows that in 1978 per capita output from such activities was lower than the provincial average and that of Jiangsu, which was famed for a thriving nonfarm rural sector led by commune and brigade enterprises. Nonetheless, the percentage was higher than the national average. Furthermore, the rural nonfarm sector of Wenzhou accounted for a slightly higher percentage of rural economic output and a much higher percentage of the rural workforce than the provincial average, suggesting greater intensity of nonfarm activities. Even more noteworthy is the role of private economic elements (as revealed by the last column of table 5.1), which contributed nearly a quarter of the nonfarm output in 1978 and provided the launch pad for the development of the private sector in the reform era. The question is why private economic elements persisted—probably to a greater extent than in many other locales—under (and despite) Maoist socialism, making Wenzhou an "outlier." The answer, as I will show below, lies in the interplay of four factors: the local entrepreneurial tradition, economic hardship, shallow socialist transformation, and the role of local officials.

---

[3]. Jiangsu province is included in the table for the purpose of comparison, as it was a showcase of early marketization led by local public enterprises during the first two decades of China's economic reform (Ho 1994; Whiting 2000).

Table 5.1 Selected indicators on economic conditions in 1978

Unit	% of rural population	GDP per capita (yuan)	Arable land per rural resident (hectare)	% of illiterates among people aged 12 and over (1982 census)	Rural nonfarm output per rural resident (yuan)	Rural nonfarm output as % of total rural output	Rural nonfarm workforce as % of rural workforce	% of commune and brigade enterprises in rural nonfarm output
Wenzhou	90	238	.035	42.5	87	36	19.1	76
Zhejiang	86	331	.055	31.4	100	35	11.2	87
National	82	381	.126	31.9	65	27	8	na
Jiangsu	86	430	.091	34.7	153	42	10	88

Sources: JSSY 1991, 1993; SCTE; CSY 1986; LSYC 1999; ZJSY 1991, 1993, 1999; WZSY 2000.

Surviving Socialism

Before the communist revolution, Wenzhou had a long-standing tradition in handicraft industries and commerce dating back to the sixth century (Shang Jingcai 1989b). Situated on the East China coast, it was opened up as a "treaty port" (*tongshang kouan*) for foreign trade in 1876 as a result of the Chefoo Convention (also known as the Yantai Treaty) between China and the United Kingdom.[4] In the following decades Wenzhou saw the rise and expansion of the production of modern industrial products and became a hub for the distribution of various handmade merchandises from the rural household sector, including homespun cloth, Chinese medicine, dry foods, and seasonings. But political turmoil (especially the war of resistance against Japan during 1937–1945 and the civil war during 1946–1949) in the first half of the twentieth century significantly constrained the growth of the modern sector. In 1949 the ratio of industrial to agricultural output was one to four (Chen Hongyuan 1999, 471).

During the first decade of the People's Republic the local economy recovered and resumed growth. But the socialist transformation in the mid to late 1950s eliminated all formal organizations of private industry and commerce. Yet the entrepreneurial spirit among locals was not wiped out. A major sustaining force was resource constraint. As noted above, farmland is scarce in Wenzhou, and the rugged terrain poses additional difficulty for farming. Moreover, Wenzhou is in the southern end of the province and close to the Taiwan Strait. It was considered by the CCP leadership as part of the "front region" (*qianxian*) in the strategic planning for armed conflict with the KMT regime in Taiwan. The concern about vulnerability to military attacks by external hostile forces limited state investment in the prefecture. In the three decades after 1949 the cumulative investment allocated to the prefecture was 559 million yuan, accounting for only 4.9% of the total received by the ten prefectures in Zhejiang province (Chen 1999, 2–3). As a result of this, modern industry and infrastructure were underdeveloped, and commerce was suppressed. To eke out a meager living and cope with rising pressures from fast population growth, many locals defied government regulations and engaged in various traditional sideline activities based on the household (Shang Jingcai 1989b).

The desire and determination among locals to improve their economic conditions through private production and exchange were further sheltered

---

4. See So and Myers 2011 for discussions on treaty ports and their economic roles in modern China.

by a shallow degree of socialist transformation in Wenzhou. The rugged terrain of the prefecture raised administrative costs, which the poorly funded local state could ill afford to fully absorb, thereby spawning slack in behavioral monitoring and control. Even more challenging to state penetration was the communication barrier. The Wenzhou dialect is one of the most difficult dialects in the Chinese language. Dialect affinity based on mutual intelligibility between Putonghua (the official spoken language) and the Wenzhou dialect features the widest gap among seventeen major dialect groups (Cheng 1997).[5] Underinvestment and fiscal deficiencies of the local government made it impossible to carry out intense propaganda activities and to make fast improvement in education, especially during the Cultural Revolution.[6] The resultant low literacy rate (see table 5.1) exacerbated the difficulty of communication and ideological indoctrination. For many local citizens, especially those in mountainous rural areas, socialism meant coercion rather than moral persuasion because of limited exposure to official propaganda,[7] loss of meaning in translation, and weak reinforcement of the essential messages of Maoism. The lack of strong ambivalence toward pursuing self-interest in light of their traditional frames of reference thus lowered self-imposed hurdles to rule-breaking behavior among local citizens.[8]

As agents of the party-state, however, local officials could still use coercive force to suppress such behavior. Indeed the postrevolution history of Wenzhou featured numerous episodes of fierce crackdowns on the private pursuits of local citizens (Shang Jingcai 1989b). Under the Leninist state local officials were driven to follow the party line so as to avoid punishment, secure their positions, and even advance their careers. But they also faced constraints. The most important constraining factor was the fact that in order to carry out

---

5. The phonological methodology of measuring Chinese dialect affinity was initially developed by William Wang at UC Berkeley in the 1960s (Wang 1970). It provides the basis for Cheng's (1997) study cited here. For a more recent variant (using experimental methods) that produces a similar finding, see Tang 2009.

6. The local public finance gazetteer (Chen Hongyuan 1999, 398–399) shows that Wenzhou's fiscal revenue peaked at 137 million yuan in 1959, when the socialist transformation was completed. It trended down significantly in the following two decades, reaching an all-time low of 23 million yuan in 1975.

7. According to a former commune official in Yongjia county (informant, 14/1997), for example, "In two of the three communes where I worked, the peasants never saw any of the *yangban xi* ["model plays" or theatrical shows filmed during the Cultural Revolution to help popularize Mao's ideas]. In fact I don't think they ever saw any movies at all [during the Mao era]."

8. When Yuan Fanglie (a native of Shandong province) was appointed party secretary of the city in 1981, his peers in the provincial government warned that the Wenzhou people were among the most recalcitrant (*nanguan*) in Zhejiang (author's interview with Yuan Fanglie in June 1998).

the basic functions of public administration and socioeconomic governance local officials needed the cooperation from local citizens. For grass-roots cadres who were members of the local community, there was also the additional social pressure to look after the well-being of their relatives and fellow citizens. When state policies met stiff resistance from local citizens, self-interest calculations could force local officials to retreat from full compliance with the rules imposed by higher-level authorities. There was a delicate balance to strike, though, as bending the rules inevitably involved a political risk. The extent to which this risk could be contained depended greatly on the plausibility and strength of the justifications the rule benders were able to offer.

In Wenzhou extreme economic hardship resulting from local geography, demographics, and state investment policy in the Mao era led many local officials to relax restrictions on private economic activities and to embrace a "moral economic" argument originating from local citizens to justify their rule-bending behavior. An illustration of this can be found in a book-length account, compiled by the Party History Research Office of Yongjia County (ZGYJXWDSYJS 1994),[9] about the repeated attempts by local officials to supplement or even replace collective farming with family farming (the presocialist mode of rural economic organization) during 1956–1978. Although the main motivation of these accounts is to give due credit for local institutional innovation in the county before national agricultural reform in the late 1970s, what they reveal sheds light on the long road of privatization in Wenzhou and beyond.

The gist of the story is that the rule bending by local officials was both driven by the enormous economic survival pressures faced by the locals and justified on the ground of such pressures. A poor and mountainous county with a very unfavorable farmland-population ratio,[10] Yongjia was highly vulnerable to the economic squeezes and mishaps under Maoist socialism. The attempts by local officials to revert to family farming intensified during periods of exogenously elevated economic difficulty, such as the Great Famine in the early 1960s, the heyday of Maoist radicalism in the mid-1970s, and various spells of natural disasters. To reinforce the defense for their behavior, local officials pointed to the chronic dependence of the county on fiscal subsidies and to the immediately demonstrable benefits of family farming, which resulted not only from

---

9. See also Dai Jietian 2002.

10. Before the reform Yongjia was a poverty-stricken county featuring "three mosts" (*sanzui*) in Wenzhou—largest poverty-stricken area, largest poverty-stricken population, and highest level of poverty (Chen Hongyuan 1999, 362).

the inherent incentive effect on agriculture but from the concurrent resumption of sideline activities and private trade that had long been part of the local household economy. There were limits, however, to the extent of rule bending under Mao. Periodic attempts to deviate from the party line were followed by periods of crackdowns and retrenchment. There were also variations in the intensity of rule bending. Some communes and brigades contracted out the bulk of the farmland to households; some contracted out only farmland of lesser quality; and some remained under collective farming all along. Such a variegated pattern of rule bending also holds true for Wenzhou at large. This raises the issue of the composition of local officials.

As noted in Liu (1992)'s study, the local leadership of Wenzhou was dominated by nonnative officials, often broadly referred to as "southbound cadres" (*nanxia ganbu*),[11] after the communist revolution. A survey of the gazetteers of all the cities and counties in Wenzhou reveals that during 1950–1980 79% of the 1,633 leading officials (i.e., party secretaries, deputy party secretaries, chief administrators, and deputy chief administrators) at the prefectural, city, and county levels were nonnative appointees from outside of Zhejiang province;[12] and 68% of them were from the northern province of Shandong. According to the memoir of Wang Fang (2006, 97), who served as acting party secretary of Wenzhou prefecture in 1965–1966 (and party secretary of Zhejiang province in 1983–1987), a special personnel policy of the CCP stipulated that the party secretaries of local governments in the "front region" of China's southeastern coast should preferably be those who had prior experience in the People's Liberation Army (and thus tended to be nonnative persons).[13] Such policy bias inevitably had a dampening effect on the career aspirations

---

11. "Southbound cadres" were recruited from political activists in the "liberated areas" (*jiefang qu*) of Northern China conquered by the CCP before the founding of the PRC. In anticipation of imminent defeat of the KMT, CCP leaders began to make preparations in early 1949 for staffing the new local governments in KMT-occupied provinces south of the Yangtze River. The new recruits for this purpose, totaling close to one hundred thousand, were given brief political training and then dispatched as special contingents attached to the People's Liberation Army (PLA). As PLA forces swept south in 1949–1950, different groups of these political functionaries were charged with the task of helping establish public administration in newly conquered locales. Many of them, along with some regular PLA officers and soldiers discharged from military service, stayed and assumed important posts at various levels of local governments in southern provinces. The term "southbound cadres" therefore is often used more broadly to refer to both types of officials in South and Southeast China who descended from the "liberated areas" of Northern China. See Ding Longjia 2010.

12. It should be noted, though, that for deputy chief administrators the percentage is 52% at the prefectural and city levels and 32% at the county level.

13. Some native officials were former members of the local guerillas, which was generally not recognized as an experience equivalent to serving in the (regular) military force of the CCP.

of native officials. But it is an oversimplification to claim that there was a factional divide between native and nonnative officials and such division led to predictably different (draconian vs. lenient or protective) orientations of regulatory behavior concerning local citizens' private pursuits.

With the potential effect of shortening social distance, native place ties indeed could provide a platform on which to forge and advance common interests. Yet this platform was unstable. Officials with common native place ties could be personal rivals and have quite different policy views and agendas.[14] In Wenzhou, despite the structural bias favoring nonnative officials in prefectural, city, and county governments,[15] neither they nor the native cadres in the local party-state apparatus were a homogenous group.[16] According to a retired official who had worked in various local offices of the CCP in Wenzhou during 1952–1986 (informant, 31/1996), in all the major political movements (e.g., the Anti-Rightist Campaign, the Great Leap Forward, the Socialist Education Movement, and different phases of the Cultural Revolution) in the Mao era, both native and nonnative officials could be found on different gradations of the local political spectrum. There were also cases where native and nonnative cadres cooperated or colluded for common interests, as well as cases where native and nonnative officials sabotaged, outmaneuvered, or conspired against their own kind to advance their careers.

Equally important to note here is that below the county level there were very few cadres from outside of the Wenzhou prefecture (informant, 31/1996; informant, 11/1998; informant, 7/2006).[17] This is where the interactions between the local state and local citizens concentrated. As suggested by the variegated pattern of cadre behavior regarding the reversion to family farming

---

14. Among the top leaders of the CCP, for example, Mao Zedong (CCP chairman), Liu Shaoqi (president), and Peng Dehuai (defense minister) were all natives of Hunan province. But Mao openly clashed with Peng and dismissed him during the Great Leap Forward campaign (1958–1960). Mao and Liu became archrivals during the ensuing years that ushered in the Cultural Revolution (1966–1976).

15. It should be noted that the nonnative officials were not even all from the same province (not to mention the same county). While a majority of them were from Shandong, several of the prefectural, city, and county leaders in Wenzhou were from Hebei, northern Jiangsu, Henan, and Anhui.

16. In Yongjia county, for example, the farmland contracting arrangement for household-based farming was started in 1956 by Li Yunhe in collaboration with Dai Jietian. Li was a "southbound cadre" from Shandong and a deputy county party secretary in charge of agriculture. Dai was a native official from the nearby Ruian county who headed a work team on rural affairs in the county government. Both of them were purged in 1958; so was Li Maogui, the county party secretary (a "southbound cadre" from Shandong too) who approved of the arrangement.

17. In all the city and county gazetteers of Wenzhou the native locale (*jiguan*) of almost every leading official is listed. But this item is not included in all the township gazetteers of Wenzhou that have been published, probably because of the nearly uniform local origins of the commune/township leaders.

in Yongjia county, native officials did not demonstrate behavioral uniformity. Indeed, some of them stayed with collective farming throughout the Mao era, and some even played an active role in the investigation and punishment of the native officials who bent the rules (informant, 14/1997). Shifting alliances in response to changes in the macropolitical environment, rather than factional loyalty along the native-nonnative divide, appear to have been the predominant force that drove local politics.

What, then, was the impact (if any) of the local political elite composition on private economic activities in Wenzhou during the Mao era? The personnel policy bias favoring nonnative officials in the top echelon of local leadership at the prefectural, city, and county levels added complications to local politics. That, I argue, was probably a contributing factor to making Wenzhou one of the most conflict-ridden regions in China during the Cultural Revolution, *which consequently undermined the governing capacity of the local state and further weakened the propensity of local citizens to comply with state authority.*

As noted above, the native-nonnative divide may blur the fact that neither group of officials was internally homogenous. But the divide did matter to local political life. It demarcated the center and periphery of power in the local party-state establishment. Yet it neither eliminated interdependence between establishment members across the divide nor provided any effective mechanism to fortify solidarity within the two sides. It was possible for players from the periphery to enhance their power through ad hoc alliances with those in the center, and for those in the center to outshine and outmaneuver their "competitive comrades" by cultivating support from the periphery. Relative to those in regions (e.g., northern and northeastern China) where the native-nonnative divide was not as stark, power relations in Wenzhou were therefore more prone to fragmentation because of an enhanced probability of additional permutations of political alliance formation and change (e.g., native-native, nonnative-nonnative, *and* native-nonnative at and across different levels of authority). The added nodes of discrete interests increased the fluidity of power struggles among the local political elite. At times of structural instability and open conflict, such fluidity could increase the difficulty of power consolidation and thus become a major debilitating force for the local state.

The history of the Cultural Revolution in Wenzhou appears to bear this out.[18] In most other regions of the country, the violent period of the revolution

---

18. For a useful account of the Cultural Revolution in Zhejiang province (including Wenzhou), see Forster 1990.

ended in 1968–1969, when the old government had been overthrown by rebels and martial law was imposed by the military forces that Mao sent to restore political order. But violence in Wenzhou continued through the mid-1970s. There were three massive waves of armed conflict with heavy casualties during the extended revolution (1967–1968, 1972–1973, and 1974–1975), as well as frequent and numerous rounds of personnel reshuffling at all levels of the local party-state. After Mao's death in October 1976, there were further rounds of purges to eradicate the remnants of "leftist" radicals and "troublemakers" in the revolution. Deeply involved in these conflicts and struggles were players from both sides of the divide, who jousted for political advantage by repositioning and regrouping themselves in response to major shifts in national politics (e.g., the purges after the Lin Biao Incident in 1971 and the "Anti–Lin Biao Anti-Confucius Campaign" in 1974). In the words of a former middle-ranked official who worked in the city government of Wenzhou during the revolution (informant, 7/1998):

> There were all kinds of factions [*paixi*] back then. . . . It's true that the northerners always had the advantage of holding leading positions, but it's hard to say there was a "northern faction." The factional conflicts were definitely not just a matter of native-versus-nonnative struggle. . . . Many of the fighting groups had both native and nonnative participants, sometimes openly, sometimes from behind the scenes. Some people switched sides too. Even those in power at any given time were not united among themselves. Few lasted long.

The open and covert conflicts and frictions in the local party-state during the Cultural Revolution increased inconsistencies in economic policy and weakened the abilities of local cadres to control the behavior of local citizens despite continued and even intensified reliance on the use of coercion. The chaos caused by power struggles and the naked manipulation by political opportunists for self-interest also exposed the dark nature of the Maoist system. This seriously undermined the legitimacy of the state authority and further hardened the determination of many local citizens to defy or overcome restrictions on the efforts to change their economic conditions. During the Cultural Revolution, a large number of local residents broke the ban on spatial movement and traveled away from Wenzhou to earn illegal income by peddling small items of merchandise and providing various urban services, such as haircutting, shoe repairing, tailoring, and quilt fluffing (Chen Hongyuan 1999; Shang Jingca 1989b).

The disruption and stoppage of production in urban public enterprises amid the long-lasting political turmoil also created opportunities for rural nonfarm activities to grow. From 1971 to 1977 the industrial output from commune and brigade enterprises (CBEs) increased by 81% (Shang Jingcai 1989b, 309). Unlike CBEs in the southern Jiangsu region that drew on the strength (e.g., human resources, technology, supplies, and subcontracting opportunities) of state-owned enterprises in nearby urban centers, CBEs in Wenzhou had to cope on their own, especially when local SOEs were paralyzed during the extended revolution. What they did instead was to draw on private economic elements. Some farmed out their work to rural households; some simply resold household-made products for a fee; and most of them relied on the hundreds and thousands of largely private supply and sales agents (*gongxiao yuan*) for securing orders and inputs and for selling products (Chen Hongyuan 1999). There were also various entirely private, "underground" factories, construction teams, and retail shops. In 1977, for example, some forty-seven hundred regular private retailers were on the tracking list of local authorities in Wenzhou, and more operated off the official record (Shang Jingcai 1989b, 309).

The "Wenzhou Model" of (Early) Privatization

Understanding the mechanisms that kept local entrepreneurial forces from being stifled by Maoist socialism helps explain the development of the private sector in Wenzhou after 1978. This process was an outgrowth of the persistent private economic elements in the prereform rural household sector, but it was by no means a smooth sail. There was continued suppression of the private sector after the start of economic reforms, as the official policy was to promote economic growth through public enterprises. In May 1982, for example, there was a major crackdown on private business in Wenzhou. Eight prominent entrepreneurs, known among locals as *ba dawang*, or "the eight kingpins," in the township of Liushi were given jail sentences for engaging in "speculative buying and selling" (*touji daoba*), which was an economic crime at that time.

The crackdown campaign took place under the aegis of Yuan Fanglie, the party secretary of Wenzhou.[19] Yuan was appointed to the post in 1981 to clean up the Maoist legacies of political divisiveness and to turn the local economy

---

19. Discussion in this paragraph and the following one is based on author's interviews with Yuan in June 1998.

around. A former vice governor of Zhejiang and a "southbound cadre" from Shandong,[20] he was a pragmatic official as well as a shrewd observer of the party line. When he first arrived, he had yet to consolidate his power base,[21] and the macropolitical environment was still quite hostile to private business. While he went along with the prosecution and sentencing of the "eight kingpins," which was initiated by a special investigation team from the provincial government, Yuan quickly realized that the local entrepreneurial force was so strong that any attempt to suppress it would likely be futile. Equally important was the realization that given the weak base of SOEs and the lack of independent ability for CBEs to grow, private business held a key to local economic growth, which was the mandate of the local government in the postreform era. During the year following the "eight-kingpin incident," for example, industrial output grew only by a lackluster 3% in Wenzhou as a whole, whereas it shrank by 53% in Liushi, the township where the incident occurred.

Concerns about the negative impact of the incident on the local economy led Yuan to make a series of policy adjustments concerning the private sector. In the month following the incident, the city government issued a note cautioning against expanding the scope of the crackdown campaign to "legitimate" businesses. In December 1982 it convened a mass meeting with some 1,200 representatives of private businesses. Thirty-five of the attendees were invited to share their stories of success, and 171 were honored with a plaque of praise for their contributions to the local economy. The political message was clear: private business would not only be tolerated but encouraged. In a number of internal documents that followed, city government departments and lower-level governments were instructed to facilitate the growth

---

20. Yuan was the last "southbound cadre" leading the city. After his departure in 1985, none of the party secretaries of Wenzhou was a northerner. At the county level, the fading of nonnative leaders started immediately after the Cultural Revolution. According to the rosters of county leaders in the county gazetteers of Wenzhou, by 1984 all the county party secretaries were natives of Zhejiang. That effectively brought to an end the three-decade-long divide between native and nonnative leaders in local governments.

21. Before Yuan's appointment, there had already been several rounds of purges throughout the local governments in Zhejiang to remove from leading posts officials actively involved in the Cultural Revolution. The merger of the prefectural government and the city government in 1981 gave Yuan a further opportunity to realign the local leadership by excluding those he called "problematic cadres" from the downsized party-state establishment. The massive retirement campaign launched by Deng Xiaoping during 1982–1983 (Manion 1993) resulted in the removal of additional old-timers in Wenzhou's local leadership teams. While seeing these developments as conducive to reducing political divisiveness, Yuan considered the shift of policy focus from class struggle to economic development, especially the new political performance assessment system, to be the most important factor that helped rebuild and consolidate local party-state authority.

of self-employment, which was the only legally allowed form of private economic activities at that time. In January 1984 the city government reversed the verdict on the "eight kingpins" and set them free. In response, private business rebounded.

Yuan was transferred back to the provincial government in December 1985 (first as head of the Political and Legal Affairs Committee of the CCP and then as head of the provincial court). His successor, Dong Chaocai, was a native of Jiangshan county in western Zhejiang and had been the party secretary of Jinhua prefecture before the appointment. Although he was instructed by the provincial party authority to try to restore the strength of SOEs in Wenzhou, he came to the same realization as Yuan Fanglie after working on the job for a few months (Dong Chaocai 2005). That is, in Wenzhou the private sector was both unrelentingly resilient and indispensable. During his tenure through January 1990, Dong continued Yuan's approach toward private business. Moreover, under his leadership a number of local regulations were instituted to facilitate the expansion and governance of the private economy in 1987. Among these was a provisional regulation that legalized the longstanding practice of *guahu*—a fee-based service where public enterprises provided organizational sponsorship to private business people who had no legal-person status under the existing system and thus had difficulty in opening bank accounts, fulfilling bookkeeping requirements, signing contracts, and issuing receipts. Also important was a set of provisional guidelines on the registration and issuance of business licenses to private economic entities with a workforce exceeding the legal limit (of no more than seven people), which effectively granted formal recognition to these organizations before the lifting of the limit in 1988. Another document, entitled *Provisional Guidelines on Issues Concerning Rural Shareholding Cooperatives*, defined entities that pooled funds from more than two shareholders as shareholding cooperatives—a new and politically less sensitive category between "collective" and "private" enterprises, thereby creating an opportunity for private business owners to gain a legitimate cover for larger-scale operations. In the following six years shareholding cooperatives proliferated in Wenzhou and provided a vital organizational platform for the elevation and expansion private economic activities beyond the confines of the household.

The accommodating policy environment under Yuan and Dong was conducive to the fast growth of the private sector in Wenzhou before it became a national trend, as can be seen from figure 5.1. What drove their decisions was the benefit of private business for the performance of the local economy, which on average grew by 13.2% per year during 1981–1990 (*WZSY 1999*, 25),

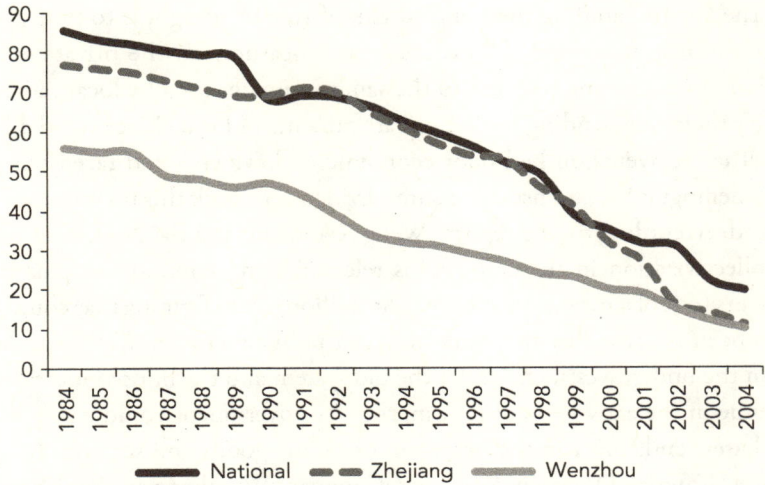

FIGURE 5.1 Share of public enterprises in nonfarm workforce, 1984–2004
Sources: CSY 2001; ZJSY 1999; WZSY 1999.

higher than the provincial average of 12.7% and the national average of 9.9% (ZJSY 2010, 7; CSY 2010, 22). Although both Yuan and Dong were subsequently given "lateral transfers" to similarly ranked positions in the provincial government instead of being promoted, they probably would not have fared better if they had chosen to adopt a hard-line policy against the private sector.

The reason, as Yuan explained more than a decade after his departure, is that "the likelihood of promotion would be next to zero if the local economy was a big mess."[22] As was the case under the prereform system, however, the act of tolerating or even facilitating private business was politically risky. Indeed throughout their tenures both Yuan and Dong faced warnings, criticisms, and challenges from conservative elements in the central leadership, the provincial party establishment, and the local party-state apparatus. As Yuan told Huang Huang, the party secretary of Anhui province who during a visit to Wenzhou in 1985 expressed admiration for Yuan's boldness in dealing with the private sector, "There would be a political price to pay" if the matter was not "handled properly" (Huang Huang 2005).

---

22. As to why he was not promoted, his answer was: "I would have fared much worse if not for the policies I adopted. Besides, I was too old [note: he was born in 1929] for a more important position. Deng Xiaoping said we old cadres should let younger people take over" (author's interview with Yuan in June 1998).

The key to handling the political risk of rule bending was to find strong justifications. To defend the extraordinary measures on the private sector, both Yuan and Dong resorted to the same argument used by local cadres to justify their rule bending for the private pursuits of local citizens in the Mao era. That is, Wenzhou had poor economic endowments and faced tremendous demographic and fiscal pressures. Evidence to back this up was not hard to find. According to one report (Wang Xiaoqiang and Bai Nansheng 1983), decollectivization in the early 1980s released some 1 million surplus rural laborers (out of a rural workforce of 1.85 million) from farming that could not have been absorbed by the weak nonfarm public sector in Wenzhou. Also, given the underinvestment under the old system and the limited increases in revenue in the early years of reform, the city government could barely make the barest ends meet in the provision of public goods and services. In 1982 six (i.e., Yongjia, Dongtou, Pingyang, Cangnan, Wencheng, and Taishun) of the nine counties under the prefectural city were unable to cover their basic spending with the revenue they collected (*ZJSY 2010*, 543–648). On the other hand, thanks to the remarkable potency of local entrepreneurial forces, there was also immediately demonstrable evidence about the positive role of the private sector in response to the policy adjustments. In 1981 the public sector accounted for some 73% of the net gain in nonfarm employment; in 1990 all the net gain came from the private sector (*WZSY 1999*, 36, 75). Of the six counties with a budget deficit in 1982, two (Pingyang and Cangnan) generated positive fiscal flows in 1990, and two (Yongjia and Dongtou) reduced the gap between revenue and spending by nearly 50% (*ZJSY 2010*, 543–648).

The political risk that Yuan and Dong took was also a calculated one. Both were fully aware of the evolving nature of the CCP's reform policies (as epitomized in the saying "crossing the river by touching stones"), as well as the division and cleavage within the central leadership over the direction, pace, and depth of reforms. They bet, by and large correctly, on the predominance of proreform leaders and figured that offense would be their best defense. In Yuan's words, "If you always hide your *xifu* (wife or daughter-in-law) from public view, people will think she must be ugly." He seized upon every possible opportunity to raise the profile of Wenzhou through the media and to pitch the case to visiting dignitaries from the proreform camp, including Premier Zhao Yiyang and the influential scholar Fei Xiaotong (who subsequently wrote approvingly about Wenzhou's private economy and served as a deputy chairman on the Standing Committee of the National People's Congress during 1988–1998). In May 1985 the term *wenzhou moshi* or "Wenzhou model" (of household-based economic development) appeared in an article by a reporter from *Jiefang Ribao* (*Liberation Daily*) in Shanghai after interviewing Yuan and touring the city. To capture the attention from higher levels, Yuan used the term to denote a path of economic development parallel to the *sunan moshi*, or "southern Jiangsu model" (of marketization led by public enterprises) in a report submitted to a proreform think tank (the Rural Policy Research Office of the CCP Secretariat) of the CCP. In 1987 Dong successfully lobbied the central government to make Wenzhou one of the twelve "experimental zones of rural reforms," where the local governments were given a certain degree of latitude in experimenting with more liberal policies of reform. This gave the city leadership an extra buffer against the political risk of going beyond centrally authorized limits.

The reshuffling of the central leadership following the June Fourth Incident in 1989 and the subsequent slowdown of reforms cast a dark cloud over Wenzhou. Six months later, Dong Chaocai was transferred out of the city, though he was not demoted.[23] Nonetheless, the policy path that he and Yuan had started continued to be followed by his successors, who used the same defense to justify their treatment of the local private sector. Deng Xiaoping's call for the resumption of reforms and opening in 1992 shifted the focus of national policy from politics back to economic development (Fewsmith 2008), thereby taking some of the pressures off the local leaders in Wenzhou. But it was the exhaustion of the once dominant strategy to promote sales expansion of public enterprises in many other regions, as discussed in the preceding chapter, that before long rendered moot the controversy over Wenzhou and led to the start of the endgame for the dominance of public ownership.

---

23. Dong was transferred out to head the provincial Economic Reform Commission. Other than the unfavorable political climate at that time, age might be a factor for his remaining career in officialdom after Wenzhou. Born in 1932, he was fifty-eight when the reassignment came in 1990. In contrast, Dong's successor, Liu Xirong, has had much greater upward mobility despite his extensive work experience (1981–1991) in the controversial policy environment of Wenzhou. Born in 1942, Liu was a deputy party secretary (1983–1989) and a deputy mayor (1983–1988) in charge of economic affairs under Yuan Fanglie. He was promoted to the position of mayor in 1988, when Lu Shengliang, the fifty-nine-year-old incumbent, was semiretired to chair the local people's congress. Liu took over Dong's position as party secretary in 1990. A year later he was appointed as the head of the provincial Discipline Inspection Commission of the CCP. He was subsequently elevated to be a deputy provincial governor, a deputy provincial party secretary, and eventually a deputy secretary of the Central Discipline Inspection Commission of the CCP. It is interesting and a bit ironic that Liu's deputy, Chen Wenxian, who was mayor when Liu Xirong left Wenzhou to head the provincial antigraft body, was not promoted to succeed him. Chen was later jailed on corruption charges, in part related to his tenure in Wenzhou. His case is a reminder of a parallel force influencing the relationship between local political and economic actors (Lin 2001).

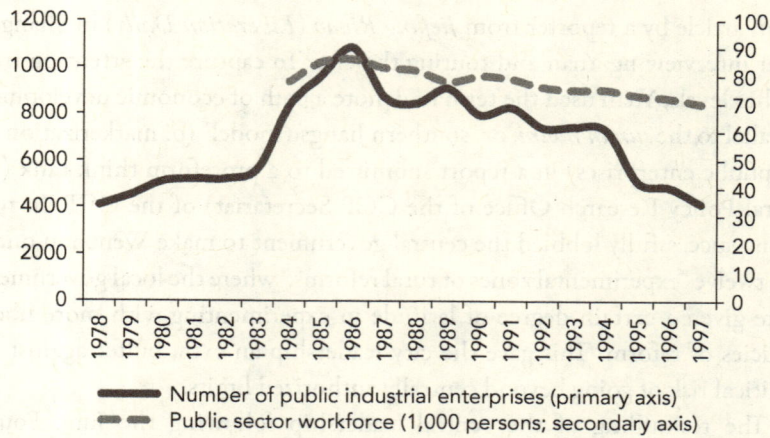

FIGURE 5.2 Size of Wenzhou's public sector, 1978–1997
Sources: SYZJS; WZSY 1999.

It should be noted, though, that the early privatization in Wenzhou was mainly driven by faster growth of private business rather than a drastic decline of public enterprises in the 1980s and early 1990s. Figure 5.2 shows that the local public sector experienced substantial expansion through the mid-1980s, suggesting that like those elsewhere, the local authorities in Wenzhou initially sought to make heavy use of public enterprises as vehicles of economic growth. The chart also shows that the subsequent erosion of the public sector was gradual. It was not until 1995 that massive closure of factories began, and it was not until after 1997 that significant downsizing of the public sector workforce took place. Table 5.2 further shows that the extent of early privatization also varied among different counties in Wenzhou, though even the county with the slowest pace still had higher level of privatization than the provincial average (to be shown in the next section). In particular, the extent of privatization was generally lower in economically less developed counties (with the exception of Lucheng District, the old city center and home to the majority of the larger SOEs and urban collective enterprises established before the reform). This is interesting in that underdevelopment was a major argument used by the prefectural leaders to justify their rule bending for private business and, given the political shield provided at the prefectural level, it would have been less risky for the poor counties to go farther beyond the national policy limits.

The twist here may be a reflection of the context-specific, multidimensional cost-benefit calculation by local officials in face of the lasting impact of history and changing structural constraints. In comparison with other

Table 5.2 Selected statistics on cities and counties in Wenzhou

Administrative unit	% of public enterprises in industrial output in 1993	% of mountains and hills in surface area	Industrial output per capita in 1949 (yuan)	Arable land per capita in 1980 (hectare)	GDP per capita in 1980 (yuan)	Industrial SOE output per capita in 1980 (yuan)	Budgetary balance in 1980
Wenzhou prefecture	48	78	16	.038	312	71	+
Wenzhou city			34	.043	602	284	+
Lucheng	63						
Longwan	16						
Ouhai	37						
Ruian	44	67	24	.039	316	40	+
Yueqing	19	72	15	.036	322	32	+
Yongjia	48	86	13	.036	204	13	–
Dongtou	67	89	5	.011	191	29	–
Pingyang	50	63	19	.043	230	25	–
Cangnan	60	67		.030			
Wencheng	62	83	10	.033	206	17	–
Taishun	62	93	6	.038	201	13	–

Note: Cangnan was separated from Pingyang in 1981. Information is unavailable for some pre-1981 indicators.
Sources: SYZJS; Chen 1989.

counties in Wenzhou, entrepreneurial forces were relatively weaker in these counties, which have more rugged terrains and thus economically less favorable natural environment than those with more flat areas and shorter distances to the coast and city center (where industrial and commercial activities traditionally clustered). The three counties (Dongtou, Wencheng, and Taishun) with the highest levels of remaining public ownership, for example, had the lowest levels of per capita industrial output in 1949. The initial weakness in the modern sector, coupled with their geographic disadvantages,[24] tended to constrain the capacity of these counties to boost the level of local private industry and commerce quickly, even with more accommodating policies, and to develop a "virtuous cycle" of positive feedback.

In the meantime, the existing public enterprises could still serve as useful vehicles of revenue generation as long as the near-term benefits (taxes—especially indirect taxes—fees, and savings on severance expenses and social governance cost associated with layoffs of existing employees) were not outweighed by the immediate costs (interest payments, nondeferrable principal repayments, and subsidies for losses). Moreover, some of the counties with slower paces of early privatization received fixed fiscal subsidies in the 1980s and early 1990s because they were included on the national list of poverty-stricken counties (Wencheng and Taishun), the provincial list of poverty-stricken counties (Yongjia), or the provincial list of less developed counties (Dongtou, which was recategorized as a district in 2015). These subsidies, however, were conditional on their fulfilling the revenue targets specified in the fiscal contracts with the provincial government. Before 1994 fiscal subsidies were largely administered as lump-sum payments without clearly earmarked spending stipulations. That left open an opportunity for the recipient governments to channel part of the funds to facilitating the cash flow of the local enterprises they owned (especially SOEs and urban collective enterprises at the county level) so that these enterprises could continue to contribute to the generation of revenue (especially sales-related taxes) required by the fiscal contracts. This loop of financing extended the longevity of some local public enterprises. But it faced increasing difficulty with the expansion of more clearly earmarked spending programs in fiscal subsidies after 1993, thus weakening the sustainability and relative significance of the remaining local public sector. The policy behavior of different local officials in the Wenzhou region, therefore, was shaped not only by their broadly shared history but by varying

---

24. Dongtou consists of islands, and Wencheng and Taishun are the most mountainous counties in Wenzhou.

strategic calculations of what would serve their best interest in concrete and evolving subregional settings.

Beyond Wenzhou

The story of Wenzhou's early privatization yields some useful clues for further exploring the variations in the evolving fate of private ownership in the reform era. What it suggests is that three important factors combined to influence the calculus of local political actors, thereby conditioning the development of private business before the exhaustion of public enterprises in the mid-1990s as the leading force of marketization. First, the tendency of local governments to tolerate or even facilitate the private sector hinged upon the initial strength and sustainability of the local public sector, which posed a major competing incentive in their decision-making. Second, to benefit from economic development led by the private sector, local political actors needed to tackle the pertinent cost—that is, the political risk of rule bending. Doing so required plausible and strong justifications, which in turn depended greatly on the economic conditions shaped by local geography and history. Third, the strength of the local entrepreneurial forces could directly affect the intensity of the initial impetus for rule bending for private business, as well as the delivery of immediately demonstrable results necessary for sustaining and expanding the rules bent.

To see these implications from a broader view, it is useful to take a comparative snapshot of Wenzhou and other regions in Zhejiang province. The year for this comparison is 1993, when industrial SOE employment ceased to increase and the fiscal contract system between central and local governments was about to end. Table 5.3 shows that in 1993 the prefectures in northern Zhejiang mostly had higher levels of remaining public ownership than those in southern Zhejiang. The strength in public enterprises at the start of economic reforms was probably what retarded early privatization in the northern region despite its strong entrepreneurial traditions (especially in places like Ningbo and Hangzhou) before the revolution and despite efforts to revive such traditions after the start of economic reforms (Shang Jingcai 1989).[25]

---

25. It should be noted, though, that during the Mao era there was more effective suppression of private economic pursuits in Ningbo and Hangzhou than in Wenzhou. This prevented the quick formation of *a critical mass* of entrepreneurial forces at the start of economic reforms. See the local gazetteers of these prefectures for accounts of the local economic policies under Mao and the revival and growth of private business in the post-Mao era.

Table 5.3 Selected statistics on privatization and initial economic conditions in prefectural cities of Zhejiang

Region	% of public sector in industrial output in 1993	% of space being mountains & hills	Industrial output per capita in 1949 (yuan)	Arable land per rural resident in 1980 (hectare)	GDP per capita in 1980 (yuan)	SOE industrial output per capita in 1980 (yuan)	Nonfarm output per rural resident in 1980 (yuan)	% of commune and brigade enterprises in nonfarm output in 1978	% of counties with budget deficit in 1980
Zhejiang	79	70	19	.055	470	216	131	87	22
Northern Zhejiang									
Hangzhou	79	66	43	.055	791	644	172	94	0
Ningbo	78	50	40	.065	634	184	288	89	0
Jiaxing	83	10	35	.095	610	318	204	96	0
Huzhou	85	39	20	.075	504	208	146	90	0
Zhoushan	80	43		.031	554	138		84	0
Shaoxing	80	62	16	.074	433	145	157		
Southern Zhejiang									
Wenzhou	48	78	16	.038	312	71	137	74	60
Jinhua	51	88	10	.052	371	136	109	79	13
Quzhou	82	85	11	.055	387	193	93	87	40
Lishui	57	88	6	.051	298	63	72	89	63
Taizhou	45	73	9	.041	338	65	107	72	25

Sources: CSY 1998; ZJSY 1987; SYZJS; gazetteers of the cities included in the table.

In contrast the generally faster paces of early privatization in the southern region were correlated with less favorable resource endowment (topography and land-population ratio), poorer initial economic conditions (industrial output, GDP per capita, and fiscal imbalances), and weaker initial strength of public enterprises (SOEs and commune and brigade enterprises). As the Wenzhou case illustrates, all these conditions were unfavorable to sustaining the expansion of local public enterprises but conducive to justifying rule bending for private business.

A twist that merits attention is that southern prefectures in Zhejiang had lower levels of industrial output per capita in 1949. This raises the question of how local entrepreneurial forces might have mattered to the pace of early privatization. What the lower levels reflect is the relative weakness of southern prefectures in modern industries at the time of the communist revolution, as the output from household-based handicraft activities was counted as part of agriculture in statistical reporting. Ironically, privately owned modern industries tended to be more completely wiped out during the subsequent socialist transformation than household sidelines in rural areas. The latter tended to be more difficult to eradicate, especially in face of shallow state penetration and deeply divisive local politics in places like Wenzhou, thereby offering a niche for the persistence of private economic pursuits. For the initial burst of entrepreneurial forces after reform, what mattered most was the private economic elements that had managed to survive socialism, rather than the level of prerevolution industrialization per se. In this regard, southern prefectures appear to have had an edge, as indicated by their lower levels of CBE share in nonfarm output in 1978.

A case in point is Taizhou. Located on the coast and with a vibrant precommunist local business culture, this prefecture had a geographic and socioeconomic profile very similar to that of neighboring Wenzhou (table 5.4). It was also a fast mover in early privatization. As in Wenzhou, local politics in Taizhou featured dominance by "southbound" officials and serious divisiveness (which affected local state governance capacity) during the Mao era, as can be seen from the accounts of recent local history in city and county gazetteers.[26] But early privatization in Taizhou proceeded without much fanfare during the 1980s and early 1990s. Such a low profile might have partly been the result of a calculated strategy to free-ride on the initial political risks Wenzhou had taken. In the words of a former deputy mayor (informant,

---

26. For a list of the local gazetteers at different administrative levels (city, district, and county) of Taizhou, see http://www.tzfz.org.cn/tzfz/class/?12.html&pcid=12.

16/1997), "We were always half a step behind Wenzhou in these matters [concerning the private sector]. That gave us an opportunity to steer clear of the land mines, so we were more than happy not to take the lead."[27]

On the other hand, post-1949 industrial buildup could have implications for the pace of early privatization. In 1993, for example, Quzhou retained the highest level of public ownership among the prefectures in southern Zhejiang. It had been given sizable industrial investment in the Mao era and developed into a major base of Zhejiang's chemical industry dominated by large SOEs. That investment had a spillover effect on the development of local support industries, including those organized both as SOEs and as collective enterprises, as well as an enhancing effect on the local economy.[28] In 1980 Quzhou had the highest GDP per capita in the southern region, though it remained far below the levels of the prefectures in northern Zhejiang. Although the prefecture is more mountainous than Wenzhou, the relief brought about by the modern sector (e.g., through revenue it generated) helped alleviate local economic hardship, making it difficult to justify policies favoring the private sector if attempts had been made in that regard during the early years of reform. In the meantime, as an inland region with limited transportation links, Quzhou did not have a significant presence of modern industry and commerce before the revolution, as indicated by the low level of industrial output per capita in 1949; nor did it have a strong tradition in rural handicraft industries, as may be inferred from the low level of nonfarm output per capita in 1980. That reality affected the development of entrepreneurial forces that otherwise could have brought about significant pressures for early liberalization of policies toward the private sector. Like many other locales in the country the local public sector experienced significant expansion in the 1980s, especially the second half of the decade (1985–1989), when industrial output on average grew at 19% per annum for SOEs and 41% for collective enterprises (*SYZJS*, 2:1403). The growth rate of these enterprises sharply slowed down to an average of 11% and 16% respectively during 1990–1997 years. But public enterprises, while experiencing some erosion, remained dominant through 1997.

---

27. A fuller account of early privatization in Taizhou cannot be offered here because of space limitations.

28. This investment also had some spillover to the cities and counties in Jinhua (as reflected in the higher SOE industrial output per capita than Wenzhou), which governed Quzhou until 1985. But most of the state-owned industries there were small and medium enterprises, which did not fare well amid growing competition after reform (Shang Jingcai 1989b). Moreover, the rural nonfarm sector of Jinhua had greater degree of surviving private economic elements at the start of reform, which was probably a major contributing factor to its faster pace of privatization than Quzhou (Shang Jingcai 1989b).

An equally interesting case in the southern region is Lishui, a prefecture adjacent to Wenzhou (map 5.1). A landlocked mountainous region, it has more rugged terrain and higher elevation than Wenzhou and has always been the poorest prefecture in the province. Such severe economic hardship should have provided a very strong ground for justifying early privatization. Yet that does not appear to be what had happened. In 1993 it had the second highest share of industrial output accounted for by local public enterprises in the southern region (table 5.4). Throughout the 1980s and early 1990s, when Wenzhou experienced fast growth in the local private sector, Lishui saw continued dominance of the public sector. Unlike Quzhou, which had received sizable government investment for the development of the chemicals industry in the prereform era, Lishui only had a moderate buildup of small and medium-sized SOEs and collective enterprises located in and around county seats in the region, which accounted for only 1.7% of the provincial industrial output in 1980 (*ZJSESY 1986*, 193, 596). Like many other regions in the country, however, both SOEs and collective enterprises experienced significant growth in the early years of reform, with an average rate of 25.7% and 29.8% per year during 1984–1988 respectively. The growth rate slowed down to 18.6% and 6.2% per year respectively during 1989–1993 (*ZJSESY 1986*, 193, 596; *ZJSY 1988*, 383–384; *ZJSY 1989*, 420–422; *ZJSY 1990*, 424–426; *ZJSY 1991*, 481–482; *ZJSY 1992*, 472–473; *ZJSY 1993*, 484; *ZJSY 1994*, 403). Yet the private sector did not achieve a concurrent growth that was fast enough to overtake the public sector as the leading force of the local economy.

The contrast between Wenzhou and Lishui was a reflection of the different attitudes of their local governments toward private business. Despite severe economic hardship, local authorities in Lishui sought to rely primarily on public enterprises to address their political and economic interests. An important reason for this is that entrepreneurial forces were much weaker in Lishui at the start of economic reforms. As can be seen from table 5.4, it had not only the lowest level of industrial development in 1949 but the lowest private share in nonfarm rural economic activities in the southern region at the start of reforms. As a result of such initial conditions, private economic elements neither generated strong enough pressures for drastic relaxation of existing restrictions nor demonstrated (through their rule-breaking behavior) sufficient supporting evidence for local officials to justify such a move. It is not surprising that local officials pursued a "play safe" strategy. As a leading official in the prefectural Economic Commission explained (informant, 18/1996):

We are different from Wenzhou. Even though we are neighboring regions, our starting point was lower. Our SOEs and collective enterprises were the weakest in the province, but they were the strongest part of the local economy. We have to count on them to invigorate Lishui's reform and development. . . . I must also admit that, overall, private entrepreneurs in Wenzhou are savvier and more enterprising. They have a long-standing tradition from before the liberation [in 1949]. They pushed the government hard, oftentimes by doing things illegally, yet the [Wenzhou] government has managed the situation quite well, and as a result their economy has prospered. That's not the case here—we have overseen more orderly changes. Of course, we have gradually relaxed the rules on private business as well, partly by learning from Wenzhou. We cannot go too far and too fast, though. What would happen if we took big steps to promote private business, but the private sector did not quite measure up? That would be very risky.

However, the expansion of public enterprises in Lishui during the 1980s and early 1990s did come with a cost that became increasingly unbearable. In 1993 the debt-equity ratio was 287% for industrial SOEs and 242% for industrial collective enterprises at or above the level of township; the percentages of loss-making enterprises were 37% and 46% for these groups respectively.[29] The fiscal restructuring and banking reform in 1994 dealt a further blow to the local public sector, making it harder to keep public enterprises afloat through manipulation of tax burdens and to leverage bank loans. The majority of local SOEs nevertheless managed to linger on until the massive privatization in 1997–1998.[30] But the decline of collective enterprises quickly became irresistible. The total number of collective enterprises in the industrial sector fell from an all-time high of 1,823 in 1992 to 1,013 in 1995 and then to 447 in 1997 (*SYZJS*, 2:1810).

Some of the causal links suggested by the Wenzhou case and the cursory cross-sectional comparisons within Zhejiang are examined more systematically in a data analysis with greater geographic coverage and time span (Li and

---

29. These figures are calculated using firm-level data from the 1993 annual industrial survey conducted by the National Bureau of Statistics. Earlier data on total liability are unavailable because 1993 was the first year for the adoption of a Western-style accounting standard. A description of the data is posted at the book site.

30. The total number of industrial SOEs in Lishui was 261 in 1993, 189 in 1997, 118 in 1998, 81 in 1999, and 59 in 2000 (*SYZJS*, 2:1810).

Lin 2016). It finds a strong correlation between early movers in private business in the post-Mao era and their prior (unauthorized) involvement in private economic pursuits under Mao. Another finding is that early slowdown of sales growth among local public enterprises and deterioration of their financial health and local fiscal conditions are not strong predictors of early privatization. But their effects on early privatization are enhanced when proxies for both local economic hardship and strength of entrepreneurial forces at the start of reform are included in the regression analysis. These results are consistent with what the Wenzhou story reveals. Finally, also noteworthy is a finding from another data analysis, mentioned earlier in the chapter (Chen and Lin 2016), of factors affecting the promotion of prefectural officials. That is, during the 1990s there was no significant difference in the likelihood of promotion between leaders in locales with early privatization and those in locales with a strong and predominant public sector. Rather it was "adequate" economic performance, however achieved, that served as a necessary enabling condition for the career advancement of local leaders. This sheds some light on the motivating forces behind local officials' behavior where the initially dominant strategy played out differently.

Summary

In a widely quoted remark, Theodore Schultz (1964) had the following words about the impact of institutions on economic behavior: "Once there are investment opportunities and efficient incentives, farmers will turn sand into gold." China's economic growth in the post-Mao era attests to the wisdom of this proposition. Yet the transformation of economic institutions that has fostered such growth also illustrates that economic actors are not simply respondents to the incentives and constraints embodied in the changing rules of the game. But rather they are active participants in making the changes. To understand how such a process of endogenously induced institutional change unfolded, it is important to investigate the interactions between economic actors and the rule makers and enforcers—that is, political actors, and how the structural conditions they face fashion the outcomes of their interactions.

The foregoing analysis of the mechanisms of early privation shows that citizens' entrepreneurial pursuits could create both the impetus for changing the rules and the political shield (i.e., demonstrable economic outcomes) for defending such change beyond centrally authorized limits. But the initial strength of entrepreneurial forces varied because of different historical and geographic conditions, especially those affecting their persistence and survivability under Maoism. Where such forces were strong at the outset of economic reform, the likelihood of early privatization tended to increase. The responses of local political actors also varied, largely because different self-interest calculations were shaped by the ecology of the local political economy. Where the dominant strategy of economic expansion through sales growth by local public enterprises was sustained, as in northern Zhejiang, early privatization did not materialize despite a strong precommunist entrepreneurial tradition and postreform efforts to revive it. Where the strategy faltered early, and where strong justifications based on both extraordinary economic hardship *and* demonstrable benefits from private economic activities could be established to tackle the political risk of rule bending for private business, early privatization was likely to occur and deepen, as illustrated by the case of Wenzhou and with suggestive evidence from Taizhou. Where the second condition was lacking or not strongly present—as was the case of Lishui, however, early privatization would be less likely to proceed at fast and steady pace. Where both conditions were weak—as exemplified by Quzhou, early privatization was least likely to gain quick momentum despite growing difficulties faced by the local public sector. Nonetheless, with the increase of the cumulative cost for relying on the local public sector and a sharp decrease of the political risk for ownership change, many of the "laggard" locales that had managed to hold onto local public enterprises with morbidity or deteriorating health would likely be among the first to react to a political bandwagon effect triggered by the drastic national policy change on private ownership in 1997–1998. That reaction, as I will show in chapter 7, contributed to the precipitous decline of public ownership thereafter.

6

FDI and Privatization

THE DEFINING THEME of the CCP's economic policy in the post-Mao era is "reform and opening" (*gaige kaifang*). Under this policy foreign direct investment (FDI)—the inflow of foreign investment that involves varying degrees of both direct ownership and direct management by foreign investors—has become an increasingly important force in the remaking of the Chinese economy. A major consequence of the inflow of foreign capital is the deepening of privatization, which has taken place both because of the quantitative growth of foreign (private) investment and as a result of the changing organizational forms of foreign capital. As highlighted in chapter 1, since 1979 foreign investment has significantly increased in volume and expanded to more and more geographic areas and economic sectors. The landscape of the foreign-invested sector has also experienced a transformation from being dominated by joint ventures with public enterprises to being dominated by organizations involving greater degrees of private ownership, that is, wholly foreign-owned companies, joint ventures with declining state-owned shares, and companies with various mixes of foreign and domestic private owners.

Understanding these developments entails an examination of the behavior of local officials, who are the primary gatekeepers and regulators of foreign investment. Under the postreform system the inflow of foreign capital may help improve the local economy, thereby contributing to the careers of local officials and increasing the resources under their control. Yet the efforts to attract foreign capital are not without constraints. While promoting foreign investment has been politically more legitimate than facilitating domestic private business, there have been centrally imposed rules on the entry and boundary of foreign capital and on the organizational forms of foreign-invested companies. In particular, there have been formal and informal restrictions on the geographic locations and economic sectors that foreign investors have sought to enter. There has also been a long-standing policy bias toward joint ventures with public enterprises, whereas joint ventures with domestic private enterprises faced severe restrictions before the mid-1990s. In reality, however, these rules have been relaxed by many local authorities, resulting in expanded institutional space for foreign capital and greater intensity of private ownership. Bending the rules nevertheless involves a risk, as such an act contradicts the ideological, political, and economic considerations behind central policies. The abilities of local officials to contain the risk vary under different conditions and at different times; so do the benefits of rule bending. The interplay of different cost-benefit calculations by local officials has led to variations in the gatekeeping and regulatory strategies of local governments toward FDI, adding further twists to the uneven process of privatization before and beyond the tipping point in 1997.[1]

Centrally Imposed Constraints and Local Rule Bending

When CCP leaders initiated the open-door policy in the late 1970s, their basic strategy was to maximize the potential gains from foreign trade and investment and minimize any "undesirable" effects of economic internationalization. The potential gains from FDI are similar to those perceived by national governments elsewhere (Caves 2007), including increase of capital supply, expansion of foreign market connections and opportunities, access to advanced technology, infusion of international management know-how, growth of employment and revenue, and stimulating effects on domestic enterprises through competition, transaction, and demonstration. The "undesirable" effects include the threat of foreign competition to domestic vested interests (e.g., SOEs), foreign control of vital economic resources and activities, political, social, and cultural influence from abroad, and erosion of the dominance of public ownership. It is the concern about these effects that has led the central government to impose restrictions on where and how foreign investment takes place in the country.

Unlike many small economies where the national government is the sole gatekeeper and regulator of FDI (Caves 2007), China is a large country with multiple levels of government that hold varying degrees of authority over

---

1. My analysis in this chapter focuses on the two decades before China's accession to the World Trade Organization in 2001. Although the findings are also relevant for understanding the ramifications of the trade liberalization thereafter, a full investigation of that issue is beyond the scope of this book.

foreign investment. To align foreign investment with its policy imperatives in face of this reality, the central government has resorted to three major measures: rule setting, direct involvement in gatekeeping and regulation, and use of informal influence on local governments.

In 1980 the central government designated Shenzhen, Zhuhai, Shantou, and Xiamen as special economic zones (SEZs). In 1984 fourteen coastal cities were given the special status as "coastal open cities."[2] A similar status was granted to Hainan Island, which was subsequently elevated to a special economic zone in 1988. In 1984–1986 the central government also designated fourteen industrial parks, which were called National Economic and Technological Development Zones (NETDZs) and mostly located in the coastal open cities (except for one located in Guangzhou). Several batches of NETDZs were added in the ensuing years, including twenty-one during 1989–1995, sixteen during 2000–2001, six during 2002–2009, and ninety-five during 2009–2014. In 2013–2014, the central government authorized Shanghai, Guangdong, Tianjin, and Fujian to pilot free trade zones in select areas under their jurisdiction. What all these centrally created special policy enclaves have in common is that they have been allowed to adopt more liberal and flexible rules than other locales on a wide range of issues related to foreign trade and investment, such as project approval, financing, custom clearance, land use, taxation, currency controls, and labor practices (Howell 1993; Zweig 2002). The intention is to make them the focal areas of experimentation of centrally defined foreign economic policies.

Along with the uneven rules concerning the geographic locations of FDI, the central government has also defined the organizational forms and laid out the sectoral entry requirements for FDI. During the first decade of reform the central government enacted three important laws that set joint venture (JV) and wholly foreign-owned enterprise (WFOE) as the basic organizational forms of FDI,[3] as mentioned in chapter 1. Starting from 1987 the Chinese government has issued a series of guidelines that stipulate the scopes

---

2. These cities include Tianjin, Shanghai, Dalian, Qinhuangdao, Yantai, Qingdao, Lianyungang, Nantong, Ningbo, Wenzhou, Fuzhou, Zhanjiang, and Beihai.

3. There are two major types of joint ventures defined by the 1979 and 1988 laws respectively: joint equity venture and contractual joint venture (Randt 1996). A joint equity venture requires that the foreign investor hold at least a 25% stake and that the decision rights, income rights, and responsibilities for losses be based on the proportion of ownership held by each of the stakeholders involved. A contractual joint venture has neither a minimum ownership requirement nor predetermined rights and responsibilities based on ownership shares. A provisional regulation adopted in 1995 authorized the formation of a third and (until recently) much less frequently used type of joint venture: foreign-invested joint stock

of FDI entry and the organizational forms that must be used for entry into different economic sectors. These guidelines, revised six times (in 1995, 1997, 2002, 2007, 2011, and 2015), classify the entry conditions of FDI in different economic sectors into four categories: "encouraged," "allowed," "restricted," and "prohibited." The guidelines are not exhaustive, though. Foreign entry into sectors not explicitly listed in the guidelines has been subject to the ad hoc review and decision by the pertinent gatekeeping authorities, mostly at subnational levels.

Before the mid-1990s joint venture with public enterprise was the dominant organizational form prescribed by the central government (Pearson 1991; Roehrig 1994; Randt 1996). Although WFOEs were legally allowed as of 1986,[4] the general rule was that wholly foreign-owned enterprises must be treated as the least preferred organizational form (MOFERT 1986, 23).[5] That policy bias persisted until the turn of the century. In the FDI entry guidelines revised in 1995, for example, joint venture was explicitly listed as the only organizational form permitted for a number of economic sectors listed as "encouraged" and "restricted." In some sectors there was the further stipulation that domestic (public) enterprises must hold the controlling stakes in the joint ventures formed. Over time the number of sectors in the "encouraged" category increased and that in the "restricted" category declined; yet the number of sectors with explicit joint venture stipulation was also expanded.[6]

Before the start of massive privatization in 1997, this policy bias toward joint ventures was further coupled with rules that steered joint ventures toward partnership with public enterprises and restricted the formation of joint ventures between domestic private owners and foreign investors.[7]

---

company. It is governed by the Company Law enacted in 1994 (and amended in 2006). The threshold of equity capital is 30 million yuan, at least 25% of which must be owned by the foreign investor(s). In this study I focus on the identity of the local partners of joint ventures and the degree of foreign ownership. The differences among different types of joint venture are not further investigated.

4. Before the 1986 law a very small number of wholly foreign-owned enterprises had been formed through ad hoc approval procedures (Pomfret 1991).

5. The implementation guidelines of the 1986 law on wholly foreign-owned enterprises also contained general statements (Articles 4, 5, and 6) on the broad sectors where wholly foreign-owned enterprises would be banned, restricted, and denied entry.

6. In 1987 there were 169 and 208 sectors in the "encouraged" and "restricted" categories respectively. These numbers changed to 171 and 113 respectively in 1995 and 354 and 80 respectively in 2011. On the other hand, the total number of sectors with joint venture stipulation increased from 34 in 1995 to 99 in 2011.

7. Before 1997 the central government required that SOEs be the Chinese partners in sectors where the controlling stakes had to be held by domestic enterprises in Chinese-foreign joint ventures.

Throughout the 1980s and early 1990s there were very few such enterprises, largely because of the highly restrictive political environment for private business and the lack of statutory ground.[8] In fact the equity joint venture law (1979) and the contractual joint venture law (1986) defined joint ventures as legal persons but did not make any provision for the formation of joint ventures between parties that were not legal persons. This in effect precluded the formation of joint ventures with domestic private owners as natural persons.

Under Chinese law *getihu*, private sole proprietorships and partnerships, are not considered legal persons and have to face unlimited liability. Private enterprises using these organizational forms thus could not directly form joint ventures with foreign investors until the mid-1990s. Although the Provisional Ordinance on Private Enterprise in 1988 allowed the establishment of private limited liability companies (with legal person status) as an organizational form of private enterprise, no implementation details were made available before the enactment of the Company Law and the corresponding implementation guidelines in 1994.[9] And it was not until 1995 that the implementation guidelines on the formation of joint ventures involving parties without legal person status were issued. Before these developments, any action taken by local licensing authorities to approve the formation of foreign-private joint ventures would inevitably involve a risk due to the lack of statutory clarity. The stigma and sectoral entry restrictions faced by the domestic private sector before the late 1990s also cast a constraining shadow over the formation of foreign-private joint ventures. The adverse institutional setting made foreign-private joint ventures the least-used organizational form for FDI in the 1980s and early 1990s despite their potentially stronger capability of limiting political meddling and containing agency problems than joint ventures with public enterprises.[10]

For economic sectors not explicitly specified in the four categories defined in central FDI guidelines, the approving authority has been divided among different levels of government. The main criterion for determining this division

---

8. It is possible that given these constraints some of the joint ventures with public enterprises (e.g., collective enterprises) were in fact formed with domestic private enterprises that disguised themselves by "donning the red hat" (falsely registering themselves as public enterprises). Such cases cannot be identified from official statistical data, though.

9. Before the amendment of the Company Law in 2006, there was no legal allowance for single-owner limited liability companies (the minimum number of owners was two), which could add organizing cost and thus pose a hurdle to the formation of foreign-private joint ventures.

10. In 1989, for example, only 5, or 4%, of the 124 industrial joint ventures in Fujian were formed between foreign owners and domestic private enterprises (1989 Fujian industrial survey data set).

is the size of initial capitalization of foreign-invested enterprises (Randt 1996). The central government has held the authority to approve and license very large investment projects. In the mid-1990s, for example, approval by the State Council was required for projects involving more than US$100 million of foreign investment. Those involving more than US$30 million but no more than US$100 million and those involving more than US$10 million but no more than US$30 million required approval by the State Planning Commission (SPC) and the Ministry of Foreign Trade and Economic Cooperation (MOFTEC) (renamed Ministry of Commerce in 2003) and by provincial-level authorities respectively. Smaller projects under the $10 million threshold were left to lower-level governments for approval and licensing.

A major consideration affecting the decisions of gatekeepers is the competitive threat posed by foreign investment to the enterprises already under their purview, especially public enterprises directly "owned" by the governments concerned and situated in the same sectors that foreign investors seek to enter. Such competition may take place on multiple fronts, including financial, physical and human resources, supply chain relations, and product sale and distribution.[11] To protect their vested interests, local gatekeepers of FDI can block the attempts at entry that they perceive as threatening. They can also defuse the threat by requiring that the prospective entrants form joint ventures with their local counterparts. For the central government, however, direct use of these strategies is often out of reach, as many centrally controlled SOEs are situated in locales and sectors where local governments are the immediate gatekeepers "on the spot." Moreover, there was no unified authority in the central government that supervised all nonfinancial SOEs before 2003 (when the SASAC was formed to take on that role through consolidating control over the surviving central SOEs after massive privatization). Instead central SOEs were controlled by various industry-specific ministries and agencies. What these authorities could do, though, was to use their clout in the central government to pressure local governments to act on their behalf by denying entry and/or demanding the use of a joint venture structure as the

---

11. "We have to be extra careful when we review applications from foreign investors that seek to enter sectors where our local [public] enterprises already operate," said a leading official in charge of foreign economic affairs in Jiangmen of Guangdong province (informant, 12/1997). "They may emerge as more attractive clients to banks, making it harder for our enterprises to maintain the existing terms of borrowing. They may drive up the prices for the common inputs used, plus electricity and even water. They may lure away valuable personnel from our enterprises, including technicians and even skilled workers. They may put more bargaining chips in the hands of our [enterprises'] suppliers and disturb and complicate the long-established business ties therewith. And they may encroach upon the sales networks of our enterprises and crowd them out with better-selling products."

only avenue for entry where face-off situations arose between central SOEs and foreign entrants.

There is no guarantee of full compliance by local governments with centrally set rules and pressures, though. Although local governments share many of the considerations behind central policies on FDI, they tend to be less concerned about the well-being of centrally owned SOEs and about the more "encompassing" issues deemed important by the central government, such as national security, cumulative hazards posed by negative externalities (e.g., environmental pollution and resource depletion), broad sectoral and interregional positive spillover effects in terms of technology and organizational practice, noneconomic influence from abroad, and even the ideological and political ramifications of (foreign) private ownership. In the meantime, they are strongly interested in parochial agendas that foreign capital may facilitate. The inflow of foreign capital may have a positive impact on local economic growth, expansion of revenue base, linkages among related local sectors and activities, and job creation, all of which are conducive to the career advancement of local officials, as discussed in chapter 4.

Under the new political performance assessment system, achievement in luring foreign investment, known as *zhaoshang yinzi* (attracting business and channeling [foreign] capital), is often a concrete performance indicator in itself. An additional benefit of FDI is that it can provide a conduit for the rescue of poorly performing local public enterprises that have become liabilities of the local government (Huang 2002). Moreover, foreign entry may also bring about opportunities for local officials to leverage bank lending and manipulate fiscal resources (e.g., by extending tax breaks with strings attached or to transaction partners of foreign-invested companies), to make personal gains (e.g., through bribe taking), and to benefit their own family members or associates who conduct business with or through foreign investors.[12]

In the meantime, local governments face competitive pressures among themselves (Zweig 2002). Unlike local governments, foreign investors are geographically mobile. They may be able to take advantage of such mobility to pit different local governments against one another and bargain for more liberal and flexible

---

12. Political corruption is an important reality that foreign investors have to cope with. This is reflected in the annual Corruption Perceptions Index compiled by Transparency International on the basis of results from opinion surveys, which include many expatriate business personnel in different countries (https://www.transparency.org). During 1995–2005 the average score for China was 3.1 on a scale between 0 (the government being totally corrupt) and 10 (the government being totally clean). A common practice used by foreign investors to enter and operate in the country is to bring personal benefits to government officials through various direct or indirect channels. Examples include outright

terms of entry and regulatory treatment. The fact that there is rent (e.g., in the form of first mover's advantage) associated with institutional unevenness across different jurisdictions (Vogel 1989; Montinola, Qian, and Weingast 1995) also drives local governments to create and maintain more accommodating policy environments for the purpose of better positioning themselves in regional competition for FDI (Zweig 2002). While undertaking this endeavor, they need to be vigilant in guarding the sectors already populated by local companies, especially public enterprises. When inconsistencies arise between addressing centrally defined policy imperatives and concerns and attending to their own short-term and parochial interests, however, local officials may be inclined to bend the rules for the latter. Such behavior is likely to be more pervasive at the sub-provincial level, as provincial governments are more closely monitored by the central government than lower-level jurisdictions, which nevertheless have been the gatekeepers of the vast majority of foreign-invested entities.[13]

In chapter 1 I have already highlighted the temporal trend of FDI growth in the reform era. Table 6.1 provides further information on such growth in the industrial sector (which was the main domain of foreign investment before China's WTO accession in 2001 and subsequent opening up of service sectors) up until the time of massive privatization. Between the 1985 and 1995 industrial censuses, for example, the total number of foreign-invested industrial enterprises increased by eighty-six times. The percentage of geographic areas (at the prefectural level) and industrial sectors (with four-digit classification) with foreign presence also experienced significant expansion—from 22.4% and 20.0% to 94.2% and 90.4% respectively.

---

cash payment, "sale" of real estate properties at deeply discounted prices, free use of expensive cars and communication devices, junkets, other types of in-kind consumption, transfer of funds or offering of lucrative contracts to officials' family members or the companies owned by them, hiring of officials' family members as highly paid employees, sponsorship and financial support for overseas education of officials' children, to list a few. A report by the private consulting firm Anbound Group claimed that of the five hundred thousand corruption cases invested by the authorities during 2000–2009, 64% were in the field of foreign trade and investment (*China Daily*, September 8, 2010). Companies implicated and/or found guilty in the investigations include not only small and medium enterprises with foreign investment but large multinationals such as Avon, IBM, Daimler, Rio Tinto, Lucent, Siemens, Walmart, GlaxoSmithKline, Morgan Stanley, to name a few.

13. From 1980 to 1990 the cumulative number of FDI establishments in China was 25,389. Only 222 of these were directly licensed by the head office of the SAIC, the central licensing agency, whereas only 4 of the 222 were wholly foreign-owned ventures (*SFYCICA*, 81, 118). An examination of the data of the 1995 industrial census reveals that the foreign equity capital of some 84% of the newly established FDI firms ($n = 4,496$) was below the threshold (of $10 million) for provincial level approval, 11% of these firms had foreign equity capital in the range (between $10 and $30 million) that would require provincial level approval, and only 5% had foreign equity capital above the threshold (of $30 million) for central-level approval.

Table 6.1 Selected statistics of foreign-invested industrial enterprises

Indicators	1985	1992	1995	1998
Total number of foreign-invested industrial enterprises	516	9,325	44,293	26,448
% of prefectural jurisdictions with industrial FDI	22.4%	67%	94.2%	86.1%
% of four-digit industrial sectors with FDI	20%	88.3%	90.4%	90.7%
% of sub-provincial jurisdictions where central or provincial public enterprises faced foreign-invested enterprises in the same four-digit sectors	3.7%	31.3%	40.4%	33.9%
% of sub-provincial jurisdictions where local public enterprises faced foreign-invested enterprises in the same four-digit sectors	1.3%	17.3%	19%	18.1%
% of joint ventures among foreign-invested enterprises located in the same prefectures and same four-digit sectors as central and provincial public enterprises	94.6%	87.7%	77.3%	70.6%
% of partnerships with sub-provincial public enterprises among joint ventures located in the same prefectures and same four-digit sectors as central and provincial public enterprises	94.3%	87.1%	78.2%	75.8%

Note: The data cover all industrial enterprises in 1985 and 1995, all industrial enterprises with independent accounting status (Holz and Lin 2002) in 1992, and all industrial enterprises with annual sales of at least 5 million yuan in 1998. Other than the total number of industrial enterprises, all the figures for 1985 are estimated using the information on inaugural year from the 1992 NBS industrial survey.

Sources: SSIC 1985; data of the 1992 NBS industrial survey, the 1995 industrial census, and the 1998 NBS industrial survey.

What is particularly noteworthy is that sub-provincial governments acted in ways that deviated from the interests of higher-level authorities. Statistics in the table show that over time FDI expanded its presence in the same regions and sectors already populated by public enterprises. The percentage of such presence was in some cases twice as high for centrally and provincially owned public enterprises as for those owned by sub-provincial authorities. The vast majority of the foreign entrants that entered the same regions and sectors already populated by public enterprises were organized as joint ventures. For central and provincial authorities, however, this was not necessarily good news. The joint ventures formed in the same regions and sectors as centrally and provincially owned public enterprises mostly partnered with public enterprises owned by sub-provincial authorities. What this implies is a reinforcement or intensification of the competitive relationship that might have already existed with sub-provincial public enterprises.

While using the joint venture form to protect and even advance their parochial interests, sub-provincial local authorities also tended to be more accommodating in allowing foreign investors to be organized as wholly foreign-owned ventures, especially where foreign entry did not pose a direct threat to locally owned public enterprises. Despite the central policy bias toward joint ventures, however, the changing balance between joint ventures and wholly foreign-owned enterprises over time was not necessarily entirely driven by the rule-bending behavior of local officials. It is possible, for example, that some foreign investors might actually have preferred joint ventures to wholly foreign-owned enterprises for reasons such as initial lack of experience in China, uncertainties in the institutional environment, and desire to tap into the social and resource networks of local enterprises. Such need, though, may have weakened over time as foreign investors accumulated more experience and as the institutional environment improved. One may also argue that the growth of WFOEs under local governments might have simply been a reflection of the delegation of gatekeeping authority and the concurrent relaxation of the restrictions by the central government on the use of WFOEs during the process of economic opening.

But there is more to the story. The statistics reported in table 6.2 illustrate a pattern of seemingly direct bending of centrally imposed rules on not only the organizational forms of FDI but the sectoral entry by FDI.[14] The increasing relative significance of WFOEs was accompanied by apparent deviations from the FDI entry guidelines mentioned earlier. In particular, there was a nontrivial and indeed increasing presence of WFOEs in the "restricted" and even "prohibited" sectors and in the sectors with explicit JV stipulations.

---

14. Detailed data on the ownership composition of industrial firms are unavailable for the years before the 1995 industrial census.

The rising percentage of foreign-controlled JVs with public enterprises and that of private-foreign JVs among all JVs, which is shown in tables 6.2 and 6.3 and figures 6.1 and 6.2, also indicate parallel developments that squarely ran counter to the policy preference of the central government.[15]

Given greater regulatory laxity at sub-provincial levels, many foreign investors also sought to evade direct regulatory control by higher-level authorities through collusive efforts with local governments. A common strategy used for this purpose was to split investment into different phases and several concurrent projects or locations (Randt 1996; Smart and Smart 1993). In 1991 the Federation of Hong Kong Industries (FHKI) conducted a survey among 511 member companies that had investment in the Pearl River Delta. It revealed that 79.5% of them had invested less than HK$20 million (US$2.5 million) in the region, which was significantly below the threshold (of US$10 million) for provincial approval. Of those that had invested HK$20 million or more, 77% had operations in more than one location.[16] While this might have been a reflection of the predominance of small and medium enterprises among FHKI member companies, the fact that the larger ones tended to split their investment was indicative of a possible link to the attempt to deal with local gatekeepers and regulators only, as there could be further differentiation of entry thresholds at sub-provincial levels. Of the 251 sub-provincially licensed foreign-invested industrial enterprises for which detailed data on foreign equity capital are available for both 1994 and 1995 from the 1994 NBS annual industrial survey and the 1995 industrial census, 15% increased their foreign capitalization above the $10 million threshold required for provincial approval in the year immediately following their formation.[17] Some of the increases might well have been attempts at bypassing, through investment delivered in phases, more stringent entry and regulatory requirements from higher-level authorities.

Another strategy that was more extensively used to cope with centrally imposed regulatory rigidity in the early years of reform is to disguise foreign direct investment through processing contracts, known as *sanlai yibu* in Chinese.[18] This was particularly common in the southern province of

---

15. What is particularly noteworthy here is that despite the lack of statutory basis for the formation of foreign-private joint ventures before the enactment of the Company Law in 1994 (as noted above) such enterprises had already had a nontrivial presence among all joint ventures, as can be seen in figure 6.2.

16. These figures are calculated using the survey data.

17. This is derived by using data from the 1994 NBS industrial survey and the 1995 industrial census.

18. These contracts involve manufacturing or assembly of products using materials, components, and samples supplied by foreign companies, as well as compensation trade where local manufacturers use sales proceeds to finance the purchase of equipment and facilities loaned by foreign companies.

Table 6.2 Selected statistics on wholly foreign-owned enterprises and joint ventures in the industrial sector

Year	% of WFOEs in total number of foreign-invested industrial firms	% of WFOEs in total number of FDI firms in "restricted" industrial sectors	% of WFOEs in total number of FDI firms in "prohibited" industrial sectors	% of WFOEs in total number of FDI firms in industrial sectors with JV stipulation	% of public-foreign JVs with foreign majority (50+%) shares	% of private-foreign JVs in all JVs
1992	15	21	12			
1995	23	24	22	17	26	29
1998	30	37	27	23	38	39

Sources: data of the 1992 NBS industrial enterprise survey, the 1995 industrial census, and the 1998 NBS industrial enterprise survey.

Table 6.3 Percentage of joint ventures with more than 50% of equity capital held by local partners

Year	All JVs	All newly formed JVs	JVs with public enterprises	Newly formed JVs with public enterprises
1995	59	51	59	51
1998	28	19	30	22

Sources: Data of the 1995 industrial census and the 1998 NBS annual industrial survey.

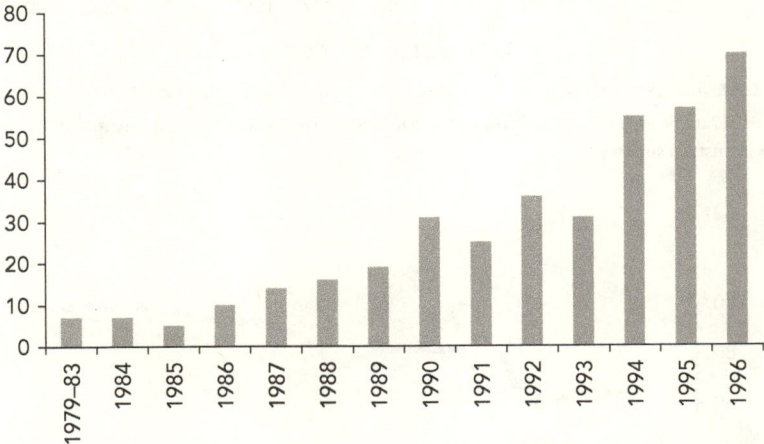

FIGURE 6.1 Percentage of newly registered JVs with foreign investors holding more than 50% of equity capital

Note: After the 1997 issue (which contains 1996 data) the *Almanac of China's Foreign Economic Relations and Trade* ceased to publish information on the percentage of equity capital held by foreign owners in newly registered joint ventures.

Source: ACFERT 1983–1997.

Guangdong, which attracted the bulk of the foreign capital inflow during the 1980s. Figure 6.3 shows the significance of foreign capital involved in processing contracts relative to that of FDI in the province. The FHKI survey mentioned above also found that even in the early 1990s some 23% of the 511 Hong Kong manufacturers that had invested in the Pearl River Delta used processing contracts as their main form of investment.

On the surface these processing contracts did not meet the twin criteria for FDI—direct foreign ownership and direct foreign participation in management—and therefore would not have to face the pertinent regulatory

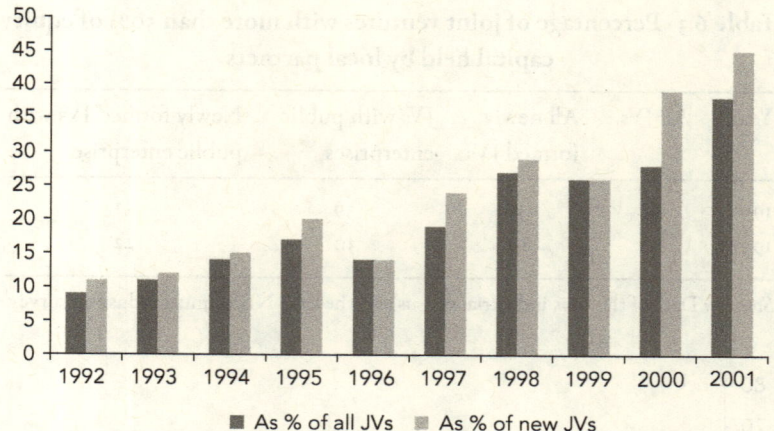

FIGURE 6.2 Number of foreign-private joint ventures in the industrial sector, 1992–2001
Sources: Data of the 1992–1994 NBS industrial surveys, the 1995 industrial census, the 1996–2001 NBS industrial surveys.

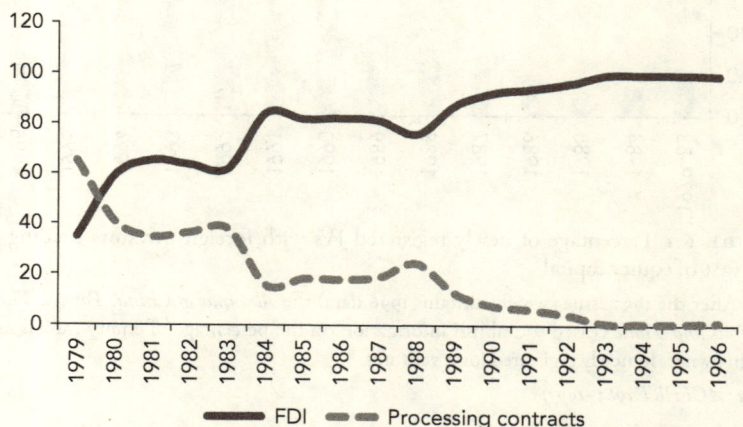

FIGURE 6.3 Foreign investment in Guangdong: FDI (%) versus processing contracts (%) 1979–1996
Source: GDSY (various years).

scrutiny required by the central authority. As contractors or subcontractors of foreign manufacturers, local companies received a processing fee (known as *gong jiao fei*) for the tasks and consignments they carried out. In reality, however, not only did many foreign investors holding processing agreements own at least part of the equity capital of these enterprises (e.g., in the form of equipment, facilities, and even factory buildings) but often they also dominated decision-making.[19] This de facto FDI status under domestic organizational shell could help foreign investors reduce approval time (e.g., from at least one month, needed for regular FDI application, to about one week); evade centrally imposed regulations on environmental protection, cost auditing (for tax purposes), and labor practices applicable to FDI companies; and provide a "backdoor" to enter sectors explicitly listed by the central authority as "restricted" or even "prohibited" for FDI.[20]

FDI Entry Mode and Resource Dependence

Deviating from centrally defined policies and preferences regarding FDI gatekeeping and regulation involves varying degrees of political risk for local officials. A relatively safe route is to stretch centrally defined limits while following the precedents set by ad hoc measures that the national government has taken to open up select areas of the economy. Inspired by the centrally initiated experiments with SEZs, coastal open cities, and NETDZs in the 1980s, for example, many local governments set up their own special foreign economic policy enclaves, where more liberal rules were often implemented to attract foreign investment and promote foreign trade (Zweig 2002; Wang 2013). A less safe step was to allow extensive use of organizational forms that the central government held a general bias against—especially during the early years of reform and in regions and sectors where the usage of these organizational forms was discouraged but not explicitly restricted or banned, including WFOEs, JVs with declining public ownership, and even Sino-foreign private JVs. A more risky move was to allow foreign investment to threaten the vested interests of higher level authorities through entry into regions and sectors already populated by centrally or provincially owned SOEs. The most risky behavior was to bypass or directly violate the stipulations, restrictions, and bans explicitly laid out in the national FDI guidelines on organizational form and sectoral access.

---

19. An interesting case study about Dongguan, which had a significant presence of various processing agreements, can be found at http://www.law-lib.com/lw/lw_view.asp?no=4139.

20. After China's WTO accession in 2001, the central government began to introduce measures to limit the space for such "backdoor" access. By 2013 Chinese companies undertaking processing contracts with foreign investors were banned from the manufacturing of some 804 types of products. An estimate by the Guangzhou office of the Hong Kong Trade Development Council claimed that some one thousand Hong Kong–invested companies in the Pearl River Delta of Guangdong province would very likely have to be closed down because of new restrictions introduced in 2013 (http://www.cre.org.cn/index.php?m=content&c=index&a=show&catid=9&id=8).

To be sure, unlike adopting accommodating policies for domestic private business during the early years of reform, providing special incentives for foreign investors beyond centrally defined boundaries was generally a less "sinful" act. Even the formation of private-foreign joint ventures might seem more legitimate than the promotion of domestic private enterprises before the drastic policy change on ownership restructuring in 1997, as it contained an element consistent with the national strategy on economic internationalization. Because of the CCP's trial-and-error approach to economic change and because of inconsistencies between old and new rules, there were also various "gray areas" where existing rules could be stretched in the name of reform experiments.

Nonetheless, the political risk of rule bending was real. In the mid-1980s, for example, several leading officials (including Lei Yu, the party secretary) in Hainan were reprimanded and removed from their positions for bypassing centrally imposed restrictions to authorize the importation of a large number of cars that were then resold by the importers for huge profits. Similar (albeit not as high-profile) cases involving lower-level officials abound.[21] The periodic anticorruption campaigns waged by the CCP leadership also cast a shadow on local officials' rule bending with weak buffers, which could become leads to the uncovering of related and/or deeper problems of deviance. Moreover, the competitive nature of the political performance assessment process made it imperative for local officials, especially local leaders, to minimize their vulnerability to decisions concerning ideologically and politically sensitive issues, which could tilt the balance in comparative evaluation with political rivals.[22]

Where the ability to manage this vulnerability was weak, local officials might not be strongly motivated to make significant concessions to foreign investors, especially during the first two decades of reforms, when restrictions on foreign capital were more stringent. Furthermore, FDI could also pose

---

21. For a sample of punishment for "serious" violations related to foreign economic policies, see the collection of cases of rule breaking by party and government officials compiled and published annually by the Central Discipline Commission of the CCP and the Ministry of Supervision during 2000–2008, and a subsequent collection of 110 cases published in 2011.

22. Such comparison has both an interlocale dimension and an intralocale dimension. This was captured in an observation made by the head of the CCP secretariat in an urban district of Guangzhou (informant, 6/1998). "Proactive efforts to open up the economy may help the local leader to move ahead of those in other regions. But unauthorized experiments have a downside. If one deviates too far [from centrally set rules], it may not be tolerated when the political climate changes. Every leading official also has enemies in the local establishment. All the moves he makes are watched closely by others in the local [political] echelon (*tidui*). Bold steps away from existing rules may be used [by rivals] as ammunition in personal attack or sabotage. The key to self-protection is to have solid ground on which to defend whatever one does."

a threat to the vested interests of local officials, especially when the foreign entrants operated in sectors already populated by local (especially public) enterprises. To contain such threats, local governments could seek to block the entry of FDI or limit it to the joint venture form in the affected sectors. In so doing, their behavior was more likely to be in line with centrally defined policies than otherwise. Since different locales do not have a uniform economic structure and since their relationships with higher-level authorities may be bound by different political and economic considerations, their gatekeeping and regulatory strategies toward FDI are likely to vary.

Accounting for such variation will provide a useful angle from which to illuminate the mechanisms whereby the privatization function of FDI has played out. Given the multiplicity in the level of FDI gatekeeping and regulation in China, it is important to consider the dynamics of intragovernmental relations. In particular, I argue that the degree of local regulatory laxity or flexibility depends greatly on the bargaining positions of local governments with higher-level authorities, which directly affect their abilities to contain the political risks in rule bending. This emphasis differs from conventional approaches to the study of the FDI entry mode, which is the focus of a large body of literature in international economics and business studies.[23]

The dominant paradigm in existing studies is a firm-centered view that emphasizes factors influencing the organizational choice of investors between joint ventures and wholly foreign-owned subsidiaries (which are called wholly foreign-owned enterprises in China). Among the factors identified as key determinants are cultural distance, risk management, proprietary asset protection, and local investing experience.[24] Most studies in the literature also recognize the importance of the gatekeeping policies of host country government regarding the entry points and organizational forms of FDI. Yet they either treat such policies as given without further probing or view the policy impact as stemming from a unitary authority (e.g., Contractor 1990; Gomes-Casseres 1990), while focusing their investigation on the formulation of strategies at the firm level.

Although the resultant findings are quite useful, the lack of close attention to the regulatory constraint faced by foreign investors leaves open serious

---

23. For overviews see Anderson and Gatignon 1986; Caves 2007; Konut 1988; and Zhao, Luo, and Suh 2004.

24. While most studies focus on the choice between a joint venture and a wholly foreign-owned subsidiary, there is also some research on other organizational forms, such as licensing (e.g., Caves 2007; Che and Facchini 2009).

questions about the relationship between FDI entry mode and the ecology of the host country's political economy.[25] When such constraint is significant and varies greatly across jurisdiction levels and boundaries, the explanatory power of a firm-centered approach may be limited. This condition, interestingly, is what foreign investors have faced in post-Mao China. On the one hand, the central government has both formal and informal entry rules and maintained a policy bias toward joint ventures; yet on the other hand, local gatekeepers have enforced the rules and bias with varying degrees of force. To account for the variations in the depth of foreign ownership and hence the privatization function of FDI, therefore, one needs to consider not only firm-level characteristics and strategies but the regulatory environments of different locales.

A key question here is what explains the varying abilities of local governments to tackle the potentially negative consequences of bending centrally imposed rules on the locational and organizational choice of FDI. Addressing this question requires an examination of the relationship between local governments and higher-level authorities. An important dimension of this relationship is interdependence between superior and subordinate authorities in the generation, pooling, allocation, and use of resources for various state functions (Bardhan and Mookherjee 2006; Treisman 2007). In this connection an extension of the analytic logic of the resource dependence theory may lend a revealing perspective.

The gist of the theory, originally formulated by Pfeffer and Salancik (1978), is that because organizations depend on external sources of resource supply for survival and growth, managing critical power relations among interdependent parties constitutes a key element in organizational strategy. The focus of the theory and its many applications largely centers on organizations outside the political system (Davis and Cobb 2010; Hillman, Withers, and Collins 2009; Pfeffer and Salancik 2003).[26] Yet a parallel can be drawn for

---

25. To a certain extent this inadequacy may be due to the fact that until the mid-1980s the bulk of FDI took place among developed economies (Markusen 1995), where there is arguably a relatively high degree of regulatory uniformity and transparency in policymaking and implementation despite complexities in large economies such as the United States. However, for transitional and emerging economies, which have become increasingly important destinations of FDI since the early 1990s, policy inconsistencies over time and across regions and at different administrative levels within host countries tend to be more pronounced. Treating a host country government as a unitary authority, not to mention holding FDI regulation constant, runs the risk of leaving out major components in the mechanisms of entry mode formation.

26. There are studies that examine the efforts of firms to manage power relations involving the government (see Hillman, Withers, and Collins 2009 for a review). Their focus, however, is

the study of the behavior of political actors, whose decision-making, like that in economic and social organizations, is both resource driven and resource constrained. Examining how the interplay of different resource dependence relationships shapes the cost-benefit calculation of local officials will help illuminate how they respond to centrally defined policy guidelines and manage the consequences of their responses.

Bipolar Concentration of Risk Taking

The most important type of resource in the state system is the fiscal revenue extracted through taxes and fees. Under China's postreform public finance system, there are three basic patterns of *net* fiscal resource flows between lower and higher-level governments: surplus, break-even, and deficit at the lower level. When the economy under a local government generates more fiscal revenue than the local government's authorized spending, part of the surplus is channeled (e.g., through direct upload known as *shangjie* under the pre-1994 system) to higher-level governments. When locally generated revenue is just sufficient for the local government to cover its authorized spending, there is little net flow to higher-level governments. When locally generated revenue falls short of authorized local spending, higher-level governments are mainly responsible for covering the gap, as it is not until recent years that local governments have been allowed to issue public debt indirectly or directly to address budgetary shortfalls (see note 32 in chapter 3). In addition, higher-level governments may download additional funds to local governments for special projects that they partially or fully finance, such as poverty eradication, conservation, and education.

Before 1994, the net flow of fiscal resources could be seen as the difference between fiscal uploads (*shangjie*) from lower-level governments and fiscal downloads or subsidies (*buzhu*) from higher-level governments.[27] The former represented the contribution of lower-level governments, whereas the latter

---

business-government relations rather than intragovernmental relations and their implications for business organizations.

27. There were two types of fiscal upload: (*a*) remittance of a portion of local (surplus) revenue to higher-level authorities as an obligation of the local government under the fiscal contract, and (*b*) remittance of funds for special purposes (e.g., the local government's share in covering the cost of tax rebates for exports) and funds from a host of locale-specific sources (e.g., port fees in Shanghai during the late 1980s and early 1990s). There were also two types of fiscal download: (*a*) subsidies for locales with revenue shortfalls, and (*b*) subsidies for special projects or purposes (e.g., infrastructure, education, poverty eradication, etc.).

embodied the obligations of higher-level governments to their subordinate governments. The 1994 fiscal restructuring brought about two major changes. Under the revenue partitioning setup (chapter 3), the "contribution" from a lower-level government now consisted mainly of the locally extracted taxes that were exclusively owned by its superior authority and the latter's portion of taxes (minus refunds benchmarked to baseline levels) in the "shared" category.[28] The obligation of the higher-level continued to be subsidies, but their amounts substantially increased—largely because of the central government's much improved fiscal power, and they were more clearly divided into general-purpose funds and funds earmarked for programs specified by the higher level.[29]

Table 6.4 sheds some light on fiscal dependence relations between counties and higher-level governments during 1988–2006,[30] when the main story of this book fully unfolded. What it shows is that some counties were regular recipients of fiscal subsidies from higher-level authorities because of chronic difficulties in revenue generation, whereas some other counties incurred budget deficit that had to be covered with ad hoc subsidies. These two categories overlapped but not entirely, as a regular recipient of subsidies might not have an imbalanced budget in a particularly year but a county not on regular fiscal transfer support might have to be bailed out when an imbalance occurred. Together they made up a sizable portion of the counties (including county-rank cities) in the country during the late 1980s and the 1990s. In contrast, an initially small number of counties were stellar performers with annual revenue of more than RMB100 million. A closer look at the detailed fiscal data from the same source (not shown here due to the limitation of space) reveals that their local economies generated more revenues (including taxes owned and shared by higher-level governments after 1993) than their

---

28. In central-provincial relations, fiscal upload remained a separate "legacy" category of fiscal flow. It referred to the annual remittance equivalent to the amount of contributions required of provincial governments in 1993 (which were in effect offset to various degrees by tax refunds benchmarked to baseline levels), and to tax rebates for exports. In 2009 these items were deducted from central fiscal downloads, effectively eliminating upload as a flow category in the central-provincial interface.

29. It should be noted that during the decade after the 1994 restructuring fiscal flows at sub-provincial levels continued to be governed mainly by different variants of the fiscal contract system (Zhang Zhihua 2006a and 2006b). Where the revenue partitioning arrangements were adopted, the demarcation of exclusive and shared ownership of tax categories between superior and subordinate governments was not as uniform and stable as that in the central-provincial interface (ibid.).

30. During the 1980s and 1990s, with the exception of Zhejiang and Hainan, public finance of most counties was placed under the purview of prefectural cities, which in turn were under the purview of provincial governments. Since the turn of the century an increasing number of provinces have carried out reforms to place counties under the direct purview of provincial governments.

Table 6.4 Selected statistics (%) on fiscal conditions of counties

Year	Regular recipients of subsidies	With current-year budget deficit	With revenue of 100 million yuan or more
1988	55	36	3
1989	55	37	5
1990	55	46	6
1991	53	50	7
1992	n/a	n/a	n/a
1993	57	59	13
1994	55	59	6
1995	n/a	n/a	n/a
1996	44	41	15
1997	43	34	18
1998	42	32	22
1999	49	35	27
2000	46	36	29
2001	44	36	32
2002	32	25	22
2003	34	23	25
2004	36	21	28
2005	35	19	31
2006	32	17	37
2007	n/a	14	42

Sources: Annual local fiscal data sets (Ministry of Finance), 1988–1991; *FSPCC 1993–2007*.

expenditures. In between were counties that had neither significant fiscal shortfalls nor surplus. Over time, the percentage of those heavily dependent on regular and/or ad hoc subsidies decreased, while more counties became fiscal "contributors" to higher-level authorities. There were nonetheless considerable variations among different provinces in terms of both the relative significance of the dependents and contributors, and the changes over time.

What these facts illustrate is that during the 1990s and the early years of the new century (when privatization progressed and deepened), the local policy environments for FDI were conditioned by a wide range of dependence relationships between the gatekeepers and their supervising authorities. Where a local government was a net fiscal contributor, it tended to be in a strong position to leverage this situation for more flexibility in FDI policy implementation, thus containing the political risk of rule bending. Where the opposite was true, such ability tended to be weak, as in the case of "break-even" locales. At the other end of the spectrum were local governments that not only made no net contribution to higher levels but absorbed large and growing amounts of fiscal subsidies for addressing the basic needs of local public administration. But there is a twist to such seeming disadvantage. These governments represented a drag on the political performance of their supervising authorities and on the fiscal resources that the latter commanded or "filtered" (e.g., from centrally allocated fiscal transfers). The need to contain or reduce such liability thus could engender a special type of dependence relationship, where the more resourceful party might be willing to "trade" policy flexibility for improvement in the self-financing ability of the less resourceful party.

It follows that the resource positions of different local governments were likely to bear a curvilinear rather than a linear correlation with their tendencies to ease centrally imposed restrictions on the entry points and organizational forms of FDI. Other things being equal, rule bending was most likely to occur where the local governments either had extremely strong or extremely weak fiscal resource positions vis-à-vis their immediate supervising authorities.

A case in point is the southern province of Guangdong. Because of its geographic proximity to Hong Kong and Macau, historical ties (as the main region of emigration during the century before the founding of the PRC) with overseas Chinese (who were the main investors in China during the 1980s and 1990s) (Wang 2003), home to three of the initial four special economic zones, and more liberal foreign economic policies adopted by local leaders (Vogel 1989), Guangdong has been the leading province in China's economic internationalization, especially during the early years of reform. In 1995 it accounted for 27.1% of the inbound FDI and 38% of the export of China (*GDSY 1996*, 238–240; *CSY 1996*, 312–314). It is also a province of enormous internal diversity and variation in terms of economic development. The Pearl River Delta is the most dynamic and developed region, whereas the eastern and western regions of the province have lagged far behind. Northern Guangdong is the least developed region. Situated in mountainous areas, it has had the lowest GDP per capita, as well as two of the three nationally designated poverty-stricken counties in the province and eleven of the thirteen provincially designated poverty-stricken counties. It also has much greater degree of dependence on fiscal transfers from higher-level authorities than other regions in the province, as can be seen from table 6.5, which also profiles some important organizational features of industrial FDI in the province.

Table 6.5 Selected statistics on foreign-invested industrial enterprises in Guangdong, 1995

Region	% of central & provincial SOEs facing FDI firms in the same prefecture & 4-digit sector	% of WFOEs in total number of FDI firms	% of WFOEs in total number of FDI firms in "restricted" sectors	% of WFOEs in total number of FDI firms in "prohibited" sectors	% of WFOEs in total number of sectors with JV stipulation	% of public-foreign JVs with foreign majority (50+%) shares	% of private-foreign JVs in all JVs	GDP per capita (yuan)	Fiscal downward as % of local spending
Pearl River Delta	39.2	20.4	29.6	26.1	20.7	37.5	36.5	22,741	20.3
Northern	37.1	45.4	31.3	22.6	19.3	41.2	26.1	3,330	62.7
Eastern	20.2	17.7	10.9	13.2	18.4	22.3	25.2	4,704	47.8
Western	13.2	9.7	7.3	9.5	13.1	21.7	17.6	5,487	46.8

Note: The Pearl River Delta consists of Guangzhou, Shenzhen, Zhuhai, Foshan, Zhongshan, Jiangmen, Dongguan, Huizhou, and Zhaoqing. Northern Guangdong includes Shaoguan, Qingyuan, Heyuan, and Meizhou. Eastern Guangdong includes Chaozhou, Shantou, Shanwei, and Jieyang. Western Guangdong includes Zhanjiang, Yangjiang, Maoming, and Yunfu.

Sources: 1995 industrial census data; *GDSY 1996*; *FSPCC 1995*.

Interestingly, it is the Pearl River Delta and the northern region where the entry and organizational patterns of FDI demonstrated the greatest degrees of inconsistency with the vested interests of higher-level authorities, as shown by the greater threats posed by foreign-invested firms to the public enterprises owned by these authorities and located in the prefectures concerned. They also had more significant deviations from the gatekeeping and regulatory biases and requirements set by the central government pertaining to WFOEs, entry restrictions and bans, foreign controlling stakes in joint ventures with public enterprises, and joint ventures with domestic private enterprises. Nonetheless, the bipolar correlation between resource dependence and apparent local rule bending as suggested by these limited descriptive statistics may be specific to the particular year shown and/or subject to distortions by other relevant factors that are not controlled for. To further investigate the possible causal link suggested by the descriptive statistics, I analyze more systematic data with greater geographic and time span.

The focal issue of my data analysis is how intragovernmental resource dependence, as a key factor shaping the bargaining positions of local governments vis-à-vis higher-level authorities, affected the tendencies of local officials to bend formal and informal rules on the entry points and organizational forms of FDI. Specifically, I explore whether resource dependence, proxied with the local fiscal subsidy-contribution ratio divided by the pertinent provincial average, had a curvilinear or bipolar effect on the likelihood of (*a*) central and provincial SOEs being directly exposed to FDI entrants in the same prefectures and (four-digit) industrial sectors, (*b*) bending of centrally imposed restrictions on the entry point and organizational form of FDI, (*c*) rising foreign shares in public-foreign joint ventures, and (*d*) growth of joint ventures with domestic private enterprises. The time span is from 1993 to 1999, for which the necessary panel data are available at the prefectural level. It was also the period when ownership restructuring in the public sector built up and reached a crescendo. Details about the data, variables, methods, and regression results are posted at the book site. The main findings are as follows.

First, prefectures that had the strongest or weakest fiscal positions relative to higher-level authorities were more likely to have greater degrees of rule bending than prefectures that were fiscally neither very strong nor very weak. This finding is consistently strong in the regression analyses on the direct local exposure of central and provincial SOEs to FDI entry, the violation of centrally imposed restrictions on the entry point and organizational form of FDI, and the growth of private-foreign joint ventures. As I have pointed out earlier, the political risks associated with these (the first two in particular) types of behavior tended to be greater than reducing public shares in joint ventures (which, as discussed below, could serve as a way to tackle organizational and financial problems faced by the enterprises concerned).

Second, the estimation results from the regressions on rising foreign shares in joint ventures with public enterprises only show a marginally significant curvilinear effect (at $p < .10$). In the meantime, however, the estimates for financial health (proxied by debt-equity ratio and profitability) yield significantly strong results. This suggests that the declining significance of public shares in joint ventures might be more strongly related to the financial health of the enterprises concerned than to the bargaining positions of the pertinent local government vis-à-vis higher-level authorities. It could be due to weak bargaining positions of the local government concerned vis-à-vis foreign investors in face of poorly performing enterprises in the local public sector, or attempts by the local governments to use FDI as a conduit to rescue financially troubled public enterprises, as argued in Huang's study (2002), or a combination of both.

Third, forming joint ventures with local public enterprises had an enhancing effect on the abilities of foreign investors to enter the regions and sectors already populated by central and provincial SOEs. This result suggests that the tendencies of local governments to grant entry sought by foreign investors against the interests of higher-level authorities were not only conditioned by their bargaining positions but were also motivated by the incentives and opportunities to address their parochial interests associated with avenues they could directly exploit. Where both conditions were present, privatization through internationalization tended to go farther and faster.

Summary

Local regulatory flexibility has been a major factor for the deepening of privatization through FDI in post-Mao China. The mechanisms at work include the entry of foreign investment in areas and sectors restricted or banned by the central government and/or populated by public enterprises owned by higher-level authorities, the growth of wholly foreign-owned enterprises (versus joint ventures), the growth of foreign shares in joint ventures with public enterprises, and the growth of joint ventures with domestic private enterprises. These developments reflect, among other things, the impact of the decisions and interactions of gatekeepers and regulators at multiple levels of the government. With more encompassing and ideologically bound agendas, the central government has imposed gatekeeping policies restricting foreign access to certain economic sectors and regions and favoring joint ventures with public enterprises. With narrower interest calculus and in the face of spatial mobility of foreign capital and interjurisdiction competition, local governments tended to deviate from the centrally defined rules and policy bias to address their parochial interests. The degree of local deviation was nevertheless uneven and conditioned by local officials' varying calculations of not only the benefit but the political cost of rule bending under different structural conditions before the late 1990s. Central to such calculations were local governments' fiscal resource positions relative to higher-level authorities'. Understanding intragovernmental fiscal relations and the (largely unintended) consequences of the responses of local officials to the changing incentives and constraints after reform, therefore, yields useful clues to explaining the geographic and sectoral distribution of FDI as well as the evolving organizational forms it has taken.

In contrast with previous research on the privatization function of FDI (e.g., Huang 2002), the foregoing analysis broadens the scope of investigation from regions to organizations cross-embedded in regions and economic sectors, and from joint ventures to the full spectrum of organizational forms in the foreign-invested sector. More importantly, it shifts the focus of analysis from the dependence of local governments on foreign capital to the interdependence within the government system, and it examines the perceived benefits of foreign capital for local governments in relation to the varying costs of different gatekeeping and regulatory strategies in face of centrally imposed entry rules and policy bias. This allows for a clearer separation of the roles played by central and local governments in the process of internationalization, thereby helping identify the causal channels through which political actors' self-interest calculus influenced and contextualized the scope and depth of foreign capital's penetration into China's new economy. It was the convergence of the ramifications from such penetration with those from the forces discussed in the preceding chapters that contributed to the generation of the momentum for the massive privatization in the late 1990s and beyond.

7

The Tipping Point and Beyond

IN SEPTEMBER 1997, two months after the outbreak of the Asian financial crisis, the Chinese Communist Party held its Fifteenth Party Congress. In the concluding report to the congress, General Secretary Jiang Zemin announced three important changes in the CCP's policy on ownership-related issues. First, public ownership could take diverse forms, including not only public sole proprietorship but various public-private shareholding arrangements with public controlling interests. Second, the state sector needed to be downsized and restructured according to market principles, whereas the remaining SOEs should consist mainly of large enterprises and concentrate in strategically important sectors. Third, the private sector should be encouraged to "play an important part in meeting the diverse needs of citizens, increasing employment, and boosting the development of the national economy" (Jiang Zemin 2006, 2:20).

What followed was a massive wave of privatization. Within a few years the size of the public sector was substantially reduced. From 1997 to 2000 the total number of industrial SOEs went down from 98,600 to 53,489. It further dropped to 34,280 in 2003, when the SASAC was established to consolidate the control over the remaining nonfinancial SOEs (*CIESY 2005*, 279). Although the collective sector was not explicitly mentioned for restructuring and downsizing at the Fifteenth Party Congress, the repercussion of the policy change was equally profound. From 1997 to 2003 the total number of township and village enterprises (TVEs) declined from 1.29 million to 0.29 million (*SCTE*, 55; *CTEY 2004*, 105). Altogether, the share of the entire public sector in nonfarm employment during the same period decreased from 57% to 23%, as shown in table 1.7.

The retreat of the CCP leadership from a full-front approach to curbing the erosion of public ownership was a response to the evolving realities in the first two decades of reform. In particular, the inability of the public sector to cope with growing job provision pressures and the deteriorating financial health of public enterprises made it imperative for the central authority to change strategy. But their subsequent decline was far more precipitous and widespread than CCP leaders had anticipated. It was hastened by a bandwagon reaction among local governments to the central policy change in 1997. The challenges faced by public enterprises were further exacerbated by a shift in the focus of the self-interest calculus of local officials from industrial development to urbanization, and by insiders' strategic manipulation and pursuit of self-enrichment opportunities during ownership restructuring. Together these forces combined to accelerate and deepen the process of privatization.

The Triggers

An immediate trigger for the CCP's policy change in 1997 was the concern about nonfarm employment. As shown in chapter 1, the 1980s saw an active role played by the public sector in the creation of nonfarm jobs. This role ceased after 1995, when public sector employment plateaued.[1] Yet job creation pressures persisted because of the lasting impact of the age structure shaped in the booming years of the population and because of the continuing movement of labor out of farming after agricultural decollectivization (chapter 2). This challenge was also coupled with the growing pressure for the provision of retirement benefits for retirees in the urban public sector due to the life-cycle effect of the postrevolution workforce (table 2.4). In 1991 the fiscal expenditure on retirees in state-owned work units was 45 billion yuan; in 1997 it almost quadrupled, totaling 173 billion yuan (*FYC 1998*, 457). Moreover, as more and more public enterprises ran into difficulties in implementing the sales growth strategy discussed in chapter 4, their ability to make use of the existing workforce declined. Over time, redundant employees became a pressing issue.[2]

Starting from 1993 the central government launched a series of "reemployment projects" (*zai jiuye gongcheng*) among urban public enterprises, especially SOEs, to cope with the redundant personnel problem. In 1995 the National Bureau of Statistics began to collect statistics on *xiagang zhigong*,

---

1. Industrial SOE employment began to decline in 1993, whereas 1994 was the year when urban collective units attained the highest level of employment (*CSY 1998*, 137).

2. In a speech delivered in 1994, Vice Premier Zhu Rongji estimated that redundant personnel accounted for up to two-thirds of the workforce of SOEs (Zhu Rongji 2011, 2:64).

Table 7.1 Redundant and furloughed employees in urban public enterprises (millions)

Year	All urban staff and workers			SOE staff and workers		
	Redundant	Newly furloughed	Furloughed and yet to be placed	Redundant	Newly furloughed	Furloughed and yet to be placed
1994	1.2					
1995	6.6	5.6	4.3	3.7		
1996	9.7	8.2	6.2	5.4		
1997	10	12.7	6.4	6.9		
1998	17.4	7.4	8.7	12.5	5.6	5.9
1999	16.5	7.8	9.4	12.1	6.2	6.5
2000	14.5	5.1	9.1	10	4.5	6.6
2001	11.9	2.8	7.4	8.9	2.3	5.2
2002	9.5	2.1	6.2	7.5	1.6	4.1
2003	7.5	1.3	4.2	5.1	1	2.6
2004	4.7	0.5	2.7	2.9	0.3	1.5

Sources: *LSYC 1995–2005*.

or furloughed employees, who had been removed from active duty because of slack or overcapacity. In 1996 the officially documented number of *xiagang zhigong* exceeded 8 million, whereas the total number of redundant personnel in the urban public sector reached 9.7 million, plus 5.5 million urban citizens formally registered as unemployed (*CSY 1997*, 273).[3] Table 7.1 shows that the total number of furloughed employees in urban public enterprises swelled from 1.2 million in 1994 to 10 million in 1997. With such a drastic increase, the burden of continuing to support redundant personnel quickly became unbearable for urban public enterprises. Alternative placement was badly needed to absorb these people back into the active workforce and to contain the political fallout of the growing problem.

A concurrent problem that triggered the policy change in 1997 is deteriorating financial performance of many public enterprises and their increasing

---

3. In Chinese government statistics, individuals removed from active duty in urban public enterprises were not classified as unemployed persons, as they had not severed organizational affiliations with their employers, which were obligated to give them a small subsistence allowance, find alternative placement, and contribute in their behalf the employers' shares to newly established social security funds (for pensions, healthcare, and unemployment).

Table 7.2 Selected financial indicators of industrial SOEs, 1980–1997

Year	Ratio (%) of taxes and profit to assets	Ratio (%) of profit to assets	Total profit (billions of yuan)	Total losses (billions of yuan)	% of enterprises incurring losses
1980	24.8	16	55.1	3.2	22.4
1981	23.8	16	52.1	4.2	27.7
1982	23.4	14.4	51.9	4.3	25.1
1983	23.2	14.4	57.1	2.9	14.6
1984	24.2	14.9	61.5	2.3	10.5
1985	23.8	13.2	62.2	2.7	9.6
1986	20.7	10.6	57.2	4.7	13.4
1987	20.3	10.6	60.9	5.1	12.8
1988	20.6	10.4	70.2	7.1	10.7
1989	17.2	7.2	57.3	12.8	15.9
1990	12.4	3.2	25.3	27.9	30.3
1991	11.8	2.9	23.7	30.0	28
1992	9.7	2.7	31.1	30.0	22.7
1993	9.7	3.2	66.0	28.2	29.8
1994	9.8	2.6	70.6	27.4	32.6
1995	7.2	1.7	63.1	36.5	33.3
1996	6.5	1	36.9	50.1	37.5
1997	6.3	0.9	29.6	60.7	43.9

Sources: CFYB 1998; CIEYB 1998.

inability to service the loans borrowed from state banks to finance earlier growth. Table 7.2 shows that both the ratio of taxes and profit to assets and the ratio of profit to assets steadily declined among industrial SOEs after the mid-1980s. In the meantime, the percentage of loss-making enterprises increased in the 1990s, and the magnitude of their losses relative to the total profits of industrial SOEs also rose, especially after 1995. Consequently, more and more SOEs were unable to generate enough revenue to pay back the loans they had taken out from state-owned banks. Figure 7.1 shows that in 1997 SOEs located in more than two-thirds of the country's provinces had "unhealthy assets" (which mostly consisted of debts and could not be recovered) equivalent to more than 20% of their equity. The problem further worsened in 1998, when this percentage equivalent doubled to 40% and three provinces (i.e., Jilin, Heilongjiang, and Qinghai) even had more unhealthy assets than equity capital.

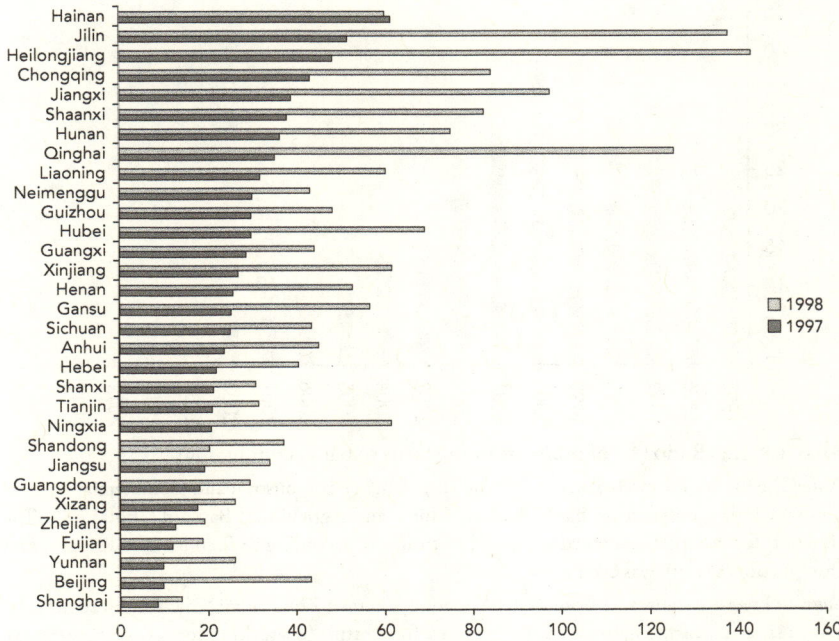

FIGURE 7.1 Ratio of unhealthy assets to equity (%) by province: Nonfinancial SOEs, 1997–1998
Source: CFYB 2000.

Since SOEs were the main recipients of bank loans, their financial woes resulted in growing strains on the banking sector. Figure 7.2 shows a sharp increase of nonperforming loans relative to bank lending after 1995. The real magnitude of the problem was likely greater than what the chart shows, as the official definition of nonperforming loans before 2002 lacked clarity and was narrower than international standard (Holz 2003). In 1995 the People's Bank (China's central bank) adopted a four-tier system to rate the quality of bank lending as "pass," "past due," "idle," and "bad." The last three categories were called "poor quality loans" or "bad loans" (*buliang daikuan*). While this categorization did capture borrowers that were clearly in default, the underlying criterion included no separate assessment of the financial risk of borrowers other than the occurrence and duration of default. This left out cases where the borrowers became financially unhealthy but were able to continue to service their loans on schedule by stretching the repayment deadlines beyond the regulatory limit for loan extension and/or borrowing new loans to cover old ones, oftentimes with the help of government agencies and officials.

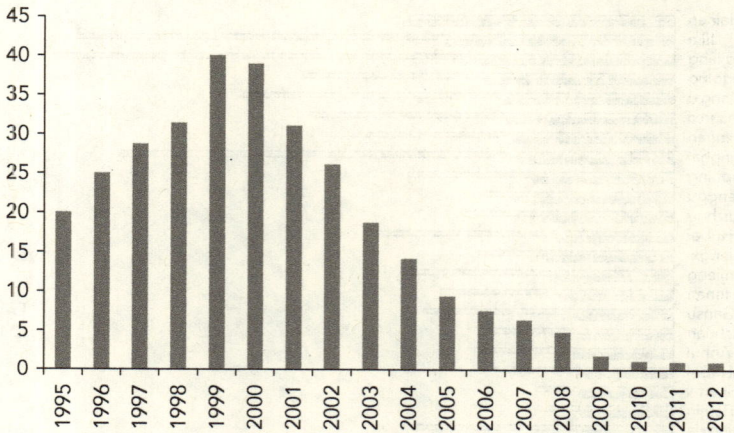

FIGURE 7.2 Ratio (%) of nonperforming loans to bank lending, 1995–2012

Note: The figures for 1998–2002 are for the "Big Four" (i.e., Industrial and Commercial Bank of China, China Construction Bank, Bank of China, and Agricultural Bank of China) only. The situation for other (state-owned) financial institutions, according to Premier Zhu Rongji (Zhu Rongji 2006, 2:477), was even worse.

Sources: Pre-2001 figures are from speeches made by Premier Zhu Rongji (Zhu Rongji 2011, 2:162, 511; 3:182; 4:113, 240). Figures for 2001–2002 are from http://www.china.com.cn/chinese/2002/Jul/175314.htm and http://www.cbrc.gov.cn/chinese/home/docView/183.html, and figures for 2003–2012 are from the website of the China Banking Regulatory Commission (http://www.cbrc.gov.cn/chinese/home/docViewPage/110009&current=1).

It was not until May 1998 that the People's Bank began to pilot a new system that would follow international practice by focusing on the assessment of the financial risks of borrowers and classifying loans into five categories: "pass," "special mention," "substandard," "doubtful," and "loss." It took some four years for this system to be fully implemented among commercial banks. During the transitional period the loan quality statistics reported by the government were based on the combined information under the two different systems. It is likely that there were more ambiguities in the statistics reported around 1997–1998 than those closer to 2002. Indeed, many foreign observers argue that China's nonperforming loan problem in the late 1990s was more serious than was indicated by the officially reported figures. A report produced by the Swiss bank UBS (2006, 91), for example, estimated that the ratio of nonperforming loans to all bank lending in 1996–1997 was in the range of 55%–65%, which was more than twice the official numbers (see also Lardy 1998).

The double crunch of redundant personnel and deteriorating financial health of SOEs drove the CCP to make policy changes. In a speech (to central economic policymakers) on risk prevention in economic development in August 1996, for example, General Secretary Jiang Zemin highlighted the job creation challenges confronting the state:

> There are 1.2 billion people in our country, with a fast growth of labor supply and tremendous pressures for urban and rural employment. . . . The challenge of job creation we face now and ahead is very formidable. 5.2 million urban residents are currently registered as unemployed. 6.6 million urban staff and workers are deployed in idle or semi-idle production processes. Hidden unemployment and underemployment total some 22 million. In addition, there are 130 million surplus laborers yet to be transferred out of rural areas. (Jiang Zemin 2006, 1:542)

Jiang's concern was echoed in a series of speeches made by Zhu Rongji (Zhu Rongji 2011, vol. 2), who as vice premier (1993–1998) and then premier (1998–2003) was in charge of economic issues. Expounding on the need to deepen reforms, he repeatedly mentioned the challenge of having to accommodate the 10 million furloughed employees in the urban public sector (e.g., Zhu Rongji 2011, 2:484). He also expressed serious concern about the financial and fiscal consequences of the problems of SOEs. According to him, state-owned banks could only collect some 62% of the interest due on their lending when the decision on ownership restructuring was announced in 1997 (Zhu Rongji 2011, 2:511). This had a major negative impact on banks' ability to fulfill their fiscal obligations and was a major contributing factor to the growth of budget deficit (Zhu Rongji 2011, 2:326).[4] At the same time the government had to resort to money printing for the unrecoverable loans that banks had to write off, which created inflationary pressures on the economy.[5] The outbreak of the Asian financial crisis as a coincidence only further heightened the seriousness of the threat posed by the growing financial risks in the state sector (Zhu Rongji 2011, 2:475–491).[6]

---

4. In 1997 the total amount of current-year unpaid interest was 157 billion yuan, whereas the cumulative sum reached 557 billion yuan (Zhu Rongji 2011, 2:511). In contrast the total budget revenue of the government in 1997 was 865 billion yuan (*CSY 2011*, 75).

5. Zhu Rongji (2011, 2:364) disclosed that the amount of extra money printed was 59 billion yuan in 1991, 120 billion yuan in 1992, 153 billion yuan 1993, 140 billion in 1994, 59.6 billion in 1995, and 100 billion in 1996. Closely correlated with these numbers was the movement of the consumer price index in these years, 103 in 1991, 106 in 1992, 115 in 1993, 124 in 1994, 117 in 1995, and 108 in 1996 (*CSY 1998*, 265).

6. Given that the timing of the Fifteenth Party Congress had been set in January 1997 (Jiang Zemin 2006, 1:613–616) and that the pertinent preparation had been underway for two years (see note 7), the

The coping strategy adopted at the Fifteenth Party Congress of the CCP was "holding onto the large (enterprises) and letting go of the small" (*zhuada fangxiao*).[7] The announced objective (known as *san nian tuokun*) was to lift SOEs, especially large and medium ones, from the plight of overstaffing and financial malaise within three years. What CCP leaders sought to do was to transform the five hundred largest SOEs into shareholding companies with predominant state ownership[8] while allowing other SOEs, especially small ones, to purse diverse avenues of ownership restructuring, including outright privatization (Zhu Rongji 2011, 2:448–451).[9] But it was not the initial intention of the CCP leadership to push the vast majority of small SOEs to the private sector. Indeed their preferred way out was to make public enterprises that still had adequate performance to absorb those with poor performance through mergers.[10] Nor was it an integral part of the CCP's strategy to restructure the ownership of TVEs along the same line as SOEs, not to mention privatizing the vast majority of them. What transpired in the ensuing five to six years, however, turned out not to be what the CCP leadership had hoped for.

The Political Bandwagon

The Fifteenth Party Congress signaled CCP leadership's willingness to take a more flexible approach toward privatization. *Gaizhi*, or organizational restructuring, immediately became a buzzword for economic policymaking in urban areas, touching off swift changes throughout the country (Yusuf, Nabeshima, and Perkins 2006; see also Lardy 1998 and Steinfeld 1998). In 1996 the total number of industrial SOEs was 113,800; by the end of 1998 it

---

outbreak of the crisis could not have "triggered" the landmark decision on ownership restructuring in September 1997.

7. This notion was first proposed at a plenary meeting of the CCP's Fourteenth Central Party Committee in September 1995, which set the tone for subsequent preparatory work leading to the formal policy change at the Fifteenth Party Congress in 1997.

8. The top five hundred SOEs contributed some 85% of the profits and taxes from the state sector (Zhu Rongji 2011, 2:500).

9. One of the major steps taken by the central government was to convert the debts of poorly performing SOEs into equity capital held by four asset management companies (established by the central government in 1999) and to recover, through reorganization or liquidation, any remaining values of the assets taken over by these companies.

10. As an incentive, the government allowed those taking over poorly performing SOEs to defer for up to five years the payment of the interest on the loans owed by the enterprises they took over.

Table 7.3 Percentage of remaining industrial SOEs relative to previous year's, 1996–2002

Year	Provincial average	Prefectural average	City/county average
1996	97.7 (13.1)	98.2 (17.2)	96.8 (18.2)
1997	67.1 (16.3)	62.7 (28.9)	59.8 (34.4)
1998	80.5 (14.2)	78.1 (26.1)	77.2 (28.7)
1999	90.4 (9.5)	88.9 (22.4)	84.2 (26.6)
2000	84.6 (12.1)	79.2 (23.2)	78.7 (24.9)
2001	79.3 (8.8)	76.4 (15.2)	77.2 (23.1)
2002	90.7 (8.4)	89.2 (11.1)	86.5 (15.8)

Note: Figures in parentheses are coefficients of variation.
Sources: CSY 1996–2003; data of the 1995 industrial census and the 1996–2002 NBS industrial surveys.

had dropped to 64,737 (*CIESY 2001*, 17). The sharpest decline came in 1997, which saw an average 33% drop in the number of industrial SOEs among different provinces, as shown in table 7.3. The rush probably had started earlier in the year, as the basic plan of ownership restructuring had been outlined (and very likely leaked out afterward) during a meeting that the CCP held in January 1997 to make preparations for the upcoming party congress in the fall (Jiang Zemin 2006, 1:613–616).

Indeed the quick responses to the central policy change during 1997–1998 prompted a series of calls by Premier Zhu Rongji for more measured paces of ownership restructuring and use of more diverse methods (especially merger) other than outright sell-off (Zhu Rongji 2011, 2:448–451, 455–457, 470–471, 501–502). The overall speed of change eased in 1999 but then accelerated again in 2000 and 2001. Contrary to the wish of central leaders, the fast disappearance of large numbers of SOEs seemed to be more of a result of net attrition than incorporation of poorly performing enterprises into the remaining SOEs. As reported in an earlier study (Lin and Zhu 2001), only a small group (less than 10%) of the industrial SOEs restructured during 1997–1998 used merger as the means of change. As the process of ownership restructuring deepened, the initial emphasis on merger between SOEs also faded, as indicated by a total absence of any mention of the term in Premier Zhu Rongji's speeches on SOE reforms after 1999. Part of the reason may be the lack of enthusiasm among SOE managers due to concerns about the opportunity cost relative to outright privatization and other alternatives, as well as doubts about the effectiveness of merger for tackling the problems of SOEs.[11]

An even more powerful driving force behind the unexpectedly precipitous decline of SOEs came from local officials, who controlled more than 90% of all SOEs before the ownership restructuring. From 1997 to 2003 (when the SASAC was formed), the total number of nonfinancial SOEs under subnational governments dropped from 26.3 million to 12.7 million, whereas that of centrally controlled nonfinancial SOEs decreased at a much slower pace—from 2.3 million to 1.9 million (*FYC 2004*, 367). The policy change announced at the party congress created an immediate impetus for many local officials to realign themselves with the new party line by demonstrating activism in ownership restructuring.[12] The sharply reduced political risk for privatization also left open opportunities for local officials to use ownership restructuring to address other agendas for self-interest, which oftentimes could be more effectively facilitated through methods other than the centrally prescribed one (i.e., merger) within the public sector. An important fact in what followed is that, while the rush toward privatization was broad-based among different provinces, there were considerable variations at sub-provincial levels, which help reveal what drove the behavior of local officials.

Variations among SOEs

The statistics reported in table 7.3 show a limited degree of variation in industrial SOE attrition rate among different provinces, though the coefficients of variation were relatively higher during the early years of restructuring. There was a similar trend of declining variability among different prefectures and among cities and counties. But the degrees of variation were greater at

---

11. In 2004 I took part in a survey of 511 private enterprises jointly conducted with researchers from the Chinese Academy of Social Sciences. During the survey I interviewed seventeen private enterprise owners who were former managers of SOEs. None of them considered merger to be a viable option of restructuring. One of them (informant, 14/2004) remarked: "Unless there was something that the stronger enterprise really wanted from the weaker one, it's not worth the trouble to have a merger. It often involved more complications in regard to personnel, placement of [redundant] employees, financing, debts, and relations with the government and business partners. Other methods of reform were more straightforward and clear-cut." Another former SOE manager (informant, 9/2004) opined: "Government-arranged mergers between SOEs only resulted in bad marriages. Instead of getting to the core of the problems of SOEs, mergers shifted all the problems from the poorly performing enterprises to those that were not losing money yet. In the end it made everyone worse off. The result is that more SOEs became candidates of privatization. It's totally self-defeating."

12. For examples of indiscriminate, campaign-style sell-off of public enterprises by local governments, see Zhu Rongji 2011, 2:501–502.

these levels of comparison, especially at the outset of the restructuring. What explains such a pattern of variability? An analysis of a large-scale national survey of ownership restructuring conducted by the National Bureau of Statistics among industrial SOEs ($n = 40,238$) in 1998 reveals that fast movers in the early phase of restructuring were those that had lighter financial and personnel liabilities and stronger profitability than laggards and nonstarters (Lin and Zhu 2001). What the finding suggests is that, although the decision on ownership restructuring was largely motivated by the problems of poorly performing SOEs, the pace of change did not bear a positive correlation with the seriousness of the problems they faced. Rather, many less unhealthy enterprises were actually rushed out of the door first. A likely driving force behind this is a political bandwagon response, highlighted above, of local officials to the centrally adopted policy change, though their abilities to respond were unevenly constrained by the varying restructuring costs associated with the preexisting organizational conditions of the enterprises under their purview.

For local governments facing similar constraints, on the other hand, their strategies toward privatization were subject to peer influence. As political rivals, local officials sought to outshine each other and would rarely turn a blind eye on the policies of their regional peers. The more risk-averse actors also tended to follow the footsteps of those who were politically more entrepreneurial, especially when the latter's deviant behavior (e.g., not focusing on mergers within the public sector) not only went unpunished but reaped benefits. In the 2004 CASS-HKUST survey of private enterprise owners ($n = 511$) mentioned above, 55% of the respondents agreed or strongly agreed that the changing attitude of their local governments toward private ownership in the preceding decade was in part due to some kind of demonstration effect from the more liberal policies adopted by governments in neighboring regions. While such an effect would hasten the tempo of privatization, it may also hold a clue to explaining the convergence that quickly followed the initial disparity in the decline of SOEs.

To examine this possibility I analyze the data from NBS annual industrial surveys during the ownership restructuring process in 1998–2005. The focal issue is how regional competition and learning may have affected the attrition rate of industrial SOEs,[13] which is defined as the ratio of the current-year number of industrial SOEs in a locale to that of the preceding year. The

---

13. It would be interesting to include urban collective enterprises in this analysis and compare them with industrial SOEs. Unfortunately the data sets after 1997 only include all industrial SOEs, and their

measure I use to proxy regional peer influence in post-1997 privatization is the local attrition rate of industrial SOEs divided by the regional attrition rate, both lagged for one year. A ratio less than 1 implies a lagging position and thus pressure for catch-up, whereas a ratio greater than 1 implies a leading position and thus a gap to be narrowed by laggards. A number of control variables are included in the analysis. Descriptions of these variables, along with regression method and results, are posted at the book site.

The data analysis yields three basic findings. First, the pace of ownership restructuring of a locale relative to the regional average in a given year was negatively correlated with the local attrition rate of industrial SOEs in the subsequent year. What this suggests is that many laggards probably played catch-up, whereas the lead of faster movers tended to be short-lived.[14] Second, such effect was similarly significant among cities and counties within the same prefecture and among prefectures in the same province. The regional influence on local attrition rates thus appears to have been widespread and contagious. Third, the significance of the effect of the explanatory variable weakened over time. This reflects a growing convergence, resulting from earlier regional peer influence, in the attrition rate of industrial SOEs among different locales. A common outcome of these forces is that they pushed ownership restructuring far beyond the initial plan of the central leadership.

Variations among TVEs

Given the important role of TVEs in the public sector before 1997, it is equally interesting to further examine what mechanisms were in play among these enterprises during their post-1996 acceleration of privatization. The change there was more precipitous than that among SOEs, as noted at the beginning of this chapter. Chapter 5 shows that privatization had actually started earlier among TVEs, though the pace was constrained by the political risks involved and varied according to the different abilities of local authorities to justify such a move with demonstrable results from the expansion

---

counterparts in the urban collective sector that had annual sales less than 5 million yuan were no longer included. It would also be useful to further distinguish between the two different sources of regional influence—competition and learning. Yet the necessary data are unavailable.

14. An enabling condition for this was furnished by the concurrent intensification of the efforts of government authorities and SOEs to find alternative placement for existing employees, including relaxing restrictions on private business. From 1998 to 2002 a total of 27.2 million state sector employees were laid off through various furlough arrangements that eventually channeled them out of the urban public sector (*LSYC 2003*, 134).

of the space for private business. Such political constraint was lifted by the policy change at the Fifteenth Party Congress.[15] Although TVEs were not explicitly mentioned as part of the plan for ownership restructuring, many local authorities sensed the new direction in central policy and pressed ahead with their own *gaizhi* programs (Zhu Rongji 2011, 2:501–502). The Ministry of Agriculture (MOA), which was the central policymaker for TVEs, also moved in sync and gave the green light for such undertaking.[16]

From 1997 to 2003 the average annual attrition rate of TVEs was 21% (*CTEY*, various years), resulting in the reduction of the number of TVEs by 1 million. In this process of change TVEs were prone to the same kind of regional peer influence faced by SOEs. But unlike many SOEs that encountered difficulties in severing organizational ties with their employees (and thus were unable to seize upon the opportunity of restructuring immediately), the privatization of TVEs was not constrained by old labor institutions inherited from the Mao era. As Walder (1995) has noted, from the very beginning of reform employment relations in TVEs were largely driven by labor market conditions and not bound by the kind of social service and welfare responsibilities appended to urban public enterprises. As a result, the initial tempo of privatization among TVEs following the party congress tended to be more heavily influenced by the preexisting strength and mix of public and private ownership in the local nonfarm sector.

In chapters 4–5 I have outlined three different local patterns of ownership structure and change: (*a*) locales where the sales growth strategy was forcefully carried forward up to the time of central policy change and public enterprises dominated the nonfarm sector; (*b*) locales where the strategy had stalled but the private sector remained underdeveloped despite the languishing of the local public sector; and (*c*) locales where the initial dominance of the strategy was eclipsed by subsequent growth of private enterprises. For local officials in pattern (*a*), the policy change in 1997 opened up an opportunity to unload poorly performing public enterprises. But they would probably not have very strong incentive to immediately privatize those that were

---

15. An indication of the reduced political risk for privatization in rural areas is the diminishing relevance of shareholding cooperatives, which had been widely used as a way to disguise privatization of TVEs before the policy change at the Fifteenth Party Congress (Tsai 2002; Whiting 2000). In 1996 there were 1.55 million TVEs and 0.144 million rural shareholding cooperatives. The number of the latter went up to 0.194 million in 1997 but quickly turned south along with the decline of TVEs. By 2002 the total number of TVEs dropped to 0.401 million, whereas that of rural shareholding cooperatives went down to fewer than 80,000 (*CTEY 1997*, 129; *CTEY 1998*, 174; *CTEY 2003*, 186).

16. The MOA's new policy guidelines and directives on ownership restructuring among TVEs can be found in the 1999–2002 issues of the *China Township Enterprise Yearbook*.

still able to maintain the existing *modus operandi* and thereby help address the revenue and employment imperatives. For local officials in pattern (*b*), the reduced political risk for privatization created a major impetus for quick action to let go of local public enterprises, most of which had been kept for lack of viable alternatives yet gradually lapsed into increasingly unbearable liabilities for the local governments due to sagging performance. For local officials in pattern (*c*), where many poorly performing public enterprises were likely to have already been rid of before 1997, the rational choice was to trim those that had been retained as window dressing while keeping those that had been and could still be of some use for various reasons. It follows that the initial response of local officials to the central policy changes was likely to be relatively modest among the strongholds of the erstwhile dominant strategy and among steady early movers of privatization, but it was likely to be very strong among laggards in both regards. Yet, once the effect of regional peer influence kicked in and intensified, such initial difference tended to fade.

A case in point for investigating these possibilities is Jiangsu. It was famed for being an exemplary model of TVE-driven economic growth up until the mid-1990s (Ho 1994; see also Whiting 2000). It is also a province for which systematic data at the county level can be found to trace both the changes among TVEs and their operating environments in the first two decades of reform. Like those in other provinces, TVEs in Jiangsu eventually succumbed to the changing policy and economic conditions around the turn of the century. Their pattern of decline thus helps illuminate some important mechanisms at work.

Figure 7.3 illustrates the rise and decline of TVEs in Jiangsu. The decline started in the early 1990s. It began to accelerate after 1995 and became precipitous after 1997. Table 7.4 further suggests that many of the enterprises that led the way down were those that had experienced substantial expansion in earlier years, as may be inferred from a contrast of the numbers for larger enterprises (with annual sales above 5 million yuan) with those for industrial TVEs of all sizes in 1995 and 1998. Table 7.4 also shows that, while the overwhelming majority of TVEs disappeared in all three regions of the province by 2004, the initial decline was much slower in southern Jiangsu, the heartland of TVE-led growth in the 1980s and early 1990s. In contrast, the rush to privatization immediately following the policy change in 1997 was faster in central Jiangsu and much faster in northern Jiangsu, where some locales had experienced significant slowdowns of TVE growth and/or even a major expansion of the private sector earlier in the decade. This is consistent with part of what is postulated above. Yet there were nevertheless considerable

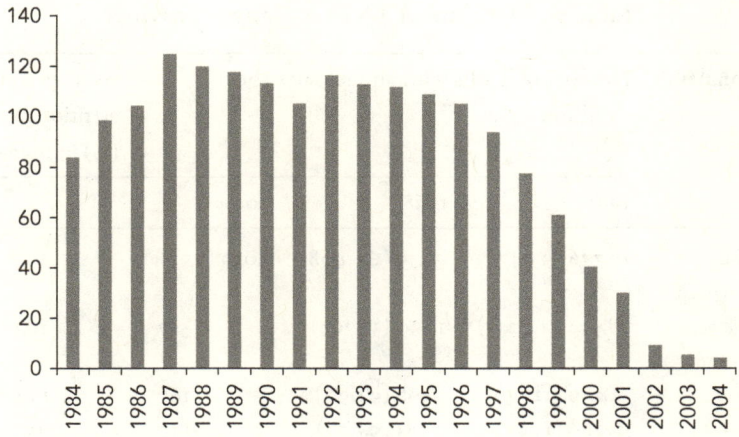

FIGURE 7.3 Total number (1,000s) of TVEs in Jiangsu, 1984–2004
Sources: JSRSY 2002; CTEY 2003, 2004, 2005.

variations among different prefectural cities within all three regions in the initial attrition rate of TVEs, as can be seen from the prefectural figures in the table.

To investigate these variations and the subsequent convergence in the outcome of decline among TVEs in the province, I probe below the prefectural level and analyze county-level data, which provide more revealing information about the sources of the forces at work. The main questions are what accounted for the different attrition rates in the initial push for privatization and how regional peer influence may have affected the pace of decline over time.

For the analysis of the first issue I run a pooled regression spanning the period of 1998–2000. I use the attrition rate of all industrial TVEs in each county-level unit of the province as the dependent variable. The main explanatory variable is the initial policy stance of each unit toward privatization in terms of the three major possibilities discussed above: stronghold of TVE-driven growth, early mover in privatization, and laggard in both regards. The hypothesis under testing is that laggards tended to move faster than the other two types of locales in the immediate aftermath of the central policy change. For the regression analysis on the issue of regional peer influence, I use a panel data set that spans the period of 1998–2004. The basic setup is similar to that for the analysis of regional peer influence among industrial SOEs in the preceding section. The dependent variable is the attrition rate of TVEs, and the main explanatory variable is the ratio of county-level attrition rate to

Table 7.4 Decline of TVEs in Jiangsu province

Regional unit	Number of TVEs with annual sales above 5 million yuan			Average annual attrition rate (%) in 1997–1999
	1995	1998	2004	
Jiangsu province	19,776 (93,476)	3,139 (64,468)	1,039 (3,994)	19.8
Southern Jiangsu	8,524 (44,235)	1,630 (35,762)	557	10.8
Suzhou	2,289 (12,091)	392 (9,090)	167	14.9
Wuxi	2,066 (13,620)	383 (9,807)	147	15.7
Changzhou	1,623 (7,667)	295 (8,367)	65	1.2
Zhenjiang	1,269 (4,913)	252 (4,043)	133	7.9
Nanjing	1,277 (6,144)	308 (4,455)	45	17.6
Central Jiangsu	5,838 (21,373)	739 (14,244)	398	19.6
Yangzhou	2,890 (13,731)	374 (4,141)	172	26.7
Taizhou		231 (4,579)	140	21
Nantong	2,948 (7,642)	134 (5,524)	86	11
Northern Jiangsu	5,414 (27,668)	770 (14,562)	84	29
Yancheng	1,602 (8,441)	205 (4,676)	27	20.3
Huaiyin/ Huaian	1,981 (6,827)	88 (1,130)	38	42.7
Suqian		127 (1,708)	2	29
Xuzhou	959 (7,381)	116 (2,948)	12	42.9
Lianyungang	872 (5,019)	234 (4,100)	5	10

Notes: (a) The figures in parentheses are for all industrial TVEs in 1995 and 1998, and the 2004 provincial figure (italicized) in parentheses is for township-owned (including nonindustrial) enterprises of all sizes; (b) annual attrition rate during 1997–1999 is for all industrial TVEs; (c) Huaian prefecture was known as Huaiyin before 2001. Taizhou and Suqian were not prefectural cities before 1996 and belonged to Yangzhou and Huaiyin respectively.
Sources: YJSTE 1997–2000; CTEY 2005; 1998 NBS annual industrial survey data; 2004 economic census data.

the prefectural average rate in the preceding year. Descriptions of the other variables included in this analysis and the preceding one, along with discussion of regression methods and summary of the main estimation results, are posted at the book site.

What the pooled regression reveals is a significantly positive effect of the leading role played by laggard counties in the initial rush toward privatization. This is consistent with the conjecture developed earlier. There is also evidence from the panel data analysis that confirms both the effect of regional peer influence on TVE attrition rates and the weakening of such effect over time. What these findings illustrate is that the initial responses of TVEs to the central policy change in 1997 were patterned by the lasting impact of their recent trajectories of development under different mixes of ownership. Like SOEs, however, the fall of TVEs thereafter was not simply a locale-specific affair, but rather a process where the pace of change followed interdependent calculus used by officials across different locales within a larger ecosystem of political governance. In tandem these two elements (initial leading role of "laggards" and growing regional peer influence) of the political bandwagon reactions among TVEs added to the precipitousness and the breadth of the decline of public ownership beyond the limits set by the central leadership in 1997.

From Industrial Development to Urbanization

The bandwagon reactions of local officials to the policy change following the Fifteenth Party Congress in 1997 were coupled with a shift in the focus of their self-interest calculus. As I have discussed in chapter 3, the 1994 fiscal restructuring redefined the revenue bases of local governments and drove them to explore and expand revenue sources beyond the industrial sector. In particular increasing attention was directed to urban development, which quickly became the "new locus of economic growth" (*xin jingji zengzhang dian*) for many locales in the mid to late 1990s and beyond. The adjustment of local officials' strategies along the way had important implications for the deepening of privatization.

A basic fact of life in the Mao era was that cities were centers of production and government administration rather than hubs of consumption. China's postrevolution industrialization was achieved in part by limiting urban development despite the fact that the industrial sector absorbed the bulk of investment and most industrial facilities were located in urban areas. What the government did during the first three decades of the People's Republic was to concentrate investment in capital goods industries that had relatively low demand for labor (Riskin 1987), to restrict rural-urban migration through the *hukou* (household registration) system (Cheng and Selden 1994), and to suppress citizens' income and thus effective demand

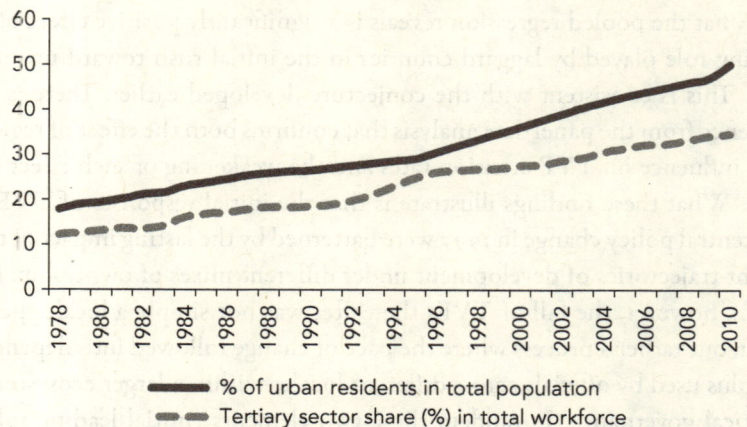

FIGURE 7.4 Urbanization and tertiary sector growth, 1978–2010
Source: *CSY* (various years).

for consumer goods and services (Whyte and Parish 1984). The result is a slow growth of urban population and a contraction of urban services relative to other economic activities. From 1952 to 1978 the share of the industrial sector in China's GDP went up from 18% to 44%; but the share of urban citizens in the total population only edged up from 13% to 18%, whereas the share of the tertiary sector in GDP declined from 29% to 24% (*CSA 1999*, 23, 77).

That pattern of urban underdevelopment has changed in the post-Mao era, with a drastic expansion of (more labor-intensive) consumer goods industries, massive rural-to-urban migration, and fast growth of service activities in response to rising income, demographic change, and pent-up demand for essential necessities (e.g., housing) and facilities that were grossly undersupplied under the old system. Figure 7.4 shows a strong upward trend of the significance of both the urban population and the tertiary sector during the three decades after reform. Figure 7.5 further shows that in the 1990s and beyond the traditional dominance of the secondary sector in cities was eclipsed by the growth of the tertiary sector, which tends to concentrate in urban areas. Since the secondary sector includes both industry and construction and since urban development also entails an expansion of construction work, the declining relative significance of industrial activities in the urban sector as implied by figure 7.5 was likely to be greater than that of the secondary sector as a whole.

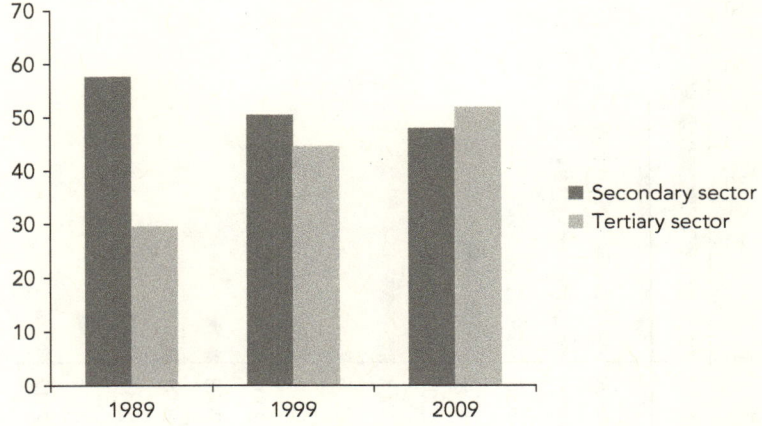

FIGURE 7.5 Share (%) of secondary and tertiary sectors in city GDP
Source: CCSY 1990, 2000, 2010.

A corollary of these developments is the rising importance of urbanization for addressing the employment and revenue imperatives of local governments (Ho 2005; Hsing 2010). Such importance was further enhanced and accentuated by the 1994 fiscal restructuring, which demarcated the lion's share of industry-related taxes as central government revenue, as noted in chapter 3. The impact of this change on the self-interest calculus of local officials is twofold. It diluted the attention of local officials to industry as a weakening source of revenue and thus drove them to focus on local and nonindustrial revenue sources, such as the business tax, which was defined as a local tax and levied on a wide range of services as well as construction activities. It also reinforced local officials' attempts to promote land acquisition and transactions for urban development, as the fees for transfers of land use rights and various other proceeds from urban and suburban land transactions were not only local but off-budget revenues (thus subject to more discretionary use).

Yet the tertiary sector and construction were not where the traditional strength of public enterprises lay. Despite the waning fiscal importance of industry-related revenue,[17] in 1995 (when public sector employment peaked) 60% of the workforce of nonfinancial SOEs was still deployed in the industrial sector (*CSOAY 1996*, 450). The percentage was 73% for

---

17. In 1980 the industrial sector contributed 77% of government revenue; in 1995 this share dropped to 44% (*FYC 1996*, 517).

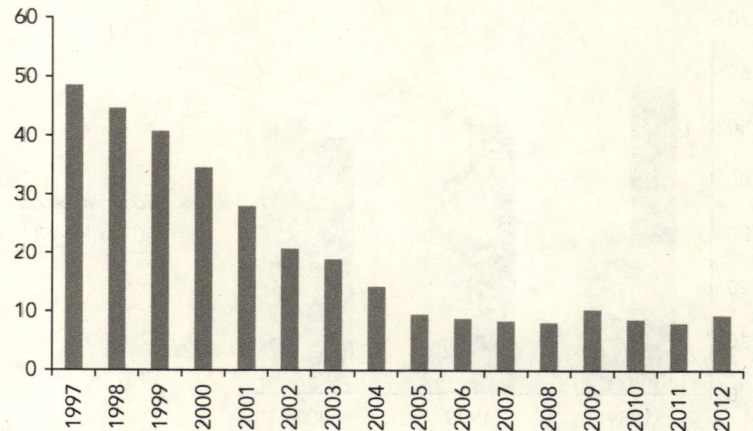

FIGURE 7.6 Share (%) of public enterprises in total real estate investment, 1997–2012
Source: CRESY 1999–2013.

TVEs in that same year (*CTEY 1996*, 99). On the other hand, private business organizations, especially *getihu*, had a significant presence in nonindustrial activities. In some sectors that did not exist before the reform, such as real estate, they had even quickly developed an early lead before massive privatization began in 1997,[18] as suggested by the statistics in figure 7.6. To promote urban development, which could also create jobs for placing redundant personnel from the predominantly industrial public sector, it was necessary for local governments to allow the private sector to play a more significant role.

Moreover, a major consequence of the industrial buildup under Mao is that many public enterprises, especially SOEs, were located in areas with close proximity to city centers or even within city centers proper. With the expansion of urbanization, the land they occupied had growing potential for more lucrative alternative uses, especially with the deterioration of their financial performance before the start of massive privatization. Opportunity cost considerations tended to drive local officials to close down the public enterprises

---

18. An interesting twist in this connection is that some of the private business people who earned their "first pot of gold" in China's first real estate boom in the early 1990s were former government officials or employees. They used their political connections to leverage opportunities and funds for land acquisition, construction, and speculation. Their activities not only directly expanded the space of the private sector but accelerated the organizational decay of the state and exacerbated the financial woes of state-owned banks (with some 400 billion yuan of bank lending lost in various misuses, according to Premier Zhu Rongji [2011, 2:511]), both of which also contributed to the decline of public ownership (Lin 2001).

Table 7.5 Industrial enterprises centrally located in urban areas

Year	Number of industrial enterprises located in urban centers	% of public enterprises in industrial enterprises located in urban centers
1995	38,332	86.3
2004	15,221	25.8

Note: Urban centers are proxied as the postal code zones where the headquarters of prefecture-level governments were located.
Sources: 1995 industrial census data; 2004 economic census data.

located in more centrally located sites or sell them at premium prices to parties that subsequently would also help generate greater benefits through alternative (especially service-related) uses of the underlying space. Table 7.5 shows that from 1995 to 2004 some 60% of the industrial enterprises located in urban centers at the prefectural level disappeared from their previous sites. In 1995 86.3% of those situated in central locations were public enterprises. In 2004 public enterprises only accounted for 25.8% of the ones remaining in the reduced pool.[19]

What these descriptive statistics suggest is a possible link between the new focus of interest for local officials and the fate of public enterprises in urban areas. To explore whether opportunity cost considerations associated with urban development had any accelerating effect on the pace of privatization, I have performed an analysis of data on industrial SOEs during the tidal years of privatization.[20] The main hypothesis tested is whether, other things being equal, the shorter the distance of firm location to the city center the earlier the demise of an industrial SOE. What the analysis reveals is that there is indeed a strong positive correlation between these factors. This suggests that

---

19. The privatization of industrial SOEs located in or near urban centers did not necessarily lead to their immediate demolition for urban development, as it might take some time to work out the financial and regulatory arrangements and to overcome the challenges of accommodating affected parties (e.g., employees, occupants, neighbors, and so on) for turning such strategic holdings into real estate projects. Nor did it necessarily take the form of a complete sell-off of the SOEs concerned, as the process could involve a dilution of public ownership through various quasi-private organizational forms and/or gradually phase into deepening private ownership. There were also cases where local governments acquired or converted poorly performing industrial SOEs for urban development through real estate companies under their control (e.g., the Greenland Group and the Shenda Group in Shanghai).

20. Descriptions of the data source, variables and methods, along with regression results, are posted at the book site.

the desideratum of vacating prime sites occupied by industrial SOEs for urban development probably hastened the elimination of many of these enterprises.

Asset Stripping and Insider Control

A concurrent contributing force to the decline of public ownership in the post-Mao era is the outright self-seeking behavior of party-state officials and public enterprise managers. In a previous study (Lin 2001), I have discussed how and why the central planning system of the Mao era faded away during the 1980s–1990s partly as a result of the growth of private exchange relations in the political process and with outsiders. By diverting resources from designated users and purposes, bending regulations, and directly undertaking for-profit activities, party-state officials weakened the abilities and tendencies of public enterprises to stay within the old system and at the same time expanded the economic space outside central planning. Since government officials were the main stewards of public ownership in China's market transition, a collateral consequence of the growing collusion between political and economic actors for private gains is that it undermined the governance of public enterprises, where deteriorating organizational health partly resulting from insiders' manipulation for private gains set the stage for the massive privatization in the late 1990s and beyond.

The corrosive effect of insiders' self-seeking behavior on public enterprises has attracted considerable attention from both policymakers and observers. A focal issue is asset stripping—the conversion of corporate assets into private assets, primarily by insiders in the public sector. It is often discussed with reference to *guoyou zichan liushi* (the erosion and loss of state-owned assets), though the scope of the problem extends beyond SOEs and encompasses collective enterprises (especially TVEs) as well. Two related questions figure most prominently in connection with this. The first one has to do with the role of asset stripping in exacerbating the plight faced by public enterprises during the years leading up to the Fifteenth Party Congress in 1997. Premier Zhu Rongji, for example, regarded it as a major cause for the sagging performance of SOEs (Zhu Rongji 2011, 2:56–61, 139, 242–247). There are also numerous reports and case studies to the same effect, including some undertaken by the government's own regulatory authorities (e.g., Chen Jian 1998; Chen Zhengyun, Yang Shuwen, and Sun Ming 1998; ZYQYGW 2003). In the 2004 CASS-HKUST private enterprise owner survey mentioned above, 66.5% of the respondents ($n = 510$) agreed or strongly agreed that asset stripping was a major contributing factor to the deteriorating organizational health that brought down many SOEs and collective enterprises before massive privatization.

The second question concerns the deepening effects on privatization as a result of the strategic moves by some public enterprise managers for self-enrichment during the process of ownership restructuring after 1997, such as exaggerating losses and/or liabilities, undervaluing assets, manipulating or distorting relevant information, and hiding or stealing enterprise funds. There has been a heated debate about the ramifications of these maneuverings in China. The debate was popularized by Larry Hsien-ping Lang in 2004, who was then a finance professor at the Chinese University of Hong Kong and has since become a prominent public intellectual in mainland China. In a series of investigative reports widely publicized through the Chinese mass media, he outlined the methods used by insiders to strip away corporate assets in the ownership restructuring of three well-known public enterprises—Haier, TCL, and Kelong, and he chastised the social injustice that such behavior rendered on society. Peking University economist Zhou Qiren (Zhou Qiren 2004) dissented by questioning some of the facts in Lang's reports and suggested that the gains (if any) accruing to insiders during the downsizing and restructuring of the public sector could be seen as a necessary price that China had to pay for speeding up the process of ownership reform.[21]

While case materials and anecdotal evidence abound (e.g., Chen 2005; Chen Jian 1998; Chen Zhengyun et al. 1998), asset stripping is in large measure a clandestine phenomenon that evades systematic investigation using observational data. The inconsistencies and opacity of China's evolving regulatory system pose further challenges to such investigation.[22] It is particularly difficult to obtain the necessary longitudinal information that would help assess the causal links pertaining to the first question stated above. What I attempt to do here is to focus on the period spanned by the second question and to search for provisional clues by examining available data on industrial SOEs before and after ownership restructuring. The issues that I seek to shed some

---

21. For a collection of Lang's reports and a sample of different views, see the edited volume by Liu Yiqing and Zhang Qinde 2005.

22. For example, before 1994 the value of land was not counted as part of the equity capital of public enterprises. That began to change after the government introduced a scheme called *qingchan hezi* (stocktaking of enterprise assets) among SOEs during 1994–1995. It was extended to urban collective enterprises in 1997 and to TVEs (by the Ministry of Agriculture) in 1998. Although there were general guidelines on how to assess and account for land values, in practice it was up to local authorities to decide on how to proceed and what criteria to use (Liu Weidong 2008; Xu Mu and Zhang Xiaohua 1995).

light on include whether insider takeover of control was a significant phenomenon immediately after privatization and whether there is any suggestive evidence of extraordinary space for insiders to maneuver for self-enrichment during ownership restructuring.[23]

To explore the first issue, I make use of the information on chief enterprise leaders in the 1995 industrial census, the annual industrial enterprise surveys conducted by the National Bureau of Statistics in 1996–2003 and 2005–2007, and the 2004 economic census. I compare the data for industrial SOEs in the years immediately before and after their disappearance from the data sets. I count as insider-controlled enterprises the cases where the chief leaders, known as *faren daibiao* or legal person representatives, of the industrial SOEs that dropped out in a given year and their names reappeared as chief leaders of nonpublic enterprises in the following year during 1998–2006.[24] The results are tabulated in table 7.6.

What the figures in the table show is that insiders did account for a sizable portion of the industrial SOEs undergoing privatization. The last two columns of the table also reveal that the debt-equity ratio of industrial SOEs in the year immediately before privatization tended to be higher among those that were subsequently controlled by insiders than those controlled by outsiders.[25] This descriptive statistic is intriguing, as it suggests that insider-controlled enterprises had taken seemingly greater financial risk than (later) outsider-controlled enterprises at the outset of privatization.[26] It is possible,

---

23. Such behavior does not necessarily fully overlap with the notion "asset stripping," though, which typically denotes illicit diversion of corporate assets. See the discussion below.

24. It should be noted that this method of estimation may be prone to measurement errors. One potential source of inaccuracy is the fact that the nonpublic enterprises headed by some of those identified as "insiders" might not be the same SOEs where they had been the chief leaders, though a check of the data based on four-digit classification sector code, postal code, regulatory authority, and in some cases firm ID code and starting year (which should have been changed to reflect the new identities and vintage of the privatized enterprises but somehow had yet to be modified in the data reported, thus exposing the common identities of the same enterprises with changed ownership) reveals a close match for more than 90% of the cases. Another potential source of problem is that some of the privatized SOEs might be headed by surrogates or people with close ties to their former chief leaders (e.g., their relatives) or by insiders who had not been listed as the chief leaders in the preprivatization year. Such cases are unobservable from the data. The overestimation and underestimation resulting from these two different sources may be mutually offsetting in summary statistics, but the extent is unknown and the distortions may introduce biases in further data analysis.

25. I report the median instead of the mean because it is much less sensitive than the latter to the impact of a small number of extreme values.

26. Another pattern it reveals is that the debt-equity ratio of industrial SOEs prior to privatization trended down after the turn of the century. This holds for both enterprises subsequently controlled

Table 7.6 Insider control of former industrial SOEs after privatization

Year	Remaining number of industrial SOEs	Number of insiders as firm leaders the year after privatization	% of insider-controlled firms after privatization	Median debt-equity ratio in the year immediately before privatization	
				Non-insider-controlled	Insider-controlled
1998	58,665	8,453	27%	1.08	1.34
1999	53,230	3,691	63%	1.03	1.35
2000	45,023	4,203	52%	1.15	1.49
2001	36,214	4,357	50%	0.99	1.23
2002	31,861	2,723	43%	0.91	1.20
2003	25,403	3,424	55%	0.96	1.28
2004	25,571	3,607	51%	0.58	0.73
2005	18,690	3,078	48%	0.78	0.97
2006	16,368	1,848	82%	0.68	0.76
2007	11,834	2,171	48%		

Sources: Data of 1995 industrial census, 2004 economic census, 1998–2003 and 2005–2007 NBS industrial surveys.

though, that the distribution patterns of the two groups of enterprises were subject to the influence of selection bias in the timing of privatization and a variety of other factors, such as sector, firm age, and recent performance and history. With these possibilities controlled for,[27] however, a regression analysis of the data finds that debt-equity ratio still shows a significantly positive correlation with the likelihood of insider control in privatization. Why, then, did insiders demonstrate a stronger tendency to take over SOEs with greater financial liabilities than outsiders? Assuming insiders and outsiders did not have sharply different risk tolerance profiles, one would not expect this to have occurred to any significant extent unless the observed difference is due to some unobserved factor(s).

The relatively higher debt-equity ratio of insider-controlled enterprises could be associated with two possibilities that may have combined to shape

---

by insiders and those by outsiders. A possible contributing factor is the efforts of the government to address the problem of nonperforming loans during the same period, which resulted in a transfer of liabilities to asset management companies and massive write-offs by state-owned banks, as noted above.

27. Details of the analysis are posted at the book site.

the summary statistic. One is that the correlation reflected in varying degrees the real financial situations of the enterprises concerned prior to privatization. The other is that the higher ratio was inflated for some undisclosed agenda(s), such as facilitating strategic bargaining and/or illicit conversion of corporate assets into private assets during and after privatization. In the former case a major factor that could have driven insiders to take on greater financial liability is their firm-specific knowledge and experience, which outsiders did not have but insiders could draw upon to help contain any potential or real threat posed by the extra level of liability. In order for this mechanism to play out during the process of ownership restructuring, however, insiders had to be given sufficiently strong incentives that would more fully reward their unique human capital. In other words, the price of selling the enterprise (and thereby unloading the financial burden) to insiders had to be attractive enough (e.g., with a huge discount). In the case of a strategically inflated debt-equity ratio (which could result from undervaluation or hiding of equity, exaggeration of liabilities, or both), two conditions would be conducive to its occurrence: information asymmetry between enterprise managers and supervising officials, and collusion between them for mutual benefits, both of which have been discussed in chapter 4. Like the incentive effect just mentioned, these conditions would enlarge the space for insiders to benefit from the process of privatization. The stronger the inducing and facilitating conditions, the stronger the tendency of insiders to embrace and speed up privatization.

Closely related to these causal channels were the corresponding roles played by government officials as duly diligent "principals," negligent overseers, and active colluders, as I have pointed out in chapter 4.[28] To account for what shaped the observed link between prior debt-equity ratio and subsequent insider control, it would be useful to clearly distinguish and compare such roles, as well as those played by enterprise managers. Unfortunately, this undertaking is not feasible because the pertinent information is lacking. There are no published statistics on the transfer prices of privatized SOEs,

---

28. These roles figure prominently in the literature on corporate governance and management buyout in the West (e.g., Cumming, Siegelb, and Wright 2007; Shleifer and Vishny 1997). A major difference, though, is that the "principals" in China's ownership restructuring were fictitious, as they were invariably government officials who had no intrinsic interest in publicly owned assets. They merely acted as agents of the public and were subject to the influence of private incentives. Moreover, ownership restructuring took place at a time when the basic structure of corporate governance was being fundamentally revamped and there existed many loopholes for insider manipulation and collusion at and between the corporate and the regulatory levels.

nor can the manipulation by managers and their collusion with supervising officials be discerned from existing observational data.

There is nevertheless one piece of indirect evidence, revealed by a two-stage regression analysis (posted at the book site), concerning a link between sales growth in earlier years of reform and the likelihood of insider control during privatization. What it shows is that earlier overexpansion of sales had an enhancing effect on the correlation between debt-equity ratio and insider control at the time of privatization. If the relatively higher debt-equity ratio of insider-controlled enterprises indeed provides a rough proxy for the extra benefits accruing to insiders (via the channels just discussed) during privatization, then the enhancing effect is of relevance for understanding the mechanisms of deepening privatization. As I have shown in chapter 4, faster expansion of sales delinked from profitability entailed greater liability; with growing organizational scale and complexity it also tended to increase information asymmetry between management and supervising authorities. These in turn could increase the space for managerial bargaining and manipulation in the process of ownership restructuring. Although it is not possible to separate and directly identify these relevant effects from the data, the finding does point to a path-dependent link to the deepening of privatization after 1997 and suggests a need to broaden the time frame in the examination of the driving forces at work.

The End Game: SASAC and the Remaining SOEs

The sharp decline of the public sector around the turn of the century was followed by a reorganization of the remaining public enterprises, especially SOEs.[29] A major theme of this reorganization was the consolidation of control authority. Before 2003 SOEs were supervised by various industry-specific agencies at different levels of government (Lin and Zhu 2001). That arrangement was brought to an end with the establishment of the SASAC in 2003 as the sole government authority to oversee the operations of the vast majority of remaining nonfinancial SOEs.[30] The SASAC at the national level oversees centrally owned nonfinancial SOEs, whereas local

---

29. As I have shown in chapter 1 and further mentioned in preceding sections of this chapter, collective enterprises have become an insignificant part of the public sector since the turn of the century. The discussion in this section therefore focuses on the remaining SOEs.

30. Since the late 1990s financial services have been placed under the supervision and regulation of four central authorities: the People's Bank, the China Banking Regulatory Commission, the China

governments have formed their counterparts to supervise locally owned SOEs that survived massive privatization. At the national level nonfinancial SOEs were regrouped into 196 very large enterprise groups or holding companies in 2003. That number has since been reduced in subsequent rounds of consolidation. It went down to 169 in 2008 and further to 102 in August 2016. A similar trend has also been demonstrated at local levels (*FYC*, various years; *SICA*, various years).

Concurrent with the reorganization of SOEs was a retreat of SOEs from the vast majority of economic sectors and from dominance in many sectors where they still maintained a presence. Table 7.7 shows that the total number of industrial SOEs decreased by more than 85% during 1995–2008. During the same period the total number of four-digit industrial sectors with SOE presence declined from 604 to 440, whereas those with a presence of more than ten SOEs experienced a far more drastic drop—from 521 to 159. Also noteworthy is that the percentage of industrial sectors with a more than 50% share of SOE presence went down from 29% to 2.5%. Small SOEs experienced faster decline than larger ones; so did local SOEs relative to central SOEs, especially after the formation of the SASAC. This change was in line with the policy of "holding onto the large and letting go of the small," noted earlier in this chapter. What, then, were the forces that shaped the landscape of public ownership in the postprivatization era?

An apparently important factor is the strategic calculation by the central leadership. In an interview with the *People's Daily* on March 13, 2005,[31] SASAC commissioner Li Rongrong pointed out that the remapping of SOEs must focus on four considerations: importance for national security and vital economic interests, strength based on existing competitive advantage and/or potential for future industry leadership, development of international competitiveness, and gravitation toward central government ownership and control. Among the nonfinancial sectors he emphasized are weaponry, aviation and aerospace, telecommunications, petroleum and petrochemicals, power, and transportation. In 2004 the last four of these sectors accounted for nearly

---

Securities Regulatory Commission, and the China Insurance Regulatory Commission. The tobacco industry has been under the State Tobacco Monopoly Administration. The railway system has been under the Ministry of Railway (until 2013, when it was abolished) and the China Railway Corporation (as of 2013). Postal services have been under the State Post Bureau. In addition, there have been several dozen state-owned units under the supervision of various central government ministries and agencies that are also categorized broadly as SOEs, including some transportation facilities (e.g., airports) and for-profit organizations in publishing, mass media, and other cultural and social affairs.

31. http://www.gov.cn/zwhd/2006-03/13/content_225540.htm.

Table 7.7 Selected statistics on industrial SOEs before and after ownership restructuring

	1995	1998	2004	2008
Number of enterprises	87,905	58,665	25,571	10,844
Four-digit industrial sectors with SOE presence	603 (521)	599 (490)	515 (336)	440 (159)
% of four-digit industrial sectors with 50+% sales produced by SOEs	29	22.1	4.6	2.5
% of large & medium SOEs	19	23	23	34
Median asset (RMB millions)	67	118	171	685
Median equity (RMB millions)	12	19	30	192
Immediate supervising authority (%)				
Central	5	7	12	17
Provincial	11	13	20	23
Prefectural	26	24	23	22
Other	58	56	45	38
Top five industries (two-digit) in terms of number of SOE establishments	Food P Building M Chemicals Food M Power	Food P Power Building M Water Coal	Power Water Food P Building M Auto	Power Water Coal Food P Building M
% of top five industries (two-digit) in total number of industrial SOEs	38	30	37	48
% of local enterprises in top five SOE industries (two-digit)	90	95	91	90

Notes: (a) Data are for industrial SOEs with independent accounting status. (b) Figures in parentheses indicate the number of four-digit industrial sectors with no more than ten remaining SOEs. "Food P," "Building M," and (c) "Food M" stand for food processing, building materials, and food manufacturing respectively.

Sources: Data of 1995 industrial census, 1998 NBS annual industrial survey, 2004 economic census, 2008 economic census.

half (48.4%) of the equity capital and 39.7% of the total assets of nonfinancial SOEs (*FYC 2006*, 429–431).

Conspicuously missing in Li Rongrong's remarks, however, is the role of SOEs (and the remaining public sector at large) in job creation. As noted in chapter 1 and chapter 4, industrial SOEs ceased to add jobs in 1993, and the share of the public sector in the total workforce steadily declined throughout the 1980s and 1990s. The reorganization of SOEs after the tidal wave of privatization had subsided continued that trend. In 2001 the total number of employees in the remaining nonfinancial SOEs was 51.4 million. It went down to 39.8 million in 2004, one year after the formation of the SASAC, and further to 35.1 million in 2008 (*FYC 2006*, 436; *FYC 2013*, 473). Realities in the new economy appear to have forced the CCP leadership to accept the overwhelmingly dominant and increasingly indispensable role of the private sector in job provision, creation, and growth. In fact the strategy that Li Rongrong spelled out for the remaining SOEs is a highly capital-intensive one, primarily aimed at addressing policy concerns other than employment due to its inhibitively high cost.

One such concern is the generation and control of fiscal revenue. As I have discussed in chapter 4, throughout the 1980s and the better part of the 1990s SOEs and other public enterprises were used extensively as vehicles of revenue generation through a sales growth strategy. That strategy was a response to both the postreform political incentives and a long-standing feature of the fiscal system that relied heavily on indirect taxes. Over time the moral hazard it fostered undermined the financial and organizational health of many public enterprises and contributed to their ultimate demise. For government officials in charge of the remaining public sector, however, the basic structural conditions that influenced their decision-making before massive privatization have persisted. Despite the use of more diverse political performance assessment criteria during the Hu-Wen years (2002–2012) and greater relative importance of income taxes in government revenue, economic growth and fiscal resources have continued to be the focal concerns of leading officials, and indirect taxes have remained the main source of government revenue. But there has been a major shift in the strategic approach to the organization and management of SOEs following massive privatization.

With much smaller number of public enterprises remaining, organizational scale has become the focus of their supervising authorities. Table 7.7 shows that industrial SOEs experienced steady growth in terms of both equity and assets after massive privatization. The increase was drastic in the years following the formation of the SASAC. A likely contributing factor is organizational consolidation that combined smaller units into larger ones. Another factor is the injection of capital, in terms of both capital investment and bank lending, to create "national champions" in key industries (Lardy 2014). From 1999 to 2008 the equity capital held by the state in nonfinancial SOEs increased from 5.1 trillion yuan to 13.4 trillion yuan (*FYC 2009*, 506). During the same period, fixed-asset investment in all state-owned units increased from 1.6 trillion yuan to 4.9 trillion yuan (*CSY 2000*, table 6.4; *CSY 2009*, table 5.3); and short- and long-term liabilities (which mainly consisted of bank loans) rose from 8.9 to 26.7 trillion yuan (*FYC 2006*, 418; *FYC 2009*, 506). Although the pace of investment and lending growth among the remaining SOEs was slower relative to that in the fast-expanding private sector (Lardy 2014), the intensity of the capital infusion was likely to be very high given the much-reduced number of fund recipients.

Still another contributing factor is the use of corporatization as a way to boost the scale of state-controlled companies with nonstate capital. As mentioned at the beginning of this chapter, at the Fifteenth Party Congress in 1997 the CCP leadership abandoned its long-standing definition of public ownership as public sole proprietorship and allowed for a "dilution" of public ownership through shareholding arrangements dominated by the state. What followed was an increase of companies with controlling stakes held by the state.[32] In 1999 these "state controlled" companies made up 16% of industrial SOEs (*CIESY 2001*, 4); the percentage went up to 28% in 2003 and 48% in 2008 (*CIESY 2004*, 4; *CIESY 2009*, 7, 52). They also accounted for a significant number of the companies listed on the Shanghai and Shenzhen stock exchanges,[33] as well as a large number of the Chinese companies listed on stock exchanges in Hong Kong, Singapore, New York, and London. In 1998 minority stakes (held by noncontrolling owners) accounted for 3.5% of the equity capital of nonfinancial SOEs; the percentage went up to 17% in 2003 and further to 19.4% in 2008 (*FYC 2004*, 372; *FYC 2009*, 506).

Closely coupled with the strategy to grow the size of the remaining SOEs is an effort to use regulatory power to reinforce the dominant or monopolistic positions of SOEs in key economic sectors, especially those at the national level. The railway system and the tobacco industry, for example, are exclusive territories for SOEs. Various entry barriers have also been erected and/or

---

32. Such dominance is not necessarily equivalent to majority shareholding by the state. See Holz and Lin 2001 for a discussion of the definition of controlling stakes.

33. In 2010, for example, of the 2,063 domestically listed companies 1,038 were nonfinancial SOEs controlled by SASACs at various levels (*CSY 2011*, table 19.12; *CSOASAY 2011*, 31). Of the 124 nonfinancial SOEs under the central SASAC, 93 had subsidiaries listed on domestic and/or foreign stock exchanges.

maintained for not only the sectors that Li Rongrong emphasized but a host of other sectors, especially at local levels (see the discussion below). With the regulatory protection and concentrated resource support, the overall financial performance of the remaining SOEs experienced some improvement. The percentage of profitable nonfinancial SOEs rose from 31.3% in 1998 to 48% in 2004 and further to 56.8% in 2008, and the return on total assets went up from 2.1% to 4.5% and 4.6% respectively (*FYC 2006*, 419; *FYC 2013*, 256).

Underneath these generally positive changes, however, are some unsettling issues concerning the strength of the reorganized SOEs. More than 40% of the nonfinancial SOEs were either unprofitable or in the red. Profitability also skewed toward a small number of sectors, such as petroleum and petrochemicals, tobacco, and electricity, that benefited from rising demand from consumers and producers and from the government's pricing policies. During 2001–2008 the combined share of these three industries in the total taxes paid by nonfinancial SOEs was 42.8%. A deeper problem, as Lardy (2014) has pointed out, is that many remaining SOEs faced difficulties in covering the cost of (borrowed) capital because of low return on assets and high leverage. The pressure was particularly strong for local SOEs, which accounted for 45% of the assets of nonfinancial SOEs in 2008 and over 80% of the number of establishment. Their debt-equity ratio was 212% in 1998 and averaged at 222% per year in the following decade.[34] During the same period the average return on assets for local SOEs was 3.5%, which was lower than the average for SOEs under the SASAC (5.7%) and nonfinancial SOEs controlled by other central government authorities (4.7%) (*FYC 2006*, 418; *2009*, 506).

Why, then, were many SOEs with lackluster financial performance retained? A likely consideration behind this phenomenon is that, other than the strategic importance assigned to them by various government authorities, the remaining SOEs continued to be useful and convenient tools of fiscal revenue generation, control, and manipulation as a result of several enabling conditions. The significantly increased unit scale of the remaining SOEs through organizational consolidation and capital infusion helped compensate for the substantial reduction in the number of organizational units during massive privatization. In contrast to the dispersed organizational pattern in the 1980s and 1990s, concentrated scale expansion provided an alternative avenue for sales growth, which continued to be important for revenue generation given

---

34. In contrast the debt-equity ratio was 117% for central SOEs in 1998 and averaged 136% during 1999–2008 (*FYC 2006*, 418; *FYC 2009*, 506).

the persistence of the importance of indirect taxes.[35] Sales growth in the new economy could also benefit from rising demand from producers and consumers for the resources, products, and services in the sectors dominated or monopolized by the remaining SOEs in upstream or exclusive sectors.[36] It is interesting to note that the overall fiscal strength of the downsized state sector did not deteriorate but actually made some gains after massive privatization. In 1998 the share of nonfinancial SOEs in total tax revenue was 30.6%. During 2001–2008 it averaged 39.9% (*FYC 1999*, 449, 482; *FYC 2006*, 432, 434; *FYC 2009*, 520, 522).

For local SOEs, which accounted for the vast majority of the remaining state sector and had poorer rates of return and higher leverage, their persistence in some sectors might have been mainly driven by fiscal considerations too. Table 7.9 shows that after massive privatization, power (mainly electricity distribution) and water supply became the sectors with the largest presence of industrial SOEs. This is not surprising in that they are both "natural monopolies" based on scale economy and have strategic importance for socioeconomic stability. Yet there also remained a sizable cluster of overwhelmingly local SOEs (representing over 95% of the remaining SOEs therein) in food processing and building materials. These sectors are by no means strategically important as defined by central leaders.[37] Many of them were unprofitable

---

35. The share of these taxes in total tax revenue was 76% in 2003 and 73% in 2008 (*FYC 2009*, 480).

36. Some of these sectors had higher tax rates too. A case in point is the tobacco industry, which also provides an example of the impact of revenue considerations on the decision to retain SOEs in some economic sectors that are not of importance for national security or long-term development. China has the largest number of smokers (totaling more than 300 million) and the largest tobacco industry in the world (Mao Zhegzhong and Hu Dewei 2008). Tobacco has been a major source of government revenue in the industrial sector, second only to the petroleum and petrochemical industry. In 2004, for example, the tobacco sector accounted for 4% of the profits earned by nonfinancial SOEs but 14% of the taxes from these enterprises (*FYC 2009*, 522–524). The lucrative gains from this sector have led the government not only to retain it as a state monopoly and (since 2006) place all tobacco companies under the direct control of the central government, but to adopt policies that help maximize revenue through state-owned tobacco companies. Most of the smokers in China are rural citizens without much or any healthcare coverage subsidized or financed by the government. Against recommendations from medical experts and international institutions like the World Health Organization to use fiscal measures to contain and minimize the health hazard associated with smoking, the Chinese government has maintained tobacco tax rates (and hence retail prices) at very "affordable" levels so as to keep a broad base of smokers for short-term revenue extraction (http://www.wpro.who.int/china/mediacentre/factsheets/tobacco_taxation/zh/).

37. A nonindustrial sector that has no apparent strategic significance but has had some SOE presence in the postprivatization era is real estate. With the booming of the sector after the turn of the century, many remaining SOEs set up auxiliary operations in the sector. One report claims that in 2008 130 of the 169 nonfinancial SOEs under the SASAC at that time had real estate business (http://www.xindichan.com.cn/article_15090.html). But the central government cracked down on such activities.

too (e.g., accounting for 60% and 53% of the sector totals respectively in 2004). A probable reason for their retention is that they were locality-specific monopolies rendered by historical patterns of industrial location, local regulatory policies, and transportation cost.

A close examination of the data reveals that of the 477 food-processing SOEs remaining in 2008, 154 were slaughterhouses and 151 were milling plants; of the 490 building material enterprises remaining, 374 were producers of cement and related products. In over 85%–90% of the cases, these enterprises were the sole businesses in their county-level locales. All of them were established before the start of massive privatization in 1997, and there had been no local peers before that. It is possible that many of the supervising authorities of these enterprises used regulatory power to block entry by potential competitors after massive privatization so that they could continue to monopolize local business and thereby lock in a stream of revenue. The main customers of these enterprises were farmers and constructors. Although the local governments concerned might not be able to effectively prevent them from going elsewhere to address their needs, transportation cost considerations could have led them to refrain from doing so.

Another industry with a significant number of remaining SOEs is coal, which has been the source of supply for some two-thirds to seven-tenths of the energy consumption in China. As shown in table 7.9, coal had the third largest number of remaining industrial SOEs in 2008, though this was not the case in earlier years. During the massive privatization around the turn of the century, many locally owned small coal mines were closed down or sold to private operators because of financial problems. But then coal prices steadily rose, partly because of the booming demand for energy in the new economy following massive privatization and China's accession to the WTO in 2001, and partly because of the rise of oil prices nearly through the end of the decade. This change not only led to a withholding of the efforts to further privatize the coal sector but drove some local governments to claw back lost territories.

In Shanxi, which is the country's largest coal-producing province and depends on the coal sector for more than half of local government revenue, a major decision was made by the provincial government in 2009 to buy

---

In 2008 it issued directives to consolidate and limit SOE involvement in real estate to fifteen centrally owned companies and to instruct local SASACs to impose similar restrictions. Although real estate only made up a small fraction of the total sales of nonfinancial SOEs (no more than 3%), its share in profits increased—from 2.2% in 2001 to 4.6% in 2008 and 7.6% in 2012 (*FYC 2006*, 432–433; *FYC 2013*, 469–470).

back over one thousand small private coal mines on the ground of improving safety and to integrate them into seven large coal-producing SOEs. As noted in chapter 1, that move, along with a few concurrent incidents of SOEs taking over private companies, triggered the debate about whether a new trend of deprivatization was in the making (chapter 1). The reorganization of the coal industry in Shanxi has taken longer to complete than planned, with mixed results in terms of the financial and fiscal gains anticipated by the local governments.[38] There is no sign of further or similar moves of deprivatization in the coal sector and other economic sectors, both in the province and nationally.[39] It is beyond the scope of this book to examine the repercussions for Shanxi province and for the relative significance of public ownership in the economy at large. What this event does seem to corroborate, though, is that revenue concerns have played an important role in shaping the decisions and actions of political actors in regard to the boundaries of the remaining public sector.

Summary

The central government played a key role in setting off the massive wave of privatization in the late 1990s. What led to the tipping point in 1997 was the growing inability and failure of public enterprises to cope with the impact of persistent demographic pressures and the deepening of their financial problems that plagued the fiscal capacity of the state. These challenges were the results of the actions and interactions of political and economic actors in response to the evolving institutional and policy environment during the first two decades of reform, as discussed in the preceding chapters. As a bitter pill taken for regime survival, therefore, the drastic decision at the Fifteenth Party Congress was driven by cumulative endogenous forces. In contrast to exogenous shocks in many processes of institutional change (North 1990), the triggers to the pivotal event in this context were also highly path-dependent despite the coincidental outbreak of the Asian financial crisis.

The trajectory of privatization subsequent to the reset point of departure in 1997 nevertheless deviated from CCP leaders' initial plan of ownership restructuring. In no way did they foresee the tempo and extent of decline in

---

38. For an interesting report, see http://business.sohu.com/20140922/n404524013.shtml.

39. Table 1.9, based on data from the three economic censuses in 2004, 2008, and 2013, shows that the shares of SOEs in the assets and sales of the coal industry actually trended down despite the episode discussed here.

public ownership in the decade to follow. Yet they had to reckon and come to terms with the new realities, however grudgingly, due to the seriousness of the problems and the exhaustion of viable alternatives, especially in regard to the issue of employment. The substantial softening of the Party's stance on private ownership has also sharply reduced the risk and difficulty of justifying the adoption of measures of ownership restructuring beyond centrally prescribed or preferred solutions (e.g., mergers).

As a vital group of change agents, local officials have contributed significantly to the precipitousness and deepening of privatization from the late 1990s onward. To explain the causal mechanisms of their behavior, it is important to consider the strategic reactions of local officials to the new opportunities and interests prompted by the pivotal event in 1997 and the coevolving structural conditions that reshaped the incentives and constraints they faced. It is equally important, though, to take account of the lasting impact from the consequences of local officials' past pursuit of self-interest, as well as the long-standing characteristics of the political and economic system. The foregoing discussions of the accelerating effects from the bandwagon responses of local governments, the shift of policy focus from industrial development to urbanization, the role of insider control in the aftermath of the Fifteenth Party Congress, and the landscape of the postprivatization public sector all show that the ramifications of the pivotal event played out through mechanisms related to both pre- and postevent conditions. In so doing, they also illustrate the relevance of both the contingency view and the lasting-impact view of path dependence, outlined in the introductory chapter, for understanding endogenously induced institutional change. I shall further reflect on the pertinent theoretical implications in the conclusion.

Conclusion

SINCE MAY 1, 1991, every day at dawn a special squad of the People's Armed Police Force has been performing a solemn and elaborate ceremony to raise the Chinese national flag at Tiananmen Square in Beijing. It is part of a concerted effort by the CCP to promote nationalism. Sometimes televised live, the ceremony always attracts a big crowd of spectators. Ironically, many of those who watch it on any given day do not know the original meaning of the national flag, as can be verified by random and repeated surveys.[1] In fact the CCP has been largely reticent about the matter. The National Flag Law (1990), for example, makes no mention of what exactly the five-star pattern means.[2] Nor can an explicit and uniform answer be found in any official document disseminated for use by schools and media organizations in civic education and political propaganda related to this subject.[3] The unforthcoming

---

1. With the help of research assistants I conducted six small-sample surveys ($n = 30$) on this issue at Tiananmen Square on May 27, 2007, September 12, 2007, September 25, 2008, March 2, 2009, February 15, 2010, and April 28, 2011. The percentages of respondents (aged fifteen or above) failing to give a correct answer are 87%, 93%, 73%, 83%, 97%, and 83% respectively.

2. As described in the introduction, two of the four small stars were originally meant to represent capitalist classes.

3. In an explanatory note on China's national flag, national emblem and capital city, the National People's Congress completely omits the rationale offered by the designer of the national flag and instead depicts the five-star pattern as symbolizing the "great solidarity of all the revolutionary people under the leadership of the CCP" (http://www.npc.gov.cn/npc/flsyywd/xianfa/2010-04/14/content_1567087.htm). The same omission is made in an article on the national flag posted at a web page of the official Xinhua News Agency (http://news.xinhuanet.com/ziliao/2003-01/18/). The only full account from an official source about the origins of the flag design is offered in an article posted at a web page of the *People's Daily*, which is nevertheless listed as an obscure information item under the heading of "What Happened in History Today" (http://cpc.people.com.cn/GB/64162/64165/70293/70320/4861365.html). Less authoritative accounts from various nonofficial sources also exist, though there is no "standard version" defined by the central authority for such accounts.

attitude of the CCP toward fully informing Chinese citizens about the historical origins of the country's best-known political symbol is indicative of the ambivalence and uneasiness with which the Party has overseen the growth of private ownership and the spread of capitalism in the post-Mao era. In struggling for regime survival, the communist leadership has had to make increasing compromises on its basic ideological principles, including the dominance of public ownership and socialism.

This book offers an account of how and why this has happened. I focus on the behavior of political actors. The basic premise of my analysis is that jobs—especially nonfarm jobs—and revenue are essential concerns of contemporary rulership. Deficiencies in addressing these concerns under the Maoist system were among the factors leading to the start of economic reforms in the late 1970s. That undertaking has served as a tool for the post-Mao rulers to tackle the twin imperatives by redefining economic institutions according to their own priorities and preferences, and by realigning the behavior of political and economic actors with the new rules of the game. The result is an extraordinary span of fast economic growth for nearly four decades.

The remaking of the rules governing economic activities, however, has not always followed the political will of the CCP leadership. It is an evolutionary and interactive process where institutional rules—both preexisting and new—have unintended consequences that subvert institutional stability and lead to paths deviating from the intended course. Such consequences may stem from compliant behavior, noncompliant behavior, or both among subordinate actors in pursuit of self-interest. I have shown that the compliant behavior of many local officials to promote the marketization and expansion of public enterprises during the 1980s and early 1990s was closely coupled with a growth of moral hazard, which gradually weakened the financial and organizational health of these enterprises and thereby contributed to their demise. I have also shown that in the reform, private enterprises and foreign capital were able to re-emerge and expand partly because the formal rules were bent in their favor by many of those holding regulatory and gatekeeping authorities, who saw the benefits of doing so as complementing or outweighing those of compliant behavior. Such noncompliance inevitably involved political risks/costs, which nonetheless were often contained with various justifications in the name of addressing the formal agendas of the party-state. As more and more public enterprises turned from carriers of the twin mission (of employment and revenue) into sinking ships of personnel and financial liabilities, the tenaciously growing private sector became an increasingly indispensable lifeboat for the CCP's political rule. Ultimately, expediency and desperation prevailed over principles, resulting in massive sell-offs of public enterprises and substantial liberalization and institutionalization of the space for private ownership.

Institutional Stability and Unintended Consequences of Rule Compliance

The process of privatization in post-Mao China represents a case of fundamental institutional change largely driven by endogenous forces. Explaining this change requires an examination of what affects institutional stability. The beginnings of the process can be traced to the end of the Mao era, when the state faced increasing difficulties in addressing the employment and revenue imperatives, as discussed in chapters 2–3. What the post-Mao leaders sought to do was to tackle the cumulative challenges by shifting their policy priority from class struggle to economic development and by ameliorating the central planning system with limited market mechanisms. But unlike the former Soviet bloc, where political revolutions ushered in drastic ownership transformations, China did not set out to privatize existing property right arrangements.[4] Instead the initial focus of reform was on changing the behavior of political and economic actors by altering the incentives and constraints within a framework of predominant public ownership. Among the measures to facilitate this dominant strategy were fiscal decentralization, use of new metrics for political performance assessment, and marketization of public enterprise (chapter 4).

These new arrangements induced active efforts by local officials to promote economic growth and marketization in the 1980s and early 1990s.[5] Yet the formative institutional platform supported by these arrangements was unstable in that the progrowth and promarket responses from local officials were mixed with pursuits of self-interest that rendered the new rules increasingly unsustainable. A major consequence of such pursuits in the face of the demographic and fiscal legacies of the old system is the delinking of

---

4. Decollectivization of agriculture and permission for off-farm self-employment in the countryside did lead to the creation of *new* private assets. But land as the most important resource in the rural economy remained publicly owned. New forms of private ownership also appeared in urban areas with the entry of foreign capital and the legalization of urban self-employment. Their significance in the economy was nevertheless insignificant in the early years of reform.

5. As noted in chapter 4, there is a sizable literature on the impact of such efforts on output (GDP) growth and on the patterns of political elite mobility. In contrast, the focus of my investigation is the implications for economic institutional change.

financial health from sales expansion among public enterprises. It was driven by a widely used strategy that served the interests of local officials (in terms of career benefits and resource control) and at the same time brought about short-term outcomes in line with what the central rule-makers intended to achieve—that is, addressing employment and revenue imperatives through the marketization of public enterprises. With the growth of the moral hazard that accompanied the rule-compliant behavior under this strategy, however, the sustainability of public enterprises became increasingly untenable. What unfolded as a result was a paradoxical story: the stewards of public ownership turned out to be its main destroyers.

My analysis of the mechanisms leading to the debacle of public enterprises illustrates that rule compliance is a necessary but insufficient condition for institutional stability. This, of course, is by no means a novel finding. There is a long-standing tradition in the study of organizations and institutions that focuses on the potential of institutional rules being used as multipurpose tools that can engender consequences unintended by rule makers (e.g., Perrow 1986; Scott 2001, 2013; Selznick 1949). While the pertinent theories are largely developed or applied to account for "aberrations" in relatively stable systems in the West, this focus is equally relevant for the study of non-Western systems that undergo fundamental transformations. Yet it appears to be sidelined in the more recent literature on institutional change, where considerable attention has been drawn to directionally predictable correlation between rule following and institutional stability.

As I have highlighted in the introduction, in explaining the sources of institutional instability and change, the "rationalist" perspective in institutional economics focuses on the breakdowns of rule-compliant behavior due to exogenous shocks and/or the ramifications of quasi-exogenous factors, whereas the "historical institutionalism" school in political science emphasizes the cumulatively eroding effects of noncompliant behavior from within an existing system. What I have presented in the preceding chapters shows that rule-compliant behavior may be a Janus-faced phenomenon. Investigating how this potential duality plays out in the process of institutional change helps bridge the gap between the two contrasting views on institutional (in)stability and complements their strengths. It also complements theories that emphasize the role of the local developmental state (e.g., Oi 1992, 1999) and federalism (e.g., Montinola, Qian, and Weingast 1995) in China's economic change. A common focus of these theories is the immediate stimulating effect of progrowth policies adopted by local officials in response to new political incentives and fiscal decentralization. What my account seeks to illuminate is the implications of these policies for institutional change over a longer time span and in ways deviating from centrally intended course.

A key factor for understanding the unintended consequences of rule-compliant behavior is opportunism. It is widely considered to be a major threat to the governance capacity of established institutions (e.g., Williamson 1985). As an extension of this view, my analysis suggests that opportunism embedded in rule compliance may also play a catalytic role in shaping and timing the ebb and flow of superseding institutional orders. In the post-Mao era this role grew partly because of the lack of effective safeguards against opportunistic uses of newly adopted rules, and partly because of the initially promising outlook of the rule-compliant behavior that accommodated such uses. I shall further discuss these issues in the later section on path dependence. What should be noted here is that opportunism is not only a widespread behavioral trait among local officials. Central leaders of the CCP have also been opportunistic in their policymaking and adjustment. Although they are preoccupied with more encompassing agendas than local officials, what ultimately drives their behavior is the calculation of their own self-interest, which is closely tied to regime survival. In seeking to address this fundamental concern under the constraint of new and evolving realities, they have had to resort to short-term fixes at the expense of further drifting away from communism, making it harder for subsequent leaders to use the Party's ideological mantle for the legitimation of their political rule.

Noncompliance and Political Risk Management

Unintended consequences of compliant behavior in the administration of public enterprises were not the only contributing force to privatization in the post-Mao era. A parallel path to the rise and spread of private ownership is rule bending by local officials for genetically private enterprises and foreign capital. This represents a form of noncompliant behavior, as it often stretched or exceeded the limits of the formal rules defined by the central leadership at different stages of the reform process. Such behavior was motivated by efforts to seek the same kind of career benefits and resource control under the new political incentive system, by responses to private incentives from collusive alliances and/or favor seekers,[6] or by both.

---

6. In a previous study (Lin 2001) I have offered an in-depth account of such responses and their consequences for institutional change. There are also numerous studies that reveal the intimate ties and

Noncompliance with institutional rules inevitably involves varying degrees of political risk for local officials. How they managed such risk during the 1980s and 1990s is a recurrent theme throughout this book (especially chapters 5–6). Four major findings are particularly noteworthy. First, noncompliance was often a corollary of the weak ability or failure of local officials to stay the course prescribed by the prevailing institutional rules. In most of the regions experiencing early privatization, bending formal rules for private business did not become the dominant strategy before the faltering of public enterprises. Even in Wenzhou—the most-cited case of early "aberration," the initial policy stance of the local government was to promote public enterprises.

Second, a common tactic for containing the risk of local officials' noncompliance with the central policy bias toward public ownership is to fabricate justifications in relation to the twin imperatives of revenue and employment. Case study findings and statistical analyses both point to the importance of such maneuvering among early movers of privatization. It should also be noted that the political risk taken by many local officials in this regard was a calculated one. It was often buffered with claims of severe economic hardship beyond the responding capacity of local public enterprises, and with attempts to portray policy deviations as innovative coping measures under the vague rubric of "reforms," as illustrated by the story about the political leadership in Wenzhou during the 1980s (chapter 5). My investigation into the relationship between risk management and variations in ownership change among different regions and locales also points to a need to expand the analysis of the role of factionalism in economic institutional change.

Existing studies of factions in Chinese politics focus on the personal characteristics of political leaders at various levels, such as policy preferences or factional affiliations (e.g., Bo 2002; Cheung, Chung, and Lin 1998; Huang 2000; Shih 2008). Considerable efforts have been made to ascertain their ideological persuasions or inclinations, to delineate factional origins and boundaries among shifting political alliances, and to separate the policy changes introduced by incumbents from those initiated by their predecessors under a generally transient tenure system. What my study shows is a different angle from which to analyze the roles of factionalism for understanding institutional change. That is, factional divisions (and more discrete personal rivalry

---

private exchanges between government officials and private business people in the reform (e.g., Shi Xianmin 1991; Tsai 2002; Wank 1999; Young 1995).

as well) are an important factor that engenders and sustains political risks, thus posing a major constraint on noncompliant behavior and conditioning its cost and outcome. Moreover, intense factional divisions may also weaken the governance capacity of the state and thus leave open opportunities for the persistence and survival of entrepreneurial forces under Maoism and for social and economic actors to break away from the existing system. A case in point at the local level is Wenzhou, discussed in chapter 4. The rule-breaking behavior of nonstate actors in turn may also affect the political strategies of state actors, which pertains to the next finding.

Third, the extent and sustainability of local policy deviation from the centrally defined focus on public ownership depended greatly on the demonstrable results it could help deliver. This is where the strength of entrepreneurship among local economic actors could have a major catalytic and reinforcing effect on institutional change. Where economic hardship was severe but both the local public sector and the local entrepreneurial forces were initially weak, early privatization often failed to materialize, partly due to the risk aversion tendencies among local officials in the absence of deliverables. In contrast, such tendencies were reversed in places like Wenzhou because of a long-standing and tenacious business culture rooted in local history, damage rendered by divisive politics to the governing capacity of the local state in the Mao era, and the initial weakness of local public enterprises in the nonfarm sector. What this analysis represents is an extension of the investigation into the role of entrepreneurship in China's economic change. Existing studies focus on the interactions between entrepreneurs and political actors (e.g., Huang 2008; Tsai 2002, 2007). My findings suggest that it is equally important to consider the impact of such interactions on those between political actors and, through the latter, on institutional stability.

Fourth, noncompliant behavior is also conditioned by the dependence relationship between rule-enforcing authorities and subordinate political actors under an organizationally potent, Leninist state system. The more the former depends on the latter, the greater the space for the latter to maneuver for leniency in enforcement against noncompliance (and hence containment of the political risk for local policy deviations); and vice versa. In the analysis of the role of FDI in privatization I have discussed two types of dependence of a superior level on a subordinate level of government in China's multilevel political system (chapter 6)—that is, dependence for contribution of revenue and employment and dependence for alleviation of resource strain on spending. This helps explain the bipolar pattern of rule bending for the organizational forms of FDI and the varying depths of privatization driven by foreign capital across different regions. It also points to an important mechanism of intragovernmental interaction that has yet to be more clearly demonstrated in the existing literature on central-local relations (e.g., Cheung, Chung, and Lin 1998; Montinola, Qian, and Weingast 1995).

The above findings are all consistent with what the "historical institutionalism" school emphasizes—that is, the impact of noncompliant behavior of change agents on institutional stability. Yet at the same time they also illustrate the importance of an issue that is not explicitly explored by the school—that is, risk management or containment for noncompliance. This issue is of particular relevance for understanding evolutionary processes of institutional change, where the degree to which deviant behavior can be sustained and expanded hinges greatly on how costly it is to break or move away from the formal rules. As I have pointed out in the introductory chapter, accounting for the role of noncompliance in institutional change may benefit from an extension of the "new institutionalist" view in sociology and organization studies, which considers the difficulty of legitimizing deviant behavior to be a key factor in institutional stability. The findings just summarized illustrate two related conditions under which such difficulty may be reduced, resulting in increased likelihood of institutional instability and change. That is, rule makers and enforcers are made to perceive certain deviant behavior as beneficial, and the perceived benefit of tolerating such behavior is deemed greater than that of suppressing it. Understanding how these mechanisms develop and how they subvert an existing institutional order in a transitional economy like China requires a close examination of the path-dependent contexts in which the choice sets and cost-benefit calculus of political actors are defined and redefined.

Path Dependence in Endogenous Institutional Change

The decline of the old economy in post-Mao China did not follow the path of the former Soviet bloc, where bottom-up revolutions created new political regimes that subsequently imposed top-down programs of "shock therapy" for a drastic transformation of economic institutions. Yet there have been several pivotal events in the Chinese case that generated significant changes in the parameter of decision-making for political and economic actors. Among the events that are most relevant for understanding the process of privatization are the CCP's decisions to initiate fiscal restructuring in 1977, to shift the focus of policy from class struggle to economic development in 1978, to open up the economy for foreign trade and investment in 1979, to decollectivize agriculture and legalize self-employment in 1980, to remove the size limit on private business in 1988, to restructure the fiscal and banking systems in 1994, and to carry out ownership restructuring of SOEs in 1997 (chapter 1). With the exception of the timing of the historic move to depart from Maoism in 1978,[7] all the other events were driven by endogenously derived forces. I have argued and shown that a major driving force leading to these events stemmed both from the efforts of the party-state to introduce new ways to fix the deficiencies carried over from the Maoist system and from those to cope with the problems and challenges arising from post-Mao ameliorating measures for addressing the policy imperatives of revenue and employment. The path of institutional change in this process of cumulative causation, involving decisions, actions, and interactions at and between central and local levels, is subject to the influence of the self-interest calculus of political actors in face of an evolving structure of incentives and constraints and the feedback from their earlier behavior and responses conditioned by the long-lasting impact of demographic forces and the preexisting fiscal system.

As noted above, the initial strategy of the central leadership to rely on public enterprises to play the leading role in marketization and internationalization was sustained for over a decade despite growing moral hazard, and the failure to contain opportunism eventually led to the demise of the vast majority of public enterprises. Cognitive constraints, such as bounded rationality (Simon 1957; Lindblom 1959), could have been a reason for such failure, especially given the adaptive and problem-driven nature of the reform process (Naughton 1995; Perkins 1994). Political expediency and compromises among different interest groups in the leadership might be another reason (Fewsmith 2008; Shih 2008), as CCP leaders wrestled and coped with circumstances by taking a path of least resistance, instead of an all-around approach, in designing reform measures. Also relevant is the fact that there were competing considerations in personnel policy that led to transient tenures and lack of clarity in cost accounting for political responsibility in local public administration, as discussed in chapter 4. An even more powerful contributing factor revealed in this book is the positive feedback that the initial strategy generated.

---

7. Two "shock" factors—i.e., Mao's death in 1976 and massive natural disasters in 1977–78—were among the forces that triggered the decision on reforms in the pivotal meeting (the Third Plenum of the Eleventh Central Party Committee) of the CCP leadership at the end of 1978. See Lin 2003 for a discussion of how the causal mechanisms played out.

To political actors at all levels, the strategy of promoting marketization through public enterprises looked like a win-win solution and thereby developed a self-reinforcing mechanism. Accounting for this mechanism entails an understanding of how the fiscal system evolved. In particular, it was a key feature inherited from the old system that induced the opportunistic behavior of local officials. That is, government revenue was heavily reliant on sales-related taxes. Efforts of subordinate levels to promote sales growth through the public enterprises under their purview, often without regard for profitability and fundamental financial health, helped boost both revenue and employment in the short run, which served both their self-interest and their superior levels' interests but undermined the sustainability of these enterprises.

As this perverse positive feedback loop progressed, it eroded the organizational foundations of public ownership and effectively "locked out" the longer-term survivability of most of its carriers. In the meantime, the growth of private economic activities under rules bent by local officials in regions experiencing early privatization generated and reinforced a different type of positive feedback—economic and political interests that helped "lock in" the prospect of private ownership as an increasingly viable alternative for addressing the key concerns for regime survival. Explaining the uneven paces of early privatization, though, requires an understanding of the varying initial conditions shaped by the recent histories of different locales, especially those concerning the strength of local public industries, the stock and vitality of local entrepreneurial forces, and the interdependence between superior and subordinate levels. As I have shown in chapters 4–6 these factors had a direct bearing on the strategies and outcomes of interaction between political and economic actors and between different levels of political authority.

The interplay between the "lock-out" and "lock-in" effects of positive feedback illustrates an important mechanism of evolutionary institutional change. The latter does not work independently of the former, but rather moves in tandem with it along convergent paths. The growing role of entrepreneurship in China's privatization, for example, cannot be fully understood by only looking at the strategies and perseverance of economic actors and without a close examination of how and why the public sector self-destructed and locked itself into a dead end under the purview of political actors. The rise and decline of the new and initially dominant institutional order in the Chinese case also suggest a need to broaden the contingency view in the literature on path dependence, which focuses on self-reinforcement (and hence a "locked-in" path) of a positive feedback loop driven by realigned political and economic interests in an initially fluid state, often rendered by exogenous shock(s), of institutional order (e.g., Mahoney 2000; Pierson 2004). Central in this broader view are the forces that affect institutional (in)stability, which in turn are subject to the long-lasting impact of past and continuing institutions and structural forces such as demographics and political and economic interests associated with the fiscal infrastructure of the state.

Furthermore, such impact is relevant for understanding not only the supersession of newly emerging institutional orders but its tempo and spatial spread. I have shown that the forces developed in the cumulative causation process of ownership change not only triggered the CCP's pivotal decision to restructure SOEs in 1997 but accounted for the subsequently precipitous decline of public ownership and pushed it beyond the initial limit prescribed by that decision (chapter 7). The political bandwagon effect driven by the pent-up reactions of "laggard" locales (in both public sector-led growth and early privatization) and by regional peer influence, the shift of local officials' policy focus from industrial development to urbanization, and the growth of opportunities for asset stripping and insider control before and during ownership restructuring, all contributed to the drastic transformation of China's economic landscape around the turn of the century and the legitimation of private ownership as a necessary evil. They all, too, embody the consequences of past decisions and responses of political and economic actors, including those of successive CCP leaders. Like countless rulers in history, these leaders have had to drift with the tide of their own making, rather than navigating against it, in order to survive. In so doing, however, they have increasingly lost control over the destiny of the party-state, as well as that of the economy and society.

Bibliography

CHINESE MATERIALS

(1) STATISTICAL YEARBOOKS, SUMMARIES, AND SPECIAL VOLUMES

Agricultural Statistics on Fifty Years of New China (ASFYNC) 新中国五十年农业统计资料. 北京: 中国统计出版社.

Almanac of China's Foreign Economic Relations and Trade (ACFERT) 中国对外经济贸易年鉴. 北京: 中国展望出版社.

China City Statistical Yearbook (CCSY) 中国城市统计年鉴. 北京: 中国统计出版社.

China Economic Census Yearbook (CECY) 中国经济普查年鉴. 北京: 中国统计出版社.

China External Economic Statistical Yearbook (CEESY) 中国对外经济统计年鉴. 北京: 中国统计出版社.

China Foreign Economic Statistics, 1979–1991 (CFES). 1979–1991 中国对外经济统计大全. 北京: 中国统计出版社.

China Industry Economy Statistical Yearbook (CIESY) 中国工业经济统计年鉴. 北京: 中国统计出版社.

China Labor and Wage Statistics, 1949–1985 (CLWS a) 中国劳动工资统计资料 (1949–1985). 北京: 中国统计出版社.

China Labor and Wage Statistics, 1978–1987 (CLWS b) 中国劳动工资统计资料 (1978–1987). 北京: 中国统计出版社.

China Real Estate Statistics Yearbook (CRESY) 中国房地产统计年鉴. 北京: 中国统计出版社.

China Second National Census of Basic Units (CSNCBU) 中国第二次基本单位普查资料汇编. 北京: 中国统计出版社.

China State-Owned Assets Yearbook (CSOAY) 中国国有资产年鉴. 北京: 经济科学出版社.

China's State-Owned Assets Supervision and Administration Yearbook (*CSOASAY*) 中国国有资产监督管理年鉴. 北京: 中国经济出版社.

China Statistical Abstract (*CSA*) 中国统计摘要. 北京: 中国统计出版社.

China Statistical Yearbook (*CSY*) 中国统计年鉴. 北京: 中国统计出版社.

China Taxation Yearbook (*CTY*) 中国税务年鉴. 北京: 中国税务出版社.

China Township Enterprise Yearbook (*CTEY*) 中国乡镇企业年鉴. 北京: 中国农业出版社.

China Township Enterprise and Agricultural Product Processing Yearbook (*CTEAPPY*) 中国乡镇企业及农产品加工年鉴. 北京: 中国农业出版社.

Comprehensive Statistical Data and Materials on Fifty Years of New China (*CSDMFYNC*) 新中国五十年统计资料汇编. 北京: 中国统计出版社.

Comprehensive Statistical Data and Materials on Sixty Years of New China (*CSDMSYNC*) 新中国六十年统计资料汇编. 北京: 中国统计出版社.

Education Statistics Yearbook of China (*ESYC*) 中国教育统计年鉴. 北京: 人民教育出版社.

Fifty Years of Jiangsu (*FYJS*) 江苏五十年. 北京: 中国统计出版社.

Fifty Years of Taxation in China, 1949–1999 (*FYTC*) 中国税制五十年 (1949–1999 年). 北京: 中国税务出版社.

Fiscal Statistics of Prefectures, Cities, and Counties (*FSPCC*) 全国地市县财政统计资料. 北京: 中国财政经济出版社.

Fiscal Statistics on Fifty Years of China (*FSFYC*) 中国财政五十年. 北京: 中国财政经济出版社.

Finance Yearbook of China (*FYC*) 中国财政年鉴. 北京: 中国财政杂志社.

Guangdong Statistical Yearbook (*GDSY*) 广东统计年鉴. 北京: 中国统计出版社.

Jiangsu Statistical Yearbook (*JSSY*) 江苏统计年鉴. 北京: 中国统计出版社.

Jiangsu Rural Statistical Yearbook (*JSRSY*) 江苏农村统计年鉴. 北京: 中国统计出版社.

Labor Statistical Yearbook of China (*LSYC*) 中国劳动统计年鉴. 北京: 中国统计出版社.

Major Figures on 2000 Population Census of China (*MF2000PCC*) 2000 年第五次全国人口普查主要数据. 北京: 中国统计出版社.

1982 Population Census of China (*1982PCC*) 中国 1982 年人口普查资料. 北京: 中国统计出版社.

Population Statistics of the PRC, 1949–1985 (*PSPRC*) 中华人民共和国人口统计资料汇编, 1949–1985. 北京: 中国财政经济出版社.

Sixty Years of Zhejiang in Statistics (*SYZJS*) 浙江六十年统计资料汇编. 北京: 中国统计出版社.

Statistical Summary of Industrial Census, 1985 (*SSIC 1985*) 中华人民共和国 1985 年工业普查资料. 北京: 中国统计出版社.

Statistical Summary of Industrial Census, 1995 (*SSIC 1995*) 中华人民共和国 1995 年第三次全国工业普查资料汇编. 北京: 中国统计出版社.

Statistical Yearbook of China's Land Resources (*SYCLR*) 中国国土资源统计年鉴. 北京: 地质出版社.

Statistics of China's Township Enterprises, 1978–2002 (*SCTE*). 中国乡镇企业统计资料 (1978–2002). 北京: 中国农业出版社.

Statistics of Forty Years of China's Industry and Commerce Administration (*SFYCICA*). 中国工商行政管理四十年. 北京: 中国统计出版社.

Statistics of Industry and Commerce Administration (*SICA*) 工商行政管理统计汇编 /工商行政管理统计. 北京: 国家工商行政管理总局.

Statistics on FDI in China (*SFDIC*) 中国外资统计. 北京: 商务部 (http://www.fdi.gov.cn/1800000121_33_5481_0_7.html).

Tabulation on the 1990 Population Census of the PRC (*T1990PC*) 中国 1990 年人口普查资料. 北京: 中国统计出版社.

Tabulation on the 2010 Population Census of the PRC (*T2010PC*) 中国 2010 年人口普查资料. 北京: 中国统计出版社.

Wenzhou Statistical Yearbook (*WZSY*) 温州统计年鉴. 北京: 中国统计出版社.

Yearbook of Industry and Commerce Administration of China (*YICAC*) 中国工商行政管理年鉴. 北京: 中国工商出版社.

Yearbook of Jiangsu's Township Enterprises (*YJSTE*) 江苏乡镇企业年鉴. 南京: 南京大学出版社.

Zhejiang Socioeconomic Statistical Yearbook (*ZJSY*) 浙江社会经济统计年鉴. 北京: 中国统计出版社.

Zhejiang Statistical Yearbook (*ZJSY*) 浙江统计年鉴. 北京: 中国统计出版社.

(2) BOOKS AND ARTICLES

Bo Yibo 薄一波. 1991. 若干重大决策与事件的回顾 (Recollection of Several Important Decisions and Events). 北京: 中共中央党校出版社.

Chen Hongyuan 陈洪源 (主编). 1999. 温州财税五十年 (Fifty Years of Public Finance and Taxation in Wenzhou). 北京: 中国财政经济出版社.

Chen Jian 陈剑 (编著). 1998. 流失的中国 (Asset Erosion in China). 北京: 中国城市出版社.

Chen Zhengyun, Yang Shuwen, and Sun Ming 陈正云, 杨书文, 孙明. 1998. 中国国资流失状况调查 (Studies of State-Owned Asset Losses in China). 北京: 法律出版社.

Dai Jietian 戴洁天. 2002. 燎原火种: 1956 年永嘉包产到户始末 (Seeds of Fire: The Full Story of Household Land Contrating in Yongjia in 1956). 北京: 新华出版社.

Deng Yingtao, Yao Gang, Xu Xiaobo, and Xue Yuwei 邓英淘, 姚刚, 徐笑波, 薛宇伟. 1990. 中国预算外资金分析 (An Analysis of China's Extra-budgetary Funds). 北京: 中国人民大学出版社.

Ding Longjia 丁龙嘉 (主编). 2010. 南下 (Southbound). 北京: 中共党史出版社.

Ding Yizhuang 定宜庄. 1998. 中国知青史: 初澜, 1953–1968 (A History of China's Sent-Down Youth: Early Waves, 1953–1968) 北京: 中国社会科学出版社.

Dong Chaocai 董朝才. 2005. "坚持改革试验大力促进温州民营企业发展—我在温州工作五年的回顾" ("Persistent Efforts to Promote the Development of Private Business through Reform Experiments: Recollections of My Five Years' Work in Wenzhou"). 载于温州民营经济的兴起与发展, 第四章. 北京: 中国文史出版社.

Fei Kailong and Zuo Ping 费开龙, 左平 (主编). 1991. 当代中国的工商行政管理 (Industrial and Commercial Administration in Contemporary China). 北京: 当代中国出版社.

Fei Xiaotong 费孝通. 1983. 小城镇, 大问题 (Small Townships, Big Issues). 费孝通文集(第九卷). 北京: 群言出版社 (1999).

Feng Junqi 冯军旗. 2010. 中县干部 (Cadres in Zhong Xian). 北京大学社会学系博士论文.

He Dongchang 何东昌 (主编). 1996. 当代中国教育 (Education in Contemporary China). 北京: 当代中国出版社.

He Guang 何光 (主编). 1990. 当代中国的劳动力管理 (Labor Force Management in Contemporary China). 北京: 中国社会科学出版社.

Huang Huang 黄璜. 2005. "我眼中的温州" ("My Observations of Wenzhou"). 温州民营经济的兴起与发展. 第二章. 北京: 中国文史出版社.

Jia Yingzi 贾英姿. 2008. 中国社会保障支出水平研究 (A Study of the Spending Levels of China's Social Security System). 北京: 中国税务出版社.

Jia Kang and Zhao Quanhou 贾康, 赵全厚. 2008. 中国经济改革三十年: 财政税收卷 (Thirty Years of Economic Reforms in China: Volume on Public Finance and Taxation). 重庆: 重庆大学出版社.

Jiang Zemin 江泽民. 2006. 江泽民文选 (Selected Works of Jiang Zemin). 北京: 人民出版社.

Jin Qiang 金强 (编著). 2005. 反腐镜鉴录 60个贪官的真实案例 (Lessons from Anti-corruption Campaigns: Sixty Real Cases of Corrupt Officials). 北京: 中国检察出版社.

Li Chengrui 李成瑞. 2006. "关于我国目前公私经济比重的初步测算" ("A Provisional Estimation of the Relative Significance of Public and Private Economic Elements in Our Country"). 探索, 第4期, 第190至192页.

Li Hanlin 李含琳. 1994. 国有资产大流失 (Serious Losses and Disappearance of State-Owned Assets). 兰州: 兰州大学出版社.

Liu Xiaomeng 刘小萌. 1998. 中国知青史: 大潮 (1966–1980年) (A History of Sent-Down Youth in China: The Great Tide, 1966–1980). 北京: 当代中国出版社.

Liu Weidong 李卫东. 2008. 城市地价评估理论探索与实践 (Theory and Practice in Urban Land Valuation). 北京: 科学出版社.

Liu Yiqing and Zhang Qinde 刘贻清, 张勤德 (主编). 2005. "郎旋风" 实录: 关于国有资产流失的大讨论 (The "Lang Whirlwind": The Great Debate about State Asset Losses). 北京: 中国财政经济出版社.

Lu Yu 路遇 (主编). 2004. 中国人口五十年 (Fifty Years of China's Population). 北京: 中国人口出版社.

Ma Jiesan 马杰三 (主编). 1991. 当代中国的乡镇企业 (Township Enterprises in Contemporary China). 北京: 当代中国出版社.

Ma Rong, John Wong, Wang Hansheng, and Yang Mu 马戎, 黄朝翰, 王汉生, 杨沐 (主编). 1994. 九十年代中国乡镇企业调查 (Case Studies in Chinese Township Enterprises in the 1990s). 香港: 牛津大学出版社.

Mao Zhengzhong and Hu Dewei 毛正中, 胡德伟. 2008. 中国烟草控制的经济研究 (An Economic Analysis of Tobacco Control in China). 北京: 经济科学出版社.

Ministry of Foreign Economic Relations and Trade (MOFERT). 1986 (4月). 对外经济贸易部外资管理局. 审批外商投资合同问答.

Pei Changhong 裴长洪. 2014. "中国公有制主体地位的量化估算及发展趋势" ("Trends and Quantitative Estimates of the Predominant Position of China's Public Ownership"). 中国社会科学, 第一期, 1至29页.

Shang Jingcai 尚景才 (主编). 1989. 当代中国的浙江 (Zhejiang in Contemporary China). 北京: 中国社会科学出版社.

Shang Ming 尚明 (主编). 1989. 当代中国的金融事业 (The Financial Sector in Contemporary China). 北京: 中国社会科学出版社.

Shenji shu fagui si (SJSFGS) 审计署法规司. 1995. 三乱治理与收费管理法规汇编 (A Collection of Laws and Regulations on Fee Collection and Correction of "Three Types of Arbitrary Levies"). 北京: 中国审计出版社.

Shi Xianmin 时宪民. 1993. 体制的突破: 北京市西城区个体户研究 (A Break-Through in the System: A Study of Self-Employed Individuals in the Western District of Beijing). 北京: 中国社会科学出版社.

Tao Ran, Lu Xi, Su Fubing, and Wang Hui 陶然, 苏福兵, 陆曦, 汪晖. 2009. "地区竞争下的中国转轨: 财政激励和发展模式反思" ("China in Transition under Regional Competition: Reflections on Fiscal Incentives and Development Models"). 经济研究, 第7期.

Tao Ran, Su Fubing, Lu Xi, and Zhu Yuming 陶然, 苏福兵, 陆曦, 朱昱明. 2010. "经济增长能够带来晋升吗?" ("Can Economic Growth Bring about Promotion?"). 管理世界, 第十二期, 第13至27页.

Unirule Institute of Economics (UIE) 天则经济研究所. 2011. 国有企业的性质、表现与改革 (The Nature, Performance, and Reform of State-Owned Enterprises). 北京.

Wang Fang 王芳. 2006. 王芳回忆录 (Memoir of Wang Fang). 杭州: 浙江人民出版社.

Wang Guangying 王光英 (主编). 1996. 当代中国反腐倡廉典型案例通览 (A Collection of Illustrative Cases in Fighting Corruption and Building Clean Government). 北京: 中国检察出版社.

Wang Hansheng and Wang Yige 王汉生, 王一鸽. 2009. "目标管理责任制: 农村基层政权的实践逻辑" ("Target Management Responsibility System: The Logic of Administrative Action in the Rural Grassroots"). 社会学研究, 第二期刊.

Wang Xiaoqiang and Bai Nansheng 王小强、白南生. 1983. 农村商品生产发展的新动向—浙江省温州农村几个专业商品产销基地的情况调查 (New

Trends in Rural Merchandise Production: Report on a Study of Several Specialized Merchandise Production Regions in Rural Wenzhou of Zhejiang Province). 人民日报 (12月8日).

Wei Jinsheng, Sheng Lang, and Tao Ying, eds. 魏津生，盛朗，陶鹰主编. 2002. 中国流动人口研究 (Studies of China's Floating Population). 北京: 人民出版社.

Wen Tiejun 温铁军. 2000. 农村合作基金会的兴衰 (1984–1999) (The Rise and Decline of Rural Cooperative Funds). 香港中文大学大学服务中心.

Xiang Huaicheng 项怀诚 (主编). 1994. 中国财政体制改革 (Reforming China's Fiscal System). 北京: 中国财政经济出版社.

Xu Dixin 许涤新 (主编). 1988. 当代中国的人口 (Population in Contemporary China). 北京: 中国社会科学出版社.

Xu Mu and Zhang Xiaohua 许牧，张晓华 (主编). 1995. 中国土地管理利用史 (A History of Land Use and Management in China). 北京: 中国农业科技出版社.

Yang Xinming and Yang Jixue 杨新铭，杨继学. 2012. "对中国经济所有制结构现状的一种定量估算" ("A Quantitative Estimation of the Current Ownership Structure of the Chinese Economy"). 经济学动态，第十期，第10至16页.

Zeng Liansong 曾联松. 1949. "国旗图案参考资料：复字第三十二号" ("Number 32, Collection of Select National Flag Designs"). 收录于中央档案馆编印的《中华人民共和国国旗国徽国歌档案》(北京: 中国文史出版社，2014年出版), 第188页.

Zhonggong yongjia xianwei dangshi yanjiushi dng (ZGYJXWDSYJS) 中共永嘉县委党史研究室等编. 1994. 中国农村改革的源头—浙江省永嘉县包产到户的实践 (Origins of China's Rural Reforms: The Practice of Household Land Contracting in Yongjia, Zhejiang). 北京: 当代中国出版社.

Zhang Xuwu, Xie Minggan, and Li Ding 张绪武，谢明干，李定 (主编). 1996. 中国私营经济年鉴 (Yearbook of China's Private Sector Economy) 北京: 中华工商联合出版社.

Zhang Zhihua 张志华. 2006a. "完善中的中国省以下财政管理体制" ("Improve the Sun-Provincial Fiscal System in China"). World Bank (http://siteresources.worldbank.org/PSGLP/Resources/4ZhihuaZhang.pdf).

———. 2006b. "完善中的中国中央对地方转移支付制度" ("Improve Central-to-Local Transfer in China"). World Bank http://siteresources.worldbank.org/PSGLP/Resources/6ZhihuaZhang.pdf).

Zhang Zuoji 张左己 (主编). 1994. 中国劳动体制改革研究 (A Study of Reforms in the Labor Employment System of China). 北京: 中国劳动出版社.

Zheng Yuchuan 郑玉川 (主编). 1998. 当代中国的土地管理 (Land Administration in Contemporary China). 北京: 当代中国出版社.

Zhou Li-An 周黎安. 2007. "中国地方官员的晋升锦标赛模式研究" ("A Tournament Model of the Promotion Pattern of Chinese Local Officials"). 经济研究，第7期.

Zhou Qiren 周其仁. 2004. "为什么回应郎咸平？" ("Why Do I Respond to Lang Xianping?"). 经济观察报，九月二十六日.

Zhu Rongji 朱镕基. 2011. 朱镕基讲话实录 (A Collection of Zhu Rongji's Speeches). 北京: 人民出版社.

Zou Yuchuan 邹玉川(主编). 1998. 当代中国土地管理 (Land Administration in Contemporary China). 北京: 当代中国出版社.

Zuo Chuntai and Song Xinzhong 左春台, 宋新中. 1988. 中国社会主义财政简史 (A Brief History of Socialist Finance in China). 北京: 中国财政经济出版社.

Zhongyang qiye gongei (ZYQYGW) 中央企业工委. 2003. 企业国有资产流失形式和对策 (Forms of State Asset Losses by Enterprises and Counter Strategies). 北京: 中国石化出版社.

ENGLISH MATERIALS

Acemoglu, Daron, Simon Johnson, and James A. Robinson. 2002. "Reversal of Fortune: Geography and Institutions in the Making of the Modern World Income Distribution." *Quarterly Journal of Economics* 117 (November): 1231–1294.

Ahmad, Ehtisham, Qiang Gao, and Vito Tanzi, eds. 1996. *Reforming China's Public Finances*. Washington, DC: International Monetary Fund.

Anderson, E., and H. Gatignon. 1986. "Modes of Foreign Entry, A Transaction Cost Analysis and Propositions." *Journal of International Business Studies* 17 (3): 1-26.

Arrow, Kenneth. 1963. "Uncertainty and the Welfare Economics of Medical Care." *American Economic Review* 53 (5): 941–973.

Arthur, W. Brian. 1989. "Competing Technologies, Increasing Returns, and Lock-In by Historical Events." *Economic Journal* 97: 642–665.

Bahl, Roy W. 1999. *Fiscal Policy in China: Taxation and Intergovernmental Fiscal Relations*. San Francisco: 1990 Institute.

Bai, Chong-En, and Yijinang Wang. 1998. "Bureaucratic Control and the Soft Budget Constraint." *Journal of Comparative Economics* 26 (1): 41–61.

Banister, Judith. 1987. *China's Changing Population*. Stanford, CA: Stanford University Press.

Bardhan, Pranab, and Dilip Mookherjee. 2006. *Decentralization and Local Governance in Developing Countries: A Comparative Perspective*. Cambridge, MA: MIT Press.

Bellier, Michael, and Yue Maggie Zhou. 2003. *Private Participation in Infrastructure in China: Issues and Recommendations for the Road, Water, and Power Sectors*. Washington, DC: World Bank.

Bernstein, Thomas P. 1977. *Up to the Mountains and Down to the Villages: The Transfer of Youth from Urban to Rural China*. New Haven: Yale University Press.

Bo, Zhiyue. 2002. *Chinese Provincial Leaders: Economic Performance and Political Mobility since 1949*. Armonk, NY: M.E. Sharpe.

Bramall, Chris. 2007. *Industrialization of Rural China*. Oxford: Oxford University Press.

Brandt, Loren, Hongbin Li, and Joanne K. Roberts. 2005. "Banks and Enterprise Privatization in China." *Journal of Law, Economics and Organization* 21 (2): 524–546.

Brandt, Loren, and Thomas G. Rawski, eds. 2008. *China's Great Economic Transformation*. New York: Cambridge University Press.

Bruun, Ole. 1993. *Business and Bureaucracy in a Chinese City: An Ethnography of Private Business Households in Contemporary China*. Berkeley: Institute of East Asian Studies, University of California.

Burns, John P., ed. 1989. *The Chinese Communist Party's Nomenklatura System: A Documentary Study of Party Control of Leadership Selection, 1979–1984*. Armonk, NY: M.E. Sharpe.

Byrd, William A., and Lin Qingsong, eds. 1990. *China's Rural Industry: Structure, Development, and Reform*. New York: Oxford University Press.

Cai, Hongbin, and Daniel Treisman. 2006. "Did Government Decentralization Cause China's Economic Miracle?" *World Politics* 58 (4): 505–536.

Cai, Yongshun. 2000. "Between State and Peasants: Local Cadres and Statistical Reporting in Rural China." *China Quarterly* 163: 783–805.

Cao, Yuanzheng, Yingyi Qian, and Barry R. Weingast. 1999. "From Federalism, Chinese Style, to Privatization, Chinese Style." *Economics of Transition* 7 (1): 103–131.

Caves, Richard E. 2007. *Multinational Enterprise and Economic Analysis*. 3rd ed. New York: Cambridge University Press.

Che, Jiahua, and G. Facchini. 2009. "Cultural Differences, Insecure Property Rights and the Mode of Entry Decision." *Economic Theory* 38 (3): 465–484.

Che, Jiahua, and Yingyi Qian. 1998. "Insecure Property Rights and Government Ownership of Firms." *Quarterly Journal of Economics* 113 (2): 467–496.

Chen, Chih-jou Jay. 2005. "The Path of Chinese Privatisation: A Case Study of Village Enterprises in Southern Jiangsu." *Corporate Governance* 13 (1): 72–80.

Chen, Jie, and Bruce J. Dickson. 2010. *Allies of the State: China's Private Entrepreneurs and Democratic Change*. Cambridge, MA: Harvard University Press.

Chen, Ting, and Yi-min Lin. 2016. "Performance Assessment and Promotion of Chinese Prefectural Leaders, 1990–2004." Working paper, Social Science Division, Hong Kong University of Science and Technology.

Chen, Ye, Hongbin Li, and Li-An Zhou. 2005. "Relative Performance Evaluation and the Turnover of Provincial Leaders in China." *Economics Letters* 88 (3): 421–425.

Cheng, Chin-Chuan. 1997. "Measuring Relationship among Dialects: DOC and Related Resources." *Computational Linguistics and Chinese Language Processing* 2 (1): 41–72.

Cheng, Tiejun, and Mark Selden. 1994. "The Origin and Social Consequences of China's *Hukou* System." *China Quarterly* 139: 644–665.

Cheung, Peter, Jae Ho Chung, and Zhimin Lin, eds. 1998. *Provincial Strategies of Economic Reform in Post-Mao China: Leadership, Politics, and Implementation*. Armonk, NY: M.E. Sharpe.

Chiu, Becky, and Mervyn K. Lewis. 2006. *Reforming China's State-Owned Enterprises and Banks*. Cheltenham, UK: Edward Elgar.

Contractor, F. J. 1990. "Ownership Patterns of U.S. Joint Ventures Abroad and the Liberalization of Foreign Government Regulations in the 1980s: Evidence from the Benchmark Surveys." *Journal of International Business Studies* 21 (1): 55–73.

Cumming, Douglas, Donald S. Siegelb, and Mike Wright. 2007. "Private Equity, Leveraged Buyouts and Corporate Governance." *Journal of Corporate Finance* 13 (4): 439–460.

David, Paul A. 1985. "Clio and the Economics of QWERTY." *American Economic Review* 75 (May): 332–337.

Davis, G. F., and J. A. Cobb. 2010. "Resource Dependence Theory: Past and Future." *Research in the Sociology of Organizations*, 28: 21–42.

Dewatripont, Mathias, and Eric Maskin. 1995. "Credit and Efficiency in Centralized and Decentralized Economies." *Review of Economic Studies* 62: 541–556.

Dickson, Bruce J. 2003. *Red Capitalists in China: The Party, Private Entrepreneurs, and Prospects for Political Change*. Cambridge: Cambridge University Press.

———. 2008. *Wealth into Power: The Communist Party's Embrace of China's Private Sector*. Cambridge: Cambridge University Press.

DiMaggio, Paul J., and Walter W. Powell, eds. 1991. *The New Institutionalism in Organizational Analysis*. Chicago: University of Chicago Press.

Djankov, Simeon, and Peter Murrell. 2002. "Enterprise Restructuring in Transition: A Quantitative Survey." *Journal of Economic Literature* 40 (3): 739–792.

Duckett, Jane. 1999. *The Entrepreneurial State in China: Real Estate and Commerce Developments in Reform Era Tianjin*. London: Routledge.

Edin, Maria. 2003. "State Capacity and Local Agent Control in China: CCP Cadre Management from a Township Perspective." *China Quarterly* 173 (March): 35–52.

Fang, Gang, and Nicholas C. Hope. 2013. "The Role of State-Owned Enterprises in the Chinese Economy." In China–United States Exchange Foundation, ed., *China-US Economic Relations in the Next Ten Years*, chap. 16 (http://www.chinausfocus.com/2022/wp-content/uploads/Part+02-Chapter+16.pdf).

Federation of Hong Kong Industries (FOHKI). 1992. *Hong Kong's Industrial Investment in the Pearl River Delta*. Hong Kong: FOHKI.

———. 1993. *Investment in China: 1993. Survey of Members of the Hong Kong Federation of Industries*. Hong Kong: FOHKI.

Fewsmith, Joseph. 2008. *China since Tiananmen: From Deng Xiaoping to Hu Jintao*. Cambridge: Cambridge University Press.

Forster, Keith. 1990. *Rebellion and Factionalism in a Chinese Province: Zhejiang, 1966–1976*. Armonk, NY: M.E. Sharpe.

Gallagher, Mary. 2005. *Contagious Capitalism: Globalization and the Politics of Labor in China*. Princeton, NJ: Princeton University Press.

Garnaut, Ross, Ligang Song, Yang Yao, and Xiaolu Wang. 2001. *Private Enterprise in China*. Canberra: Asia Pacific Press.

Garnaut, Ross, and Ligang Song, eds. 2004. *China's Third Economic Transformation: The Rise of the Private Economy*. New York: RoutledgeCurzon.

Garnaut, Ross, Ligang Song, Stoyan Tenev, and Yang Yao. 2005. *China's Ownership Transformation: Process, Outcomes, Prospects*. Washington, DC: World Bank.

Gold, Thomas B. 1985. "After Comradeship: Personal Relations in China since the Cultural Revolution." *China Quarterly* 104: 657–675.

Gomes-Casseres, B. 1990. "Firm Ownership Preferences and Host Government Restrictions: An Integrated Approach." *Journal of International Business Studies* 21 (1): 1–22.

Granick, David. 1990. *Chinese State Enterprises: A Regional Property Rights Analysis.* Chicago: University of Chicago Press.

Greenhalgh, Susan, and Edwin A. Winckler. 2005. *Governing China's Population: From Leninist to Neoliberal Biopolitics.* Stanford, CA: Stanford University Press.

Gregory, Neil F., Stoyan Tenev, and Dileep Wagle. 2000. *China's Emerging Private Enterprises: Prospects for the New Century.* Washington, DC: International Finance Corp.

Greif, Avner. 2006. *Institutions and the Path to the Modern Economy: Lessons from Medieval Trade.* Cambridge: Cambridge University Press.

Greif, Avner, and David Laitin. 2004. "A Theory of Endogenous Institutional Change." *American Political Science Review* 98 (4): 4–48.

Guo, Gang. 2007. "Retrospective Economic Accountability under Authoritarianism: Evidence from China." *Political Research Quarterly* 60 (3): 378–390.

———. 2009. "China's Local Political Budget Cycles." *American Journal of Political Science* 53 (3): 621–632.

Guo, Kai, and Yang Yao. 2005. "Causes of Privatization in China: Testing Several Hypotheses." *Economics of Transition* 13 (2): 211–238.

Hall, Peter A., and Rosemary C. R. Taylor. 1996. "Political Science and the Three New Institutionalisms." *Political Studies* 44: 936–957.

Hamm, Patrick, Lawrence P. King, and David Stuckler. 2012. "Mass Privatization, State Capacity, and Economic Growth in Post-Communist Countries." *American Sociological Review* 77 (2): 295–324.

Harwit, E. 2008. *China's Telecommunications Revolution.* New York: Oxford University Press.

Hassard, John, ed. 2007. *China's State Enterprise Reform: From Marx to the Market.* London: Routledge.

Hausner, Jerzy, Bob Jessop, and Klaus Nielsen, eds. 1995. *Strategic Choice and Path-Dependency in Post-socialism: Institutional Dynamics in the Transformation Process.* Aldershot, UK: Edward Elgar.

Hay, Donald, ed. 1994. *Economic Reform and State-Owned Enterprises in China, 1979–1987.* Oxford: Clarendon Press.

Hillman, A. J., M. C. Withers, and B. J. Collins. 2009. "Resource Dependence Theory: A Review." *Journal of Management* 35 (6): 1404–1427.

Ho, Peter. 2005. *Institutions in Transition: Land Ownership, Property Rights, and Social Conflict in China.* Oxford: Oxford University Press.

Ho, Sam P. S. 1994. *Rural China in Transition: Non-agricultural Development in Rural Jiangsu, 1978–1990.* Oxford: Clarendon Press.

Holz, Carsten. 2003. "China's Bad Loan Problem." Working paper, Social Science Division, Hong Kong University of Science and Technology.

———. 2004. "China's Statistical System in Transition: Challenges, Data Problems, and Institutional Innovations." *Review of Income and Wealth* 50 (3): 381–409.

———. 2014. "The Quality of China's GDP Statistics." *China Economic Review* 30: 309–338.

Holz, Carsten, and Yi-min Lin. 2001. "Pitfalls of China's Industrial Statistics: Inconsistencies and Specification Problems." *China Review* 1 (1): 29–71.

———. 2002. "The 1997–1998 Statistical Break: Facts and Appraisal." *China Economic Review* 13 (4): 1–13.

Howell, Jude. 1993. *China Opens Its Doors: The Politics of Economic Transition*. Boulder, CO: Lynne Rienner.

Hsing, You-tien. 2010. *The Great Urban Transformation: Politics of Land and Property in China*. New York: Oxford University Press.

Hsueh, Roselyn. 2011. *China's Regulatory State: A New Strategy for Globalization*. Ithaca, NY: Cornell University Press.

———. 2016. "State Capitalism, Chinese-Style: Strategic Value of Sectors, Sectoral Characteristics, and Globalization." *Governance* 29 (1): 85-102.

Huang, Jing. 2000. *Factionalism in Chinese Communist Politics*. Cambridge: Cambridge University Press.

Huang, Yasheng. 1996. *Inflation and Investment Controls in China: The Political Economy of Central-Local Relations in the Reform Era*. New York: Cambridge University Press.

———. 2003. *Selling China: Foreign Direct Investment during the Reform Era*. Cambridge: Cambridge University Press,

———. 2008. *Capitalism with Chinese Characteristics: Entrepreneurship and the State*. Cambridge: Cambridge University Press.

Jackson, Sukhan. 1992. *Chinese Enterprise Management: Reforms in Economic Perspective*. New York: Walter de Gruyter.

Jefferson, Gary H., and Thomas G. Rawski. 2008. "China's Emerging Market for Property Rights: Theoretical and Empirical Perspectives." *Economics of Transition* 10 (3): 585–617.

Jia, Hao, and Zhimin Lin, eds. 1994. *Changing Central-Local Relations in China: Reform and State Capacity*. Boulder, CO: Westview Press.

Jin, Hehui, and Yingyi Qian. 1998. "Public versus Private Ownership of Firms: Evidence from Rural China." *Quarterly Journal of Economics* 113 (3): 773–808.

Jin, Hehui, Yingyi Qian, and Barry Weingast. 2005. "Regional Decentralization and Fiscal Incentives: Federalism, Chinese Style." *Journal of Public Economics* 89: 1719–1742.

Kamath, S. J. 1990. "Foreign Direct Investment in a Centrally Planned Developing Economy: The Chinese Case." *Economic Development and Cultural Change*: 107–130.

Katznelson, Ira. 2003. *Desolation And Enlightenment: Political Knowledge after Total War, Totalitarianism, and the Holocaust*. New York: Columbia University Press.

Kelliher, Daniel. 1992. *Peasant Power in China: The Era of Rural Reform, 1979–1989*. New Haven: Yale University Press.

Khan, Z. S. 1991. "Patterns of Direct Foreign Investment in China." World Bank Discussion Papers 130, Washington, DC.

Kogut, B. 1988. "Joint Ventures: Theoretical and Empirical Perspectives." *Strategic Management Journal* 9 (4): 319–332.

Kornai, Janos. 1979. "Resource-Constrained versus Demand-Constrained Systems." *Econometrica* 47 (4): 801–819.

———. 1980. *Economics of Shortage*. Amsterdam: North Holland.

Kraus, Willy. 1991. *Private Business in China: Revival between Ideology and Pragmatism*. Honolulu: University of Hawaii Press.

Krueger, Ann. 1974. "The Political Economy of the Rent-Seeking Society." *American Economic Review* 64 (June): 291–303.

Kueh, Y. Y. 1992. "Foreign Investment and Economic Change in China." *China Quarterly* 111: 638–690.

Krug, Barbara, ed. 2004. *China's Rational Entrepreneurs: The Development of the New Private Business Sector*. London: Routledge.

Kung, James Kai-sing, and Shuo Chen. 2011. "The Tragedy of the Nomenklatura: Career Incentives and Political Radicalism during China's Great Leap Famine." *American Political Science Review* 105 (1): 27–45.

Kung, James Kai-sing, and Yi-min Lin. 2007. "The Decline of Township-and-Village Enterprises in China's Economic Transition." *World Development* 35 (4): 569–584.

Landry, Pierre F. 2008. *Decentralized Authoritarianism in China: The Communist Party's Control of Local Elites in the Post-Mao Era*. Cambridge: Cambridge University Press.

Lardy, Nicholas. 1994. *China in the World Economy*. Washington, DC: Institute for International Economics.

———. 1995. "The Role of Foreign Trade and Investment in China's Economic Transformation." *China Quarterly* 144: 1065–1082.

———. 1998. *China's Unfinished Economic Revolution*. Washington, DC: Brookings Institution Press.

———. 2002. *Integrating China into the Global Economy*. Washington, DC: Brookings Institution Press.

———. 2014. *Markets over Mao: The Rise of Private Business in China*. Washington, DC: Peterson Institute for International Economics.

Lee, Hung Yong. 1990. *From Revolutionary Cadres to Party Technocrats in Socialist China*. Berkeley: University of California Press.

Lee, James Z., and Feng Wang. 1999. *One Quarter of Humanity: Malthusian Mythology and Chinese Realities, 1700–2000*. Cambridge, MA: Harvard University Press.

Lee, Keun. 1991. *Chinese Firms and the State in Transition: Property Rights and Agency Problems in the Reform Era*. Armonk, NY: M.E. Sharpe.

Leung, Chi Kin. 1990. "Locational Characteristics of Foreign Equity Joint Venture Investment in China, 1979–1985." *Professional Geographer* 42: 403–421.

Levi, Margaret. 1988. *Of Rule and Revenue*. Berkeley: University of California Press.
Li, Bing, and Yi-min Lin. 2016. "Organizational Legacies and Early Privatization in Post-reform China." Working paper, Social Science Division, Hong Kong University of Science and Technology.
Li, David D. 1998. "Insider Control and the Soft Budget Constraint: A Simple Theory." *Economics Letters* 61 (3): 307–311.
Li, David D., and Minsong Liang. 1998. "Causes of the Soft Budget Constraint: Evidence on Three Explanations." *Journal of Comparative Economics* 26 (1): 104–116.
Li, Hongbin. 2003. "Government's Budget Constraint, Competition and Privatization: Evidence from China's Rural Industry." *Journal of Comparative Economics* 31 (3): 486–502.
Li, Hongbin, and Li-An Zhou. 2005. "Political Turnover and Economic Performance: The Disciplinary Role of Personnel Control in China." *Journal of Public Economics* 89 (9–10): 1743–1762.
Li, Hongbin, and Scott Rozelle. 2004. "Insider Privatization with a Tail: The Screening Contract and Performance of Privatized Firms in Rural China." *Journal of Development Economics* 75 (1): 1-26.
Liang, Zai, and Zhongdong Ma. 2004. "China's Floating Population: New Evidence from the 2000 Census." *Population and Development Review* 30 (3): 467–488.
Lin, Justin, and Zhigang Liu. 2000. "Fiscal Decentralization and Economic Growth in China." *Economic Development and Cultural Change* 49 (1): 1–21.
Lin, Shuanglin, and Shunfeng Song, eds. 2007. *The Revival of Private Enterprise in China*. Aldershot, UK: Ashgate.
Lin, Shuanglin, and Xiaodong Zhu, eds. 2007. *Private Enterprises and China's Economic Development*. New York: Routledge.
Lin, Yi-min. 2001. *Between Politics and Markets: Firms, Competition, and Institutional Change in Post-Mao China*. Cambridge: Cambridge University Press.
———. 2003. "Economic Institutional Change in China: Reflections on the Triggering, Orienting, and Sustaining Mechanisms." In Alvin Y. So, ed., *China's Developmental Miracle: Origins, Transformations, and Challenges*, 32–54. Armonk, NY: M.E. Sharpe.
Lin, Yi-min, and Zhanxin Zhang. 1999. "The Private Assets of Public Agencies." In Jean C. Oi and Andrew G. Walder, eds., *Property Rights and Economic Reform in China*, 203–225. Stanford, CA: Stanford University Press.
Lin, Yi-min, and Tian Zhu. 2001. "Ownership Restructuring in Chinese State Industry: An Analysis of Evidence on Initial Organizational Changes." *China Quarterly* 166: 305–341.
Lindblom, Charles E. 1959. "The 'Science' of Muddling Through." *Public Administration Review* 19 (Spring): 79–88.
Liu, Yia-ling. 1992. "Reform from Below: The Private Economy and Local Politics in the Rural Industrialization of Wenzhou." *China Quarterly* 130: 293–316.
Lu, Xiaobo, and Elizabeth J. Perry, eds. 1997. *Danwei: The Changing Chinese Workplace in Historical and Comparative Perspective*. Armonk, NY: M.E. Sharpe.

MacFarquhar, Roderick, and John K. Fairbank, eds. 1987. *The Cambridge History of China*. Vol. 14: *The People's Republic, Part 1: The Emergence of Revolutionary China, 1949–1965*. Cambridge: Cambridge University Press.

Maddison, Angus. 2007. *Chinese Economic Performance in the Long Run*. Paris: Development Centre of OECD.

Mahoney, James 2000. "Path Dependence in Historical Sociology." *Theory and Society* 29 (4): 507–548.

Mahoney, James, and Kathleen Thelen. 2010. "A Gradual Theory of Institutional Change." In James Mahoney and Kathleen Thelen, eds., *Explaining Institutional Change: Ambiguity, Agency, and Power*, 1–37. Cambridge: Cambridge University Press.

Markusen, J. R. 1995. *International Trade: Theory and Evidence*. New York: McGraw-Hill.

Manion, Melanie. 1993. *Retirement of Revolutionaries in China: Public Policies, Social Norms, Private Interests*. Princeton, NJ: Princeton University Press.

Maskin, Eric, Yingyi Qian, and Chenggang Xu. 2000. "Incentives, Information, and Organizational Form." *Review of Economic Studies* 67 (2): 359–378.

McMillan, John, John Whalley, and Lijing Zhu. 1989. "The Impact of China's Economic Reforms on Agricultural Productivity Growth." *Journal of Political Economy* 97: 781–807.

Megginson, William L., and Jeffrey M. Netter. 2001. "From State to Market: A Survey of Empirical Studies of Privatization." *Journal of Economic Literature* 39 (2): 321–389.

Montinola, Gabriella, Yingyi Qian, and Barry R. Weingast. 1995. "Federalism, Chinese Style: The Political Basis for Economic Success in China." *World Politics* 48 (October): 50–81.

Moore, Thomas Geoffrey. 2002. *China in the World Market: Chinese Industry and International Sources of Reform in the Post-Mao Era*. Cambridge: Cambridge University Press.

Naughton, Barry J. 1995. *Growing Out of the Plan: Chinese Economic Reform, 1978–1993*. New York: Cambridge University Press.

———. 2007. *The Chinese Economy: Growth and Transformations*. Cambridge, MA: MIT Press.

———. 2013. "The Return of Planning in China: Comment on Heilmann-Melton and Hu Angang." *Modern China* 39 (6): 640–652.

Naughton, Barry J., and Kellee S. Tsai, eds. 2015. *State Capitalism: Institutional Adaptation and the Chinese Miracle*. New York: Cambridge University Press.

Naughton, Barry J., and Dali L. Yang, eds. 2004. *Holding China Together: Diversity and National Integration in the Post-Deng Era*. Cambridge: Cambridge University Press.

Nee, Victor, and Sonja Opper. 2012. *Capitalism from Below: Markets and Institutional Change in China*. Cambridge, MA: Harvard University Press.

North, Douglass C. 1990. *Institutions, Institutional Change and Economic Performance*. New York: Cambridge University Press.

Obinger, Herbert, Carina Schmitt, and Stefan Traub. 2016. *The Political Economy of Privatization in Rich Democracies*. New York: Oxford University Press.

O'Brien, Kevin J. 1990. *Reform without Liberalization: China's National People's Congress and the Politics of Institutional Change*. Cambridge: Cambridge University Press.

Odgaard, Ole. 1992. *Private Enterprises in Rural China: Impact on Agriculture and Social Stratification*. Aldershot, UK: Avebury.

Oi, Jean C. 1992. "Fiscal Reform and the Economic Foundations of Local State Corporatism in China." *World Politics* 45: 99–126.

———. 1999. *Rural China Takes Off: Incentives for Industrialization*. Berkeley: University of California Press.

———, ed. 2011. *Going Private in China: The Politics of Corporate Restructuring and System Reform*. Stanford, CA: Walter H. Shorenstein Asia-Pacific Research Center.

Oi, Jean C., and Andrew G. Walder, eds. 1999. *Property Rights and Economic Reform in China*. Stanford, CA: Stanford University Press.

Oksenberg, Michel, and James Tong. 1991. "The Evolution of Central-Provincial Fiscal Relations in China, 1971–1984." *China Quarterly* 125: 1–32.

Ong, Aihwa, and Li Zhang. 2008. *Privatizing China: Socialism from Afar*. Ithaca, NY: Cornell University Press.

Organisation for Economic Co-operation and Development (OECD). 2005. *Governance in China*. Paris: OECD Publishing.

Park, Albert, and Minggao Shen. 2003. "Joint Liability Lending and the Rise and Fall of China's Township and Village Enterprises." *Journal of Development Economics* 71: 497–531.

Pearson, Margaret M. 1991. *Joint Ventures in the People's Republic of China*. Princeton, NJ: Princeton University Press.

———. 1998. *China's New Business Elite: The Political Consequences of Economic Reform*. Berkeley: University of California Press,

Perkins, Dwight Heald. 1988. "Reforming China's Economic System." *Journal of Economic Literature* 26: 601–645.

———. 1994. "Completing China's Move to the Market." *Journal of Economic Perspectives* 8: 23–46.

Perrow, Charles. 1986. *Complex Organization: A Critical Review*. New York: Random House.

Pfeffer, J., and G. R. Salancik. 1978. *The External Control of Organizations: A Resource Dependence Perspective*. New York: Harper & Row.

———. 2003. *The External Control of Organizations: A Resource Dependence Perspective*. Stanford, CA: Stanford University Press.

Pierson, Paul. 2000. "Increasing Returns, Path Dependence, and the Study of Politics." *American Political Science Review* 94 (2): 251–267.

———. 2004. *Politics in Time: Politics in Time: History, Institutions, and Social Analysis*. Princeton, NJ: Princeton University Press.

Pomfret, R. 1991. *Investing in China*. Ames: Iowa State University Press.

Qian, Yingyi, and Gerand Roland. 1998. "Federalism and the Soft Budget Constraint." *American Economic Review* 88 (5): 1143–1162.

Qian, Yingyi, and Chenggang Xu. 1993. "Why China's Economic Reforms Differ: The M-Form Hierarchy and Entry/Expansion of the Non-state Sector." *Economics of Transition* (2): 135–170.

Randt, Clark T., Jr., ed. 1996. *Obtaining PRC Approvals: Foreign Investment Enterprises, Infrastructure Projects*. Hong Kong: Asia Law & Practice.

Rawski, Thomas. 1994. "Progress without Privatization: The Reform of China's State Industries." In Vedat Milor, ed., *Changing Political Economies: Privatization in Post-Communist and Reforming Communist States*, 27–52. Boulder, CO: Lynne Rienner.

———. 2001. "What Is Happening to Chinese GDP Statistics?" *China Economic Review* 12 (4): 347–354.

Riskin, Carl. 1987. *China's Political Economy: The Quest for Development since 1949*. Oxford: Oxford University Press.

Roehrig, Michael Franz. 1994. *Foreign Joint Ventures in Contemporary China*. New York: St. Martin's Press.

Samuelson, Paul A. 1954. "The Pure Theory of Public Expenditure." *Review of Economics and Statistics* 36 (4): 387–389.

Schultz, Theodore W. 1964. *Transforming Traditional Agriculture*. New Haven: Yale University Press.

Schurmann, Franz. 1968. *Ideology and Organization in Communist China*. Berkeley: University of California Press.

Scott, W. Richard. 2001. *Organizations: Rational, Natural, and Open Systems*. 4th ed. Englewood Cliffs, NJ: Prentice-Hall.

———. 2013. *Institutions and Organizations: Ideas, Interests, and Identities*. Thousand Oaks, CA: Sage Publications.

Selznick, Philip. 1949. *TVA and the Grass Roots: A Study of Politics and Organization*. New York: Harper & Row.

Sewell, William H., Jr. 1996. "Historical Events as Transformations of Structures: Inventing Revolution at the Bastille." *Theory and Society* 25 (6): 841–881.

Shih, Victor C. 2008. *Factions and Finance in China: Elite Conflict and Inflation*. Cambridge: Cambridge University Press.

Shih, Victor C., Christopher Adolph, and Mingxing Liu. 2012. "Getting Ahead in the Communist Party: Explaining the Advancement of Central Committee Members in China." *American Political Science Review* 106 (1): 166–187.

Shirk, Susan. 1993. *The Political Logic of Economic Reform in China*. Berkeley: University of California Press.

———. 1994. *How China Opened Its Door: The Political Success of the PRC's Foreign Trade and Investment Reforms*. Washington, DC: Brookings Institution.

———. 2007. *China: Fragile Superpower*. Oxford: Oxford University Press.

Shleifer, Andrei, and Robert W. Vishny. 1994. "Politicians and Firms." *Quarterly Journal of Economics* 109 (4): 995–1025.

———. 1997. "A Survey of Corporate Finance." *Journal of Finance* 52 (2): 737–783.

Shue, Vivienne. 1980. *Peasant China in Transition: The Dynamics of Development toward Socialism, 1949–1956*. Berkeley: University of California Press.

Shue, Vivienne, and Christine Wong, eds. 2007. *Paying for Progress in China: Public Finance, Human Welfare and Changing Patterns of Inequality*. London: Routledge.

Simon, Herbert. 1957. "A Behavioral Model of Rational Choice." In his *Models of Man: Social and Rational—Mathematical Essays on Rational Human Behavior in a Social Setting*. New York: Wiley.

Smart, Josephine, and Alan Smart. 1993. "Personal Relations and Divergent Economies: A Case Study of Hong Kong Investments in South China." *International Journal of Urban and Regional Research* 15 (2): 216–233.

Smyth, Russel, ed. 2005. *China's Business Reforms: Institutional Challenges in a Globalized Economy*. London: RoutledgeCurzon.

So, Billy K., and Ramon H. Myers, eds. 2011. *The Treaty Port Economy in Modern China: Empirical Studies of Institutional Change and Economic Performance*. Berkeley: Institute of East Asian Studies.

Solinger, Dorothy J. 1984. *Chinese Business under Socialism: The Politics of Domestic Commerce, 1949–1980*. Berkeley: University of California Press.

Steinfeld, Edward S. 1998. *Forging Reform in China: The Fate of State-Owned Industry*. Cambridge: Cambridge University Press.

Swidler, Ann. 1986. "Culture in Action: Symbols and Strategies." *American Sociological Review* 51 (April): 273–286.

Tang, Chaoju. 2009. "Mutual Intelligibility of Chinese Dialects: An Experimental Approach." Doctoral thesis, Center for Linguistics, Leiden University.

Tong, Daochi. 2002. *The Heart of Economic Reform: China's Banking Reform and State Enterprise Restructuring*. Aldershot, UK: Ashgate.

Treisman, Daniel. 2007. *The Architecture of Government: Rethinking Political Decentralization*. Cambridge: Cambridge University Press.

Tsai, Kellee S. 2002. *Back-Alley Banking: Private Entrepreneurs in China*. Ithaca, NY: Cornell University Press.

———. 2007. *Capitalism without Democracy: The Private Sector in Contemporary China*. Ithaca, NY: Cornell University Press.

UBS Investment Research. 2006. "How to Think about China?" Global Economic & Strategy Research, Asia, Hong Kong.

Unger, Jonathan. 1996. "'Bridges': Private Business, the Chinese Government and the Rise of New Associations." *China Quarterly* 147: 795–819.

Vogel, Ezra. 1989. *One Step Ahead in China: Guangdong under Reform*. Cambridge, MA: Harvard University Press.

Walder, Andrew. 1986. *Communist Neo-traditionalism: Work and Authority in Chinese Industry*. Berkeley: University of California Press.

———. 1992. "Local Bargaining Relationships and Urban Industrial Finance." In Kenneth G. Lieberthal and David M. Lampton, eds., *Bureaucracy, Politics, and Decision-making in Post-Mao China*, 308–333. Berkeley: University of California Press.

———. 1995. "Local Governments as Industrial Firms: An Organizational Analysis of China's Transitional Economy." *American Journal of Sociology* 101: 263–301.

Walter, Carl E., and Fraser J. T. Howie. 2012. *Red Capitalism: The Fragile Financial Foundation of China's Extraordinary Rise*. Hoboken, NJ: Wiley.

Wang, Gungwu. 2003. *China and the Chinese Overseas*. Singapore: Eastern Universities Press.

Wang, Jifu. 2006. *Strategic Challenges and Strategic Responses: The Transformation of Chinese State-owned Enterprises*. Oxford: Chandos.

Wang, Jin. 2013. "The Economic Impact of Special Economic Zones: Evidence from Chinese Municipalities." *Journal of Development Economics* 101: 133–147.

Wang, Shaoguang. 1996. "The Institutional Foundation of China's Fiscal Reform." Paper presented at Social Science Division, Hong Kong University of Science and Technology, October.

———. 1997. "China's 1994 Fiscal Reform: An Initial Assessment." *Asian Survey* 37: 801–817.

Wang, William S.-Y. 1970. "Project DOC: Its Methodological Basis." *Journal of the American Oriental Society* 90: 57–66.

Wang, Yong. 2015. "State-Owned Enterprises under China's State Capitalism." Working paper, Department of Economics, Hong Kong University of Science and Technology.

Wank, David L. 1999 *Commodifying Communism: Business, Trust, and Politics in a Chinese City*. Cambridge: Cambridge University Press.

Wen, James Guanzhong. 1993. "Total Factor Productivity Change in China's Farming Sector: 1952–89." *Economic Development and Cultural Change* 3: 1–41.

White, Tyrene. 2006. *China's Longest Campaign: Birth Planning in the People's Republic, 1949–2005*. Ithaca, NY: Cornell University Press.

Whiting, Susan. 2000. *Power and Wealth in Rural China: The Political Economy of Institutional Change*. Cambridge: Cambridge University Press.

———. 2004. "The Cadre Evaluation System at the Grassroots: The Paradox of Party Rule." In Barry Naughton and Dali Yang, eds., *Holding China Together*, 101–119. New York: Cambridge University Press.

Whyte, Martin K., and William Parish. 1984. *Urban Life in Contemporary China*. Chicago: University of Chicago Press.

Williamson, Oliver. 1985. *The Economic Institutions of Capitalism*. New York: Free Press.

Wong, Christine, ed. 1997. *Financing Local Government in the People's Republic of China*. Hong Kong: Oxford University Press.

Wong, Christine, Christopher Heady, and Wing T. Woo. 1995. *Fiscal Management and Economic Reform in the People's Republic of China*. Hong Kong: Oxford University Press.

World Bank. 1997. *China's Management of Enterprise Assets: The State as Shareholder*. Washington, DC: World Bank.

———. 2014. *Corporate Governance of State-Owned Enterprises: A Toolkit*. Washington, DC: World Bank.

World Bank, and Development Research Center of the State Council, the PRC. 2013. *China 2030: Building Modern, Harmonious, and Creative Society*. Washington, DC, and Beijing.

Wu, Huiying, and Chris Patel, eds. 2015. *Adoption of Anglo-American Models of Corporate Finance and Financial Reporting in China*. Bingley, UK: Emerald.

Xu, Chenggang. 2011. "The Fundamental Institutions of China's Reforms and Development." *Journal of Economic Literature* 49 (4): 1076–1151.

Yang, Chen. 2007. *Ownership in China's Transitional Economy: The Limitations of Conventional Property Rights Theory*. Lewiston, NY: Edwin Mellen Press.

Yang, Dali L. 1996. *Calamity and Reform in China: State, Rural Society, and Institutional Change since the Great Leap Famine*. Stanford, CA: Stanford University Press.

———. 2004. *Remaking the Chinese Leviathan: Market Transition and the Politics of Governance in China*. Stanford, CA: Stanford University Press.

Yao, Yang. 2005. "Chinese Privatization: Causes and Outcomes." *China and World Economy* 13 (1): 66–80.

Young, Susan. 1995. *Private Business and Economic Reform in China*. Armonk, NY: M.E. Sharpe.

Yusuf, Shahid, Kaoru Nabeshima, and Dwight H. Perkins. 2006. *Under New Ownership: Privatizing China's State-Owned Enterprises*. Stanford, CA: Stanford University Press.

Zhang, Li, and Aihwa Ong, eds. 2008. *Privatizing China: Socialism from Afar*. Ithaca, NY: Cornell University Press.

Zhang, Qi. 2011. "The Communist Revolution and the Political Origin of the Private Economy in China: Evidence from Zhejiang Province." PhD dissertation, Department of Political Science, Northwestern University.

Zhao, H., Y. Luo, and T. Suh. 2004. "Transaction Cost Determinants and Ownership-Based Entry Mode Choice: A Meta-analytical Review." *Journal of International Business Studies* 35 (6): 524–544.

Zheng, Shiping. 1997. *Party vs. State in Post-1949 China: The Institutional Dilemma*. Cambridge: Cambridge University Press.

Zweig, David. 1989. *Agrarian Radicalism in China, 1968–1981*. Cambridge, MA: Harvard University Press.

———. 2002. *Internationalizing China: Domestic Interests and Global Linkages*. Ithaca, NY: Cornell University Press.

Index

accounting system reform, 44
administrative allocation of land, 87, 88, 99, 100, 101
age structure, 60, 61, 65, 66, 67, 196
aging, 78, 79
agricultural decollectivization, 16, 72, 84, 97, 156, 196, 233
arable land, 66, 143, 144, 159, 162
Asian financial crisis, 101, 195, 201, 229
asset stripping, 17, 23, 103, 128, 135, 216, 217, 218, 241
assets, 11, 24, 28, 37, 38, 41, 43, 44, 45, 46, 47, 53, 55, 97, 126, 128, 133, 135, 198, 199, 202, 216, 217, 218, 220, 224, 226, 229, 233
attrition rate (of public enterprises), 204, 205, 206, 207, 208, 210, 211

baby boomers, 4, 65, 67
Banister, Judith, 61, 77
bank loans, 64, 101, 107, 114, 124, 125, 133, 166, 198, 199, 200, 201, 219, 225
banking reforms, 10, 14, 104, 107, 239
bargaining, 19, 20, 26, 100, 174, 185, 192, 193, 220, 221,
bi-polar pattern (of local rule bending), 187, 192, 237
Bo Yibo, 29

book site (where additional materials are posted), 27, 33, 84, 108, 110, 118, 120, 122, 129, 134, 135, 166, 192, 206, 210, 215, 219, 221
budget constraint, 10, 14, 15, 16, 17, 20, 111, 114
budget deficit, 82, 88, 93, 156, 162, 189, 201
"bursary service" for local governments and officials, 127, 134
business culture, 140, 237
business tax, 87, 94, 96, 213

capital goods industries, 60, 64, 65, 72, 84, 211
capital-intensive development, 16, 65, 224
capitalism, 2, 3, 231
careerism, 22, 106, 118, 126
Caves, Richard, 170, 185
census (population), 62, 63, 67, 76, 144
Central People's Government (see also State Council), 32, 34, 35, 48, 86, 100, 174
central planning, 2, 16, 31, 36, 44, 64, 65, 72, 76, 77, 83, 84, 85, 97, 106, 112, 117, 128, 129, 133, 216, 233
central revenue (see fiscal revenue)
change agent, 8, 21, 24, 230, 238,

Index

Chinese Communist Party (CCP), 1, 2, 3, 4, 5, 9, 10, 12, 21, 22, 23, 24, 26, 28, 29, 30, 31, 33, 34, 35, 36, 37, 38, 62, 64, 65, 69, 80, 81, 107, 108, 109, 113, 134, 137, 139, 145, 148, 154, 156, 157, 169, 170, 184, 195, 196, 200, 201, 202, 203, 204, 205, 225, 229, 231, 232, 235, 238, 239, 241, 251
CCP Organization Department (CCPOD), 108
Chinese constitution, 13, 21, 32, 34, 35, 84, 97, 98
Chinese People's Political Consultative Conference (CPPCC), 1, 28
city / urban center, 158, 160, 214, 215
coal industry, 37, 53, 223, 228, 229
coastal region, 55, 56, 75, 171, 183
cohort effect, 24, 60, 65, 66, 71, 77, 81
collective enterprise / sector, 23, 29, 35, 39, 41, 42, 44, 45, 46, 48, 49, 50, 54, 64, 77, 87, 89, 91, 119, 120, 133, 164, 165, 166, 195, 206, 217,
commune and brigade enterprise (CBE), 74, 116, 152, 153, 163
communism, 3, 6, 21, 26
communist revolution, 62, 139, 140, 145, 148, 163,
Company Law, 39, 40, 42, 172, 173, 179
competition, 4, 10, 14, 18, 22, 35, 36, 78, 103, 109, 111, 116, 124, 127, 129, 137, 164, 170, 174, 194, 205, 206,
constitutional amendment, 34, 35, 98
construction (industry), 73, 94, 96, 104, 213, 214
controlling stake, 33, 37, 40, 41, 42, 43, 172, 192, 225
cooperatives, 28, 29,
corruption (political), 3, 140, 157, 175, 176, 184
Cultural Revolution (1966–76), 22, 24, 29, 30, 60, 68, 69, 70, 71, 80, 82, 97, 124, 146, 149, 150, 153
cumulative causation, 239, 241

debt-equity ratio, 125, 133, 134, 166, 193, 218, 219, 220, 221, 226
debt-revenue ratio, 126, 133
demographic transition, 61, 79
demonstrable results, 147, 156, 161, 167, 168, 205
Deng Xiaoping, 2, 33, 76, 153, 155, 157
Deng Xiaoping's "southern tour", 76
dependency ratio, 63, 66
DiMaggio, Paul, 8
"dining in separate kitchens" (*fenzao chifan*), 86
discrimination against private business, 2, 11, 19
dominant strategy, 23, 25, 102, 112–113, 121, 135, 137, 157, 168, 208, 233, 236
Dong Chaocai, 154, 157

early privatization, 104, 126, 136, 137, 138, 141, 152, 158, 160, 161, 163, 164, 167, 168, 208, 209, 214, 236, 237, 240, 241
"early stage socialism", 2
economic census, 44, 46, 53, 55, 56, 215, 218, 223
economic growth, 101, 106, 109, 118, 119, 137, 153, 158, 175, 208, 211, 232
economic hardship, 25, 26, 143, 147, 164, 165, 167, 168, 236, 237
economic internationalization, 19, 190, 193
economic reforms, 4, 9, 15, 16, 17, 18, 21, 33, 34, 37, 76, 81, 83, 108, 111, 138, 143, 157, 168, 169, 232, 236
economic transition, 3, 15, 17, 238
employee shareholding cooperative (*gufen hezuo qiye*), 39, 41, 42
employment, 4, 5, 13, 14, 15, 16, 20, 22, 26, 30, 38, 49, 50, 51, 52, 55, 60, 65, 66, 67, 68, 70, 71, 72, 74, 75, 77, 78, 80, 81, 112, 117, 119, 126, 130, 134, 156, 161, 170, 195, 196, 197, 201, 207, 208, 213, 224, 230, 232, 233, 234, 236, 237, 239, 240

endogenously induced change, 5, 7, 9, 59, 81, 111, 167, 229, 230, 233, 238, 239
enterprise affiliation relationship (*lishu guanxi*), 88, 89
entrants into workforce pool, 67, 68
entrepreneurs / entrepreneurship, 4, 10, 11, 12, 13, 14, 20, 22, 25, 31, 59, 137, 138, 139, 140, 141, 143, 145, 152, 153, 156, 160, 161, 163, 164, 165, 166, 167, 237, 240
entry restrictions (on FDI), 59, 173, 178, 183, 190, 192
excise tax, 94, 96, 97
extra-budget funds / revenue, 85, 89, 90, 91, 92, 93, 98, 125, 126

factionalism, 21, 108, 109, 110, 110, 112, 113, 139, 140, 150, 151, 236, 237
family planning, 61, 62, 73, 75, 80, 114
Fan Gang, 49
farmland, 30, 31, 44, 94, 97, 102, 145, 147, 148, 149
fees and levies, 85, 88, 89, 90, 91, 95, 119, 127, 160, 187, 213
Fei Xiaotong, 74, 156
Feng Junqi, 110, 113, 114
fertility, 61
financial leverage, 22, 107, 128, 133, 136, 227
fiscal contract, 17, 82, 83, 86, 87, 89, 90, 91, 93, 94, 95, 96, 102, 103, 126–127, 128, 160, 161
fiscal decentralization, 14, 17, 22, 25, 82, 102, 107, 109, 110, 233, 234
fiscal dependence, 20, 26, 147, 187, 188, 190, 192, 194
fiscal flows, 4, 17, 20, 127, 187
fiscal revenue, 4, 10, 14, 16, 17, 20, 22, 24, 25, 26, 82, 83, 84, 85, 86, 87, 88, 90, 91, 93, 94, 95, 96, 97, 98, 102, 103, 104, 107, 109, 111, 112, 114, 120, 126, 127, 131, 132, 133, 134, 156, 160, 175, 187, 188, 189, 201, 211, 213, 224, 226, 227, 229, 234, 239, 240
fiscal spending, 4, 20, 78, 83, 84, 85, 86, 87, 88, 93, 160, 191
fiscal transfer, 20, 97, 105, 190
"floating population", 75, 76
foreign direct investment (FDI), 10, 11, 18, 19, 20, 25, 26, 29, 41, 54, 55, 56, 57, 58, 59, 169, 170, 171, 172, 173, 174, 175, 176, 177, 178, 179, 180, 181-187, 189, 190, 191, 192, 193, 194
Forster, Keith, 150
furloughed staff and workers, 197, 201, 206

gaizhi (see ownership restructuring)
gatekeeping (FDI), 18, 19, 34, 57, 169, 170, 171, 172, 174, 176, 178, 179, 183, 185, 186, 189, 192, 193, 194, 232
GDP, 2, 38, 44, 47, 48, 49, 65, 85, 88, 93, 108, 109, 112, 117, 121, 122, 131, 143, 144, 159, 162, 163, 164, 190, 191, 212, 213, 233,
getihu (see also self-employment), 31, 32, 39, 40, 42, 44, 71, 173, 214
global financial crisis, 36
governance capacity of local state, 163, 237
governance problems (public enterprises), 4, 23, 134, 216
Granick, David, 84
gray area, 9, 17, 22, 184
Greif, Avner, 7, 8
Guangdong, 52, 102, 118, 119, 129, 171, 174, 181, 182, 183, 190, 191, 199,
guojin mintui ("the state advances, the private sector retreats"), 36, 38, 47
guoyou cangu (companies with state-held shares), 42
guoyou konggu (see state-controlled companies)

Hall, Peter, 7, 8
Hangzhou, 139, 142, 161, 162
Holz, Carsten, 44, 131, 177, 199, 225
housing, 30, 65, 76, 77, 212
Hu Angang, 37
Hu-Wen era (2002–12), 38, 224
Huang, Yasheng, 10, 11, 18, 33, 35, 41, 108, 138, 175, 193, 194, 237
hukou (household registration system), 65, 211

ideology, 2, 3, 5, 11, 12, 21, 26, 70, 135, 140, 170, 175, 184, 193, 132, 135
incentives, 7, 8, 16, 66, 72, 82, 85, 87, 91, 106, 108, 110, 112, 118, 127, 140, 148, 161, 167, 184, 193, 194, 202, 207, 220, 224, 230, 233, 234, 235, 239
income tax (enterprise), 16, 84, 87, 90, 91, 92, 94, 95, 117, 125, 224
independent accounting status, 45, 177
indirect taxes, 16, 22, 89, 92, 96, 102, 103, 107, 112, 122, 127, 133, 160, 175, 224, 227
industrial census, 56, 128, 129, 176, 178, 179, 181, 182, 191, 203, 215, 218, 219, 223
industrial sector, 17, 38, 53, 54, 55, 56, 57, 58, 64, 65, 72, 102, 104, 166, 176, 177, 180, 182, 191, 192, 211, 212, 213, 214, 222, 223
industrialization, 16, 64, 65, 66, 81, 83, 117, 163, 211
information asymmetry, 17, 128, 135, 220, 221
insider control, 43, 216, 218, 219, 220, 221, 230, 241
institutional change, 5, 6, 7, 8, 9, 26, 33, 55, 81, 82, 111, 167, 229, 230, 233, 234, 235, 236, 237, 238, 239, 240
institutional owner, 39, 40, 41, 54, 58
institutional reversal, 5

institutions, 5, 7, 8, 10, 12, 21, 81, 111, 167, 207, 232, 234, 235, 236
interest payment, 122, 125, 133, 160, 202
inventory turnover, 118

Jiang Zemin, 35, 195, 201, 203
Jiangsu, 52, 86, 102, 119, 143, 144, 149, 152, 157, 199, 208, 209, 210
job creation (see employment)
joint ownership enterprise, 39, 40, 42, 97
joint stock company, 39, 40, 42, 43, 51, 171
joint venture (JV), 11, 19, 32, 39, 40, 41, 42, 44, 45, 46, 50, 51, 55, 57, 58, 59, 89, 169, 170, 171, 172, 173, 174, 177, 178, 179, 180, 181, 182, 183, 184, 185, 186, 192, 193, 194
June Fourth Incident, 33, 34, 119, 121, 157
justification, 2, 8, 9, 13, 26, 116, 138, 147, 156, 157, 158, 161, 163, 164, 165, 168, 206, 230, 236

Kornai, Janos, 15
Krueger, Anne, 7
Kuomintang (KMT), 1, 28, 145, 148

"label-less companies", 40, 41, 43, 45, 46
labor market, 71, 72, 207
labor service companies, 74
labor supply, 90, 201
"laggard regions", 23, 136, 168, 205, 206, 208, 209, 211, 241
land, 28, 30, 31, 44, 66, 97, 98, 99, 100, 101, 102, 104, 134, 143, 144, 145, 147, 148, 149, 159, 161, 163, 164, 208, 213, 214, 233
land acquisition, 98, 213
Land Administration Law, 97, 98, 99, 100
land sale proceeds, 94, 97, 98, 99, 100, 101, 179, 213
land use rights, 97, 98, 99, 100, 101, 213
Landry, Pierre F., 108, 109, 113,
Lang, Larry Hien-ping, 217

Lardy, Nicholas, 11, 34, 36, 38, 124, 200, 202, 225, 226
lateral transfer of local officials, 119, 156
legal person, 39, 40, 54, 173, 218
Li Chengrui, 49
Li, Hongbin, 109, 110
Li Rongrong, 222, 224, 226
Li Yining, 71
licensing, 32, 33, 71, 173, 174, 176, 185
lifetime employment, 78
limited liability company, 33, 39, 40, 42, 44, 173
Lin, Yi-min, 17, 90, 103, 113, 137, 205, 214, 216, 225, 235
Lishui, 142, 162, 165, 166, 168
Liu, Yia-ling, 11, 139, 140, 148
loan rollover, 124
local dialect (Wenzhou), 146
local history, 140, 237
local revenue (see fiscal revenue)
loss (financial), 10, 85, 128, 131, 133, 198

Ma Yinchu, 61
Mahoney, James, 6, 7, 241
managerial corruption, 107, 115, 127, 128,
Mao era, 13, 16, 29, 62, 66, 71, 77, 80, 82, 83, 84, 116, 139, 147, 149, 150, 156, 164, 167, 207, 211, 216, 233
Mao Zedong, 1, 28, 149, 151, 167
Maoism, 22, 61, 70, 81, 146, 152, 232, 237, 239
marketization, 6, 23, 106, 128, 143, 157, 161, 232, 233, 234, 239, 240
markets, 4, 5, 10, 14, 16, 31, 37, 77, 93, 98, 100, 101, 106, 116, 118
marriage age, 62
median age, 63
merger, 29, 202, 203, 204, 205, 230
migrants, 75
migration, 69, 75, 76, 190, 211, 212
Ministry of Agriculture (MOA), 72, 74, 207, 217

Ministry of Commerce, 174
Ministry of Finance, 79, 82, 87, 91, 98, 102, 133, 189
Ministry of Foreign Economic Relations and Trade (MOFERT), 174
Ministry of Land and Resources, 97, 98,
mobility (foreign capital), 175, 194
monitoring cost, 18, 33, 107, 128
moral hazard, 4, 7, 16, 20, 25, 78, 106, 107, 112, 114, 115, 135, 232, 234, 239
mortality, 61, 67

National Bureau of Statistics (NBS), 39, 40, 42, 58, 166, 177, 179, 180, 181, 182, 196, 203, 205, 210, 218, 219, 223
National Economic and Technological Development Zones (NETDZs), 171, 193
national flag, 1, 2, 28, 231
National People's Congress (NPC), 34, 35, 156
natural disaster, 147, 239
natural person, 40, 173
natural rate of population growth, 62, 63
Naughton, Barry, 36, 77, 87, 106, 112, 117, 128, 239
"New Democracy Theory" (Mao), 1, 2, 28
Ningbo, 139, 142, 161, 162, 171
noncompliance with rules, 7, 8, 9, 19, 26, 232, 234, 235, 236, 237, 238
non-farm employment / jobs / workforce, 14, 16, 50, 51, 55, 73, 74, 75, 103, 112, 117, 119, 126, 138, 155, 195, 196, 232,
nonfinancial SOEs, 44, 46, 174, 195, 199, 204, 213, 221, 222, 224, 225, 226, 227, 228
nonperforming loans, 199, 200, 219
nonpublic enterprises / sector, 2, 35, 45, 47, 48, 49, 50, 97, 218
North, Douglass, 229

Index

Oi, Jean C., 109, 117
old age support, 65, 76
open door policy, 32, 34, 170
opportunism, 17, 22, 112, 128, 235, 239
opportunity cost, 15, 20, 104, 203, 214, 215
output, 22, 25, 30, 43, 47, 53, 66, 103, 108, 109, 111, 112, 117, 118, 119, 120, 121, 122, 128, 129, 130, 143, 144, 145, 152, 153, 159, 160, 162, 163, 164, 165, 233
organizational form (of FDI), 19, 57, 58, 172, 173, 178, 183, 185, 186, 190, 192, 194, 237
ownership restructuring, 6, 34, 83, 184, 192, 196, 201, 202, 203, 204, 205, 206, 207, 217, 218, 220, 221, 223, 230, 239

paid-in capital, 54
partnership, 33, 38, 40, 42, 57, 172, 173
party congress (of the CCP), 33, 34, 195, 201, 202, 203, 204, 207, 211, 215, 229
path dependence, 6, 9, 12, 26, 115, 127, 221, 229, 230, 238, 240
Pearl River Delta, 179, 181, 183, 190, 191, 192,
Pearson, Margaret, 11, 32, 41, 172
Pei Changhong, 38, 44, 48, 49
pension, 76, 77, 79, 80
People's Armed Police Force, 231
People's Bank, 199, 200, 221
people's commune, 28, 30, 31, 39, 44, 64, 70, 72, 74, 76, 84, 97, 115, 116, 143, 146, 147
People's Daily, 222, 231.
People's Liberation Army, 148
People's Republic of China (PRC), 1, 28, 145, 211
periodization, 38
Perkins, Dwight H., 31, 65, 128, 202, 239
personal rivalry, 21, 236
Pierson, Paul, 6, 241

political bandwagon, 23, 26, 168, 202, 205, 211, 230, 241
political performance assessment, 16, 22, 81, 82, 102, 106, 107, 108, 109, 110, 111, 113, 114, 117, 118, 121, 128, 129, 135, 137, 153, 175, 184, 224, 233
population growth, 16, 60, 62, 66, 67
population size, 15, 60, 61, 143
positive feedback, 6, 160, 239, 240
post-communism, 3, 5
poverty-stricken counties, 143, 147, 160, 190
Powell, Walter, 8
pre-1949 entrepreneurial tradition, 12, 25, 141, 143, 145, 152, 160, 161, 163, 237, 240
principal payment, 124, 125, 133, 160
private business, 3, 4, 11, 12, 13, 14, 23, 24, 25, 31, 33, 35, 36, 59, 83, 107, 111, 116, 119, 128, 136, 137, 138, 139, 140, 141, 152, 153, 154, 155, 156, 161, 163, 165, 166, 169, 206, 207, 214, 236, 239
private enterprise, 3, 11, 12, 17, 18, 19, 20, 24, 25, 30, 31, 33, 36, 39, 40, 42, 43, 44, 46, 50, 51, 81, 89, 97, 103, 133, 135, 137, 154, 170, 173, 184, 192, 193, 204, 205, 207, 216, 232, 235
private ownership, 3, 4, 5, 6, 9, 10, 11, 21, 22, 23, 24, 28, 29, 30, 31, 33, 34, 35, 38, 43, 59, 64, 67, 71, 81, 137, 161, 169, 175, 207, 215, 230, 232, 233, 235, 240, 241
private sector, 2, 3, 12, 13, 14, 18, 19, 20, 24, 32, 33, 34, 36, 38, 39, 75, 81, 139, 140, 152, 154, 155, 156, 157, 161, 164, 166, 173, 195, 202, 207, 208, 214, 232,
privatization, 3, 4, 5, 6, 8, 9, 10, 11, 14, 15, 18, 19, 22, 24, 25, 26, 27, 29, 33, 36, 38, 41, 46, 47, 50, 53, 54, 55, 57, 60, 79, 80, 81, 101, 104, 105, 106, 110, 111, 114, 121, 126, 128, 135, 136, 137, 138, 139, 141, 147, 152, 158, 160, 161, 162,

163, 164, 166, 167, 168, 169, 170, 172, 174, 176, 185, 186, 189, 194, 195, 196, 202, 203, 204, 205, 206, 207, 208, 209, 211, 214, 215, 216, 217, 218, 219, 220, 221, 222, 224, 226, 227, 228, 229, 230, 233, 235, 236, 237, 240, 241
processing agreements / contracts, 179, 181, 182, 183
product tax, 87, 94, 96
profit, 4, 10, 14, 16, 17, 30, 32, 38, 40, 54, 78, 82, 83, 84, 85, 87, 88, 90, 91, 92, 93, 94, 117, 118, 119, 120, 121, 122, 123, 124, 125, 129, 131, 132, 133, 184, 198, 202, 216, 227, 228,
profitability, 16, 22, 25, 37, 103, 107, 112, 117, 118, 121, 123, 127, 131, 136, 193, 205, 221, 226, 227, 240
promotion (officials), 109, 110, 114, 155, 167, 184
property rights, 3, 4, 6, 9, 11, 13, 31, 35, 82, 86, 96, 107, 111, 135
public enterprise, 3, 4, 6, 7, 9, 10, 12, 14, 15, 16, 17, 18, 20, 21, 22, 23, 24, 25, 26, 30, 31, 32, 33, 34, 37, 38, 40, 41, 42, 44, 45, 46, 47, 48, 50, 55, 57, 59, 74, 79, 81, 82, 83, 84, 85, 87, 88, 89, 97, 102, 103, 104, 106, 107, 111, 112, 113, 114, 115, 125, 127, 134, 135, 136, 137, 138, 139, 141, 143, 152, 154, 155, 157, 158, 159, 160, 161, 163, 164, 165, 166, 167, 168, 169, 170, 172, 173, 174, 175, 176, 177, 178, 179, 181, 185, 192, 193, 194, 196, 197, 204, 207, 208, 213, 214, 215, 216, 217, 218, 221, 224, 229, 232, 233, 234, 235, 236, 237, 239, 240
public finance, 12, 13, 20, 29, 81, 82, 83, 84, 85, 88, 97, 104, 115, 120, 146, 187, 188
public ownership, 2, 4, 5, 7, 9, 19, 21, 22, 23, 24, 29, 31, 32, 33, 34, 37, 38, 39, 41, 44, 55, 57, 58, 81, 138, 157, 160, 161, 164, 183, 195, 211, 214, 215, 216, 225, 229, 230, 232, 233, 234, 236, 237, 240, 241
public sector, 2, 3, 4, 13, 14, 15, 22, 23, 26, 28, 33, 35, 36, 38, 40, 41, 47, 48, 49, 50, 51, 59, 61, 73, 77, 78, 79, 80, 103, 104, 136, 138, 139, 141, 156, 158, 160, 161, 162, 164, 165, 166, 167, 168, 192, 195, 196, 197, 201, 204, 205, 206, 207, 213, 214, 216, 217, 221, 224, 230, 237, 240, 241

quasi-private enterprises, 40, 41, 42, 43, 46, 47, 50, 51, 215
Quzhou, 142, 162, 164, 165, 168

real estate development, 18, 43, 176, 214, 215, 227, 228
Real Right Law (*wuquan fa*) 35, 36, 38
"recall" of exempted taxes, 91, 127
"red hat" (faking as public enterprises), 33, 173
redundant personnel, 126, 196, 197, 200, 204, 214
re-employment projects (*zai jiuye gongcheng*), 196
regime survival, 3, 12, 26, 81, 229, 232, 235, 240
regional peers, 110, 205, 206, 207, 208, 209, 211, 241
"regional property rights", 82, 88, 135
resource dependence, 183, 186, 187, 190, 192, 237
retirees, 71, 77, 78, 79, 80, 132, 196
retirement (urban), 23, 76, 77, 79, 80, 196
retirement age, 76
revenue hiding, 107, 111, 127
revenue partitioning, 17, 93, 94, 95, 104, 188
revenue sharing, 91, 95, 98, 111, 126
revenue sources, 82, 83, 84, 91, 96, 104, 112, 117, 211, 213
re-zoning, 98

Index

risk (political), 4, 8, 12, 19, 20, 21, 23, 25, 40, 107, 113, 116, 118, 135, 136, 138, 140, 141, 147, 155, 156, 157, 158, 161, 163, 168, 170, 173, 183, 184, 185, 187, 190, 192, 204, 205, 206, 207, 208, 230, 232, 235, 236, 237, 238

Riskin, Carl, 29, 65, 128, 211

rule bending, 4, 11, 12, 13, 14, 18, 19, 20, 23, 25, 137, 147, 148, 156, 158, 161, 163, 168, 170, 178, 184, 185, 186, 190, 192, 194, 235, 236, 237

rule compliance, 8, 147, 175, 233, 234, 235,

rural credit cooperative / cooperative funds, 124, 154

rural nonfarm enterprises, 16, 31, 42, 43, 44, 48, 52, 72, 74, 75, 84

rural shareholding cooperatives, 207

rustication of urban youths (see also "sent-down youths"), 60, 69, 70, 71, 81

sales growth strategy, 23, 25, 26, 102, 103, 104, 106, 107, 111, 112, 113, 114, 115, 116, 118, 120, 121, 125, 126, 127, 128, 131, 134, 141, 167, 168, 196, 207, 208, 224, 234, 240,

sanlai yibu (see processing agreements)

schooling, 68, 81

Schultz, Theodore, 167

Scott, W. Richard, 8, 234

self-employment (see also *getihu*), 4, 13, 40, 31, 32, 33, 59, 60, 67, 71, 81, 154, 233, 239

sent-down youths, 70

separation of taxes (see revenue partitioning)

services (see also tertiary sector), 18, 28, 30, 31, 34, 35, 36, 64, 65, 72, 74, 79, 88, 104, 156, 212, 213, 221, 222, 227

shared revenue / taxes, 87, 94, 95, 96, 127, 188,

shareholding enterprises, 40, 41, 42, 50, 51, 119, 202

shareholding system, 39, 225

"shock" events, 6, 114, 229, 239

social security reform, 79, 80

"socialist market economy", 13, 34, 35

soft budget constraint, 10, 14, 15, 16, 17, 20, 111, 114

sole proprietorship, 33, 34, 40, 42, 173, 195, 225

"southbound cadres", 148, 149, 153, 163

Soviet bloc, 3, 233, 238

Soviet-style system, 2, 47

special economic zones, 171, 190

special policy enclaves, 171, 183

State Administration for Industry and Commerce (SAIC), 30, 32, 42, 71, 176

state capitalism, 36

state-controlled companies, 38, 39, 40, 42, 44, 46, 51, 225

State Council, 32, 34, 35, 48, 86, 100, 174

state-owned Assets Supervision and Administration Commission (SASAC), 36, 37, 38, 42, 53, 129, 174, 195, 204, 221, 222, 224, 225, 226, 227, 228

state-owned enterprise (SOE), 10, 11, 14, 19, 23, 29, 30, 34, 35, 36, 37, 38, 40, 41, 42, 43, 44, 45, 46, 47, 48, 49, 53, 59, 77, 79, 84, 85, 86, 87, 88, 90, 91, 92, 94, 106, 112, 117, 119, 125, 126, 128, 129, 130, 131, 132, 133, 134, 135, 152, 153, 154, 158, 159, 160, 161, 162, 163, 164, 165, 166, 170, 172, 174, 175, 183, 191, 192, 193, 195, 196, 197, 198, 199, 200, 201, 202, 203, 204, 205, 206, 207, 209, 211, 213, 214, 215, 216, 217, 218, 219, 220, 221, 222, 223, 224, 225, 226, 227, 228, 229, 239, 241

State Statistical Bureau (see also National Bureau of Statistics), 49

stigma (of private business), 32, 173
stock exchanges, 33, 79, 225
subcontracting, 152, 182
subsidies, 10, 20, 38, 75, 86, 88, 147, 160, 187, 188, 189, 190

Taishun, 141, 142, 143, 156, 159, 160
Taizhou (Zhejiang), 142, 162, 163, 164, 168,
tax-for-profit (reform), 87, 90
taxes, 16, 22, 55, 84, 85, 87, 88, 89, 91, 92, 93, 94, 95, 96, 98, 102, 103, 104, 107, 112, 115, 117, 119, 120, 121, 122, 123, 126, 127, 129, 131, 132, 133, 134, 160, 187, 188, 198, 202, 213, 224, 226, 227, 240
tax exemption, 79, 91, 104, 112, 122, 126, 127, 131, 134,
tax rate, 91, 93, 126, 131, 227
tertiary sector, 17, 46, 49, 52, 73, 96, 104, 212, 213,
Thelen, Kathleen, 7
Third Plenum of the Eleventh Central Party Committee, CCP, 37, 107, 239
tipping point, 15, 26, 59, 104, 136, 170, 195, 229
tobacco industry, 3, 53, 93, 131, 222, 225, 226, 227
touji daoba (speculative buying and selling), 31, 152
township and village enterprise (TVE), 14, 42, 74, 91, 92, 106, 111, 112, 115, 116, 117, 118, 119, 120, 121, 122, 123, 124, 125, 126, 127, 128, 129, 130, 131, 133, 134, 195, 202, 206, 207, 208, 209, 210, 211, 214, 216, 217
transient tenure (local leaders), 16, 23, 107, 112, 113, 114, 118, 135, 236, 239
triangle debt, 124
Tsai, Kellee S., 10, 11, 12, 29, 36, 138, 207, 236, 237

under-employment, 16, 201
unemployment (see also employment), 15, 20, 74, 79, 197, 201
unemployment allowance, 79, 197
unified revenue and spending (*tongshou tongzhi*), 83, 84, 86
unintended consequences, 2, 7, 8, 25, 26, 118, 194, 232, 233, 234, 235
unlimited liability, 173
urban development, 23, 57, 98, 100, 101, 102, 211, 212, 213, 214, 215, 216
urbanization, 15, 18, 62, 100, 104, 196, 211, 212, 213, 214, 230, 241

value-added tax, 87, 94, 95, 96, 97, 126
Vanke, 43
vested interests, 128, 170, 183, 185, 192
Vogel, Ezra, 176, 190

Walder, Andrew G., 30, 117, 207
Wencheng, 141, 142, 143, 156, 159, 160
Wenzhou, 25, 139, 141, 142, 143, 144, 145, 146, 147, 148, 149, 150, 151, 152, 153, 154, 155, 156, 157, 158, 159, 160, 161, 162, 163, 164, 165, 166, 167, 168, 171, 236, 237
western systems, 5, 47, 234
Whiting, Susan, 10, 12, 108, 111, 112, 113, 114, 115, 116, 117, 139, 143, 207, 208
wholly foreign-owned enterprises (WFOE), 19, 32, 34, 39, 41, 42, 57, 58, 169, 171, 172, 176, 178, 180, 185, 193
workforce, 2, 14, 16, 23, 32, 43, 49, 50, 51, 55, 57, 58, 62, 64, 65, 66, 67, 68, 69, 72, 73, 74, 75, 76, 77, 78, 81, 103, 116, 117, 128, 138, 143, 144, 154, 155, 156, 158, 196, 197, 212, 213, 224,
World Bank, 48, 49, 118, 120, 121, 124, 129, 131, 132, 133
World Trade Organization (WTO), 18, 25, 34, 57, 176, 183, 228
Wu Jinglian, 36

xiagang zhigong (see furloughed workers)
Xu Dixin, 60, 61

Yongjia, 141, 142, 146, 147, 149, 150, 156, 160
Yuan Fanglie, 146, 152, 154, 157

Zhejiang, 25, 52, 102, 119, 139, 141, 142, 143, 144, 145, 146, 148, 150, 153, 154, 155, 161, 162, 163, 164, 166, 168, 188, 199

Zhou, Li-An, 109, 110
Zhou Qiren, 217
Zhu Rongji, 79, 196, 200, 201, 202, 203, 204, 207, 214, 216
zhuada fangxiao ("holding onto the large and letting go of the small"), 34, 202
Zweig, David, 11, 18, 31, 72, 171, 175, 176, 183